W9-BOA-057

Get Into College

WARNING:

This guide contains differing opinions. Hundreds of heads will not always agree. Advice taken in combination may cause unwanted side effects. Use your head when selecting advice.

Get Into College

RACHEL KORN, ED.M.
JENNIFER YETWIN KABAT, ED.M.
SPECIAL EDITORS

HUNDREDS OF HEADS BOOKS, LLC
Atlanta, Georgia

Copyright © 2009 by Hundreds of Heads Books, LLC, Atlanta, Georgia
Brody's Guide to the College Admissions Essay © Jay Brody 2005, reprinted with permission.

All rights reserved. No portion of this book may be reproduced—mechanically, electronically, or by any other means, including photocopying—without written permission of the publisher. Trademarks: Hundreds of Heads, Because Hundreds of Heads are Better Than One!, and related trade dress are trademarks or registered trademarks of Hundreds of Heads Books, LLC, and may not be used without written permission. All other trademarks are the property of their respective owners. Hundreds of Heads Books, LLC, is not associated with any product or vendor mentioned in this book.

Illustrations © 2009 by Image Club
Cover photograph by Jupiter Images
Cover design by The Cadence Group
Book design by Elizabeth Johnsboen

Library of Congress Cataloging-in-Publication Data

Get into college / Rachel Korn, Jennifer Yetwin Kabat, special editors.
   p. cm.
ISBN 978-1-933512-15-0 (pbk.)
1. Universities and colleges—United States—Admission. 2. College choice—United States.
3. College student orientation—United States. I. Korn, Rachel. II. Kabat, Jennifer Yetwin.
LB2351.2.G46 2009
378.1'610973--dc22
                   2009006306

See page 536 for credits and permissions.

Limit of Liability/Disclaimer of Warranty: Every effort has been made to accurately present the views expressed by the interviewees quoted herein. The views expressed herein reflect those of their respective authors, and not necessarily those of Hundreds of Heads Books or any other entity. The publisher and editors regret any unintentional inaccuracies or omissions, and do not assume responsibility for the opinions of the respondents. Neither the publisher nor the authors of any of the stories herein shall be liable for any loss of profit or any other commercial damages, including but not limited to special, incidental, consequential, or other damages.

HUNDREDS OF HEADS® books are available at special discounts when purchased in bulk for premiums or institutional or educational use. Excerpts and custom editions can be created for specific uses. For more information, please e-mail sales@hundredsofheads.com or write to:

HUNDREDS OF HEADS BOOKS, LLC
#230
2221 Peachtree Road, Suite D
Atlanta, Georgia 30309

ISBN-10: 1-933512-15-6
ISBN-13: 978-1-933512-15-0

Printed in U.S.A.
10 9 8 7 6 5 4 3 2

CONTENTS

THE HEADS EXPLAINED

With hundreds of tips, stories, and pieces of advice in this book, how can you quickly find those golden nuggets of wisdom? We recommend reading the entire book, of course, but you can also look for these special symbols:

 Remember this significant story or bit of advice.

 This may be something to explore in more detail.

 Watch out! Be careful! (Can we make it any clearer?)

 We are astounded, thrilled, or delighted by this one.

 Here's something to think about.

P   Advice from a parent of a college student.

—*THE EDITORS*
AND HUNDREDS OF HEADS BOOKS

Introduction

"**C**ome on, give me something great!" This isn't just what we say to ourselves as we walk to our mailboxes or open our e-mail in anticipation of "the decision" at the end of the college application process. These are also the words of admissions officers all across the country, as they crack open every application they receive. As you embark on the college admissions process, you should know that every admissions officer *wants you to succeed.* They want you to give them compelling evidence that you will be an invaluable asset to their campus community. *They want to admit you.* This is your call to action. This is where your work begins.

As someone who has sat on the "other side of the desk" – as a former admissions officer and as a current college admissions consultant – I've repeated the "give me something great" mantra with thousands of applicants. Sure, it's a big challenge to convey your "best you" on paper, but you can do it.

Get Into College is a toolbox at your fingertips. From the moment you (and your parents) start to think about the college process, this book will deliver a wealth of advice you may not have accessed before: real "battle-tested" advice from hundreds of college students, plus lots of expert wisdom from college counselors and admissions officers.

What should you do first? Start the college admissions process early! Not so much so that you can quickly cross things off your "to-do" list, but so that you have ample opportunity to reflect on yourself, where you might best "fit" in college, and how best to present yourself to those schools. Time allows you to write and think about what you want in a college when you feel inspired and relaxed. I guarantee that the quality of your college list, your essays, your test scores, and your overall applications will be significantly higher, the less pressure you feel to just "get it done."

Take time to consider the experiences and advice of the many people we've interviewed for this book. Use *Get Into College* on your journey as a resource, a comfort, a go-to for expert guidelines, or just for the occasional well-needed laugh. From SAT/ACT preparation, to interviewing advice, to how to select the right college (from the huge list of schools that have admitted you!), Hundreds of Heads will be your companion through it all.

JENNIFER YETWIN KABAT

College might be called the best four years of your life, but you have to get there first. With selectivity rising, SAT and ACT tests to study for and take, applications and essays to complete, school visits and presentations to manage, grades and activities to maintain—and then the nerve-wracking wait for colleges and universities to select *you*—getting into college has become, truly, a grinding "process" in recent years.

As a former admissions officer and current private college counselor, I know how complicated it can seem, and how hard it can be to sort out all the options, advice, and suggestions. There are times of the year when college admissions dominates the media. Somewhere in the middle of it all, we hope, there's the school of your dreams, looking for the student of its dreams—you! A perfect match.

Applying to college is a stressful period for families. It has spawned several cottage industries, such as test preparation and private counseling, and plenty of books and websites purporting to tell all and give you secrets and keys to admission (hey, you are reading this book, aren't you?). In some communities, college prep begins well before high school! Parents are more involved in the process than ever before: in some cases, their involvement has turned into over-involvement, and their children's colleges have also become their personal status symbols. Parents have been heard to speak of "our" application, instead of about "my child's" application. These changes have increased the race for the "edge" in the application that will yield that letter of admission. Families believe they have to play games of strategy to gain admission into "brand-name" schools—nothing less will do—and, along the way, the ideals of higher education may get lost.

But here's the truth: Admissions officers are bound by their instructions about whom to admit, and there is no way to *really* have an edge.

An accomplished student who is merely building his resume is as obvious to an admissions officer as the truly curious and passionate student who does things for love. Believe me, they will "get" you.

So how do you interpret and survive this rat race? Trust that there is some logic and sanity to it all, and that admissions officers invest themselves personally in their applicants. Assess your realistic chances of admission by genuinely evaluating your grades and skills against the colleges' averages. Make sure that there is at least one true safety school on your list at which you can really be happy. Craft thoughtful and reasoned applications to each school, and only apply to schools that you can honestly imagine attending. Know that admissions are never guaranteed. Know that you are not defined by your rejection from—or even your admission to—a particular school. Great students can receive rejection letters simply because there's no room, and it is no reflection on their skills or character. This is all the more important to remember in these days of increased applications for an unchanging number of spots.

There are plenty of guides to help you get to college. What makes this one different? We don't rely solely on the advice of one or two experts: Oh sure, we have wisdom from plenty of experts too. But, we've also consulted hundreds of people who have "been there, done that," and have a story to tell and advice to share.

In *Get Into College*, part of the Hundreds of Heads series, we asked a variety of students, from Ivy Leaguers to small-college scholars to students at Big Ten universities, about their admissions experiences. We've also complemented our stories with hard facts and clear guidance on issues such as choosing schools, essay writing, interviewing, getting recommendations, dealing with financial aid, and taking the SAT. You'll hear what admissions officers, or AO's, are really thinking about on the other side of the desk, and the resident expert (that would be me) will answer some questions you've been afraid to ask: Trust me, AO's know and understand the secret thoughts, schemes, and fears of high school students.

We've talked to parents of students as well—after all, more and more parents provide support to their kids in the college search, whether as research assistants, travel agents, proofreaders, or bankers. And although this book is primarily for students, we all know who else will be reading it. (Note to students: Parental comments are headlined as such, or marked with a *P*, to make it easy for you to avoid any more parental advice. But you should take a look; they have some pretty smart things to say.)

Think of this book as a companion guide to your college admission process, one that will help you reach the goal of this long journey: To find a place where you can be yourself, grow up, and enjoy the best four years of your life. Here's to the first steps on the path.

RACHEL KORN

> ## Expert Advice　A NOTE ON
> ## IECA⁺ *COUNSELOR'S CORNERS*
>
> **SPRINKLED THROUGHOUT THE BOOK**, you'll find several expert articles written by professional college counselors. These counselors are members of the Independent Educational Consultants Association (IECA), which is widely recognized as the country's leading professional organization for those educational placement advisors working in private practice. You can find contact information for these consultants on page 540.

1

First Steps: Launching The College Process

Your guidance counselor wants to see you. You get brochures in the mail from places you've never heard of. Yes, it's time to start thinking about college. And while you have a lot of dreamy ideas about colleges, you also have a lot of competition for the top spots. Your graduating class is likely to be among the largest—if not the largest—in U.S. history. So: When, where, and how do you start? Read on to hear about other students' first steps toward college.

APPLYING TO COLLEGE IS HARD. The organization that is required to get all these things out and the time and the effort you put into the essays is phenomenal. And the terror that you feel: Is it worth all of this? Am I going to get in? Or am I going to get the thin envelope? You just have to remember: It will be over someday. You'll get in somewhere. It will work out.

—CHRISTIANA
NEW YORK, NEW YORK
COLUMBIA UNIVERSITY

YOU DON'T HAVE TO IDENTIFY YOUR NUMBER ONE CHOICE AT THIS POINT.

—STEVE DETETRIADIS
PARKERSBURG,
WEST VIRGINIA
WEST VIRGINIA
UNIVERSITY

HEAD**LINES**
Best Advice and Top Tips

- It's never too soon to start preparing for college.
- Take advantage of information sessions when college representatives visit your school.
- Start refining your search in general first: Big campus vs. small; public vs. private.
- Organization is essential to keep information and deadlines from slipping through the cracks.
- If you know what you want, early decision can spare you a lot of stress.

FIRST, CONSIDER the important things: big city, college town, or something in between? Big school, small school? Liberal arts or specialist? Close to home or far away? Do they have the major you are considering?

—*SARAH BORMEL*
BALTIMORE, MARYLAND
BOSTON UNIVERSITY

• • • • • • • •

DON'T APPLY SOMEWHERE just because it has a name. It is no good being unhappy in a school that is too demanding or too far from familiar surroundings, or where the culture is alien. Try to be happy.

—*ANONYMOUS*
NEW YORK, NEW YORK
P CARLETON COLLEGE

KNOW YOURSELF. I've proven that I have some difficulty making big decisions and feeling confident in my choices. Early decision was definitely the best way to go for me. If you have an idea where you want to be, single out one school where the location, academics, atmosphere, etc., would please you. If you're leaning towards one school, apply early. This way if you get in, the decision is made. If you don't get in, you still have the opportunity to get into other schools through regular decision.

—*KATIE*
NEW YORK, NEW YORK
NEW YORK UNIVERSITY

● ● ● ● ● ● ● ●

" You can't prep for college too soon. I have injected myself with the SAT guides so that my unborn children can get an earlier start than I got! "

—*DANIEL*
TORONTO, ONTARIO
YORK UNIVERSITY

THE GOOD NEWS

Even though the acceptance rate at the most selective colleges has plummeted, the overall rate among the more than 2,500 four-year colleges and universities in the country—70 percent—hasn't changed since the 1980s.

WHEN TO START?

Most colleges send information by mail only to sophomores, juniors, and seniors. Putting yourself on a college mailing list earlier than that is not necessary.

IT'S EASIER TO GET THROUGH THE PROCESS, and get what you want out of it, if you get an early start. I wouldn't want to enter my senior year without any idea of where I wanted to go to college or what I had to do to get there. But starting earlier in your high school years, you have a chance to do things slowly and do them right. I never felt any panic because my parents and I had developed a schedule for when we wanted to get each step in the process done, and we pretty much stuck to it. You can't do that if you wait until the last minute.

—*BILL LAWRYK*
FREDERICK, MARYLAND
GEORGE WASHINGTON UNIVERSITY

● ● ● ● ● ● ● ●

THE FIRST YEAR IN HIGH SCHOOL is when you start to create a record that will play a role in the college admission decision. A picture is being painted by what you do in 9th, 10th, 11th, and 12th grades. Don't think you're going to turn it on in your last year and schools will just ignore the prior years. I had one college tell me that a "D" I got in 9th grade English could have kept me from getting in.

—*MILLER SMATHERS*
FINDLAY, OHIO

AREN'T <u>YOU</u> THE LUCKY ONE?

The swelling population of 18-year-olds peaks in 2009, when the largest group of high school seniors in the nation's history, 3.2 million, graduates.

ADMISSIONS ARITHMETIC

Why all the hysteria about college admissions? Take a look at today's college math:

> Population bubble of high school students
> + the Common Application (easier to apply)
> + more applications to more schools
> + pressure to improve college's rankings
> + static university class size
> —————————————————————
> = increasing difficulty to gain admission to top universities.

Today's high school students face this "perfect storm" of admissions factors, and the convergence of all these factors in the admissions process increases the competition at the "hot" schools. Quite simply, college admission is all about supply and demand. Right now, there is limited supply and great demand. Schools have the luxury of being even more selective, and the average, good student is struggling more than ever to stand out.

But there is good news: there are thousands of colleges and universities in the U.S. and Canada. Although it feels like a race for the prestigious, "name" schools, those are not always the best places for you. There are marvelous educational opportunities everywhere. Yes, admission is harder than ever right now, but with thorough research, a positive attitude about the college search, and thoughtful applications, you will succeed.

R.K.

Click creatively. Most college and university websites don't give a real sense of the student life that goes on there. One way to catch that flavor is to check out the Web section that's meant for current students, for a sense of day-to-day campus life.

I HAD HEARD THAT SMALLER COLLEGES and universities offered a more personal experience, which was very important to me. I surfed the Web, requested information about the schools, and interviewed students. My research led me to Marylhurst University and Concordia, both for their small size and close-to-home locations. I chose Marylhurst after meeting with one of their advisers to discuss goals and options. She took the confusion out of scheduling classes by helping me map out a plan that matched my needs. I don't believe I would have received such personal attention at a larger public college or university.

—*ANONYMOUS*
PORTLAND, OREGON
MARYLHURST UNIVERSITY

THE FIRST TIME I started thinking about college was when schools started sending stuff to me. They all looked good in the brochures. Then it was a matter of thinking, "I like how this looks. Does it have the program I want? What does it cost? What are the scholarship opportunities?"

—*JULIE COLLINS*
DES MOINES, IOWA
DRAKE UNIVERSITY

Expert Advice

IECA⁺ COUNSELOR SURVEY

SHOULD STUDENTS APPLY EARLY DECISION?

Yes – 40%
No – 60%

HANDS-OFF PARENTING

REMEMBER, IT'S YOUR KID WHO IS GOING TO SCHOOL, and not you. As a parent you tend to think in terms of what you would want for yourself. But you have to adjust that thinking for what is best for your child. It's a different kind of thinking, but it is really important. For instance, if I was the one going to school, being away from home would be important. But for my son, he needs to have the support of his friends. He'd struggle away from here. You have to keep that sort of thing in mind.

> —*JIM INGE*
> *MORGANTOWN, WEST VIRGINIA*
> *P*

• • • • • • • • •

I ALLOWED MY DAUGHTER TO GO THROUGH THE PROCESS on her own. If she is old enough to attend college, she should be independent enough to write her college essays and fill out the applications. However, stay involved with your children's progress. Discuss their goals with them. And help them be realistic about where they are applying.

> —*ANONYMOUS*
> *P*

PARENTS' PAGES: WHEN TO START

MY SON DIDN'T START THE COLLEGE APPLICATION process until he was a senior, and for him that worked. I think it's different with each kid. Some are ready to get down to brass tacks in eighth grade. Jeremy was not. We would have been knocking our heads against a wall if we tried to get him to think about college four years ago. But this year he was ready.

—*JIM INGE*
MORGANTOWN, WEST VIRGINIA

• • • • • • • •

I TOLD MY DAUGHTER IN 9TH GRADE to start thinking about what she wanted out of life and to figure out how she was going to get there. That's the thing kids don't get: Until you set the goal, you can't determine the right path. She blew off most of the college prep stuff until she was a junior. I would have liked her to start earlier, but it worked out OK.

—*TRINA AMAKER*
NIKEP, MARYLAND
P ▪▪ UNIVERSITY OF MARYLAND

• • • • • • • •

I STARTED LOOKING FOR COLLEGES when my daughter was in middle school and began taking her, at any opportunity I could, to see the campuses. I wanted to be sure we had enough time to be involved in this without being stressed.

—*ANONYMOUS*
PHILADELPHIA, PENNSYLVANIA
P ▪▪ SARAH LAWRENCE COLLEGE

• • • • • • • •

TO GET YOUR CHILD TO APPLY to a broad range of schools, make it a condition of writing the checks for the application fees. First, point out that although the student is wonderful, the competition is fierce, as are the demographics. The reality is you have to try to increase your chances by applying to a range rather than within a narrow band, be it region, academics, status, or something else.

—*ANONYMOUS*
BROOKLYN, NEW YORK
P ▪▪ STATE UNIVERSITY OF NEW YORK, PURCHASE COLLEGE

I STARTED AN EXCEL SPREADSHEET FOR each of my kids when they were freshmen in high school, and it was really helpful when applying to colleges and for scholarships. List all awards (academic, athletic, everything), community service, jobs, and anything else relevant. Make sure to include dates, contacts, hours volunteered, and any other specific information. That way, when you or your student starts to fill out all those wonderful forms, you will have all the information at your fingertips, in chronological order. I found it to be invaluable.

—SANDY
LOVELAND, OHIO
P 🏫 OHIO STATE UNIVERSITY

• • • • • • • • •

UNLESS YOU ARE CERTAIN that you can afford it, don't apply ED to a school. My son applied this way to an Ivy League school, and was accepted. But in the end, they didn't offer enough aid, so he couldn't go. When you back out like this, no other top schools will accept you, so my son ended up spending a year at a community college before transferring to a better school.

—G.V.
HOUSTON, TEXAS
P 🏫 UNIVERSITY OF TEXAS, AUSTIN;
UNIVERSITY OF MICHIGAN

• • • • • • • • •

ONE THING I WISH I had discovered earlier: College Parents of America (www.collegeparents.org). It is a national membership organization that provides access to test-prep courses like Kaplan and Thomson Peterson's, as well as scholarship searches through FindTuition.com. They maintain a parents resource center and distribute a quarterly e-newsletter for parents, customized to a student's high school graduation year.

—NANCY NELSON-DUAC
GRANBURY, TEXAS
P 🏫 GEORGE WASHINGTON UNIVERSITY

Expert Advice **FROM THE ADMISSIONS OFFICE**

PEARLS OF WISDOM

WHAT IS THE BEST PIECE OF ADVICE YOU CAN OFFER A PROSPECTIVE STUDENT?

BEFORE YOU START LOOKING AT COLLEGES, take time to reflect on who you are as an individual, and what you want to get out of your college experience. Then you can begin to search for colleges that might fit your particular needs. Don't be afraid to ask lots of questions, visit the campus, and go with your gut!

> —*TONY BANKSTON*
> *DEAN OF ADMISSIONS*
> *ILLINOIS WESLEYAN UNIVERSITY*

• • • • • • • • •

TWO PIECES OF ADVICE: READ. ACT. Well-read students seem to have more active, flexible, creative minds. They put the pieces together. They see contradictions. They're great to have in class. And students who do things, who take their real interests and turn them into action, who follow through on their commitments, who are willing to explore something in depth, those are the students who make for a vibrant, exciting, and fun college community.

> —*CHRISTOPH GUTTENTAG*
> *DEAN OF UNDERGRADUATE ADMISSIONS*
> *DUKE UNIVERSITY*

• • • • • • • • •

IF YOU ARE GOING TO DO SOMETHING, do it well.

Be yourself and have some fun with this process. It's an exciting time in your lives and an opportunity to show off all you've accomplished and achieved in a thoughtful and concise manner.

> —*JEAN JORDAN*
> *DEAN OF ADMISSION*
> *EMORY UNIVERSITY*

THE MATCH IS SO IMPORTANT. Talk to parents. Talk to friends who might currently attend an institution that you may want to attend. Talk to your school counselor and teachers who may also be thinking about good matches for you.

It's really all about the match. There are some terrific guidebooks out there that all add an interesting perspective different from the other. Do a thorough reading of guidebooks. The other piece: if at all possible, visit as many colleges as possible. If you can, visit the college more than once. Stay overnight. Live the life! I was one of those who thought I wanted a small beautiful college in the country and then I decided I wanted to go to Harvard after my visit. There's also a lot information online. None of this, though, is a substitute for going to the place, picturing yourself on campus, and talking with students on campus to get a real sense of how it would be for you there.

> —*WILLIAM R. FITZSIMMONS*
> *DEAN OF ADMISSIONS AND FINANCIAL AID*
> *HARVARD COLLEGE*

• • • • • • • •

BE YOURSELF. Successful applications are often those in which a compelling consistency emerges.

> —*MATS LEMBERGER*
> *ASSISTANT DIRECTOR OF ADMISSIONS*
> *DARTMOUTH COLLEGE*

• • • • • • • •

THERE ARE LITERALLY THOUSANDS OF COLLEGES and universities that will prepare you for a wonderful life. Don't buy into the hype and anxiety. Use reputable websites, such as the College Board, to conduct your search and the college websites to conduct research, and by all means, before you decide where you will enroll, visit campus and spend time outside the tour and program.

> —*CHRIS LUCIER*
> *VICE PRESIDENT FOR ENROLLMENT MANAGEMENT*
> *UNIVERSITY OF VERMONT*

Expert Advice

IECA⁺ COUNSELOR'S CORNER

STEP AWAY FROM ALL OF THE VOICES in your head – your English teacher's, your best friend's, your parents', your guidance counselor's – and "take a picture" of what you want to feel after graduation from college...Who are you at the end of those four years? What do you see? How is this vision different from what you think you want/need now? What do you want to take away from the college experience that is more tangible than the diploma and your future career path? How can you be true to your "best self" in this decision of selecting a school?

—*SANDRA CLIFTON*
CLIFTON CORNER, A TUTORING & COACHING CENTER

Begin early.

—*NANCY*
NELSON-DUAC
GRANBURY, TEXAS
P ▫▯ *GEORGE*
WASHINGTON
UNIVERSITY

NOT ALL COLLEGE CATALOGS are the same. Sarah Lawrence College expressed its unique philosophy on every page. My daughter kept an extra copy in her bag. It gave in-depth information far beyond course descriptions. She could see more clearly who they were. She understood why she would be so happy there.

—*MICKIE MANDEL*
RIVERDALE, NEW YORK
P ▫▯ *SARAH LAWRENCE COLLEGE*

STUDENTS SHOULD START PREPARING for college in their junior year of high school. Personally, I did not start until my first semester of senior year. My school did not give any assistance, and I was the firstborn in my family, so my parents got to make all their mistakes with me. We had to cram in college research and interviews in just three months.

—*ELIZABETH BRISTOL*
NORTH ATTLEBORO, MASSACHUSETTS
MOUNT HOLYOKE COLLEGE

• • • • • • • •

A HIGH SCHOOL GUIDANCE COUNSELOR gave me really practical advice: There are over 4,000 colleges in this country – you will get into one. Remember that!

—*ANONYMOUS*
MILWAUKEE, WISCONSIN

Look for a school that is nearby but far enough away that your parents can't check in on you on a whim.

—*ADAM GUZOWSKI*
SOUTH BEND,
INDIANA
BALL STATE
UNIVERSITY

THIS IS YOUR MOTHER TALKING

Don't relax when it comes to college admissions. This is the one time when you have to be alert and get this right. This is no joke. This is the rest of your life you're talking about. If you don't get the right education, there will be no more relaxing, because you're going to get stuck in a bad job until you're 65, working most of your adult life. But get it right and you can get a wonderful career that will let you retire on a yacht in the Pacific at 45. See the difference?

—*COLLEEN BAKEY*
FREDERICK, MARYLAND
P GEORGETOWN UNIVERSITY

WHY GO TO COLLEGE?

*You are not the first to wonder if college is for you. And with every-
one and his mother (not to mention your own mother) telling you
that you need to go to college, there naturally comes the voice of the
devil's advocate who wants you to consider other options—like
going to Europe, or Colorado, or a desert island, and just "being."
So, why go to college?*

IN TODAY'S WORLD IT'S VIRTUALLY IMPOSSIBLE to get a really good job
without college. There are just too many grads out there looking for
work to think that you are going to walk into some HR office and
have them hire you. I want to be an engineer, and I have a good aptitude for science and math, but without a college background and a
college degree, nobody in the world is going to hire me. There are no
Good Will Hunting situations going on out there in the real world.

> —BILL LAWRYK
> FREDERICK, MARYLAND
> GEORGE WASHINGTON UNIVERSITY

• • • • • • • • •

YOU GO TO COLLEGE TO BETTER YOURSELF. You don't want to be a loser
your whole life.

> —KIRA
> ST. PETERSBURG, FLORIDA
> SPC/PTA PROGRAM

IF YOU NEED A GOOD REASON

A four-year college graduate earns 70 percent more than a
high school graduate does.

WHY *NOT* GO TO COLLEGE? Why not live on your own, gain independence, meet new people, and get a degree that will get you a rewarding job doing what you love?

—*MAREN REISCH*
GENEVA, NEW YORK
KNOX COLLEGE

• • • • • • • •

I WANTED TO GO TO COLLEGE SO THAT I could achieve the highest level of education possible, and so I could provide for and be in control of my future and my family's future. I also really like school, so college was the obvious choice for me. If I could get paid to be a professional student and take a variety of different classes for the rest of my life, I would do it!

—*JULIE ROBERTS*
EDMOND, OKLAHOMA
UNIVERSITY OF OKLAHOMA

• • • • • • • •

I DECIDED THAT I DIDN'T WANT TO GO TO COLLEGE out of high school. I thought I was great enough and smart enough not to go. But then I realized that people need to go to college in order to operate in the world. And I think you learn not only how to operate in the world as an adult, but you make connections with other people, and you meet people you wouldn't meet someplace else.

—*ANGIE BENTFIELD*
NEW YORK, NEW YORK
HUNTER COLLEGE

A PARENT'S (ULTIMATELY HAPPY) TALE

OUR DAUGHTER WENT to an ultra-competitive high school with plenty of ultra-competitive parents in the wings. We parents got the message that applying to college was a blood sport that took brains, guts, strategy, and tactics to succeed. Failure was not an option.

Rachel did not buy into this point of view. She seemed to feel that if she just lived long enough, college would, somehow, inevitably happen to her, without her having to do much planning or choosing. The school (and the culture) had us geared up early in junior year for college reading, plotting, and visiting. Rachel didn't get with the program until almost a year later. She absolutely refused to be packaged: She would not work with a private counselor; she would not read books on how to get into college; she would not do extracurriculars just to pad her resume; she wrote an unconventional essay (on learning to draw, instead of one on helping to make the world a better place). In other words, she presented herself completely as herself.

The downside: If she had paid attention earlier, she might have decided to apply to certain other, even more prestigious schools, which would have taken advance planning—and she might have been accepted, and that might have been very good for her.

The upside: She applied to seven schools, was accepted at six, and wait-listed at one. She was offered two merit scholarships. She was able to turn to me (repeatedly) and say, "You see? And you said I wouldn't get in anywhere!" Ultimately, she chose to go to a prestigious, very rigorous college, and is happy there so far. It was her decision, and it was a good one. So she can say, "I told you so" as much as she likes.

—ANONYMOUS
NEW YORK, NEW YORK
P ⌂ CARLETON COLLEGE

Expert Advice

IECA⁺ COUNSELOR'S CORNER

THE FIRST TWO QUESTIONS ANY college bound student should ask him or herself are: Do I want to go to college? and Why? If you can answer both of these questions with confidence, you will go to college and you will be able to make the most of the experience.

—GINGER FAY
FAY COLLEGE COUNSELING, LLC

CREATE AN E-MAIL ACCOUNT that you will use exclusively for college admissions information, and make sure you check it often. There are so many free e-mail sites, you have plenty to choose from.

—LINDA ROADARMEL
PARKERSBURG, WEST VIRGINIA
WEST VIRGINIA UNIVERSITY

• • • • • • • •

I BEGAN THINKING about and searching for colleges around the start of senior year. This put me at a disadvantage because other kids I knew had been planning for college, in one way or another, since 9th grade. While I was playing on sports teams, other kids were planning out every extracurricular activity based on whether it would help them get into a better college. Although these kids probably had an advantage over me in searching for colleges, I think that I had a more exciting and enjoyable high school experience.

—NATHANIEL COHEN
WEST HARTFORD, CONNECTICUT
NEW YORK UNIVERSITY

FACEBOOK AND YOUR COLLEGE APP

THERE ARE CERTAIN THINGS YOU SHOULD keep private and not put on your MySpace or Facebook profile. I had a few friends that had colleges contact them through Facebook. One example was this girl who decided to go to NYU, so she joined the network on Facebook but hadn't told the other colleges that she wasn't going to attend. Another college she had gotten accepted to messaged her and asked her if she was in fact going to NYU.

I think as social networks become even more popular, colleges will use them more to learn about an applicant. Especially as it becomes increasingly competitive to get into a selective school, I would advise people to hold off putting up risky pictures - at least until they're enrolled.

>—ANONYMOUS
>LOS ANGELES, CALIFORNIA
> UNIVERSITY OF SOUTHERN CALIFORNIA

• • • • • • • • •

FACEBOOK WAS BOTH A COMFORT AND A NUISANCE in my college application experience. It was a great tool for seeing and learning about the people in the schools I was applying to, and joining groups with other students in my situation. But I would strongly recommend that high school students limit how much they let Facebook influence their final decision. The only way to really get to know a school and its student body is to visit and talk to them in person.

>—CASEY HEERMANS
>DECATUR, GEORGIA
> UNIVERSITY OF NORTH CAROLINA AT CHAPEL HILL

• • • • • • • •

DON'T POST PICTURES of yourself drinking/naked/etc.

>—S.R.
>ATLANTA, GEORGIA
> EMORY UNIVERSITY

I REALLY BEGAN THE PROCESS during my brother's third year of high school, when I was in 8th grade. As a result, I really got a leg up on the process. If you have older siblings, I suggest going on the family trips to tour and check out college campuses. During my junior year, my family and another family went all around California checking out schools. Bring a friend to look at schools: It takes some of the pressure off and makes it more enjoyable.

—*DAVID LICHTENSTEIN*
SAN DIEGO, CALIFORNIA
UNIVERSITY OF SOUTHERN CALIFORNIA

NO DIPLOMA? NO PROBLEM
Many colleges, public and private, two-year and four-year, will accept students who have neither graduated from high school nor earned equivalency degrees.

I STARTED VISITING SCHOOLS my sophomore year, but only because my friend's mom was the over-prepared type and I was invited to tag along. I didn't really start learning and looking until the beginning of my senior year. For me, it was just about learning the names of schools and their reputations and then applying to the best ones.

—*SETH*
SUNNYVALE, CALIFORNIA
UNIVERSITY OF CALIFORNIA, BERKELEY

TRY TO FIGURE OUT WHAT you want and go after it as best you can. Admissions officers and guidance counselors are only interested in positive outcomes (less trouble for the guidance office) and high yield (impressive numbers for the college). But this is *your life!* So, if your heart is set on a particular school and everyone tells you you'll never get in, apply anyway. The worst that can happen is that you're rejected and you go somewhere else, which is what would've happened if you'd never applied.

—*ANONYMOUS*
BROOKLYN, NEW YORK
P BELOIT COLLEGE

DON'T LET THE RUMOR MILL GRIND YOU DOWN

One of the biggest frustrations college admissions officers face is the rumor mills that crank out stories about their universities and their admissions policies that are not based on fact but nevertheless are circulated as gospel: X University hates students from a certain high school; Y University only accepts students with high test scores; Z University wants only athletes and student-government presidents.

The most dangerous elements in this rumor mill are websites and blogs where people share their experiences and supposed "insider knowledge" about admissions. The truth is, no one knows how applications are evaluated except admissions officers, and no person who has simply been through the process knows how admissions officers think. The advice on these websites can really mislead you. Make sure to separate fact from fiction by taking anything not relayed by official college admissions materials or by college professionals with a shaker of salt.

R.K.

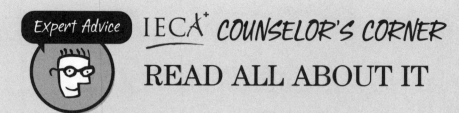

READ ALL ABOUT IT

BE SURE TO READ STUDENT NEWSPAPERS and literary magazines, either online or during your campus visit. Google the local newspaper for stories about campus life. This will help give you a feel for the school. Want to know what awaits you after graduation? The alumni magazine will give you a glimpse into the lives of grads.

—*JOAN BRESS*
DIRECTOR, COLLEGE RESOURCE ASSOCIATES

I CUT IT SO CLOSE WITH MY application that my parents had to take it down to the 24-hour post office so it could be postmarked by the deadline date. My waiting until the last minute made the whole process more stressful than it had to be.

—*EMILY ROSE*
ATLANTA, GEORGIA
AGNES SCOTT COLLEGE

• • • • • • • •

APPLYING TO SCHOOL and getting ready for college was insanely easy for me because I'm a local *and* I had taken college courses in high school, so it was a direct transfer to my college. If you can take a few courses in advance, I'd recommend it!

—*KYLE*
FT. COLLINS, COLORADO
COLORADO STATE UNIVERSITY

If you know what you want to study, see who recruits for that field on the campus and make the connection before you apply to the school.

—*AMANDA NELSON*
NEW YORK,
NEW YORK
UNIVERSITY OF
WISCONSIN-MADISON

Expert Advice **FROM THE ADMISSIONS OFFICE**

MORE WISDOM

WHAT IS THE BEST PIECE OF ADVICE YOU CAN OFFER A PROSPECTIVE STUDENT?

TAKE OWNERSHIP OF THIS PROCESS, and be sincere. Too often we see students pressured by those around them to pursue curriculums that aren't appropriate for them, or participate in activities because they "look good" on a college resume. With so much counseling (and increasingly "coaching") involved in the process, the student and his or her sincere aspirations can be lost in the process. I would tell a student to take advice from others, but ultimately pursue the courses and activities that truly motivate and inspire him or her.

This is YOUR education and YOUR college application. Having that dedication, ownership, and sincerity will not only shine through to the admissions committee, but will ultimately make for a more fulfilling high school experience.

—*JACINDA OJEDA*
REGIONAL DIRECTOR OF ADMISSIONS
UNIVERSITY OF PENNSYLVANIA

• • • • • • • • •

RELAX, APPLY DURING THE FALL of your senior year to provide the opportunity for the most consideration possible, and apply to several schools where you realistically have the potential to be admitted.

—*TED SPENCER*
ASSOCIATE VICE PROVOST AND EXECUTIVE DIRECTOR OF UNDERGRADUATE ADMISSIONS
UNIVERSITY OF MICHIGAN-ANN ARBOR

APPLY TO A WIDE RANGE OF SCHOOLS with respect to selectivity, location, academic programs, and size—many students are surprised at how what they wanted in the fall of their senior year has changed by the time they have to graduate. Also, attend the college that you believe will give you the overall best experience for the next four years and go in open-minded; you never know whom you might meet or what you might learn.

> —*MARK BUTT*
> *SENIOR ASSISTANT DIRECTOR OF ADMISSIONS*
> *JOHNS HOPKINS UNIVERSITY*

• • • • • • • • •

REALIZE THAT ADMISSIONS IS A "TWO-WAY STREET"...that we will be evaluating them and they need to evaluate us. BE A CONSUMER and ask questions. When applying to highly-selective colleges, they must realize that our decision is not a commentary on them as individuals, nor is it a reflection on any concern we might have regarding their ability to be successful at our institutions. Our decision is a reflection of the intense competition for a limited number of spaces. And, should we be unable to offer them admission, they should see that it is our loss and that they will do well some place else.

> —*DANIEL J. SARACINO*
> *ASSISTANT PROVOST FOR ENROLLMENT*
> *UNIVERSITY OF NOTRE DAME*

• • • • • • • • •

TAKE TOUGH COURSES and do your best in them.

> —*DOUGLAS L. CHRISTIANSEN, PH.D.*
> *ASSOCIATE PROVOST FOR ENROLLMENT AND DEAN OF ADMISSIONS*
> *VANDERBILT UNIVERSITY*

PARENTS' PAGES

WE STARTED TALKING about different colleges during my daughter's junior year and she attended a day for high school students at Kansas University that year. I think that this timeline was about right. Earlier would have given us too much time to think about it, but later would have rushed the process too much.

> —*JAYNE ROBERTS*
> *EDMOND, OKLAHOMA*
> *P* ☗ *UNIVERSITY OF OKLAHOMA*

· · · · · · · · ·

THE BEST TIME FOR YOUR CHILD to start thinking about college is during middle school, because college is an aspiration and you have to cultivate a mentality to go to college. Students have to want to know how to do things and you have to inform them that their skills are going to support them for the rest of their lives. The earlier you do that, the easier it is for your child to get into the college-prep mode.

> —*GLYNIS RAMOS-MITCHELL*
> *ATLANTA, GEORGIA*
> *P* ☗ *MIDDLEBURY COLLEGE;*
> *UNIVERSITY OF MASSACHUSETTS, AMHERST*

· · · · · · · · ·

WE STARTED THINKING about colleges the summer before David's junior year of high school. The process began by looking at types of schools, not specific schools. For example, we went to a big-city school, a campus school in a small town, and a campus school in a big city. It was good to see many different campuses.

> —*J.K.D.*
> *PITTSBURGH, PENNSYLVANIA*
> *P* ☗ *KENT STATE UNIVERSITY*

WE STARTED TOURING COLLEGES during our daughter's sophomore year in high school; looking back now, I think it was too soon. What my daughter liked and disliked in schools in tenth grade actually changed by the time she was a senior. They change so much in those three years.

—*T.S.*
LOS ANGELES, CALIFORNIA
P DUKE UNIVERSITY

● ● ● ● ● ● ● ● ●

IT IS NEVER TOO EARLY to prepare your child for college. We must prepare our children for college from the moment they begin attending grade school. We must emphasize that education does matter and that going to college is not a choice. There should be an unspoken rule in the house that college is just the transition from high school to the real world. Also, we must give our children the proper tools they need to succeed. These should include providing a good environment to study, showing that we are truly interested in what they do, and encouraging them to *have fun.* Also, offer them help at any time and provide the financial means. Most important, we must be good role models in our everyday life.

—*MERYL SHER*
WESTON, FLORIDA
P UNIVERSITY OF FLORIDA

● ● ● ● ● ● ● ● ●

OUR COLLEGE SEARCH PROCESS was both fun and rewarding. Make it a team effort. My husband and I attended a college prep meeting for parents. The idea is to talk openly and often about after-high-school options, including technical schools, two-year colleges, universities, and military options. Starting early allows for fitting campus visits into vacations without creating anxiety.

—*NANCY NELSON-DUAC*
GRANBURY, TEXAS
P GEORGE WASHINGTON UNIVERSITY

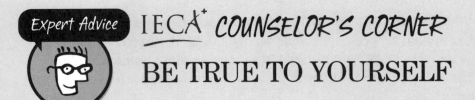

Expert Advice

IECA⁺ COUNSELOR'S CORNER
BE TRUE TO YOURSELF

BEING HONEST WITH ONESELF IS THE KEY to finding compatible colleges. This may sound obvious, but it's not always easy to do. You may have a vision of yourself at Stanford, or Colgate, or Berkeley, because that's the picture you'd like to see – maybe you know someone there, or you saw a movie you liked that showed the campus in a favorable light, or your parents want you to go to a certain kind of school. But is that really the place that fits for you? Don't be afraid to identify your true needs and desires!

> —*BRIGID DORSEY, PH.D.*
> *IECA, HECA, NYACAC*

I RESEARCHED SCHOOLS' DANCE PROGRAMS, and whether or not I could see myself there. Location was also very important to me: I wanted to live in a city, preferably New York. I had made a list of about 10 schools that I was interested in. Then I started applying.

> —*JENNIFER KEYS*
> *BALTIMORE, MARYLAND*
> *NEW YORK UNIVERSITY*

Consider

I STARTED LOOKING FOR A COLLEGE about two years after graduating from high school. I decided that working a terrible job wasn't very fun at all!

> —*KEVIN BUTTS*
> *NILES, MICHIGAN*
> *INDIANA UNIVERSITY*

DON'T START THE PROCESS TOO EARLY. You might have to make a commitment that you're not ready for. I was only 13 years old entering my freshman year of high school. I think you have to take a little time and allow the child to mature to a certain degree. For me, it worked out because I always knew I wanted to go to U.Va., and I liked it. But some of my friends ended up limiting their options and not being happy with the schools they went to.

—*KEN KEEL*
WINCHESTER, VIRGINIA
UNIVERSITY OF VIRGINIA

WORKING YOUR HIGH SCHOOL

Here's what you need to figure out:

- When can you meet with your guidance counselor to work on your school list?
- Does your school run any college admissions programs about planning the process?
- Is there a library of college catalogs and admissions materials? How do you access it?
- Are there other students who help out in the college guidance office? How do you use them?
- What is the policy about getting out of class to meet admissions officers when they visit your high school?
- How do you arrange for your guidance letter of recommendation and transcripts to be sent to the schools?

R.K.

THE ABC'S OF COLLEGE RESEARCH

There are more than 4,000 colleges and universities in the United States. How do you know where to start? Here are the top five resources:

1. **Internet.** Hands down, college and university websites have the most information. These days, printed materials from the college are helpful, but they are not necessarily thorough. You can check out a broader range of information online, from academics to clubs to atmosphere to statistics.

2. **University publications.** Definitely check the "send me material" box on the PSAT and PACT—colleges buy names of students they think could be competitive applicants, so you will get information arriving directly to your mailbox. Additionally, fill out forms on other college websites requesting information.

3. **Books/videos.** Hopefully, your high school will have a library of college catalogs and information. Spend some time in your college guidance office and ask for help from the staff, volunteers, and students working there.

4. **Parents/Siblings/Close Friends.** People who know you well will be able to suggest places where they think you will thrive. Ask questions of older high school students or any college students you know, about the application process. People can be biased, though, so be prepared to take advice with a grain of salt.

5. **College Alumni.** They will share detailed information with you, but again, be careful to always consider the source. They will likely think the place where they attended college is the perfect place for anyone.

R.K.

I STARTED LOOKING AT COLLEGES when I was only in the 8th grade. My next-oldest sister was a senior in high school, so I rode on her coattails. I was interested in languages and literature, so I researched what the best schools were in those areas. I recommend doing research and doing it early. Also, look into what the school feels like. Is it a party school or a pressure cooker where everyone has to do so well that no students can enjoy themselves at all? Measure that against your own personality and your own needs.

> —*NANCY MITCHELL POEHLMANN*
> *GRANGER, INDIANA*
> *AGNES SCOTT COLLEGE*

TO AVOID STRESS, SET CERTAIN TIMES OF EACH DAY to worry about admissions, and during the rest of the time, try not to deal with it. Go out with friends, go to the movies, go tip a cow... anything but worrying about school.

> —*K.R.*
> *WINCHESTER, VIRGINIA*
> *UNIVERSITY OF VIRGINIA*

JUST THE FACTS

On first contact with a college, don't go overboard: Writing a long letter detailing your many accomplishments and reasons you want information from a school will not make any impact at this stage. Your data (name, address, high school, year of graduation, and possible internal division/school/major) is simply entered into a computer by student workers or clerical staff. The best way is to fill out the school's online form so they can just upload your information.

PARENTS' PAGES

MY DAUGHTER GOES TO A WEST LOS ANGELES prep school, and the peer pressure to do well and prepare is intense. And as a parent, there is pressure too. It's subtle. For example, I know a lot of her friends are applying to top schools, and for years their parents have been enrolling them in classes and clubs that would look good on their college applications. I don't believe in that. Everyone is constantly talking about college and where their kids are going. I just ignore the other parents and I am secure in knowing that whatever happens will be for the best. I truly believe that regardless of where my daughter goes to college, she will do well in life.

> —*VICKI*
> *LOS ANGELES, CALIFORNIA*
> *P* ⚏ *CALIFORNIA STATE UNIVERSITY, NORTHRIDGE*

· · · · · · · ·

WHEN MY DAUGHTER WAS APPLYING TO COLLEGE, a lot of our close friends were parents of kids of the same age. It was amazing how competitive and how charged the energy was around grades and scores. I can't say that I didn't get caught up in it. I tried not to, but it really affected friendships temporarily. When my daughter was rejected from Stanford it was actually almost embarrassing. Other parents were bragging about their kids, and if your kid didn't get into her top choice it was somehow a reflection on you, the parent. It's really hard not to get into the competing aspect. I don't think we ever viewed each other as enemies, but what we tended to do was project ourselves onto our children and to see their accomplishments - or lack thereof - as our own. As you are getting older and you are settled in your career and you are not achieving great things anymore, you sort of absorb your children's achievements as your own. You have to work really hard to not see what they are doing as your own goal and accomplishment.

> —*KAREN BARCHAS*
> *TRUCKEE, CALIFORNIA*
> *P* ⚏ *UNIVERSITY OF CALIFORNIA, BERKELEY*

YOU CAN'T REALLY RELY ON YOUR KID'S SCHOOL guidance counselor to know all the information you will need. Go to those after-school nights where they discuss financing, testing and other issues. And you should start going when your child is in the 10th grade; don't wait until their senior year. Some would say 9th grade!

—S.A.
WASHINGTON, D.C.
P ᐧ JOHNSON & WALES UNIVERSITY

• • • • • • • • •

DON'T WAIT UNTIL THE LAST MINUTE to do anything. Get as much done as possible in the summer before your senior year so you can work hard but still enjoy your last year of high school.

—K.F.
BASKING RIDGE, NEW JERSEY
P ᐧ LAFAYETTE COLLEGE

• • • • • • • • •

DON'T FORCE YOUR KIDS to start looking at colleges if they aren't ready. I bought a college guide and moved it around the house every so often, but my son didn't get around to reading it until the summer after his junior year. I had friends who had kids who were motivated during their freshman years, so I thought maybe there was something wrong with mine. But then I went to a college-admissions website and found other parents who were also tearing out their hair over their late bloomers. It was very reassuring to find so many other parents who couldn't get their kids motivated. It's like toilet training; you can go on about it for years, but they aren't going to learn it until they are ready.

—C.K.
LARKSPUR, CALIFORNIA
P ᐧ WHITMAN COLLEGE

Expert Advice

IECA* COUNSELOR'S CORNER

IS EARLY DECISION (ED) OR EARLY ACTION (EA) FOR YOU?

APPLYING EARLY DECISION (ED) OR EARLY ACTION (EA) increases your chances of admission at most schools. With application volume increasing, admissions committees are looking more closely at a student's genuine interest in the schools to which he or she is applying. Applying early is a great way to demonstrate this. Because most ED programs are binding (while EAs are not), promising that you will enroll if admitted is a key way to show your commitment to a school.

However, applying ED or EA may not be the best strategy for you. If you haven't completed your campus visits, want to learn more about a college's academic or social envrionment, or aren't 100% certain that a school is your first choice, you may want to spend the first couple months of the school year researching colleges rather than preparing your ED or EA application. The decision as to where to spend the next four years of your life learning and socializing is very important, so you want to thoroughly assess your options to find the best fit, rather than rushing through the process. Also, if your junior year grades and previous extracurricular activities aren't as strong as you would like, waiting to apply regular decision in January will give you time to both improve your grades and make an impact outside of the classroom.

—*SUSAN JOAN MAURIELLO*
APPLY IVY LIMITED

MY FIRST STEP WAS TO FIND the universities that offered programs I was interested in. My final decision was actually based on laziness. The school I chose for my undergraduate degree is only one block from my parents' home.

—*NATALIA JIMENEZ*
MEDELLIN, COLOMBIA
INDIANA UNIVERSITY

BRIDGING SCHOOL WITH THE GAP YEAR

Although taking a year off in between high school and college is not as prevalent here as it is in the UK and Europe, there are a number of excellent gap year programs in the United States. It can be a very maturing experience, which often translates to an academic advantage. Check out these websites to learn more:

- www.gap-year.com
- www.yearoutgroup.org
- www.leapnow.org
- www.bunac.org
- www.interimprograms.com
- www.transitionsabroad.com/listings/work/shortterm/gap_year_jobs_abroad.shtml
- www.traveltree.co.uk

TIP

Make a file for each college that interests you. Include brochures, maps, any important names and contact numbers, deadlines for admission, and financial aid forms.

IT IS NEVER TOO SOON TO START preparing for college. You really have to assess your interests and skills well before you are accepted to a college and choose a major. Then you can properly choose the right career path for yourself and take relevant steps that will serve as a solid foundation for the first steps of your career. For instance, if you know you are good at writing, work at a newspaper during high school. Experience is key in any field.

—*CARLY JACOBS*
PHILADELPHIA, PENNSYLVANIA
LA SALLE UNIVERSITY

• • • • • • • •

I STARTED LOOKING ON THE INTERNET my sophomore year and narrowed my search to small to midsized schools with journalism majors. Look at collegeboard.com. It's a very good site. You can see size, location, personal testaments from current students, majors, cost, and reputation from reputable sources (ranking, articles, awards, and so on).

—*ADRIENNE LANG*
OLATHE, KANSAS
TEXAS CHRISTIAN UNIVERSITY

EARLY DECISION IS WRONG IF ...

- You are not completely sure about any one school over another;
- You will need to or want to compare financial aid packages;
- You are hoping you will be awarded a scholarship at one or several schools;
- You see ED as a way of upping the admission odds in the game of college admission; or
- You have not visited the campus, as well as other college campuses for comparison.

COLLEGEBOARD.COM WAS MY NUMBER ONE
resource through the application process. It lays
out everything you need to know about different
schools in a really comprehensive format. It can
tell you pretty quickly if you stand a chance at
getting in, or not.

—*NATE BATCHELDER*
STRATHAM, NEW HAMPSHIRE
UNIVERSITY OF NEW HAMPSHIRE

• • • • • • • •

I RECOMMEND THE WEBSITE Zinch as a technologi-
cal aid for the college search. Zinch enables
students to create a profile, upload a photo and
essays, list activities, as well as search and compare colleges. It has average SAT and ACT scores,
cost, rankings, etc. It is the more streamlined,
user-friendly, aesthetically pleasing version of
The Princeton Review.

—*KAITLYN*
ATLANTA, GEORGIA
GEORGIA INSTITUTE OF TECHNOLOGY

EARLY DECISION IS RIGHT IF ...

- You have identified a true front-runner school, at which you
  can see yourself above all others, by visiting in person;
- You and your parents can afford the cost (either fully or with
  estimated aid);
- There are no doubts about the fit between you and the
  school—you are committing to it; and
- You have time to complete all testing in advance and are confident that your grades have so far been a good representation
  of your ability.

FROM THE ADMISSIONS OFFICE

EARLY OR NOT

WHO SHOULD APPLY EARLY?
WHO SHOULD NOT?

ONLY STUDENTS WHO ARE CERTAIN that their college choice is truly their first choice, and who are willing to commit if admitted (and withdraw other applications once admitted) should use Early Decision programs. Students who wish to compare offers of admission, financial aid and scholarships, should apply Regular Decision.

—*DOUGLAS L. CHRISTIANSEN, PH.D.*
ASSOCIATE PROVOST FOR ENROLLMENT AND DEAN OF ADMISSIONS
VANDERBILT UNIVERSITY

• • • • • • • •

'EARLY' IS REALLY FOR A STUDENT who has narrowed their choices to one or two schools. Students who are still broadly considering a variety of options should probably reconsider the early option.

—*TED SPENCER*
ASSOCIATE VICE PROVOST AND EXECUTIVE DIRECTOR OF UNDERGRADUATE ADMISSIONS
UNIVERSITY OF MICHIGAN-ANN ARBOR

• • • • • • • •

EARLY DECISION IS LIKE MARRIAGE—you have to know that it's right for you. Students who know a specific college is perfect for them and have 'fallen in love' should consider Early Decision. These students should have no desire to compare financial aid packages. They should ask themselves "Is there any amount of money that could lure me away from this 'dream school'?" If there is, then maybe Early Decision is not the best option. That said, it is very nice to be admitted in Early Decision because you've completed the process by mid-December. Conversely, students who believe that they have to 'go Early' somewhere, though they just aren't sure where, are most likely not a fit for an Early Decision program.

—*MARK BUTT*
SENIOR ASSISTANT DIRECTOR OF ADMISSIONS
JOHNS HOPKINS UNIVERSITY

IF YOU HAVE ABSOLUTELY DONE ALL OF YOUR HOMEWORK on all of your options, zeroed in on the school you feel most confident provides the best fit, and you know your parents are committed to meeting the financial expectations of that institution, then you should feel free to take advantage of an Early Decision program. Otherwise, take your time. Applying ED because you think it will enhance your chances of getting in is one of the worst things you can do, especially if you haven't thoroughly investigated all of your options.

—*TONY BANKSTON*
DEAN OF ADMISSIONS
ILLINOIS WESLEYAN UNIVERSITY

• • • • • • • • •

APPLY EARLY TO AN EARLY DECISION school like Dartmouth if you know it is your first choice. ED is binding, meaning that you commit to enroll if admitted. Students who want to weigh need-based financial aid against merit or athletic based scholarships would do well to wait until RD.

—*MATS LEMBERGER*
ASSISTANT DIRECTOR OF ADMISSIONS
DARTMOUTH COLLEGE

• • • • • • • • •

THERE'S A COMMON MISPERCEPTION out there that you must apply somewhere early. Indeed, I can clearly recall a conversation with a parent I had a few years ago where the mother called my office and said that her son was considering applying to Colleges X, Y, & Z early, and just couldn't make up his mind. Clearly, that student shouldn't be applying early at all! Typically, students who apply early (particularly Early Decision, which is binding) should be certain that a particular college is their first choice. Ideally they've been researching schools for a number of years, they know the school has academic offerings that fit their interests, and they've visited the campus and "fallen in love." If a student doesn't have a clear first choice and/or isn't prepared to submit a complete and polished app by mid-fall, he or she is not a good candidate for an early program.

—*JACINDA OJEDA*
REGIONAL DIRECTOR OF ADMISSIONS
UNIVERSITY OF PENNSYLVANIA

WHERE TO APPLY (I): MAKING A FIRST LIST

SURF MAJOR WEBSITES with information about all U.S. schools and develop a large list of about 20 to 30 schools. Just think about personality match at this stage - you will narrow this list later and add in more safety schools and dream schools. Important tip: Make sure you take any "advice" and opinions you find with a grain of salt - be wary when statements are opinions and not facts.

Look for sites that:
- Let you plug in your academic profile and personality traits and get a list of possible matches.
- Compare and contrast schools.
- Give student feedback.
- Point you in specific directions by major.
- Show you all the schools within a certain geographic area.

Here are some good places to start your Web search:
- The College Board: www.collegeboard.com
- Peterson's Education Center: www.petersons.com
- US News & World Report: America's Best Colleges: http://colleges.usnews.rankingsandreviews.com/college
- Go College: www.gocollege.com
- College Confidential: www.collegeconfidential.com

R.K.

I HAD A COUNSELOR TELL ME that it was more beneficial to get a lower grade in a tougher class than a higher grade in an easy class, which really surprised me. I learned not to be afraid to get a lower grade in a more challenging course. While the ideal is getting the best grade possible in the most difficult class, colleges will be impressed with your willingness to stretch your mind rather than just protect your GPA. And don't think they can't tell. They know when you have put it on cruise control and when you're still pushing yourself.

> —SAM ULMER
> NEWARK, DELAWARE
> UNIVERSITY OF DELAWARE

• • • • • • • •

FIRST, FIGURE OUT WHAT you want to study. The degree I wanted—marine biology—wasn't a popular one. And I'm from Chicago, so there were limited options around there. The degree automatically ruled out a lot of schools, which was a bummer. But I researched and eventually found a few places for me.

> —DUSTIN JOHNSON
> ST. PETERSBURG, FLORIDA
> ECKERD COLLEGE

It helps if you have learned to take responsibility for yourself at an early age and through-out your high school career.

—TRINA COOKE
STRUTHERS, OHIO

SAT/ACT:
How to Prepare?

*T*he SAT is just one determining factor that colleges use in an
alphabet of academic qualifications: other important "letters"
include your GPA, your ACT and SAT II scores, and your AP or IB
classes. But for most colleges, the SAT is a biggie: Schools that
receive many thousands of applications often make their first cut
based on these test scores. So - it's pretty important to put your best
test foot forward. We asked other students how they prepared for
these tests, so that you could learn from their successes - and, well,
lesser successes. Here are their stories and tips.

SAT AND ACT: six letters that every high school
student dreads! Most important when studying:
Learn your weaknesses. If you are really good at
math, work on the reading and logic sections,
and vice versa. It is important to know what
skills you lack and hone those for these tests.

—ANDREW J. BURKE
CINCINNATI, OHIO
🏛 UNIVERSITY OF CINCINNATI

**DON'T BE AFRAID
TO ASK FOR HELP!
I'M GLAD I DID.**

—DANIELLA KANAL
PITTSBURGH,
PENNSYLVANIA
🏛 STERN COLLEGE

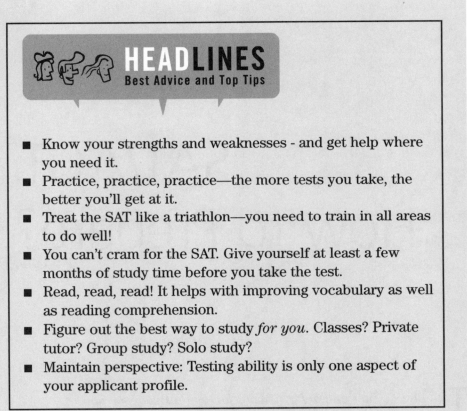

HEADLINES
Best Advice and Top Tips

- Know your strengths and weaknesses - and get help where you need it.
- Practice, practice, practice—the more tests you take, the better you'll get at it.
- Treat the SAT like a triathlon—you need to train in all areas to do well!
- You can't cram for the SAT. Give yourself at least a few months of study time before you take the test.
- Read, read, read! It helps with improving vocabulary as well as reading comprehension.
- Figure out the best way to study *for you*. Classes? Private tutor? Group study? Solo study?
- Maintain perspective: Testing ability is only one aspect of your applicant profile.

TAKE THE PSAT AS A SOPHOMORE to prepare for the SAT, which will be given during your junior year. That way, you are ahead of the game. I learned so much more about the actual SATs by taking the PSAT than from any of the study guides I read.

—*TRINA COOKE*
STRUTHERS, OHIO

You need to be realistic about your strengths and weaknesses. And if you're not, hopefully you will have someone close to you who can help you to see where you need tutoring. I was smart enough to know that I wasn't going to do well on the English portion of the SAT and got myself some tutoring before I ever took the test and screwed it up. You have to figure out where you need the help, and then be a big enough person to admit it and to seek it out.

> —*Ken Keel*
> *Winchester, Virginia*
> *University of Virginia*

• • • • • • • •

SAT scores don't measure your intelligence. They are a measure of how much money you or your parents were able to spend on classes and private tutors. Since you have to do well on them to get into college, I highly recommend spending as much as you can for help. I used Kaplan and The Princeton Review, and I had private tutors. They teach you tricks that help you during the test. For example, they teach you ways to know the answers to a section without reading the entire passage.

> —*Anonymous*
> *Los Angeles, California*
> *University of California, Los Angeles*

SHOULD YOU TAKE THE SUBJECT TESTS?

Deciding whether to take the SAT Subject Tests depends on where you want to go. Not all colleges require these tests, but more competitive programs want to see scores from two separate areas, along with your regular SAT. Several Ivies want to see scores from three tests.

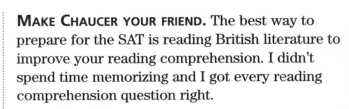

MAKE CHAUCER YOUR FRIEND. The best way to prepare for the SAT is reading British literature to improve your reading comprehension. I didn't spend time memorizing and I got every reading comprehension question right.

—*BRIAN WU*
CORONA, CALIFORNIA
UNDECIDED

• • • • • • • •

❝I did horribly on my SAT. What did I learn? Use the book, pay for the course, and pay attention to your math and grammar classes in school! And it's never too early to start preparing. ❞

—*WILLIAM WATTS*
BERKELEY, CALIFORNIA
UNIVERSITY OF CALIFORNIA, BERKELEY

• • • • • • • •

FIND A GOOD TEACHER. My teacher for the Kaplan SAT prep course was a young graduate from Lehigh University. He made it fun to come to class twice a week and encouraged the class to do the work: If we did, he would tell us a story about his adventures in college. Finding a class that was fun encouraged me to participate, and doing the work is what caused my scores to go up. I felt relaxed when I went to the test because I felt the class prepared me to the best of my ability.

—*ROB FEHN*
BASKING RIDGE, NEW JERSEY
LAFAYETTE COLLEGE

I TOOK A COURSE AT KAPLAN TEST PREP. The great thing about a course is not just that it gives you strategies you might otherwise miss out on, but it also forces you into a regimented study schedule, which ensures that you'll actually do the work. It's also a good way to meet people who are in the same boat and form study groups.

—*LAUREN ELIZABETH LEAHY*
DALLAS, TEXAS
SOUTHERN METHODIST UNIVERSITY

• • • • • • • •

THE FIRST TIME I TOOK the SAT I scored 2090, which is very good by most standards, but kind of disappointed me because of the average scores of the schools I was looking at. So I bought the College Board book and started buckling down. A lot of people turn to those review classes, but the book, with all its practice tests, is much more valuable. I tried to do about a 20-minute section a day, and corrected my errors as I went. There are always going to be things you don't understand, but the SAT is simple enough that usually an English or a math teacher offers the best help you can get. I gained 150 points after taking five practice tests. I feel confident I could have done even better with a little more practice.

—*ANONYMOUS*
ILLINOIS
YALE UNIVERSITY

The prep books can get costly, so if you know someone who's finished taking the tests you might want to trade your books. I traded my SAT II books for a friend's SAT I books, which cut down on costs.

—*QUINCY CHUCK*
HONG KONG
UNDECIDED

SAT = $$$

An estimated 12 to 17 percent of students who take the SAT spend from $400 into the thousands on prep classes and tutors, and many other students spend lesser amounts for school-sponsored, online and print resources.

WHAT IS AP?

AP (Advanced Placement) courses are advanced, college-level courses offered in high schools. There are exams for each of these courses, graded on a scale of 1 to 5, from which students may be able to gain college credit. Colleges have individual policies on what test scores, if any, are acceptable for credit. Top schools accept only a 5 for credit. In general, students competing for places at top universities are taking these courses and scoring 5 on the exams.

Use the book *10 Real SATs* and just keep doing practice problems. Also, learn a lot of vocabulary words.

—ALLISON LEVE
BALTIMORE,
MARYLAND
NEW YORK
UNIVERSITY

I WASN'T SATISFIED WITH MY SCORES, so I got the name of a private tutor from my friend who had raised his scores on the ACT. After a month or two of being tutored by this guy, I took the test. I got my scores back and they had gone up significantly. Get a private tutor: It really benefits you.

—ANGELA FRIEDMAN
PEORIA, ILLINOIS
BRADLEY UNIVERSITY

• • • • • • • •

I ENROLLED IN AN SAT PREP CLASS and it was a complete waste of money. I paid almost $1,000 for the course, "taught" by a guy who barely spoke English. The teacher just gave us practice tests; he didn't go over anything unless we asked about it. He would just sit there and wait for us to finish the test. What a waste! If I did it again, I would try to learn with a private tutor instead of taking a class. Ask around and see if anyone has recommendations.

—BARAK KRENGEL
DALLAS, TEXAS
UNIVERSITY OF KANSAS

WHETHER READING OR IN A CONVERSATION, whenever I encountered a word that I didn't recognize, I would take the time to look it up in the dictionary. Then I would attempt to use that word in daily conversation. This habit allowed me to further develop my vocabulary, to write on a more advanced level, and to improve my SAT writing scores.

—*BRITTANY RYAN*
DALLAS, TEXAS
UNIVERSITY OF OKLAHOMA

" Those courses they offer for the SAT's might sound like a waste of time, but they're not. My score went up 150 points after taking one, and I had a pretty decent score already. That definitely helped my chances. "

—*WILLIAM ALVAREZ*
LYNDHURST, NEW JERSEY
LA GUARDIA COLLEGE

Need reading inspiration? Check out The New York Times Best-Seller List:
www.nytimes.com/pages/books/bestseller/index.html

Or one of the 100 Greatest Novels:
www.randomhouse.com/modernlibrary/100bestnovels.html

Consider

I WISH I'D SPENT MORE TIME studying for the SAT and the ACT, and I wish I'd known a little more about the SAT subject tests. I just randomly chose U.S. history for the subject test and didn't score so well on it. I still scored fairly well on the SAT, but it would have helped if I'd studied more and brought my score up, even if it was just by 50 points—even 50 points is a pretty big deal for most colleges.

—*Dane Karl Skilbred*
Saint Paul, Minnesota
Santa Clara University

• • • • • • • • •

I TOOK THE SAT's THREE TIMES. I was never happy with my scores. The only time I was satisfied was after I did the CD-ROM prep course. I didn't believe it was going to be useful, but it was. What really helped me was the way they focused on test strategies, such as that the math questions are ordered in increasing magnitude and how you should pick one in the middle and work your way up or down. That helped.

—*David*
Newark, Delaware
Villanova University

WHAT IS IB?

The IB (International Baccalaureate) is a challenging, inter-national, standardized curriculum replicated in all countries around the world. The IB requires a specific set of courses, including a senior-year thesis, and several tests throughout the process, scored on a scale of 1 to 7. Colleges and universities may grant college credit based on the test scores. The IB is becoming more popular in U.S. high schools as an alternative to the AP curriculum for top students, but it is still not widely available.

GETTING TO KNOW YOU

Familiarity with the test — the question types and what they're looking for — helps students do better, says Brian O'Reilly of the College Board, which administers the tests. So, he advises: "Don't walk in cold. Every minute you spend reading the test directions is a minute you're not dealing with test material and answering questions." He recommends taking the PSAT and one or two other practice tests on your own right before taking the SAT.

AS FAR AS **SAT** PREP CLASSES GO, you need to know the levels of the class you've signed up for. I was in a much more advanced class than I should've been in, and it was hard to keep up. You may want to opt for a lower-level class so you feel as if you're at the same pace as the others practicing with you.

> —*ZACH HANDLER*
> *ST. LOUIS, MISSOURI*
> *BRANDEIS UNIVERSITY*

· · · · · · · · ·

I TOOK AN **SAT** PREP COURSE the summer before junior year and followed it up with individual tutoring sessions before each SAT that I took. I also took many practice SAT's through the tutoring center I used. After those tests, we'd go over my mistakes.

> —*ERICA ROGGEN*
> *SYRACUSE, NEW YORK*
> *SYRACUSE UNIVERSITY*

You cannot cram for the SAT. Instead, you must study over a period of time—preferably six months or more.

> —*TIMOTHY MICHAEL COOPER*
> *NEW YORK, NEW YORK*
> *YALE UNIVERSITY*

ASK THE EXPERT

HOW IMPORTANT IS THE SAT?

High schools and their grading processes are not created equal, so AO's need to look at national testing to help gauge talent on a single, measurable scale. A student can earn an A by learning in class, but also by cramming for a test. AO's want to know who has been learning. Also, the SAT tests some concepts that aren't always an official part of the high school curriculum. Grammar, vocabulary, certain types of math problem solving, and time-pressured reading comprehension are all areas tested on the SAT that students may not be explicitly tested on in high school. AO's understand that testing can be particularly challenging to some people, and that family income and access to test preparation influence students' scores.

Desirable students may not need the top scores if they can score well enough to show that they can do the work at the college, but students from major "feeder" areas for colleges will likely need strong scores.

While exact figures are of course impossible to ascertain, you can <u>very roughly</u> expect a more exclusive college to give your standardized test scores around a 30% weighting, with your high school record getting 40%, extracurriculars 10-20%, and the rest attributed to essays, recommendations, and other factors.

R.K.

GOOD SAT STUDY HABITS

START EARLY. Studying properly will require at least dozens of hours of preparation. While cramming may have worked for you in the past, it won't work here. You should begin studying during the spring of your junior year - at the latest.

PLAN YOUR STUDYING. When you first start preparing for the SAT, map out a plan of attack. Figure out what you need to learn and practice, and understand which materials you're going to work through for each section.

STUDY IN A CONSISTENT TIME AND PLACE. You'll be more relaxed and efficient if you set aside a consistent time and place to study, whether it's your bedroom on Tuesday nights or 3rd period study hall.

WORK FOR AT LEAST AN HOUR AT A TIME. The SAT is an ordeal that takes more than four hours to get through. Patience and improving your attention span are key skills. Studying for 15 minutes at a time may help you review concepts, but it won't help your brain get in shape for the actual SAT testing environment.

TIME YOURSELF. The SAT is what's known as a "speeded" test—time is definitely a factor. If you haven't been practicing doing questions with a clock or timer, then you're not ready for the test.

THINK <u>YOU'VE</u> GOT IT TOUGH?

Yeah, sure, you're putting in lots of hours boning up for the SAT. In South Korea, competition to get into college is so fierce, that more than 50 boarding "cram schools" have cropped up around Seoul. Students study from 7:30 a.m. until after midnight, 7 days a week, for the national college entrance exam. No cellphones are allowed on campus, no fashion magazines, no television, no Internet. No dating, no concerts, no earrings. Wanna trade?

WHEN YOU STUDY VOCABULARY WORDS, don't just look at the definition. Look at the word, get the part of speech, and look at it in a sentence. Define the word from context and then write a sentence that someone else could use to define the word. After that, look up the definition. It's slow and tedious but it really gets you to learn.

—*ANONYMOUS*
SIMI VALLEY, CALIFORNIA
UNDECIDED

• • • • • • • • •

THE MATH SECTION WAS the most challenging part for me. Not because I didn't know how to do the problems, but because I took calculus during my junior year in high school, so by that time I had forgotten all of the elementary stuff like fractions. So I bought some Princeton Review books and used them to review the materials and to refresh my memory.

—*ALICE HU*
REDMOND, WASHINGTON
STANFORD UNIVERSITY

DURING SAT SEASON, you will look (and be) tired, cranky and overworked. Use that to your advantage. Make your sister turn off that god-awful reality show. Put off cleaning your room for an entire month. The sky's the limit.

—*JAWON LEE*
SAN DIEGO, CALIFORNIA

• • • • • • • •

I DO NOT THINK THE SAT questions necessarily prepare you for college or real life, but the SAT does help you hone certain skills you need in real life—managing pressure, dealing with stress, and preparing for the test with seriousness and maturity.

—*DREW SILVERMAN*
ELKINS PARK, PENNSYLVANIA
SYRACUSE UNIVERSITY

• • • • • • • •

I GET REALLY NERVOUS ABOUT TESTS, so taking the SAT my sophomore year helped me relax. I focused on how to take the test and how to handle the pressure. It was amazing how much I learned about my test-taking skills when I was not focused on the grade. When I took the SAT in my junior year, I felt calmer and more confident in my test-taking ability.

—*LAURA BOUTWELL*
WINCHESTER, VIRGINIA
COLLEGE OF WILLIAM AND MARY

• • • • • • • •

DO TONS OF PRACTICE QUESTIONS. Then go over all the answers and figure out why you missed the ones you got wrong. There is no magic bullet; this is the only way to improve at taking the test.

—*TIMOTHY MICHAEL COOPER*
NEW YORK, NEW YORK
YALE UNIVERSITY

The key is to do lots of practice tests, make flash cards, and get a good night's sleep before the day of the test.

—*ELANA JUDITH SYRTASH*
NEW YORK, NEW YORK
YESHIVA UNIVERSITY

I LIKE TO THINK OF THE SAT as some sort of physical test. Let's compare it to a triathlon and its three sections. Swimming, running, and biking well are three things that would signify a good athlete. A person who is a great athlete will probably do well in a triathlon, but not always. Some people will never be able to swim well or bike well, no matter how hard they try. Some people may not be great long distant runners, but they may be great sprinters. Maybe they are top gymnasts or baseball players; their talents aren't exactly suited to a triathlon, but they are talented nonetheless. The SAT is much the same.

—*JOHN*
  VENICE, CALIFORNIA
  UNDECIDED

• • • • • • • •

IT'S A GOOD IDEA TO TAKE THE PSAT. I took mine in 10th grade and it really helped me prepare. All of my friends, except for one, did better on the SAT than they did on the PSAT, and I think that it's because the PSAT helps you prepare. The PSAT is very similar in style to the SAT, and you also get the experience of taking the PSAT in the same type of setting and environment that you will later have with the SAT.

—*BURTON DEWITT*
  MELVILLE, NEW YORK
  RICE UNIVERSITY

BLAME IT ON CALIFORNIA!

The University of California made the SAT a requirement for admissions in 1967. As a result, the test was quickly adopted as an admission requirement for universities nationwide.

I STUDIED FOR ABOUT TWO HOURS a week for two months from the College Board book. What worked for me was finishing a practice test, going back and looking at my mistakes. Figure out why you are getting problems wrong. Mark those problems. A month later, go back to it. Make sure you understand it this time.

> —ANONYMOUS
> ORADELL, NEW JERSEY
> UNDECIDED

• • • • • • • •

COMING FROM CANADA, I hadn't had the slightest preparation for the SAT's or what they really were. Kaplan helped me with answer strategies, study guides, and they stimulate tests so that we can adapt to other pressures like time and following instructions. It's those types of things (like time management) that most people tend not to focus on or even realize until they actually take their SAT's.

> —ELANA JUDITH SYRTASH
> NEW YORK, NEW YORK
> YESHIVA UNIVERSITY

Learn to use your time well, and you're already halfway to a high score.

> —JAWON LEE
> SAN DIEGO,
> CALIFORNIA

BUT I'M TOO BUSY AT SCHOOL TO FOCUS ON THE SAT!

Love it or hate it, the SAT is a huge part of the admissions process and you need to respect it as such. School is definitely the most important place for you to spend your time, and your grades in school are indeed the most important factor in college admissions. But test scores are a close second, and if you think about it, the time you spend on the SAT should do justice to the test's real importance. Between class time and homework, you'll probably devote at least 6,000 hours to schoolwork during your high school career. Doesn't the SAT warrant at least a good 40-50 hours of study?

HEADS UP: ACT vs. SAT

THE ACT MEASURES what you have learned in school while the SAT measures your verbal and reasoning aptitude. With the SAT's new Score Choice option, the SAT and ACT score reporting structures are more similar than before. Now, you may choose to send only the scores (from a single sitting) you think most reflect your capabilities for either the ACT or SAT. Here are some differences that remain:

- The ACT includes up to five sections: English, Math, Reading, Science, and an optional Writing Test. The SAT includes three: Critical Reasoning, Math, and a required Writing Test.

- The ACT is scored according to the number of correct answers; there is no penalty for incorrect answers. The SAT is scored based on the number of correct answers minus a portion for incorrect answers.

- The ACT is 3 hours and 25 minutes (including the optional writing test); the SAT is 20 minutes longer.

- The ACT has a total composite score of 1-36 based on the average of the 4 required sections; the SAT has a maximum total score of 2400 with 3 scores of 200-800 for each section.

- Most schools accept both exams.

PARENTS' PAGE

MY SON STARTED PREPARING for the SAT in ninth grade by taking practice exams. He took one at home about once a month, and with my help we simulated the testing environment as best as we could. When it came time to take the actual test, it was a breeze for him, and he only had to take it once. I really believe that this was a great way to prepare; no cramming, just part of a routine.

—*J.M.*
RENO, NEVADA
P ▪♟▪ UNIVERSITY OF PENNSYLVANIA

• • • • • • • • •

MY EXPERIENCE WITH BOYS THAT AGE: You need to give them a little bit of pushing and guidance. They tend to be less mature. Our son hadn't done particularly well on his SAT's the first time. So we enrolled him in a private SAT class. He went very regularly with a lot of pushing from us, three times a week, off and on for months. He didn't need us to convince him; he knew he needed to do well. He just needed to be prodded. He ended up doing very well, scoring in the 700s on all three sections.

—*ANONYMOUS*
COOPER CITY, FLORIDA
P ▪♟▪ DUKE UNIVERSITY

• • • • • • • • •

IT'S REALLY IMPORTANT TO KNOW your kid's strengths and weaknesses. My son can just sit down and ace standardized tests, but trying to get him to write essays is like pulling teeth. So, I had to get on him about that. Plus, he's more of a geek type, so it's harder for him to sell himself in interviews. My daughter, on the other hand, is great in interviews, but it is really difficult for her to study for the SAT's; I had to push her to take an SAT prep course. It's important to understand who they are as people, so you can tailor the way you help them prepare.

—*JORDAN CASELL*
STAFFORD, VIRGINIA
P ▪♟▪ UNDECIDED

SUGGESTED SAT CALENDAR

IF YOU'RE READING THIS BOOK as a sophomore or even a junior, you've got time to plan out—yes, and write down!—everything you need to do to get ready for the SAT. (And don't forget about SAT II's, if you need those too.) Keep a calendar or plan of action, and tack it on the fridge, wall, or bulletin board.

JUNIOR YEAR

- Find out when the PSAT is given at your school (assuming you haven't taken it in 10th grade) and put it on the calendar. If you're a very good test taker you might want to prepare for the PSAT, because it's the qualifying test for National Merit scholarships (only relevant for the top few percent of students).
- In the fall or winter, make a decision about whether you want to get a tutor or enroll in a course for the SAT. Note: The best teachers can fill up months in advance, so call in October or November to get into January or February courses.
- Decide whether to take the SAT, ACT, or both.
- Take the test for the first time in the spring (March or May for the SAT, April for the ACT). Put the test date on your calendar, as well as the deadline for signing up for the test.
- Make sure you plan out a study schedule that concludes before you take the exam. If you're taking a class or hiring a tutor, make sure the sessions all finish before the SAT test date.
- If you don't have the score you need for the colleges to which you're applying, take the test again in June.

SENIOR YEAR

- Assess your SAT score in light of where you plan to apply.
- Reconsider your study plan and think about hiring a tutor or joining a class if you haven't already.
- If necessary, take the test again (and, possibly, again).
- Relax—it's all over!

I THINK EVERYONE should at least practice each test so they can see which one fits them better. I preferred the SAT over the ACT, because I felt that breaking it up into a lot of sections made it less overwhelming, and I did not feel as rushed for time. If I had to do it all over again, I would not take the ACT, because the SAT seemed to fit my test-taking abilities better.

—*BEN*
SPRINGFIELD, ILLINOIS
UNIVERSITY OF ILLINOIS AT URBANA-CHAMPAIGN

• • • • • • • •

IT'S A GOOD IDEA to have at least one SAT and two or three SAT II's done by the end of your junior year. This way, if you are dissatisfied with your scores, you can get a few retakes in by the beginning of your senior year. Keep in mind that you will not see your October SAT scores before most top colleges' early-decision deadlines. Many schools will accept scores from October and even November and December, but you will not be able to evaluate your chances if you're using those scores.

—*MICHAEL WYMBS*
BEACH HAVEN, NEW JERSEY

Take the ACT's. I took the SAT's three times, and did so much better taking the ACT's once.

—*ADAM KRESSEL*
MIAMI, FLORIDA
CORNELL UNIVERSITY

A PERFECT 2400?

About 1.5 million students took the SAT in 2007, and only 269 nationwide achieved a perfect score (we interviewed a few of them for this book!).

AT FIRST I USED FLASH CARDS for vocabulary, but once I started taking practice tests, I realized that the same base of about 400-500 words were used repeatedly. I knew about half of them right off the bat. Just by taking the tests I was able to figure out some of the words I didn't know right away, and I looked up the words that I was really having trouble with and couldn't figure out from the prefixes and suffixes and just common ideas of what the word might be. There were maybe about 20-30 words that I had to study and memorize. There's a definite cycle of words that they use.

—AARON
BEVERLY HILLS, CALIFORNIA
UNIVERSITY OF CALIFORNIA, BERKELEY

• • • • • • • •

I ACTUALLY WISH that my parents had pushed me to study.

—BEN
SPRINGFIELD, ILLINOIS
UNIVERSITY OF ILLINOIS AT URBANA-CHAMPAIGN

PREP AND SAVE

- Stress can sometimes hurt SAT scores more than a lack of academic knowledge. Familiarity with the test can help test-takers calm down.
- Take advantage of test-preparation tools such as the free timed practice tests, complete with monitors, run by Kaplan and The Princeton Review.

THE WAY TO WORD POWER

The best way to train for the SAT Reading sections involves no studying at all: Just read. Read as much as possible. If you read just a few articles in The New York Times every day for a year, you will have come across a huge percentage of the words you'll encounter in the SAT. The test won't even seem like a test anymore. Other tips for vocabulary:

- While you're reading, watching TV, etc., carry a notebook around with you. List all the words you don't know. Look them up when you get home. This is the best way to really learn new words. There's no way you're going to learn every word in the English language, nor do you need to.
- Concentrate on the words the SAT uses the most, which can be found on Sparknotes.com, in The Princeton Review's guidebooks, and elsewhere.

—TIMOTHY MICHAEL COOPER
NEW YORK, NEW YORK
YALE UNIVERSITY

I WORKED FOR AN SAT PREP COURSE in exchange for private tutoring lessons. They really helped with my scores, so if you don't have the money, I would definitely approach a local test preparation center and see if they are up to some kind of bartering.

—LINDSAY
LOS ANGELES, CALIFORNIA
UNIVERSITY OF CALIFORNIA, SANTA BARBARA

I recommend SAT flash cards. They are a stress-free way to study and you can use them alone or with a partner.

—*Blayne Alexander*
Edmond,
Oklahoma
Duke
University

Don't think that just because you're taking lots of advanced placement classes in an academic school that these will prepare you for the SAT; they won't. The only thing that will specifically prepare you is a review class. And although a review class may be expensive, it's worth it. I took a review class and did tons of practice tests to help prepare. I'm convinced that all those practice tests helped me do better.

—*Michal Rosenoer*
Corte Madera, California
University of California, Berkeley

• • • • • • • •

I would not study with friends because it is too distracting. I invited some girlfriends over to study one time and we ended up playing drinking games all night. That was the last time I studied with a group. Not only didn't I accomplish anything that night, but the next day I was so hung over that I missed studying that day too.

—*Ashley*
San Francisco, California
University of Southern California

ASK THE EXPERT

How do you prepare for the SAT or ACT? Prepare!

It's really that simple. At least ten weeks before your exam, make sure you have a study plan in place. I find my students have much more success working with a tutor or in a prep class as opposed to relying on themselves to study on their own. It isn't that you *can't* do it on your own, but you're human! A class or tutor forces you to show up physically and mentally each time, versus letting procrastination take over.

J.Y.K.

QUITE THE FEAT

In 2008, a Birmingham, Alabama student named Lauren Faraino earned a perfect score on the SAT. Amazing enough. But what's more amazing is that Lauren was born with limited use of her arms – she took the entire test writing with her feet!

" I studied with my friends for the Math part of the SAT. Some of us were better at certain problems, like Algebra II, and others were better at logic word problems. We all gained from each other's expertise. "

—*Molly*
Las Vegas, Nevada
University of Arizona

• • • • • • • •

THE THIRD TIME I TOOK IT, all I did was buy one of those Kaplan books. I had friends who spent over $1,000 on a tutor, but if you're willing to do the work you can get just as much out of a $15 book.

—*Andrew Timberlake*
Birmingham, Alabama
Yale University

Expert Advice

IECA* COUNSELOR SURVEY

If a student could do only one thing to prepare for the SAT, which of these should s/he do?

Read books – 11%
Take SAT practice tests – 50%
Take a preparatory course – 22%
Hire a consultant – 0%
Other – 17%

TAKE THE PRACTICE TESTS. I found that my Math score went up without me really doing anything from junior to senior year. You just have to practice. The more you answer those types of questions the more comfortable you will be when you actually take the test. There are no "new" questions, so the more familiar you are with samples, the better it will be.

—*MERYL BRANCH-MCTIERNAN*
BROOKLYN, NEW YORK
SYRACUSE UNIVERSITY

• • • • • • • •

IF YOU TAKE A PREP CLASS and then take the test multiple times, it's important to review the material they taught you in that class between tests. I took a class for the SAT through my school, and then took the test at the end of that class, in the spring of my junior year. After the class, I did very well. But when I took the SAT again in the fall of my senior year, my score went down 110 points because I didn't review.

—*TERESA*
PLANTSVILLE, CONNECTICUT
UNIVERSITY OF CONNECTICUT

I TOOK A HALF-SEMESTER-LONG COURSE at my school to prepare before I took the test. It met once a week for three hours and we took practice tests and discussed test-taking strategies. We worked out of a big SAT workbook-type thing, and we had practice tests to do for homework as well. Take the course close to the test date: The second time I took the test, I performed worse than I did the first time because I hadn't really prepared well and I'd forgotten simple little strategies that I'd picked up during the class.

—CARRIE BERTOLOZZI
CHAPEL HILL, NORTH CAROLINA
UNIVERSITY OF NORTH CAROLINA AT CHAPEL HILL

• • • • • • • •

I REALLY WANTED TO TAKE THE SAT courses but there was no way my family could pay for that. So I went to the Princeton and Kaplan centers and bought their curriculum/lesson plan books. I also purchased numerous SAT books, including the one provided by the College Board. And whenever I had time, I solved problems and took test after test. Of course, I had school, friends, and, you know, life, so I did all this mostly late at night or during breaks. It was all worth it when my scores went up over 400 points.

—JIKYU CHOI
FAIR OAKS, CALIFORNIA
STANFORD UNIVERSITY

You will get so sick of taking tests, but I guarantee that nothing will surprise you on the day of the actual exam.

—SARAH CARRIER
NORTH GRANBY,
CONNECTICUT
WASHINGTON
UNIVERSITY IN ST.
LOUIS

REPEAT PERFORMANCE

The average scores for the three sections of the exam were identical for the classes of 2007 and 2008: 502 in the critical-reading section, 515 in mathematics, and 494 in writing.

SERIOUSLY!

GO BUY A PRACTICE TEST COMPILATION. Don't borrow it from the library or pay for it, skim over it, then return it to the bookstore and get $20 back. Buy it! This is so that you can mark, scrawl and notate all over it without reservation. (Or, if you'd like, stab it repeatedly with a pencil in frustration.)

Then take the test, just as you would when you're taking the real test. Lock the door, close the window, shut down the computer, turn off the stereo, put away the iPod and snacks, clear the desk, and kick the cat and/or dog and/or younger sibling out of the room. There should only be you, the test, writing utensils and a clock to keep the time. And do keep the time, especially if you find yourself running out of it frequently.

You need to learn how to work quickly and accurately. Do write the essay, before you start on everything else, just like in the real test. Afterward, ask someone else to grade it for you, unless you think you can be honest with yourself.

> —*JAWON LEE*
> *SAN DIEGO, CALIFORNIA*

SOME PEOPLE THINK IT'S DUMB to take SAT prep classes because the SAT is just supposed to test your aptitude. True, but how would you feel if a dumb friend of yours somehow got into Duke while you're stuck at a community college, all because you were unfamiliar with the structure of the exam and the types of questions they provide, thereby resulting in a low SAT score? Think of prep classes as an investment to make your profile that much more appealing.

—*SOLOMON CHANG*
PROVIDENCE, RHODE ISLAND
COLLEGE OF WILLIAM AND MARY

• • • • • • • • •

THE FORMULA REALLY DOES come down to stretching one's mind from a young age with things like math team and reading The New York Times every day. I could take an intellectually average (but willing!) 6th grader, and after five years of math enrichment, essay work, and bookworming (hopefully with a love of reading instilled since age 5 or so), and have them turn out at least a 2000 combined score. Does that mean the trick is 50 percent parenting, 30 percent good teachers, and 20 percent plain mental horsepower? Yeah, that sounds about right.

—*STEVE ESTES*
NEW YORK, NEW YORK
COLUMBIA UNIVERSITY

S'POSE IT CAN'T HURT

At Bowdoin College, which hasn't required SAT scores since 1969, an estimated 80 percent of applicants submit their scores anyway.

DEALING WITH PARENTS

THEY MEAN WELL. THEY REALLY DO. But sometimes parents can add an unbelievable amount of stress to the SAT process. Here are some tips for dealing with them:

- Take ownership of your own SAT preparation. Think of it from their perspective: their pride and joy is taking an important test, and they want to do everything in their power to make sure you get the highest possible score. If they see that you're signing up, studying, etc., on your own, they'll realize they don't need to worry and nag.
- Give them updates. Keep your parents in the loop about your SAT plans, and be loud and obvious about all of the studying you're doing.
- Manage expectations. It's tough to know in advance how you'll do on the SAT. But when you do have an idea of how you're doing based on practice exams (and the PSAT), you should tell your parents. If your parents understand your possible college admissions outcomes, it will spare them an emotional roller coaster (and spare you the fallout!).

R.K.

TRY TO GET YOUR STUDYING DONE on your own schedule when you have the free time, because that way you'll be able to really concentrate on what you're doing. If your parents have to force you to study when they think you need to, you won't be able to focus because you'll be mad about the party or the game or some other fun you're missing out on.

—*JOHN STEPHEN REBER*
CINCINNATI, OHIO
GEORGETOWN UNIVERSITY

IT CAN BE HELPFUL to prepare for and take the test at the same time as your friends. When my friends and I found out that we were going to be testing on the same day, I would keep in mind that the others were studying, so I probably should too. And we all had to wake up early on Saturday morning, so staying out late with them was not likely to happen.

—RONALD JORDAN HINSON
LENOIR, NORTH CAROLINA
CLEMSON UNIVERSITY

• • • • • • • •

FIRST, I STARTED WITH BASIC VOCABULARY, high-school level; then I moved on to Word Smart by The Princeton Review. After memorizing those words, I raised my score about 100 points. Then, I started reading magazines, newspapers and books: The New York Times, The Economist and U.S. News & World Report. My score improved every year.

—JOON NAM
MURRIETA, CALIFORNIA
UNDECIDED

What really helped prepare me for the Reading and Writing sec-tions were the books *Eats, Shoots & Leaves, The Elements of Style,* and *The Grammar Bible*.

—JIAHAO
SINGAPORE
MIDDLEBURY COLLEGE

Expert Advice IECA⁺ *COUNSELOR SURVEY*

Do SAT preparatory courses usually boost a student's score by 75 points or more (on all components of the SAT I combined)?

Yes – 67%
No – 22%
Not sure – 11%

I DON'T BELIEVE IN MEMORIZING vocabulary at all. There's no point—you either have the knowledge to begin with, or you don't. It takes years of reading to develop a full vocabulary. You can't cram. It's better to do some questions and learn the question style. Most of the time you don't need to understand all, or even most of it. You just need to be able to get a general idea of what's going on. I got an 800 in Critical Reading and there were definitely two or three words in there I wasn't sure about.

—ANONYMOUS
MIAMI, FLORIDA
COLUMBIA UNIVERSITY

• • • • • • • • •

VIEW DISCOURAGING **PSAT** subsection scores as springboards rather than vexations. My advice for math is pretty generic (unfortunately): note the question types that present the greatest problems for you, and practice them. Since I have trouble completing an entire practice test, I focused on the "hard" problems and skipped the ones classified as easy (the ones I knew I could get right). I'd usually do the last 10 problems of each Math section and found that this conserved time while allowing me to focus on the true problem areas.

—STEPHANIE
NEW FAIRFIELD, CONNECTICUT
UNDECIDED

S.A. WHAT?

Several hundred colleges no longer require either the SAT or ACT for admission. For a list, see www.fairtest.org.

OTHER SAT STUDY OPTIONS

Not all of these will work for everyone, but one or more of them might work for you:

STUDY WITH FRIENDS. A study group can be a fun (and free!) way to make sure you're devoting time to the SAT. Having a group of friends nearby can make SAT prep easier to deal with and you can help each other with tough problems. Just make sure to stay focused!

GO ONLINE. The Internet is full of SAT study options. While the big companies offer expensive online courses (not always a great choice), there's also lots of free help. The College Board offers free practice questions and even a free sample practice test at http://www.collegeboard.com/student/testing/sat/prep_one/test.html.

STUDY ALONE. If you've got the discipline and can set aside the time, simply studying on your own with prep books can be a perfectly good option. You can either buy practice books from the top test prep firms or simply use the College Board's *Official SAT Study Guide*.

FINDING A GOOD SAT CLASS OR TUTOR

CONSIDER YOUR LEARNING STYLE. Are you comfortable learning in a large group setting, where you can take notes and absorb strategies but not interact much with the instructor? Do you do better studying in small groups? Would you prefer to work one-on-one with a private tutor?

DO YOUR RESEARCH. There's no advanced degree or certification required to be an SAT instructor. That's why instructors run the gamut, from established professionals who aced the SAT to jokers without any real SAT knowledge. So before you choose a teacher or tutor, find out a little background, including years of experience and what he or she scored on the actual exam. Also, don't just assume that a big company will have the best people.

FIND AN OPTION THAT FITS YOUR ABILITY LEVEL. Classes usually work best when everyone is at *roughly* the same level. If you're way ahead of, or behind, the rest of the pack, you may want to consider a course designed for someone at your level or to hire a private one-on-one tutor.

TAKE BOTH TESTS. I think that colleges like to see the SAT because it has been around for so long that they feel it is a good benchmark. But how you do depends on the type of person you are, so why not take both? The best thing about the ACT is that if you do poorly on it, you don't have to send your scores.

—*VIDYA SATHYAMOORTHY*
ROCKVILLE, MARYLAND
UNDECIDED

JUST PUT TIME INTO IT. I enrolled in a six-week SAT tutorial program. The only real advantage to the program was that it forced me to sit down for at least an hour each week, and focus my full attention on SAT preparation. In comparison, most of my peers were probably devoting half of that or even less to their own SAT study guides. The program's selling point was that it guaranteed to raise my score 100 points over the course of the program, and I did meet that goal. However, I think that my progress was due more to the simple time spent practicing problems and less to the tricks and gimmicks that the program taught me.

> —MAX MALON MALLORY
> NEW YORK, NEW YORK
> SARAH LAWRENCE COLLEGE

It's funny: I found when I didn't study as much my overall score went down - but my math score went up a little.

> —JEREMY
> ARCADIA,
> CALIFORNIA
> JOHNS HOPKINS
> UNIVERSITY

" I wasn't happy with my SAT score, so I decided to try the ACT. I had heard encouraging things, that it works for students who have trouble with the SAT. Either I got 100 points smarter overnight, or people were actually right. "

> —NATALIE ROSE SPITZER
> DECATUR, GEORGIA
> GUILFORD COLLEGE

Studying with your friends can be really helpful if your friends are as serious as you are.

—TIM
PHOENIX, ARIZONA
UNDECIDED

WHAT MADE ME STUDY the hardest for the ACT exam was not my conceited parents or my desire to make them proud of me. I wanted an extremely high test score because my two best girlfriends and I made a bet that, whoever scored the highest would never have to pay when we went out—for the whole summer before college. Plus, the winner was to receive a weekly allowance of ten dollars per loser. We were women of our word, so we took that bet.

—MARIJOSEPHE BROWN
PLANO, ILLINOIS
ELMHURST COLLEGE

TRAIN YOUR BRAIN

If you want a real gauge of how you'll do, set yourself up each weekend for a month with a real practice test. Create as-close-to-real-testing-conditions as possible. Score the exam yourself. No one has to see but you! Ask yourself: have I studied and prepared as much as I can for this exam? If the answer is yes, you will never look back and say "I could have done more."

Prep work is as much about training your brain, anticipating the next step to each question, and feeling confident. Nerves play a role. If you feel prepared, trained, and confident, you'll breeze through with ease and ultimate success.

J.Y.K.

 **Expert Advice** IECA⁺ *COUNSELOR'S CORNER*

TIMING YOUR SAT SUBJECT TESTS

The SAT Subject Tests are offered in several areas, including Math, Language, History & Social Studies, English, and Science. It's best to take the Subject Test in the spring after you have completed the subject in school. For example, if you are taking AP U.S. History, take the Subject Test around the same time you are preparing for the AP exam. Take the Chemistry exam right after you've finished a full year of the course. Math 1 is best to take towards the end of honors algebra 2 and when you still have a good handle on geometry. For Math 2 you'll need to be almost done with trigonometry. If you plan to major in engineering or something science- or math-related, it's important to take a math and science Subject Test.

—LISA BLEICH
PRESIDENT, COLLEGE BOUND MENTOR, LLC
COPYRIGHT © 2008 COLLEGE BOUND MENTOR, LLC. ALL RIGHTS RESERVED.

I GOT HELP AT A SYLVAN PROGRAM. The help they give you is great, if you are willing to do the work! Thirty minutes a day is really all you need.

—JENNIFER KEYS
BALTIMORE, MARYLAND
NEW YORK UNIVERSITY

• • • • • • • •

A GOOD STRATEGY for reducing stress is tuning out people who harp on how hard the test is. It only intimidates you and fails to inspire the confidence that adequate preparation should bring.

—CLAIRE
EL PASO, TEXAS
CLEMSON UNIVERSITY

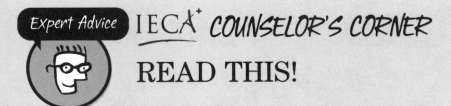

IECA⁺ *COUNSELOR'S CORNER*

READ THIS!

EVEN IF YOUR DAYS ARE CRAMMED WITH SAT TUTORS, community service in Costa Rica, or resume-boosting courses at Ivy League colleges, a trip to your local public library might be your most effective college prep strategy. Besides the simple pleasure of getting lost in a good book during a heavy thunderstorm, reading will have many benefits.

Need help figuring out black hole questions like your college major or career? Reading is a great way to pursue topics that interest you. If you think you might be interested in politics after watching *The Daily Show* and *The Colbert Report*, try picking up a good newspaper or a weekly news magazine to follow the candidates on the campaign trail. Biographies and autobiographies are also informative. For students contemplating a career in medicine, books covering health care issues at home and abroad, ranging from Tracy Kidder's *Mountains Beyond Mountains* to Atul Gawande's *Better* are eye-opening. *A Civil Action* by Jonathan Harr is a non-fiction introduction to one lawyer's big case.

The more of the world you see by reading on your own couch, the stronger your voice in your college essays and interviews. In fact, some application supplements or interviewers ask specifically about books you've read. Why not exude enthusiasm about a topic of interest rather than relying upon your junior year required readings? *The Grapes of Wrath* and *The Great Gatsby* get old fast for seasoned admissions officers.

Reading might help too, with those nasty SAT and ACT retakes still looming. As you read, have index cards and a dictionary handy. Sure, flash cards are dorky, but looking up words is a great way to increase vocabulary for those challenging SAT sentence completions. When those Fall tests roll around, you might even notice that you're moving through the reading passages faster and with better comprehension.

—*ELISE R. EPNER LLC*
COLLEGE ADMISSIONS CONSULTING
© *2008 ELISE EPNER*

I FOLLOWED THE ADVICE of an upperclassman friend of mine and signed up to have the College Board e-mail me The Official SAT Question of the Day. You can sign up on their website. I did one of those practice questions every day for about three months prior to taking the test, and that really helped me feel prepared.

—CAITLIN MYERS
CINCINNATI, OHIO
MIAMI UNIVERSITY

• • • • • • • •

IN THE FALL OF MY JUNIOR YEAR I started going to an SAT tutor who prepped me in the math and verbal sections, as well as the writing. It was very helpful, as the tutor picked up on my individual areas of weakness and helped me remedy them. I ended up increasing my score by almost 200 points. I imagine that an SAT class would not have helped me as effectively in that way.

—SAM
PALO ALTO, CALIFORNIA
STANFORD UNIVERSITY

Expert Advice **IECA* COUNSELOR SURVEY**

Although all students are different, generally speaking how many hours should a student devote to studying for the SAT?

1-20 – 31%
21-50 – 38%
51-100 – 19%
More than 100 – 12%

PRIVATE TUTORING WORKED BEST FOR ME. I took The Princeton Review class in the fall. Then I began self-studying around the first week in December for the January SAT, and I met with a tutor once a week to go over practice problems. Classes like the one I took are easy to lose concentration in and you can be easily distracted, especially with friends in the class. Private tutors force you to practice on your own, and you need to have stuff completed to go over with them.

—*TOM O'BRIEN*
SCRANTON, PENNSYLVANIA
UNDECIDED

• • • • • • • •

MY PARENTS STARTED PLANNING for me to take the SAT the day I was born. I didn't know it at the time, but now I realize that all of those verbal and math software programs they've been buying me throughout my lifetime were preparatory classes in disguise. I guess I owe them a lot because I felt really prepared for the SAT and I barely studied at all.

—*ASHLEY*
SAN FRANCISCO, CALIFORNIA
UNIVERSITY OF SOUTHERN CALIFORNIA

THE SAT SUBJECT TESTS

In addition to the SAT, some universities require SAT Subject Tests, which measure knowledge in specific areas. These tests help admissions committees assess how much you are learning in your classes—the SAT reflects math and English, but the SAT Subject Tests address other areas.

SAT/ACT: Strategies & Tips for Besting the Test

S ometimes it feels like there is a mysterious order of evil wizards who conspire to make the SAT or ACT as distressing as possible for everyone. Not so! Remember that the SAT and ACT will not single-handedly determine your future. More important, there are some basic, straight-forward strategies and tips that will help you succeed. There's no great secret to it—read on to hear from others how they've demystified the tests. Try some of these techniques, and see which work best for you.

DON'T OVERTHINK the Writing portion. I wanted to knock their socks off, so I spent a good 10 minutes outlining and thinking of something great to write. I had intended to write a five-paragraph essay. I got through one pretty good paragraph and then one more—and the time was up!

—ANONYMOUS
ST. LOUIS, MISSOURI
UNDECIDED

WATCH OUT FOR THE SAT "SUCKER ANSWER."

—C.B.
NEW YORK, NEW YORK
SYRACUSE UNIVERSITY

FOR THE WRITING PART, you have to get their attention right off the bat. You need a really clear opening paragraph, including a clear, concise thesis statement. If you lose the people who grade these tests at the start, you'll likely never get them back. Take extra time, if necessary, but come out of the gate strong. If you don't, it won't matter how you finish the essay.

—ANONYMOUS
BROWNSVILLE, MARYLAND
UNIVERSITY OF MARYLAND

• • • • • • • •

MAKE THE ESSAY VERY SHORT and concise and don't try to write anything amazing. I wrote about the necessity of perseverance and dedication to success. I tried to find a historical example, a literary example and a personal example. The books say you should do that, and it worked pretty well for me.

—ALEXANDER
PROVIDENCE, RHODE ISLAND
BROWN UNIVERSITY

• • • • • • • •

WHENEVER I SKIPPED A QUESTION, I used different symbols (like stars, circles, etc.) to mark the questions I had no clue on, and the ones I thought I might be able to figure out when I looked over the test again. That way, if I had only a few minutes left in the testing session, I could focus on the questions that I felt I could work out, instead of wasting time on questions that I knew I didn't know how to do.

—LAURA BOUTWELL
WINCHESTER, VIRGINIA
COLLEGE OF WILLIAM AND MARY

SPECIAL CIRCUMSTANCES

FOR ME, THE SAT's WERE THE MOST DIFFICULT PART of the college application process. The first time I took the SAT's, I was right in the middle of Lyme disease treatment. I had an IV in my arm. I had to get up very early on the day of the test, and I wasn't used to doing that. It took a long time to think about things, and I had to muddle through. My score wasn't bad, but if I hadn't been sick I would have done a lot better. I'd suggest that anyone who's sick look into special accommodations. I didn't do that because I didn't want to be different. I was still at the beginning of my illness and was still coming to the realization that I needed special help. I made it a lot harder on myself than it needed to be.

> —*KELLY*
> *HERNDON, VIRGINIA*
> *GEORGE MASON UNIVERSITY*

• • • • • • • •

TO ACCOMMODATE MY DAUGHTER'S ADHD, I tried to talk to her about the true value of the SAT's, so she could approach them with less anxiety. The true value means that she's good at taking the test; that's the only thing it tells. This wouldn't be a true measure of whether she was smart or would succeed in college. In preparation for the SAT's, I had an SAT tutor to help her. When it came time to take the test, she was allowed to take untimed tests. You have to go through the guidance counselor to do this. As it turned out, she applied to a school—Sarah Lawrence College—that asked for test results but didn't put a lot of emphasis on them.

> —*ANONYMOUS*
> *PHILADELPHIA, PENNSYLVANIA*
> *P SARAH LAWRENCE COLLEGE*

HEADLINES
Best Advice and Top Tips

- Use any extra time you have to double-check your work.
- The SAT is a marathon: Give it your all. At the end of the test, you should have nothing left in the tank.
- Finish all the questions you know the answers to as quickly as possible. Then go back and tackle the ones that gave you trouble.

I WAS REALLY INTIMIDATED by the Math section at first. The first time I ever took a real practice test after the PSAT, I think I got nine wrong in one section! I tried not to be discouraged and went back and reviewed why I had gotten each problem wrong. I started to recognize patterns and similar types of questions that the College Board tends to ask. From that point on, the sight of a familiar type of question prevented me from panicking. I also stopped consuming valuable time by refusing to stay stuck on a particular question. I moved on, found one that I could answer with confidence, and then went back to it.

—*STEPHANIE*
NEW FAIRFIELD, CONNECTICUT
UNDECIDED

I'M A SLOW READER SO I really had to strategize when it came to the Reading part. I had to use short cuts; one of the things I did was read the questions relating to the passage, then go back and read. Then I knew what I was looking for. Otherwise I would have gotten bogged down thinking every detail was important. It's also really important to follow the clock. You should bring your own clock; the clock was behind me and it was distracting to keep looking back at it.

—HALEY
   PETALUMA, CALIFORNIA
   UNIVERSITY OF CALIFORNIA, DAVIS

. . . .

AS FAR AS TIMEKEEPING GOES, I SAY: practice, practice, practice! Timekeeping was my biggest trouble spot when I took the SAT. I had to do countless sections from practice tests (and time myself!) before getting the timing right, especially in the Math section. Try to pace yourself.

—CHRISTINE TODD
   VERO BEACH, FLORIDA
   NORTHWESTERN UNIVERSITY

. . . .

I DID REALLY WELL ON THE VERBAL, but I still had to pay close attention to the trick questions. On the sentence completion questions there would often be answer choices that sounded like the right word. You have to be alert to these tricks because there are so many words that sound the same and even have almost all of the same letters. There are points in the test where you just get so tired and can easily fall victim to the slight variances.

—EMMA
   WASHINGTON, D.C.
   PITZER COLLEGE

SAT math questions are arranged in ascending order of difficulty. Don't spend too much time on the first questions; you'll probably answer them easily.

—B.T.
   WILMINGTON,
   DELAWARE
   UNIVERSITY
   OF DELAWARE

SAT STRATEGY I:
YES, GUESS

WHILE STUDENTS ARE TYPICALLY TOLD *not* to guess randomly on the SAT, on average the wrong answer penalties will exactly cancel out the points you get from correct guesses. So if you have no clue on a question, you can either guess or not guess. And if you can eliminate even one answer, guessing is a no-brainer. Just don't spend time on crazy guessing theories such as, "'C' hasn't come up for a while, so the answer to this question must be 'C'!" They simply don't work.

On the ACT there is *no* guessing penalty, so you must fill in absolutely every bubble.

Use your calculator to go back and check your math if you have time at the end. Use every minute to double check.

—*MICHAL ROSENOER*
CORTE MADERA,
CALIFORNIA
UNIVERSITY OF
CALIFORNIA,
BERKELEY

SOMETIMES A PASSAGE in Critical Reading will bore you to tears and you'll want to come back to the whole thing later. But if you walk in with enthusiasm, thinking "these passages are sure gonna be fun to read," as I do, it's usually not a problem. The passages usually *are* fun to read, and when I studied with others the passages occasionally sparked good discussions.

—*JESSICA*
BOCA RATON, FLORIDA
CALIFORNIA INSTITUTE OF TECHNOLOGY

PC ADVICE

Remember that the correct answers on the SAT's are always politically correct! For instance, in a passage about Native Americans (perhaps, "What attitude does the author have towards Native Americans?"), let's say the answer choices are: A) They are a primitive, uneducated race; B) Their culture is interesting and worth learning about; C) Their craft skills are second-rate in comparison to our modern industrial skills; and D) They are a beautiful people with important social and religious beliefs. Right away, you can rule out choices A and C because they put Native Americans in a bad light by calling them primitive and uneducated and by downplaying the level and importance of their skills. Your choice between the remaining answers, B and D, will depend on the specifics in the passage you have read.

—*Christine Todd*
Vero Beach, Florida
Northwestern University

THE WORST PART ABOUT TAKING the SAT is the length. Just sitting through the whole thing was a challenge in itself. After a while, I just couldn't concentrate. I was on the last Reading section and I got to the point where I would read the entire section and not even remember what I read. I panicked a little bit, then forced myself to concentrate and went back over it.

—*Elizabeth*
Denver, Colorado
Claremont McKenna College

ALL QUESTIONS COUNT EQUALLY, so don't worry if you don't get to the hardest ones. In fact, if you know you're not going to get to every question, just focus on the easier questions (the ones closer to the beginning of each section), since they count as much as the ones toward the end of the section. As you get closer to the end of one section of a particular type of question, the answers almost always get less and less obvious. So if you see a question in the last half or especially the last third of a section of questions and the answer jumps out at you, that's almost definitely the wrong answer.

—*TIMOTHY MICHAEL COOPER*
NEW YORK, NEW YORK
YALE UNIVERSITY

> I circled all the answers right on the test booklet and then went back later and transferred my answers to the answer sheet. That way, I stayed in the 'answering mode' and there was no going back and forth wondering, 'What number was I on?'

—*TORI*
BIRMINGHAM, ALABAMA

IT IS OKAY TO LEAVE SOME of the answers blank. On high school tests, you're told to answer every question. But with the SAT, if you cannot make a good guess and are absolutely clueless, then leave it blank. It goes against what I was taught, but it helped to relieve the stress by allowing me to focus my time on questions I knew the answer to or could make a good guess on. I scored much higher on the SAT when I left a few blank than when I answered every single question.

> —*LAURA BOUTWELL*
> *WINCHESTER, VIRGINIA*
> *COLLEGE OF WILLIAM AND MARY*

MAKE SURE TO ANSWER all of the questions about one passage before continuing to the next passage. You may think that you'll remember everything once you return to the first passage towards the end of your allotted time. But you will be much better off if you complete each passage's block of questions in the same group, as opposed to mixing them up with other passages.

> —*CHRISTINE TODD*
> *VERO BEACH, FLORIDA*
> *NORTHWESTERN UNIVERSITY*

On multiple-choice tests, there is always the right answer and the sucker choice. I always fell for the latter.

—*C.B.*
NEW YORK, NEW YORK
SYRACUSE UNIVERSITY

SAT STRATEGY II: TAKE SHORTCUTS

The SAT is not like any old test in school. On the SAT, only the right answer matters—no one is grading *how* you got to your answer, or whether you did a good enough job of showing your work. So don't write out every step to a math problem unless you need to. Feel free to test answers to see which ones work, ignoring the "proper" way of doing the problem. If you found an easy way to eliminate an answer, go for it.

SAT STRATEGY III: SKIP THE TOUGHEST QUESTIONS (FOR YOU)

Unless you're planning to get a nearly perfect SAT score, there will probably be a handful of questions that you should skip. Giving up on questions is, of course, never ideal, but on a very difficult, time-pressured test it can be a valid strategy. Skipping questions means that you run out of time on the *hardest* questions (the ones you skipped) instead of simply the ones at the end, which may not be the hardest ones for you.

WHENEVER I TEST, I MARK THE answer in the book, and cross out whatever I eliminate in the book. This helps keep my choices in elimination more visible. After every five questions, I transfer all circled responses into the answer sheet to save time spent going back and forth between the sheet and the booklet. When time starts to run out, though, I fill the bubble as soon as I get the answer. To skip questions, I circle the number and move on. I can't afford to waste any time on something I have to think too long on. Once I'm done with the section, I go back to the circled problems and can usually figure them out by then. Sometimes simply having time on other questions can clear your mind to tackle the hard question you skipped, with full force.

—JOSEPH ANDA
LITTLE ROCK, ARKANSAS
UNDECIDED

WHEN READING LONG PASSAGES, look ahead to the questions for the section and underline the parts of the paragraph that apply to each question. This way, when you read through it the first time, you'll pay special attention to the underlined parts, and when you are looking between the paragraph and the questions, the underlined portions catch your eye much faster, saving you many precious seconds.

—*ALLISON FOREMAN*
COLUMBIA, SOUTH CAROLINA
CLEMSON UNIVERSITY

• • • • • • • •

" After skimming each passage, I answered those questions that referred back to particular lines of the passage before answering the one on the main point of the selection. "

—*BROOKE*
ST. LOUIS, MISSOURI
PRINCETON UNIVERSITY

• • • • • • • •

DON'T SPEND TOO MUCH TIME on each question. If you don't know the answer in a minute, just leave it blank. This really helped me because I found that I was able to get through the entire test and answer the questions that I knew really quickly and go back to the more difficult ones.

—*ELISA VIERA*
WHITTIER, CALIFORNIA

CRITICAL READING:

- Make sure to answer based on what the text says - rather than on what you want it to say!
- Finish each Reading Comprehension section as quickly as possible. If you fall behind, you'll have to tackle your next section that much faster.

THE COLLEGE BOARD PRIDES itself on being extremely open-minded and liberal. No correct answer in the Reading Comprehension section would ever be the least bit negative about women or minorities. Thus, any answer that could possibly be interpreted as saying that women or minorities are incapable of any achievement is definitely wrong. Correct answers in the Reading Comprehension section tend not to make blanket statements—that is, statements that use all-encompassing words like "all" or "always" or "every" when discussing a group. Therefore, an answer like, "All British citizens were in complete agreement about how to handle the problem of colonization" is pretty much guaranteed to be incorrect.

—TIMOTHY MICHAEL COOPER
NEW YORK, NEW YORK
YALE UNIVERSITY

FOR THE CRITICAL READING SECTION, too many kids answer what they feel they *want* the answer to be, rather than choose the answer that portrays best what the text says. I did well by never giving an answer that wasn't clearly in the text. Historical passages really catch people off guard. They are confusing and they try to make the test taker answer the question with whatever coincides with their stance or their prior knowledge, rather than what the text says.

> —*NIKITA BIER*
> *PALOS VERDES, CALIFORNIA*
> *STANFORD UNIVERSITY*

• • • • • • • •

I DID BETTER WHEN I followed my own instincts rather than my tutor's directions, who told me to read the questions first and then read the actual passage. I took the SAT twice using that strategy and made about the same score each time. But on the third try, I did the opposite and I raised my score by 100 points in just that section.

> —*JACK ALTMAN*
> *ST. LOUIS, MISSOURI*
> *UNDECIDED*

SAT STRATEGY IV:
KEEP YOUR OWN TIME

Don't rely on the wall clock or on the proctors who are supposed to remember to call out time. They have the final word, of course, but it's dangerous to rely on a clock that you may not be able to see well or on monitors who may forget to call out warnings. Besides, a wall clock with hands isn't the best way to time a 25-minute test section. If a section starts at, say, 9:48, you'll practically have to do a math problem each time you look at the clock just to figure out how much time is left!

TOP CRITICAL READING STRATEGIES

DON'T FOCUS TOO MUCH ON VOCABULARY. Vocabulary is a part of the SAT, but it doesn't account for nearly as much of the test as it once did. It's probably not the best use of your time to study thousands of vocabulary words.

BROWSE OR SKIM THE PASSAGE BEFORE ANSWERING QUESTIONS. Most students will do best on the passage-based questions if they look through the passage before doing the questions. Sometimes it's tempting to do the questions first, looking back into the passage for answers. But using roughly one-third of your time quickly reading the passage—getting the important parts, looking for meaning, and establishing a roadmap in your head—will make the questions more understandable.

WATCH THE CLOCK. Timing is probably more important on the passage-based Reading portion of the SAT than anywhere else on the test. If you spend too much time on one passage, you'll do poorly on the next because, in addition to being forced to speed up, you won't have time to read the passage carefully before answering the questions.

HEAD**LINES**
Best Advice and Top Tips

MATH:

- You're better off skipping the hardest three questions instead of the three that happen to be last in the section.
- Quickly check your work after each question; it takes five seconds.

AFTER EVERY QUESTION, I quickly checked my work to make sure I didn't make careless mistakes; it only took about five seconds. Even doing this, I had about two to three minutes left over on all three sections to review. While I was taking practice tests for the Math section, I used to get a couple wrong, on average, each time. When I went back and reviewed my answers, I felt like a total idiot. I was committing careless mistakes that a 4th grader could probably recognize, and I decided this had to change to get the 800 I wanted. After some time, I discovered that the best time to check your work was right after you did the problem, because the question's information is fresh in your mind. Five to ten seconds of checking time should do it, and you still won't run out of time.

—*NEIL SHAH*
ENCINO, CALIFORNIA
UNDECIDED

IF A SKETCH DOESN'T SAY, "Not drawn to scale," that means that it *is* drawn to scale. For geometry problems there is almost always a sketch. One time I couldn't figure out the answer, but I could tell that line Y was about 3 times the size of line X, so that was my answer. It was the difference between a 780 and an 800. So sometimes when you can't figure out a problem, the answer is right there in front of you in the picture.

—*ANONYMOUS*
ORADELL, NEW JERSEY
UNDECIDED

66 On one problem in the Math section, I was not getting an answer that matched any of the choices, so I moved on. I ended up only missing that one question, so it was probably a good idea not to get stuck on it. 99

—*RAHUL RAJ MALIK*
BIRMINGHAM, ALABAMA
UNDECIDED

TOP MATH STRATEGIES

USE YOUR CALCULATOR WISELY. It's important to know what your calculator can do, and how to use it, before the SAT. Today's calculators not only do simple arithmetic functions, but also help you deal with a number of more complicated parts of the SAT Math section. Once you're certain that your model of calculator is allowed, make sure you integrate its features fully into your SAT study.

DON'T BE AFRAID TO 'PLUG AND CHUG'. For the SAT only, forget everything you've been told about showing your work. No one's looking to test whether you remember the proper approach.

SKIP THE HARDEST PROBLEMS. Unless you think you can ace the Math section, it's important that you not spend too much time on any one question. If you run out of time -- and you almost surely will -- you're better off skipping the three *hardest* questions (for you) instead of the three that were randomly last in the test order.

ALLOW FOR INCREASING DIFFICULTY. The math questions generally get harder from the front to the back of each section. Don't be fooled when pacing yourself: if you're halfway done with the test after half of the time is gone, you're actually way behind, because the problems in the second half of the section will probably take much longer.

WRITING:

- On the essay, write as much as you can. Studies have shown that longer essays grade out better.
- Take a few minutes to plan out your essay. It will help you avoid rewriting it!

FOR THE ESSAY SECTION you are given a prompt and you pretty much have to take one side of the argument and support it in your writing. The prompt is on a topic that most people can answer; you just have to apply your writing skills. It helps if you really focus on only one side, though; be for it or against it. Use lots of examples to support your side and squeeze as much information as you can in the small space and limited amount of time you are given.

—*SHARLA*
KAUAI, HAWAII
UNIVERSITY OF SOUTHERN CALIFORNIA

• • • • • • • •

IN THE WRITING SECTION, the more you write, the better. Try to fill up the entire space. Use your neatest handwriting. That's the fastest way to improve your score other than writing intelligently, making a coherent argument, and using specific details from literature and history, which are also good tips.

—*TIMOTHY MICHAEL COOPER*
NEW YORK, NEW YORK
YALE UNIVERSITY

SAT STRATEGY V: STAY FOCUSED

The SAT is a marathon, not a sprint. This may be the most important test you ever take, and you should treat it as such. Hunker down over your answer sheet, move quickly, and answer each question as if it were the most important thing in the world. When you leave the SAT you should have no gas left in your tank. If you can still think straight, you probably didn't work hard enough.

BEFORE READING THE ESSAY PROMPT, it helps to have a skeletal outline in mind; in addition to writing an introduction and a conclusion, I planned to support my thesis with three paragraphs: one discussing a novel, another a historical event, and a third a current event. I had a couple of books, historical events, and current events in mind that I thought I could easily adapt to whatever topic was given.

> —*BROOKE*
> *ST. LOUIS, MISSOURI*
> *PRINCETON UNIVERSITY*

• • • • • • • •

I TOOK AS MANY PRACTICE TESTS as I could and I tried to find similarities between them. I noticed, for example, that a lot of them were written in a quasi-narrative form, just talking about an experience that made the writer have the opinion that they do. So I basically used that form. I answered the prompt by explaining how one day convinced me of a certain idea.

> —*ANONYMOUS*
> *MIAMI, FLORIDA*
> *COLUMBIA UNIVERSITY*

INSTEAD OF SIMPLE SENTENCES, mix it up by using reverse syntax, starting with participial phrases. Throw in a few ostentatious words, like "ostentatious." Put a colon in, use semicolons, cut a few dashes; they look impressive and could help boost your score.

> —*JIAHAO*
> *SINGAPORE*
> *MIDDLEBURY COLLEGE*

• • • • • • • •

I'M AN ENGLISH AS A SECOND LANGUAGE student. The essays were a problem. When I took my first SAT, I had to make the outline in Korean (because I thought a lot faster in Korean than I thought in English) and then translate into English, and then fill in the rest. So in the first SAT, I did not have the time to finish the essay, and for the first few practice tests I never seemed to finish the essay on time. This is where I got outside help from friends; they told me to use the simple five-paragraph format, with an introduction, body paragraphs, and endings. As I got better with English, I was able to gradually think better in English, write up the five-paragraph outline, and write the essay on time.

> —*JIKYU CHOI*
> *FAIR OAKS, CALIFORNIA*
> *STANFORD UNIVERSITY*

• • • • • • • •

THEY GIVE YOU A SINGLE PAGE of writing so it's not even an essay; it's about how tight you can squeeze your words and how many cool facts you can throw out there. Remember that the reader is only going to look at your essay for a minute or less.

> —*AARON*
> *BEVERLY HILLS, CALIFORNIA*
> *UNIVERSITY OF CALIFORNIA, BERKELEY*

TOP WRITING SECTION STRATEGIES

WRITE A LONG ESSAY. Investigations have shown, and common sense dictates, that human essay graders tend to assume students are better writers when they write long essays.

PLAN YOUR ESSAY. If you spend three to four minutes planning your essay before beginning to write, you'll do a much better job keeping it organized, integrating examples, and knowing what you want to write about.

IDENTIFY THE SPECIFIC MISTAKE IN MULTIPLE-CHOICE QUESTIONS. Don't just answer these questions by chosing the selection that you think "sounds" or "feels" right. Almost always there will be something that's objectively, definitively wrong about a wrong answer choice. Try to find the problem, rather than just relying on your instincts.

CHECK ALL OF THE ANSWERS. Answer C may sound good until you take a good look at D. If you have time, look at every answer choice before you choose one.

Expert Advice I E C A⁺ **COUNSELOR SURVEY**

Of your students who take both the SAT and ACT, do you find that they tend to perform better on one versus the other?

Yes, they often perform better on one – 61%
No, their scores are pretty much the same on both – 39%

Write as much as you possibly can. That seems to be what the graders care about.

—*ANONYMOUS*
ST. LOUIS,
MISSOURI
WILLIAMS COLLEGE

I TOOK THE PSAT with no prep at all, just to see what I would get, and I got a 230, which is comparable to getting a 2300 on the SAT. I felt that I did not need to prepare for the SAT. But the PSAT doesn't have an essay, and my Writing score ended up dropping 70 points because I didn't really prepare for the essay enough. Practice writing essays in 20 minutes, and have general "fallback topics" in mind ahead of time. The essay prompt will generally ask for examples—literary, historical or personal—to help prove your point. For me, having made a list of four or five books that I had read recently would have helped me a lot, because you get in there and your mind freezes.

—*BECKY*
NEWTON, MASSACHUSETTS
SWARTHMORE COLLEGE

＂No matter what you do, don't go off topic on the essay. The length doesn't matter; the test scorers just want to see that you can focus on one idea and see it through to the end of the essay. ＂

—*CHRISTIE*
CINCINNATI, OHIO
UNIVERSITY OF CHARLESTON

SAT HORROR STORY #72: READ THE FINE PRINT

My friend once wrote an entire SAT essay on being Jewish because he thought the essay question was asking about ethnics, not ethics.

—*ELIZABETH*
MADISON, WISCONSIN
UNIVERSITY OF SOUTHERN CALIFORNIA

I WAS SURPRISED TO FIND THAT the Science section on the ACT had absolutely nothing to do with the science or chemistry or biology that I had been learning in school. It's more about proficiencies and reasoning than actual scientific content. Don't think that just because you do well in those subjects you'll do fine on the test—you should still take some practice tests so you get a feel for what it's about.

—*TEKLA TOMAN*
YOUNGSTOWN, OHIO
XAVIER UNIVERSITY

• • • • • • • •

DON'T SKIP AHEAD! When I took the SAT in October, a guy in my room went ahead to the next section since he finished early. The proctor caught him, kicked him out, and informed us that the College Board would actually put in his score report to colleges that he cheated on the test.

—*ANONYMOUS*
SIMI VALLEY, CALIFORNIA
UNDECIDED

SAT/ACT: Test Day . . . and Beyond

Y ou've woken up early for more Saturdays than you want to recall for that SAT prep class. Your ACT study guide is the only thing in your bedroom that isn't dusty. You've studied like mad; you know in your gut you've done all you can to prepare. Now it is 5pm on the evening before test day. What do you do besides bow to the SAT gods and rub your lucky charm like crazy? Hear from others how they made it through the lead–up to, the morning of, and that blissful moment: when it's all over!

I LEARNED THAT THE SAT means nothing. A few years after taking it, I do not even recall my scores, nor are they important, nor did they predict my success thus far in college. Try to do well, of course, but you aren't labeled by your SAT score.

—NICOLE SPENCE
WYCKOFF, NEW JERSEY
🎓 EMORY UNIVERSITY

CHECK GOOGLE MAPS BEFORE YOU LEAVE YOUR HOUSE.

—MIKE MELLENTHIN
MENLO PARK,
CALIFORNIA
🎓 STANFORD
UNIVERSITY

HEADLINES
Best Advice and Top Tips

- Get a good night's sleep for several nights before the test. Eat a good breakfast on the morning of the test.
- Have everything you need—including your calculator and directions to the testing site—laid out the night before.
- Leave plenty of time to travel to the testing site.
- Relax: high anxiety won't help you test well.
- Expect the unexpected; students have been known to get physically ill at these tests!
- Don't let clueless proctors and cheating students distract you; stay focused on your work.

I read a magazine or a newspaper before I took each test to get my mind going and get myself focused.

—*Laura Elaine Goldsticker St. Louis, Missouri*

IF YOU TRULY BELIEVE YOUR SAT was scored incorrectly, you can pay $50 to have it scored by hand. My scores were a lot lower than I expected and I believed that the cause was eraser marks. I paid the $50 and it turned out that there was a scoring mistake.

—*Brian Wu Corona, California Undecided*

• • • • • • • •

I TOOK BOTH THE SAT AND ACT twice in an attempt to better my score. In both cases, when I received the higher score, I had been with friends the night before at a theater cast party, relaxing and having fun. The best advice I can give is just relax about it. Yes, it's important, but keep in mind that it's just words, bubbles to fill in, and a couple of pencils. It does not and cannot truly define you as a person.

—*Jessica Pauley Chillicothe, Ohio University of Cincinnati*

I TOOK THE SAT'S TWICE, and did significantly better the second time. I did not study for the second one, but rather I just had the confidence of knowing what to expect. Confidence is the key with these tests; it is very important to not worry about it for too long. When people would try to talk to me about being nervous about the test, I would always change the topic.

—*NATHANIEL COHEN*
WEST HARTFORD, CONNECTICUT
NEW YORK UNIVERSITY

. . . .

" Don't carpool to your SAT exam. It's hard to see a friend walk out at the end of the test and feel as if you have to rush to get out and get a lift home. "

—*LAUREN SHER*
GAINESVILLE, FLORIDA
UNIVERSITY OF FLORIDA

. . . .

KNOW WHEN THE SAT TAKES PLACE! I forgot about my SAT's! I was not motivated at all to take it since I was already content with my ACT score and was confident that I wouldn't do any worse than I had on the PSAT. So one night I came home at 1 a.m. and saw my SAT registration paper on the table, and I realized I had to wake up in five hours to take it.

—*ANDREW*
MEQUON, WISCONSIN
DUKE UNIVERSITY

FOOD FOR THOUGHT
(OR AT LEAST FOR THE SAT'S!)

THE SAT RULES SAY NO FOOD DURING THE TEST, but I can't do without
food for even a minute. Since I've broken every food law on earth, I
naturally brought food into the test. My advice, though, is to bring
something that doesn't melt. I brought chocolate, but when I reached
into my pocket to get it, it was completely melted. I had to keep lick-
ing my fingers throughout the test.

> —*JANET*
> *LOS ANGELES, CALIFORNIA*
> *UNIVERSITY OF CALIFORNIA, LOS ANGELES*

. . . .

I DRANK COFFEE AND I WAS FINE for the first section and then I
crashed. I hit that caffeine low, which is something you definitely
don't want to do when you have four hours of rigorous test work
ahead of you.

> —*BRADLEY HOUSTON*
> *AUSTIN, TEXAS*
> *RICE UNIVERSITY*

. . . .

MY DAD TOLD ME TO EAT a chocolate bar about 20 minutes before taking the test, because chocolate releases endorphins in your system
and helps your brain react quicker. I'm not sure if it's true, but it gave
me a good excuse to eat a bar of chocolate at nine in the morning!

> —*JENNIFER STEWART*
> *MURFREESBORO, TENNESSEE*
> *MIDDLE TENNESSEE STATE UNIVERSITY*

. . . .

ON THE MORNING OF THE TEST, I drank purple grape juice. There was
an article in the newspaper about a couple of kids who both made
perfect scores on the old SAT and they said they drank grape juice in
the morning.

> —*ALEX*
> *BIRMINGHAM, ALABAMA*

I NEVER REALIZED HOW HUNGRY and thirsty I would get, and I didn't realize that eating wasn't allowed in the testing room. I prepared for this the second time by bringing a granola bar and eating it and getting a drink quickly during the three-minute breaks. I basically learned after taking the SAT for the first time that even the smallest things that occur can make a big difference. Being prepared for the little things that you didn't expect can add up to big point increases.

> —*MATTHEW HABER*
> *HOLLAND, PENNSYLVANIA*
> *CORNELL UNIVERSITY*

• • • • • • • •

MY SAT-DAY ROUTINE was very specific: I got up early and ran around the block twice, to get my blood pumping. I had my favorite breakfast (eggs and toast), wore my favorite college sweatshirt and used pencils that were my favorite colors (blue and purple). It was all very comforting.

> —*MICHAEL GOODWIN*
> *PROVIDENCE, RHODE ISLAND*
> *WASHINGTON UNIVERSITY IN ST. LOUIS*

• • • • • • • •

ON THE DAY OF THE TEST, I made sure to wake up extra early so that I wouldn't be groggy. I ate a good breakfast (salmon and eggs; my mom always made that before a test or a track meet). Also, music helps me wake up and get excited, so I played loud music all the way to the test. Silence would have made me nervous and sluggish.

> —*BLAYNE ALEXANDER*
> *EDMOND, OKLAHOMA*
> *DUKE UNIVERSITY*

• • • • • • • •

BRING A SOMEWHAT HEALTHY SNACK to the test. I was starving by the time we had our break, and I was so glad to have it. It helped me gain back a little energy for the rest of the test—something I doubt the old chocolate bars in the vending machines did for other test-takers.

> —*TEKLA TOMAN*
> *YOUNGSTOWN, OHIO*
> *XAVIER UNIVERSITY*

I WAS TAKING THE TEST and we had our first break. For some wacky reason I had brought a huge Asian pear to eat. I ate it and we went back to testing. I was doing math and suddenly my stomach started grumbling very loudly so that other kids could hear it. It was a little embarrassing once I noticed other kids snickering. I'm going to take the test again, and next time I'll eat a better breakfast and bring a granola bar or something.

> —*AMAR PANJWANI*
> *APPLE VALLEY, CALIFORNIA*
> *UNDECIDED*

I THOUGHT THAT DRINKING VITAMIN WATER was a good idea but then I really had to go to the bathroom and couldn't leave! I was ready to burst at the seams and I think that may have been distracting for me. Don't drink a lot before the test and be careful—those little sips can add up and you'll be sitting with your legs crossed!

> —*STEFANIE LAMPRECHT*
> *TIBURON, CALIFORNIA*
> *SANTA CLARA UNIVERSITY*

BRINGING A HEALTHY SNACK for the longer breaks really helps you to refocus when your energy level gets low after sitting at a desk for hours.

> —*TERRAHNEY WILSON*
> *LITHONIA, GEORGIA*
> *UNDECIDED*

MAKE SURE THE TWO MEALS you have before the test have a significant amount of protein. I had steak for dinner, and eggs for breakfast. And make sure you bring a snack for the break of the test. Otherwise you will become more tired as the test drags on.

> —*ZACH LEVY*
> *ATLANTA, GEORGIA*
> *UNIVERSITY OF GEORGIA*

MY MOM WOULDN'T LET ME eat eggs the morning of the SAT because eggs look like zeros, so they're bad luck. It's an Asian thing.

—*FEI ZANG*
CAMARILLO, CALIFORNIA
WASHINGTON UNIVERSITY IN ST. LOUIS

• • • • • • • • •

I WAS ALWAYS TOLD THAT you should drink white grape juice the night before a test because it helps the neurons in your brain fire faster.

—*MAX MALON MALLORY*
NEW YORK, NEW YORK
SARAH LAWRENCE COLLEGE

ONE TIME I GOT REALLY ANXIOUS BEFORE A TEST and I took this pill called Klonopin. It's a prescription pill that you take to calm down. I couldn't stop shaking and throwing up before my test, so I just took it. Well, I got about 20 minutes into the test when I realized the test pages were turning colors. I just sat there and watched the pages change colors for a while. I stayed for the whole test and I don't even remember if I finished it because I was too interested in watching the pages change colors. Never resort to a one-time fix to calm you down. I'm on anti-anxiety pills that are daily and those are fine. But I wouldn't take any medication beforehand that you don't have a lot of experience with.

—*RAYNA*
NEEDHAM, MASSACHUSETTS
CLAREMONT MCKENNA COLLEGE

REMEMBER THIS NAME
In 1999, Vinodhini (Vino) Vasudevan made national headlines as the first 12-year-old to earn a perfect SAT score.

YOU CAN DEFINITELY RAISE YOUR SAT scores by more than 100 points: I raised my math score by more than 150 points. I wasn't happy with my score the first time I took the test, and then I studied a lot with books. I set a goal of getting above a certain score in math and I kept going at it until I got it. I wanted to prove to myself that I could do it. I was in heaven when I got the scores back. That was more fun than getting into my school. I just remember walking around so happy, smiling all the time.

—*DOV KAUFMANN*
RA'ANANA, ISRAEL
PRINCETON UNIVERSITY

• • • • • • • •

THE FIRST TIME I TOOK THE SAT, I was scared: I thought if I didn't get a certain score, I wouldn't be accepted to my top schools. I did decently, but I wasn't satisfied. I ended up taking it a second time, this time feeling that I had nothing to lose, since colleges only look at your best score. My score went up considerably, even though I didn't prepare any more than I did the first time. I attribute it to being a lot calmer when I was taking it. I didn't feel rushed, the words didn't blur together in the reading section like the first time.

—*KATHERINE BELL*
STANFORD, CALIFORNIA
STANFORD UNIVERSITY

Expert Advice **IECA⁺** *COUNSELOR SURVEY*

Do students generally improve their scores if they take the SAT more than twice?

Yes – 44%
No – 56%

MY FRIEND AND I WERE on spring break during our junior year of high school and came up with the terrible idea to take the test while we were in Florida. We stayed up until 5 a.m. the night before and walked in after about three hours of sleep. Neither of us had taken classes or prepared in any way. I pretty much stared into space during the entire test. I got a decent score, but I could've done better if I'd been better prepared.

—*SCOTT COOLBAUGH*
KNOXVILLE, TENNESSEE
UNIVERSITY OF TENNESSEE

' Make sure you know where the test site is *before* the day of the test. I've heard way too many horror stories about getting lost on the way to the test site on the morning of the test. ''

—*CARRIE BERTOLOZZI*
CHAPEL HILL, NORTH CAROLINA
UNIVERSITY OF NORTH CAROLINA AT CHAPEL HILL

BE PREPARED FOR ANYTHING. I had to take my SAT partly in the dark because the school lost power. But my score was OK, and I didn't want to go through that again, so I didn't retake it.

—*ANONYMOUS*
BREMEN, INDIANA
INDIANA UNIVERSITY

BEFORE THE MORNING OF THE EXAM, make sure you have lots of pens and pencils, and a calculator with an extra battery. If you like using a timer, bring one. And if you're taking the test for the first time, just keep reminding yourself that you can take it many more times.

—DANA
LAWRENCE, NEW YORK
HARVARD UNIVERSITY

• • • • • • • •

I took the SAT at my high school. The familiar setting calmed my nerves.

—WHITNEY TRITT
ATLANTA, GEORGIA
WAKE FOREST UNIVERSITY

MY BEST FRIEND WENT TO A DIFFERENT high school than I did. Since we didn't see each other every day, whenever we got together, we were always out of control. The second time I took my SAT, she happened to be in the same room with me, since our last names are right next to each other in the alphabet. Just being in the same room with her threw off my concentration because we couldn't stop laughing at each other. Needless to say, I scored below my first SAT results. Moral of the story: Don't take the SAT's in the same room as your best friend, because you won't be able to take *anything* seriously.

—JESSICA
SARATOGA, CALIFORNIA
UNIVERSITY OF SOUTHERN CALIFORNIA

A NUMBER TWO PENCIL AND A STICK OF GUM

Research has found that chewing gum stimulates certain areas of the brain, which may have a relationship to reducing tension. Furthermore, one recent study showed that chewing gum appeared to improve people's ability to retain and retrieve information.

DRESS FOR SUCCESS

IF YOU TAKE THE TEST ANY TIME other than summer, make sure you take a jacket or sweater. A lot of schools turn off their heat over the weekend, which is when the test takes place. At one of my test-taking sessions, they forgot to leave it on for the test, and I froze the whole time!

>—*JOHN STEPHEN REBER*
>*CINCINNATI, OHIO*
>*GEORGETOWN UNIVERSITY*

WEAR SOMETHING THAT YOU'LL be comfortable in for a few hours, but not sweats or pajamas; doing that will make you want to go to sleep.

>—*CASEY PONTIOUS*
>*LOCUST GROVE, OKLAHOMA*
>*FREE WILL BAPTIST BIBLE COLLEGE*

I'M A JEANS-AND-SANDALS TYPE of girl so I went to my SAT dressed comfortably. But don't dress too sloppy, or you'll get too relaxed and probably fall asleep, like one guy next to me, who came to the test in his pajamas. And don't get too dressed up because you might get uptight. And please, no heels. I remember one girl who kept going to the bathroom, and I can still hear her three-inch heels clicking in my ear. I'm sure I got a couple of answers wrong listening to those heels.

>—*BETH HARVEY*
>*CHICAGO, ILLINOIS*
>*KENTUCKY WESLEYAN COLLEGE*

THE SECOND TIME I TOOK IT, I had already decided where I hoped to go to school. So I wore my school-of-choice Washington University shirt for good luck. It worked!

>—*CAITLIN ASTRUE*
>*BOSTON, MASSACHUSETTS*
>*WASHINGTON UNIVERSITY IN ST. LOUIS*

SLEEP—BEFORE, NOT DURING

DON'T FREAK OUT. I exercised a lot the week of the test. I slept well, and the day of the test I did the best that I could.

> —*HANNAH ASSADI*
> *SCOTTSDALE, ARIZONA*
> *COLUMBIA COLLEGE*

• • • • • • • •

GET A GOOD NIGHT'S SLEEP. I actually fell asleep for five minutes during the SAT! I still answered all the questions and did well, but if you need the full allotted time, falling asleep would definitely be a problem.

> —*B.A.R.*
> *HILTON HEAD, SOUTH CAROLINA*
> *WASHINGTON UNIVERSITY IN ST. LOUIS*

• • • • • • • •

GET SOME SLEEP BEFORE THE SAT. I only took it once, and I fell asleep halfway through. As you can imagine, my scores weren't as good as I hoped. I mean, I did OK. But I was nervous about them for a while, because I had been drooling on my test.

> —*JESSAMYN GOSHOM*
> *WASHINGTON, D.C.*
> *UNIVERSITY OF MARYLAND, COLLEGE PARK*

• • • • • • • •

IT'S REALLY IMPORTANT TO GET A FULL NIGHT'S SLEEP the night before your test, but don't try to go to bed too much earlier than you are used to because your internal clock will be completely off and it will really mess you up. I usually go to bed at midnight, but decided to go to bed at ten the night before my SAT, and I woke up feeling more tired than ever.

> —*A.C.*
> *BERKELEY, CALIFORNIA*
> *UNIVERSITY OF CALIFORNIA, BERKELEY*

• • • • • • • •

FORGET CRAMMING. Get some sleep.

> —*JAWON LEE*
> *SAN DIEGO, CALIFORNIA*

I GOT A **2360** ON THE **SAT** the first time I took it, and as much as I would like a 2400, I'm not going to go through that again. I decided that it wasn't worth it. With my score I knew I would be in the top 25 percent of applicants to my schools of choice. Look at the colleges you want to go to and if your scores are significantly lower than the top 25 percent of applicants, I would advise doing more prep for the SAT and retaking it. Otherwise, you don't need a perfect score; stop worrying and go celebrate.

—*PATTY LU*
TINTON FALLS, NEW JERSEY
UNDECIDED

Turn off your phone—they *will* take your test if it rings!

—*COLLEEN DAVIS*
LEXINGTON,
KENTUCKY
WASHINGTON
UNIVERSITY IN ST.
LOUIS

‘The only people in college who will care about your SAT score are the admissions officers, and their opinions cease to matter once your freshman year starts. ’’

—*JAWON LEE*
SAN DIEGO, CALIFORNIA

PAIR OF ACES

In the summer of 2006, Jakub Voboril, a 17-year-old from Kansas, aced both the ACT and the SAT. It's not known how many students have accomplished the feat, but a College Board spokesman admitted, "It's a very, very small number."

I KNEW THAT IT WAS IMPORTANT that I get a good score and I did everything I could to prepare. But I also knew that it was necessary for me to have good grades, extracurricular activities, essays, and interview, and I focused on those as well. In the end, I scored lower than some of my classmates on the SAT, but I got into several schools that they didn't.

—*BLAYNE ALEXANDER*
EDMOND, OKLAHOMA
DUKE UNIVERSITY

• • • • • • • •

SIGN UP EARLY. LOCATION IS SO IMPORTANT, and if you don't sign up early, you may not get to take the test at your first choice. Many of my friends ended up taking the exam at faraway locations. They told me they were uncomfortable, people were cheating left and right, and it was loud. I got to take my exam at Beverly Hills High; it was quiet and I was really comfortable because it was my actual high school.

—*AARON*
BEVERLY HILLS, CALIFORNIA
UNIVERSITY OF CALIFORNIA, BERKELEY

EAU DE SAT

Whenever I studied for the SAT's I wore the same perfume (Ralph Lauren's *Romance*) and sucked on the same candy (Lemonheads). When it came time to actually take the test, I again wore *Romance* and sucked on Lemonheads. Your senses of smell and taste are very strong; they can put you back in the same element so you'll remember better.

—*DANIELLE SILBER*
ST. LOUIS, MISSOURI
WASHINGTON UNIVERSITY IN ST. LOUIS

WHEN YOU FINISH A SECTION EARLY ...

Frankly, you shouldn't be finishing *any* section of the SAT with lots of extra time to spare. It's a hard test. But if you *do* finish early, even with just a few extra minutes, here's what you can do:

CHECK TOUGH PROBLEMS FIRST. It's nearly impossible to go back and catch silly mistakes with just a few minutes to spare. Instead, you should mark the most difficult questions as you proceed and go back to them at the end if you have extra time.

ON THE ESSAY, CHECK FOR ERRORS. Make sure you used punctuation properly, didn't make any of the grammar mistakes that sometimes trouble you, and write legibly throughout the essay.

DON'T BE AFRAID TO TAKE A SHORT BREAK. If you have just a few minutes and don't see a good way to use your time, go ahead and take 1-2 minutes to close your eyes, focus, and prepare for what you know lies ahead.

R.K.

I SIGNED UP LATE FOR MY TEST, so I couldn't get the location I wanted. I ended up taking my exam in a place where I noticed there was a lot of cheating going on. It made me really uncomfortable, especially when I realized there were people trying to look at my answers. I never said anything because I was scared, but I also ended up canceling my scores because I could not concentrate at all and I knew I wouldn't do well. The next time I signed up, I made sure to do it well in advance.

—*ASHLEY*
SAN FRANCISCO, CALIFORNIA
UNIVERSITY OF SOUTHERN CALIFORNIA

I TOOK THE SAT in two very different environments: a prestigious private school, and an urban public school in the city. It seemed to me that the kids in the first setting were taking it more seriously, and somehow it was easier for me to concentrate in that setting. Even though it was my second time and I theoretically was more prepared, I scored lower in the city classroom. I don't want to sound snobby, but try to take the test in the best setting possible, where the kids are the most serious about it.

—*ANONYMOUS*
TIBURON, CALIFORNIA
UNIVERSITY OF CALIFORNIA, LOS ANGELES

• • • • • • • •

" Make plans with your friends to do something fun immediately following the exam, and the whole experience will be more enjoyable. "

—*GRAHAM LEDERER*
BROOKEVILLE, MARYLAND
COLLEGE OF WILLIAM AND MARY

• • • • • • • •

DO NOT FORGET YOUR CALCULATOR! I forgot mine in my locker and my teacher would not let me go get it. I cried to him and he still wouldn't let me go. Needless to say, I did not do well on the Math section.

—*ALEXXA CONDON*
CHANNAHON, ILLINOIS
SOUTHERN ILLINOIS UNIVERSITY, CARBONDALE

GETTING SCORES

THE SECOND TIME MY SON TOOK THE SAT, he had dropped over 200 points in one of the sections. I thought, "This is weird. Something is wrong." I requested the actual test. We found out there was a glitch in the grading, and we had his score fixed. Don't be afraid to request the backup that shows what questions were missed. At the very least, you can see where the student might have issues or problems.

—*ANONYMOUS*
BROOKLYN, NEW YORK
P ⛪ BROWN UNIVERSITY

• • • • • • • •

I DON'T THINK THAT MY PARENTS or my friends really understood the significance of it. I mean, there is maybe one person in a thousand who can get a 35 on the ACT, but to everyone else it was more like "Oh, cool." I think everyone was happy for me, but in this town, for better or worse, we celebrate beating the next town over in football, not test scores on any level.

—*ANONYMOUS*
ILLINOIS
⛪ YALE UNIVERSITY

• • • • • • • • •

SOMEONE WILL ALWAYS DO BETTER than you, so there is no need to be arrogant and self centered. Just be happy for your friends if they score better than you do.

—*TIM*
PHOENIX, ARIZONA
⛪ UNDECIDED

• • • • • • • •

THE BEST WAY TO PREPARE for getting your test scores back is to set reasonable goals for yourself in the first place. Setting goals too high often leads to discouraging moments.

—*CHRISTINE TODD*
VERO BEACH, FLORIDA
⛪ NORTHWESTERN UNIVERSITY

THREE THINGS TO REMEMBER

Do not let yourself get distracted during the test. Just ignore the guy next to you who is picking his nose with his pencil while talking to himself.

Make sure you're filling out the correct section of the Scantron sheet for that section of the test!

As soon as you're done with one part of the test, don't worry about it anymore; not only are you not allowed to go back, but it's over, so concentrate on doing the best you can on this section.

> —TIMOTHY MICHAEL COOPER
> NEW YORK, NEW YORK
> YALE UNIVERSITY

Give yourself plenty of time to get there in the morning.

> —TORI
> BIRMINGHAM,
> ALABAMA

WEAR A WATCH. The worst feeling in the world is getting into the room and realizing you can't see the clock from your assigned seat! Especially when the proctors won't tell you what time it is. But make sure your watch doesn't have an alarm that goes off every hour, because then you will get kicked out, or at least get mean stares from everyone around you for the next three hours.

> —GENEVIEVE OTTO
> ST. LOUIS, MISSOURI
> WASHINGTON UNIVERSITY IN ST. LOUIS

RIDE WITH A PARENT if you have to take the test at a location other than your own high school. I had a horrible experience finding the testing center, and when I got there the front gate was locked and I had to try and find the back entrance through a neighborhood. The drive caused a lot of stress, which is the last thing anyone needs before the SAT. If you ride with a parent you don't have to worry about whether you'll be able to find the place, or if there will be enough parking available.

—*PHILLIP LAVIN*
MARIETTA, GEORGIA

• • • • • • • •

"The most important thing to remember—and this is not a joke—is to visit the bathroom before the test starts. It sounds obvious, but a lot of people forget. You'll be glad you did! "

—*S.M.*
MAHWAH, NEW JERSEY
PENNSYLVANIA STATE UNIVERSITY

• • • • • • • •

YOU NEED TO MAKE SURE you follow the ID instructions they give you. I had a school ID with me and not my driver's license. Luckily a bunch of my classmates were there and they vouched for me, but really they should have sent me home.

—*ANDREW TIMBERLAKE*
BIRMINGHAM, ALABAMA
YALE UNIVERSITY

FROM THE ADMISSIONS OFFICE

TESTS AREN'T ALL

WHAT IS YOUR ADVICE TO ALL THOSE STUDENTS WHO JUST DON'T TEST WELL?

DON'T FOCUS ON A WEAKNESS, focus on your strengths. In most cases, testing is *one* variable used by colleges to assess academic achievement and preparedness. We consider roughly twelve different criteria for each applicant. Instead of becoming fixated on the one criterion where you may not be as strong, focus on the other eleven that can help overcome any challenges you might face because of a test score. And don't let it be the 300-pound gorilla in the room. Take the opportunity to talk about it in an essay or with an admission counselor. There is absolutely nothing wrong with saying "This is my test score. I know it isn't as high as many of the other students being admitted each year, but here are all the reasons I think you should still give my application strong consideration."

> —*TONY BANKSTON*
> *DEAN OF ADMISSIONS*
> *ILLINOIS WESLEYAN UNIVERSITY*

• • • • • • • • •

CLEARLY REVEAL THROUGH YOUR CURRICULUM and your academic performance within that curriculum that you are well prepared for college work. In other words, take tough courses and do well!

> —*CHRIS LUCIER*
> *VICE PRESIDENT FOR ENROLLMENT MANAGEMENT*
> *UNIVERSITY OF VERMONT*

• • • • • • • • •

HIGHLIGHT YOUR OTHER ACADEMIC STRENGTHS: grades, curriculum, teacher recommendations, that all indicate your ability to succeed academically.

> —*TED SPENCER*
> *ASSOCIATE VICE PROVOST AND EXECUTIVE DIRECTOR OF UNDERGRADUATE ADMISSIONS*
> *UNIVERSITY OF MICHIGAN-ANN ARBOR*

IF YOU LOOK AT THE BIG PICTURE, most of our applicants who don't "test well" actually have quite strong test scores in comparison to the population as a whole. It's just within the context of our applicant pools that they feel that they haven't done as well as they'd like, or as well as their academic work suggests they "should" have done. They should try to keep two things in mind. First, that we are all interested in our applicants as individuals, that we always read every application through from beginning to end multiple times, and that standardized test scores are only a small part of what we consider in reviewing an application. And second, that there are hundreds and hundreds of wonderful colleges for students to consider, and that no matter what a student's test scores are, he or she can easily find plenty of colleges that will be a terrific match.

> —*CHRISTOPH GUTTENTAG*
> *DEAN OF UNDERGRADUATE ADMISSIONS*
> *DUKE UNIVERSITY*

STUDENTS WHO BELIEVE THAT THEIR TEST SCORES are not an adequate representation of their academic ability should spend time highlighting what they can offer to a college campus. Generally, spend time on the parts of your application that you can control (essays!) and consider applying to schools that de-emphasize standardized testing or do not require it for admission.

> —*MARK BUTT*
> *SENIOR ASSISTANT DIRECTOR OF ADMISSIONS*
> *JOHNS HOPKINS UNIVERSITY*

CONTINUE TO WORK HARD EACH and every day. In Emory's holistic application review, challenging oneself with the most rigorous courses and achieving at a high level in the classroom are incredibly important. Test scores, activities, essays, and recommendations help us to gain a better sense of how the student will contribute to our community, but demonstrated ability to meet the expectations in the classroom are certainly second to none.

> —*JEAN JORDAN*
> *DEAN OF ADMISSION*
> *EMORY UNIVERSITY*

UNDERSTAND THAT THE TEST SCORES "support" the decision, but do not *make* the decision. A student who tests well but has not taken a rigorous academic program and done well, will not be considered a strong candidate for admission.

—*DANIEL J. SARACINO*
ASSISTANT PROVOST FOR ENROLLMENT
UNIVERSITY OF NOTRE DAME

• • • • • • • •

REMEMBER THAT STANDARDIZED TESTING is only one factor in a holistic admissions process. If you are not a strong tester, be sure to do your best in class, and to spend a good deal of time making the remaining pieces of your application as perfect and strong as you possibly can.

—*DOUGLAS L. CHRISTIANSEN, PH.D.*
ASSOCIATE PROVOST FOR ENROLLMENT AND DEAN OF ADMISSIONS
VANDERBILT UNIVERSITY

• • • • • • • •

DON'T DESPAIR. Testing is one of many important factors. Rarely would testing alone be the determining factor in the outcome of an application. Keep in mind that we'll be looking at standardized testing in the context of resources available.

—*MATS LEMBERGER*
ASSISTANT DIRECTOR OF ADMISSIONS
DARTMOUTH COLLEGE

• • • • • • • •

PRACTICE TAKING THE TEST a few times…the more accustomed a student becomes to the format of a particular exam, the better he or she will do. At the same time, test-taking should not become an extra-curricular activity! Students who aren't strong test-takers should sit for it more than once, but not let it become an obsession. It also seems that an increasing number of students are taking the ACT and many are more comfortable with the exam since it covers classroom material. Still, prepare!

At the end of the day, many colleges and universities practice holistic admissions, such that the testing is only one factor of many in the evaluation process. Students who have difficulties with standardized exams should also be aware of the many colleges out there that are SAT/ACT optional.

—*JACINDA OJEDA*
REGIONAL DIRECTOR OF ADMISSIONS
UNIVERSITY OF PENNSYLVANIA

I TRY TO EXPLAIN TO MY PARENTS that scores aren't everything; people with perfect scores get turned down if they're lacking in other areas. They're constantly pressuring me to quit my extracurricular activities and job to focus more on the academics and testing. There's really no easy way to cope with them, so I just try to ignore them.

—*YUEYUE GUO*
CUMBERLAND, RHODE ISLAND
UNDECIDED

• • • • • • • •

ALWAYS HAVE A CHECKLIST of what to bring, or have all of your papers set out the night before the test. During spring of our junior year, one of my less conscientious friends and I were scheduled to take the SAT on the same day in a neighboring town. I picked him up, and we drove over to the school with enough time to park, sign in and settle ourselves, but no more. As we were walking in the door, he realized that he had forgotten to bring any form of ID with him, and he wanted me to drive him home to get it. He was able to talk to the test administrators, who phoned our high school and confirmed his identity, but we could easily have both missed the test.

—*SANDI BRYNN CONROY*
HADDON TOWNSHIP, NEW JERSEY
PENNSYLVANIA STATE UNIVERSITY

• • • • • • • •

BRING SEVERAL PENCILS. I even brought my own sharpener, which was a good thing because the room had no sharpener and everyone was using mine! Some people brought their own clocks, or pillows—whatever is comforting and makes you feel secure.

—*MICHAL ROSENOER*
CORTE MADERA, CALIFORNIA
UNIVERSITY OF CALIFORNIA, BERKELEY

Wearing earplugs on test day is a great way to eliminate distractions! You won't get fouled up by the ticking clock or by someone else's sniffling.

—*ERICA*
SOUTH ORANGE,
NEW JERSEY
WASHINGTON
UNIVERSITY IN ST.
LOUIS

BRING EXTRA BATTERIES TO THE EXAM and if you can, an extra calculator. My calculator died during the exam, so I winged it. I called the instructor over to see if I could get batteries or a calculator, but I couldn't. Sometimes they will help you, but I've learned that if you have a mean instructor they won't give you batteries or another calculator; I had one of those mean instructors.

—*RAYNA*
NEEDHAM, MASSACHUSETTS
CLAREMONT MCKENNA COLLEGE

• • • • • • • •

THE FIRST TIME I TOOK THE TEST I had four strikes against me: I didn't study, my alarm clock didn't go off, I forgot my calculator, and I rushed out of the house without eating breakfast. The next time, I practiced, got my stuff together, enlisted my mom's help in making sure I was up and ate a good breakfast. What a difference—my score went up a hundred points!

—*TAMMI COOKS*
ST. LOUIS, MISSOURI
WASHINGTON UNIVERSITY IN ST. LOUIS

• • • • • • • •

BE SURE TO STAY UPDATED on where your test center is. After I registered they sent me a notice with the location of my testing center. A few weeks later, when I got another notice, I just assumed it was a confirmation of that previous one and didn't look at it closely. Turns out they had moved my test to a different high school, which I didn't find out until the day of the test, when I arrived at the first school and no one was there. I eventually made it to the new location, but it was a really stressful way to start out the day!

—*LAURA*
CINCINNATI, OHIO
FRANCISCAN UNIVERSITY OF STEUBENVILLE

Some people do poorly, and some do well. But 10 years from now, you won't even remember your test score, and employers won't ask.

—*BRIAN STANLEY*
CHICAGO, ILLINOIS
ROBERT MORRIS COLLEGE

TAKING THE SAT AGAIN (AND AGAIN)

MANY STUDENTS TAKE THE SAT more than once. Here's what you need to know about retaking the test:

- As of March 2009, you have the option to take advantage of the new SAT Score Choice feature. You may select which SAT (from one sitting) and/or individual SAT Subject Tests you wish to send to each college. The College Board recently instituted this new policy in the hopes that it will reduce test-day stress.

- Colleges will usually look at your best score as an indication of your ability. They're further motivated to do so because they want to report the highest possible SAT scores to those who rank colleges.

- You *can* improve your score. The less you prepared the first time you took the test, the more likely you are to improve your score by trying again (but only if you study the second or third time around!). On the other hand, if you've been studying like crazy and haven't improved your score in four separate attempts, you've probably reached or neared your peak.

RESTED, READY, AND RARING TO GO

Some tips for test day:

EAT, PREFERABLY SOMETHING WITH PROTEIN. If you think you can eat in the morning without giving yourself a stomach ache, you'll be glad you did so. Nothing's more distracting than extreme hunger and lightheadedness. If you can add a little protein into your breakfast (eggs, bacon, soy, etc.), it'll help feed your brain.

USE CAFFEINE. Whether it's coffee, tea, or diet soda, caffeine can help you keep alert and perform better. If you don't typically drink anything with caffeine in it, experiment a few weeks in advance rather than risk making yourself anxious, giving yourself a stomach ache, or being forced to go to the bathroom constantly.

GET A GOOD NIGHT'S SLEEP FOR SEVERAL NIGHTS BEFORE THE SAT. Try to get to bed at a decent hour on Thursday as well as Friday— being well rested is something that builds up in your system.

STAY RELAXED THE DAY BEFORE THE TEST. Try not to study (very much), party, or do anything illegal the day before you take the SAT. The ideal evening probably consists of a fun, relaxing dinner, some TV or a movie, and then a slightly early bedtime.

I TOOK THE SAT THREE TIMES and scored best the time I took it in January. Most people say that the best time to take the test is January because that is when the curve is easier. The hardest curve is October. The reason for this is because in January you are competing with non-seniors.

—*M.C.*
  KALAMAZOO, MICHIGAN
  UNDECIDED

· · · · · · · ·

" I always stretched and did some very light exercise before a major test. It helps me to relax, and it spends a little physical energy. The last thing you want is to be antsy at the desk. "

—*PETER WILLIAM FINNOCCHIARO*
  BALDWINSVILLE, NEW YORK
  UNDECIDED

· · · · · · · ·

THE FIRST TIME I TOOK THE SAT, I took it at a different location from my high school. I was already terrified, but having to go to a different school was frightening. I was nervous and uncomfortable the entire time. The second time I took it at my high school and I did much better. I don't know if it was because of the comfort of being at my own school.

—*JOCELYN*
  BEVERLY HILLS, CALIFORNIA
  UNIVERSITY OF ARIZONA

ON THE SATURDAY MORNING I was scheduled to take the test, I just happened to check my e-mail. It was a good thing I did because they had changed the location and e-mailed me the new information.

—*MICHELLE WADDELL*
HOLLYWOOD, FLORIDA
WASHINGTON UNIVERSITY IN ST. LOUIS

Don't look up. Once you start looking up you might notice someone else is sweating it and that can make you nervous.

—*DAVID*
ST. LOUIS,
MISSOURI
UNIVERSITY OF
WISCONSIN

I TOOK THE SAT TWICE, and both times I made it to my room just in time. The first time I took the SAT I looked up my room assignment and I ended up in the wrong room. The second time, I took it at a school and there were other activities going on. When I arrived, there were a bunch of students waiting in the cafeteria. I just assumed that they were all waiting for the rooms to open, but they were just students doing something else. After waiting with them for a while, I had to run upstairs to find my room but fortunately the test hadn't started yet.

—*LOUIS S. WU*
SILVER SPRING, MARYLAND
UNIVERSITY OF MARYLAND

THE NIGHT BEFORE I TOOK THE ACT, I took practice tests all night long. I was exhausted the next morning. During the test, I finished a few parts really early, so I decided to take a nap. I fell half-asleep, and had a dream that I was walking on ice. I slipped on the ice in the dream and jolted upright awake in my seat. It was embarrassing to find that everyone in the test room was staring at me.

—*GREGORY JAMES FRIEND*
EVANSTON, ILLINOIS
NORTHWESTERN UNIVERSITY

DON'T RELY ON WEBSITES like MapQuest for directions to your test-taking site! Call the school itself and speak to a real person there so you can count on getting accurate information. My brother and I got incredibly lost on our way to the test because we got bad directions from an online source. Luckily, we had left early enough that we still got there in time, but it just added more stress to an already stressful day.

—*TEKLA TOMAN*
YOUNGSTOWN, OHIO
XAVIER UNIVERSITY

. . . .

"Don't be afraid to request something. During the SAT, there was a clock hanging in the back of the classroom. I asked the proctor to move the clock to the front, and she ended up hanging it on a tack on a bulletin board."

—*LAUREN*
POTOMAC, MARYLAND
CORNELL UNIVERSITY

. . . .

DON'T STRESS. The night before my test, I relaxed and watched movies, and I did much better than the time before.

—*JANET*
LOS ANGELES, CALIFORNIA
UNIVERSITY OF CALIFORNIA, LOS ANGELES

EXPECT THE UNEXPECTED

You should be ready for anything to happen on test day. *Anything.*

CLUELESS PROCTORS: While most of the people hired to monitor the SAT do a great job, sometimes they mess up. Try not to be fazed. It will be tough to do anything about minor mistakes, but if the proctor is doing something very wrong (e.g. not giving you enough time for a section, or not allowing you to use a calculator that meets the requirements) you should speak up.

CHEATING STUDENTS: Someone might try to look at your paper or ask you for the answer to a question. Act appropriately, and realize that being caught cheating can have disastrous consequences.

TIME PROBLEMS: In addition to the proctor making a timing mistake, the wall clock may be broken or other test-takers may loudly complain (even incorrectly) about how time is announced.

LOUD DISRUPTIONS BY OTHER STUDENTS: Someone might freak out during the test, start an argument with a proctor, or otherwise disrupt the rest of the room. The proctor might not know how to appropriately deal with the situation. Stay focused.

R.K.

I WAS IN LINE TO TAKE THE **SAT,** and the guy standing directly behind me ran out of the line and threw up! I was just glad it wasn't on me. It actually sharpened my focus to realize how much he was worried. I thought, "Oh, wow, I really do need to do well."

—*LAURA ELAINE GOLDSTICKER*
ST. LOUIS, MISSOURI

I PERSONALLY DO NOT BELIEVE THAT the SAT prepared me for college, and found that the material I studied had no more to do with college classes than it did with high school. The SAT tests a very specific type of intelligence, one that is insensitive to economic and cultural differences, and not necessarily relevant to college academic performance. However, it is weighted very heavily in the college admissions process, so I do suggest that everyone take it extremely seriously. When the SAT was finally over, there is only one word that encompasses my feelings: relief.

—*BETH LORI WECKSELL*
GREAT NECK, NEW YORK
TUFTS UNIVERSITY

" Sometimes you make friends during these tests. It's such a stressful situation that it brings people together. You just start talking and later you Facebook each other and become friends. My older brother actually dated a girl that he met at the SAT. "

—*ANONYMOUS*
CLAYTON, MISSOURI

DURING MY SAT, the proctor instructed us to save all questions until the end of the directions. She reads out all the instructions, and at the end a boy raises his hand and says, "I'm supposed to be taking the SAT II. What should I do?" We were all laughing our heads off because he had clearly known for 10 minutes that he was in the wrong room and didn't say anything because he didn't want to interrupt. There are obviously exceptions to every rule, and I think most people don't really anticipate how much being nervous can interfere with things like common sense!

—*BECKY*
NEWTON, MASSACHUSETTS
SWARTHMORE COLLEGE

• • • • • • • •

I MADE SURE TO FINISH all of my reviewing and practicing two days before I actually took the test so that I could feel confident and ready. The day before the test I didn't concentrate on having to take the test the next day, and chose to relax. I also made sure that I laid out my admission ticket, pencils, calculator, snack and all other materials the night before so I wouldn't be in a rush to find them in the morning.

—*TERRAHNEY WILSON*
LITHONIA, GEORGIA
UNDECIDED

• • • • • • • •

KNOW WHAT SCORE RANGE you are aiming for before you take the SAT. Use your PSAT scores as a benchmark to help you set those goals. This will help you determine whether you are satisfied with your score and whether you should take it again. Using PSAT's as a standard (as opposed to the SAT range for your dream college) will help you be realistic.

—*S.N.*
RALEIGH, NORTH CAROLINA

SOMETHING TO CONSIDER

How important are your standardized test scores? Sixty percent of colleges assign "considerable importance" to them, according to a survey by the National Association for College Admission Counseling.

I TOOK THE **SAT** TWICE because my score wasn't good enough to get me into the college I wanted to go to the first time I took it. The second time I took it my scores increased. I didn't study more, I just think having taken it once made me feel more at ease the second time. I think it's a good idea to use your first time as a warmup.

—*TIFFANY*
SHERMAN OAKS, CALIFORNIA
CLAREMONT MCKENNA COLLEGE

• • • • • • • •

I THINK YOU SHOULD TAKE THE **SAT** two times. I ended up taking it again and did much better. After the second time I stopped because I didn't think that any amount of studying would improve my scores after that. My sister will be taking hers soon and I would definitely tell her to take it twice. I do believe you improve your scores the second time because you are more confident about what to expect. By the third time I think you reach a plateau, and to increase your scores by ten or twenty points just isn't worth all of the stress and time.

—*JOCELYN*
BEVERLY HILLS, CALIFORNIA
UNIVERSITY OF ARIZONA

Bring extra pencils. When I took the SAT, I lost my only pencil and had to ask the weird girl next to me for hers.

—*NATHANIEL COHEN*
WEST HARTFORD,
CONNECTICUT
NEW YORK
UNIVERSITY

FROM THE TOP ...

A commission headed by William R. Fitzsimmons, the Dean of Admissions and Financial Aid at Harvard, has recommended that colleges and universities move away from their reliance on SAT and ACT scores in the admissions process, and shift toward exams more closely tied to the high school curriculum and achievement.

Making a List, Checking it Twice: Where to Apply?

*A*t this point in the process, your goal is to create options for yourself when admissions decisions roll in. Remember that you do not have to decide which college is the right one for you now. It's your job now to devise a smart combination of several colleges that may be the one for you.

Advice for your college list: stay grounded but still reach for the stars. You can—and should—do both. Your college list should be a balanced, realistic mix of backup, target, and reach schools. Good research and solid soul-searching will enable you to find schools that match your interests. Why shouldn't you have a couple of dream schools on your list? Just make sure to balance those with several solid backup and target schools. Look broadly, stay grounded, dream big. The pay-off will be big. Read on to see how some students crafted their lists, and for more wise advice from consultants and admissions officers.

Best Advice and Top Tips

- Make sure to apply to a mix of schools - including 'reach' schools and 'safety' schools.
- Rankings can be useful but don't give them excessive weight; they don't indicate whether a school is a fit for you.
- Think about what you like about your 'dream' school - see what other schools may offer the same things.
- Pick the schools that are right for you - not the one that was right for your parents 30 years ago!

KNOW WHAT YOU'RE LOOKING for instead of going in blind and thinking, "Oh, that school sounds nice." I applied to a lot of schools I wouldn't have wanted to go to. The counselors at my school tried to make it seem you had to go to a school they thought was good. I was trying to apply to swanky schools even though they didn't offer programs I wanted or were too far away.

—*ASHLEY LITTLE*
FLOSSMOOR, ILLINOIS
MARQUETTE UNIVERSITY

Expert Advice IECA⁺ *COUNSELOR SURVEY*

Most students should apply to:

3 or fewer schools – 0%
4-5 schools – 17%
6-7 schools – 44%
8 or more schools – 39%

I HAD A BOOK ON THE 100 BEST SCHOOLS from *U.S. News & World Report*. Those books are helpful because you find a lot of schools you may not have heard of. I went through that with my mom, looking for what majors the schools offered, whether they were big or small, or whether they were in a city. We started eliminating and got it down to a list of 20. I did more research on those and whittled it down to eight that I applied to.

—ASHLEY LITTLE
FLOSSMOOR, ILLINOIS
MARQUETTE UNIVERSITY

• • • • • • • •

ONLY APPLY TO SCHOOLS THAT you really like. If you are only somewhat impressed with a school, don't apply there – it's just a waste of time and money because you know in the back of your mind you won't end up there.

—PAUL
MIDDLEBURY, VERMONT
MIDDLEBURY COLLEGE

OTHER SIDE OF THE DESK: UNDERSTANDING "YIELD"

Yield: The percentage of accepted students who say "yes" to a college's offer of admission. Colleges want the highest yield they can achieve every year because it raises their perceived prestige or popularity, and changes the way they admit students (high yield equates with a lower number of applicants admitted). Students who carelessly apply with sloppy applications to yield-sensitive schools will likely not be admitted.

R.K.

WHERE TO APPLY (II): NARROW YOUR LIST

TAKE THE LARGE LIST OF SCHOOLS you made back in Chapter 1, and create new columns according to your academic and activity profile:

- "Reach" schools: any schools with extremely selective admissions or schools where you do not have a high chance of admission because your profile is well below that of the average admitted student;
- "Solid" schools: where you fit into the rough average student profile; and
- "Safety" schools: where your data essentially assures you a spot (usually at least one state school).

With the surge in applications due to both a population bubble and students applying to more and more schools, admissions can be harder to estimate than ever. Don't get into a situation where you only apply to schools where you fit the average student profile (or worse, schools that are all "reaches" for you). They could all say no—it happens . . .

To be sure that you'll have at least one school saying "yes" to your application, you need to apply to a so-called "safety" school. This could mean looking no further than your local state school, or a private school with less competitive admissions.

How can you assess which schools are a good fit, which are "safety schools," and which are "reach" schools for you—and the odds of admission to them? Look at the data that the schools will consider first and foremost, along with extracurriculars—your test scores and level of academic achievement. You can get a sense of your general testing ability through the PSAT and PACT—tests typically given in the sophomore year. Of course, your scores may improve, but estimate conservatively. Schools where you fall into the middle range of test scores will be solid possibilities. Otherwise, they are "reaches." Also, assess your GPA and course load. Admission to top schools will require the most rigorous course load available at your high school as well as top grades in those courses. Your test scores may be high, but if your GPA and course load are not in the same range, top schools may well be a "reach."

Develop a new list of about 10 to 20 schools combining a majority of safety and solid schools with a few favorite reach schools. You will narrow the list again later, but the goal now is to develop the list of schools you will be investigating closely.

GETTING ORGANIZED

Make a box or dedicate a desk drawer to college admissions materials. Label a **manila folder** for each school to which you plan to apply. Use it to hold:

- All snail mail and brochures the school sends
- Important names and contact information
- Printed e-mail correspondence you have with a school
- A list of all deadlines and required essays
- Financial aid forms

On a large **wall calendar** write:

- Actual deadlines for all schools and sections of the applications
- Personal deadlines (weeks before the actual ones) to spread out your work
- Days off after you've met deadlines, as a reward for your hard work

R.K.

Expert Advice **FROM THE ADMISSIONS OFFICE**

DREAM SCHOOLS

CAN YOU OFFER ADVICE TO THOSE STUDENTS WHO HAVE THEIR ONE 'DREAM' SCHOOL AND CAN'T ENVISION BEING HAPPY ANYWHERE ELSE?

CAST A WIDE NET! Having a 'dream school' is great—in fact, many students have a 'dream school'. What cannot happen is having that 'dream school' thwart the entire college search process, especially if it is a highly selective school. The student has to be comfortable enrolling at every school to which they apply and it is important to not let that 'dream school' diminish or downplay the other opportunities that other colleges offer.

> —*MARK BUTT*
> *SENIOR ASSISTANT DIRECTOR OF ADMISSIONS*
> *JOHNS HOPKINS UNIVERSITY*

• • • • • • • •

THINK HARD ABOUT WHICH OTHER COLLEGES meet your needs equally well. There's no guarantee that you'll be admitted to your dream school, and you want to have great choices if that happens. And you may be surprised at how your dreams change once you're faced with real choices.

> —*CHRISTOPH GUTTENTAG*
> *DEAN OF UNDERGRADUATE ADMISSIONS*
> *DUKE UNIVERSITY*

• • • • • • • •

UNDERSTAND HOW COMPETITIVE the college admissions process is and be open to the possibility that there are many outstanding programs. Going into the admissions process knowing this, will result in a healthy attitude that can carry you through what can be a turbulent process.

> —*MATS LEMBERGER*
> *ASSISTANT DIRECTOR OF ADMISSIONS*
> *DARTMOUTH COLLEGE*

FEW PEOPLE MARRY THE FIRST PERSON THEY DATED or who they felt they "loved" after the first date. There are literally thousands of colleges and universities, and you could "love" many of them. Ultimately, if you enroll at something other than your "dream school," that school can also be your "dream school" based on your willingness to engage the academic and social life of the campus community.

—*CHRIS LUCIER*
VICE PRESIDENT FOR ENROLLMENT MANAGEMENT
UNIVERSITY OF VERMONT

THEY NEED TO VISIT OTHER COLLEGES so that they can compare the qualities of each institution. Sometimes a student becomes so focused on one college that they fail to see that the qualities they love at this institution actually exist at other colleges as well.

—*DANIEL J. SARACINO*
ASSISTANT PROVOST FOR ENROLLMENT
UNIVERSITY OF NOTRE DAME

CHRISTOPHER COLUMBUS WAS SAILING FOR INDIA and discovered the Americas. History is full of scientists who were looking for something rather ordinary only to discover something even more amazing by accident. I have dealt with countless students who thought they knew what they wanted and then discovered that a better opportunity existed in a place they never expected. There is no such thing as only one perfect school for every student. No one has just one dream, we all have many dreams. Some students just haven't had the right dream yet.

—*TONY BANKSTON*
DEAN OF ADMISSIONS
ILLINOIS WESLEYAN UNIVERSITY

BROADEN YOUR VISION. Develop a list of the pros and cons of that "dream school." Once you've compiled the list, investigate your options of other schools with similar characteristics to your first choice school.

—*TED SPENCER*
ASSOCIATE VICE PROVOST AND EXECUTIVE DIRECTOR OF UNDERGRADUATE ADMISSIONS
UNIVERSITY OF MICHIGAN-ANN ARBOR

FIND MULTIPLE FIRST CHOICE COLLEGES! In today's competitive environment, it is irresponsible to apply to only one college, especially if your dream college is a selective or higly selective institution.

—*DOUGLAS L. CHRISTIANSEN, PH.D.*
ASSOCIATE PROVOST FOR ENROLLMENT AND DEAN OF ADMISSIONS
VANDERBILT UNIVERSITY

• • • • • • • • •

IT'S GREAT TO HAVE A DREAM SCHOOL, but students should try to be open-minded. There are SO MANY excellent colleges and universities out there, several of which could be a great fit for a particular student. When students compile a list of colleges to which they are going to apply, they need to make sure they'd be happy at every one of those schools. I can't tell you how many times I've taken calls from very upset applicants who were denied admission from our University, only to hear several months later that they're extremely happy at their current school. Your college experience is what you make of it!

—*JACINDA OJEDA*
REGIONAL DIRECTOR OF ADMISSIONS
UNIVERSITY OF PENNSYLVANIA

• • • • • • • •

THERE ARE THOUSANDS OF great colleges and universities in this country. Doing extensive research during your college search is critical. Informed people make informed decisions and are generally happy with the outcome. This is an exciting time for students and they need to have some fun with this process. But a successful college search requires students to be responsible and introspective, to identify what factors are most important to them, and then to gather as much information about schools that might meet their expectations. If you apply to a range schools you have researched, knowing that you'd be happy at any of them, then you can't go wrong in this process. But it takes a considerable commitment by the student at the beginning of the college search.

—*JEAN JORDAN*
DEAN OF ADMISSION
EMORY UNIVERSITY

ASSESS YOURSELF

Picking schools from a list of rankings is NOT the way to form a potential college list, as each school has a unique personality and culture. To figure out the best college for you, the very first step is to know yourself well. By assessing who you are, you can determine the right community for you.

Start by assessing your goals and your academics. Ask yourself:

- What do I want to do "when I grow up"?
- What subjects fascinate me?
- What subjects might I have to study?
- What is my GPA and estimated class rank?
- How many honors/AP courses am I taking?
- What is my PSAT or PACT score - what might my testing look like?

Now, make a list of your personal characteristics.

Some questions to ask yourself about your personality type:

- Are you loud or quiet?
- Do you like to be in the middle of the action or in a smaller, more communal environment?
- Are you conservative or liberal (or somewhere in the middle)?
- Are you religious?
- Are you a leader/adventurer or would you rather join clubs as a "member"?
- What weather do you love - do you like snow?
- Are you a "city person" or do you prefer the suburbs?

Together, the answers to these questions will help you - and your high school guidance counselor – develop a list of the best potential schools for you.

R.K.

PARENTS' PAGES

PARENTS MUST BE REALISTIC. First, anything you recall about college is at least a quarter century out of date. Second, if you can, rely on Web-based tools that show recent acceptance statistics (even results for applicants from your own child's high school) based on GPA and SAT/ACT results. Use the data to find realistic target schools—no point in urging the student to try for the Ivy League if your kid's stats aren't even on the same page.

> —*Tom*
> *San Francisco, California*
> *Pa€m University of Arizona*

* * * * * * * *

IF THERE IS ANYTHING YOUR CHILD is interested in, use it to help narrow down the choices. My first daughter plays field hockey and she knew that she wanted to play at a Division III school. Also, she was a very good student, so she focused on small, high-ranking liberal arts schools that offered varsity field hockey. Using those criteria, a lot of schools were immediately eliminated.

> —*Lucy Rumack*
> *Brooklyn, New York*
> *Pa€m Swarthmore College*

* * * * * * * *

MY SON AND I SPENT A SOBERING EVENING looking at acceptance scattergrams for various schools, which allow you to see how many students of a specific GPA and SAT score were accepted from a particular high school. This experience led him to remove some colleges that never accepted a student with his GPA, and led to a more realistic set of expectations. It's fine to have some reaches and to apply to several schools, but applications are time-consuming, and those $75 fees really add up.

> —*Richard Tyler*
> *Redmond, Washington*
> *Pa€m New Mexico Institute of Mining & Technology*

HELP YOUR CHILDREN RESEARCH SCHOOLS and have them give you very specific reasons why they want to go. My daughter has always been pretty independent, so when she said she wanted to do it on her own, I trusted that she knew what she was talking about. She ended up applying to 15 schools, got accepted to most of them, chose one of them and hated it. Since then she's transferred twice and is still unhappy. I didn't realize until after the fact

that she was randomly choosing colleges based on where her friends were going. If I could do it all over again, I would sit down with her and make her write down three reasons for choosing each school. And if she didn't have three reasons, I would discourage her from applying.

—*G.V.*
HOUSTON, TEXAS
P ⚏ *UNIVERSITY OF TEXAS, AUSTIN;*
UNIVERSITY OF MICHIGAN

• • • • • • • • •

IF YOUR CHILD IS RIGHT in the middle academically, I don't think there is a reason to pay a high-priced advisor to help with the application process. My daughter has good grades and scores, but we knew there was no way she would get into an Ivy League school. We didn't need someone with a relationship with an Ivy school, because we knew we couldn't get there.

—*LAURIE BRESNICK*
BEVERLY HILLS, CALIFORNIA
P ⚏ *UNIVERSITY OF ARIZONA*

MOTHER, FATHER AND ALMA MATER

"WOW, I WANT TO GO BACK TO COLLEGE" is a comment admissions officers frequently hear when talking to parents of visiting high school students. They hear it most often when parents are visiting their own alma maters.

Visits stir up your old college memories, especially if you are touring your own college. As nostalgia starts to flow, be careful that your memories of the past do not cloud the future. Your school was clearly *your* match—you loved it and you thrived—but your child is not you, and the school is not the same place 30 years later. Encourage your child to consider your alma mater, but do not be wounded if it is not her match.

As a legacy applicant, your child might get a boost in the admissions process, but be sure to research each school's policy. At some schools, your child could get a big boost. At others, it is only influential in the decision if your child is already 98-percent admissible on her own. If a legacy applicant is well below the admissions standard, you would be a kinder parent not to encourage that application, as many schools will not stretch too far to admit alumni-related students.

It bears repeating: your child's success depends on being at a school where she can thrive. This means she is spiritually comfortable, feels academically confident, and can play a role in campus life. Encouraging applications to schools where children are not within the statistical parameters can be hurtful. You can harm your child by encouraging applications to too many "reach" schools. The school's name on your bumper sticker may make you happy, but this is not about you. If your child will be overwhelmed in class, or by people too unlike him, or in an uncomfortable location, your dreams of high achievement will be dashed. With the right fit, the grades will come, and so will the launching pad for life.

R.K.

DEVELOPING THAT COLLEGE INTUITION

You have thousands and thousands of colleges from which to choose, but that's what makes it hard, right? Here are some tips to figuring out what colleges might be good fits for you:

- Visit schools whenever you can, even if they're not on your "list." You learn to rely on and trust your intuition as to what you want from your college experience. You'll become more discerning with every visit.
- Spend time with students. Walk around with the throngs of students during lunch and ask yourself, "Do I see myself here?"
- Trust your gut! This may be *the* most important advice. Remember: this process is part analytical and part instinct. Embrace the power of how the school makes you *feel*.

AS SOMEONE WHO APPLIED to only one school, I happen to think it's a phenomenal idea: I wrote only one essay, sent in only one application fee. However, take that with an entire shaker of salt, since I got into the one school to which I applied. Also, I applied early, meaning that while I put a significant share of my eggs in one basket, if I had been rejected, I would have had just enough time to spend every waking hour banging out a few more essays for my backups.

—*NAFI ISRAEL*
NEWTON, MASSACHUSETTS
COLUMBIA UNIVERSITY

I BEGAN LOOKING AT COLLEGES during my junior year of high school and sent away for information for about 10 schools. That's when I began to get bombarded with information. To narrow my choices down, I went to the schools that offered the specific program I was looking for (in my case, journalism). And I weighed the pluses and minuses of my other options, such as whether the college was liberal or conservative, whether or not the school had an honors program, whether or not it offered scholarships, and its size.

—*JASON PAUL TORREANO*
LOCKPORT, NEW YORK
STATE UNIVERSITY OF NEW YORK, BROCKPORT

• • • • • • • •

I KNEW I WANTED TO APPLY to engineering schools, so I first picked out the best one that was free (in-state), which was Georgia Tech. I then picked the one that was the most highly regarded, which was Berkeley. Finally, just to have a third option, and on the advice of a neighbor, I added a third that my neighbor's daughter had attended, which was Purdue.

—*P.T.*
CHICAGO, ILLINOIS
PURDUE UNIVERSITY

PUBLIC & PRIVATE

Public colleges and universities are state and federally funded, and therefore abide by guidelines set forth by the state and federal governments. Private universities are funded through donations and tuition and are free to set their own charters, rules and guidelines, as long as they remain accredited.

REQUEST INFORMATION AT SCHOOL WEBSITES

Getting on the mailing list and into the database is important for both you and the school - you'll get relevant info (either via snail mail or e-mail), and the school can keep track of of your application. Find the "Admissions" page on the school's website. Somewhere on there will be a link to a form which you can fill out online requesting information.

Most schools' website addresses are intuitive, so it's probably easy enough to guess the URL (and all end with .edu!). The University of Texas (yup, www.utexas.edu) has a handy list of all the colleges and universities in the US with links to their sites: www.utexas.edu/world/univ/state.

APPLYING ONLY TO SCHOOLS you are genuinely interested in is a big help. One of the schools on my initial list was U-Penn, and they had a writing-intensive application. When I got to a question that asked why I wanted to go there, the only sentence I could honestly write was, "I like the campus." It would have been a huge waste of time to finish the application after that, so I crossed it off my list.

—*LAURA DATTARO*
ELKRIDGE, MARYLAND
UNIVERSITY OF DELAWARE

• • • • • • • •

DON'T BE INTIMIDATED BY COLLEGES. I probably should have applied to the University of Michigan. My grades weren't perfect, and my high school is full of overachievers who didn't get in. I compared myself to my peers and didn't apply. I felt almost like it was too good for me.

—*MINEHAHA FORMAN*
SAN ANTONIO VILLAGE, BELIZE
OAKLAND UNIVERSITY

HEADS UP: ON IVIES

Although the term Ivy League was originally coined to refer to a collegiate athletic conference, the eight universities that form the Ivy League—Brown, Columbia, Cornell, Dartmouth, Harvard, Princeton, Yale and the University of Pennsylvania—are certainly among the best in the world. All the Ivies are old—most were founded during the colonial period—private Northeastern institutions. All were founded as men's colleges but have accepted women since the late 1960's. Here are some things to consider about the Ivy League:

- In today's highly competitive world of admissions, Ivies have among the lowest rates of acceptance. There is not nearly enough room for all the students who are qualified.

- Each Ivy is unique, not only in size and atmosphere, but also as a result of location. You will have a different experience at Columbia in urban New York City than at Dartmouth in quiet Hanover, New Hampshire.

- An underachieving and lazy student at an Ivy League school will likely not go as far as a top student and leader from a non-Ivy school.

- A student will achieve where he can thrive; not every student will do best in any one or every one of the Ivies' cultures and atmospheres. Attending an Ivy is not a guarantee of future success: Academic superstars, political and business leaders, prizewinning scientists and artists have attended—and are teaching at—a wide range of colleges across the country.

R.K.

WHERE TO APPLY (III): THE "FINA-LIST"

After you've taken all the tours and done the necessary research—read websites and colleges' publications and talked to people 'in the know' (alumni, admissions officers, current students, your guidance counselor...)—it will be time to develop your final list.

Solidifying this list allows you to assess—and limit—the work required for your applications, so that you can make a time schedule for your summer and fall. You will likely find a pattern in the schools on your final list—they'll probably be similar in character, size, type of location, academics, etc. This means you know your needs and what you want on a campus.

Take your longer list and cross out:

- Schools where you really cannot see yourself studying;
- Schools where you had a bad visit/tour;
- Schools that you want for their "name" but for little else.

Make sure to keep:

- A state school (or at least one in your home state);
- A school or two where your grades and testing are well within the average/above average for the school (you need some safeties!);
- One or two schools of your dreams.

R.K.

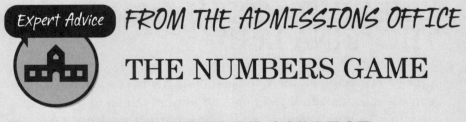

Expert Advice *FROM THE ADMISSIONS OFFICE*

THE NUMBERS GAME

WHAT IS YOUR VIEW OF COLLEGE RANKINGS?

I THINK IT IS ONE OF THE WORST CRITERIA you can use in the college search process, and I work at an institution that does very well in most rankings! There are important statistics to consider during the college search process, but trying to group them together in different ways to create a definitive rank order is ridiculous. Is there really a substantial difference or advantage in attending a school ranked #8 versus #80? Not in any research I've ever seen. When you apply for a job, graduate school, or professional school, no one asks you for your college's U.S. News rank. I have yet to see it on any resume I've ever received. No one cares about the rank. What they care about is whether or not you have picked up the required skills and experiences necessary to make you an effective addition to whatever community they are building or maintaining, and you can do that at colleges with a wide variety of ranks.

Don't get me wrong, there are certainly qualitative differences between different academic experiences, but those are not captured or presented adequately by rankings. Are there differences between schools ranked from 1 to 100 and schools ranked from 300 to 400? Definitely. But as you move from school 1 to school 100 the differences are incredibly minimal from one spot to the next. And none of this is helpful at all in determining which college is the best "fit" for a particular student. It only shows how that particular college fares regarding the specific criteria used for that ranking. In the end, it provides absolutely no assistance whatsoever in establishing a good college match for a particular student.

—*TONY BANKSTON*
DEAN OF ADMISSIONS
ILLINOIS WESLEYAN UNIVERSITY

I FIND THEM VERY PROBLEMATIC, since they take these wonderful, multi-faceted, complex institutions and reduce them to a single number that has absolutely nothing to do with how good a match there might be between a student and a college. They also are based on a limited number of factors that may not at all be relevant to a student's college needs. In an ideal world they wouldn't exist, which would help students make better college choices.

> —CHRISTOPH GUTTENTAG
> DEAN OF UNDERGRADUATE ADMISSIONS
> DUKE UNIVERSITY

• • • • • • • •

COLLEGE RANKINGS CAN BE USEFUL to gain specific information (alumni giving rates, etc.) however they cannot tell a student which school is the best fit for them. The leg work has to be done by the student in order to find a fit. Visit campuses, meet with current students, and get online. Many colleges are very different, and the idiosyncrasies of each college cannot be captured through a general ranking schema, so while the statistical information may be accurate, the most important information will not be captured in a numerical rank.

> —MARK BUTT
> SENIOR ASSISTANT DIRECTOR OF ADMISSIONS
> JOHNS HOPKINS UNIVERSITY

• • • • • • • •

I DON'T THINK MUCH OF COLLEGE RANKINGS. There are so many of them, and they are often based on nothing that helps a student understand the academic and social atmosphere at a college or university. Many are based on poor statistical analysis and faulty survey techniques. There are reputable websites to support college search, and nothing replaces visiting campus, talking to current students and faculty, and discussing your interests and goals with your parents, teachers, counselors, and family friends.

> —CHRIS LUCIER
> VICE PRESIDENT FOR ENROLLMENT MANAGEMENT
> UNIVERSITY OF VERMONT

I AM TORN. They provide great context but can be misleading. There are many wonderful colleges and universities in this country that students may choose from to continue their education. We hope that students will strongly consider the wide variety of opportunities available to them academically as they make their college enrollment plans, rather than narrowly focusing on just a few.

—*TED SPENCER*
ASSOCIATE VICE PROVOST AND EXECUTIVE DIRECTOR OF UNDERGRADUATE ADMISSIONS
UNIVERSITY OF MICHIGAN-ANN ARBOR

IT IS A "TOOL" LIKE MANY in helping the student compare colleges. But it certainly is not a critical tool. The more information a student can learn about the colleges he/she is considering, the better the decision on "what school is a better match for me" can be made. Information from objective parties should certainly be weighed in the evaluation process. Being an "educated consumer" is essential. Asking the right questions of all the colleges and using various guide books (including those that "rank" colleges) is part of the process.

—*DANIEL J. SARACINO*
ASSISTANT PROVOST FOR ENROLLMENT
UNIVERSITY OF NOTRE DAME

COLLEGE RANKINGS ARE A REALITY, so use them responsibly.

—*JACINDA OJEDA*
REGIONAL DIRECTOR OF ADMISSIONS
UNIVERSITY OF PENNSYLVANIA

STUDENTS REALLY NEED TO DIG BELOW the surface during their college search to better understand the academic expectations of school, the way the education is delivered, and the school community, before they decide where to apply. The rankings, if you read between the lines and look at the individual factors driving the final mark, may be a helpful resource if used as one of many factors in choosing the best school for you. But, to get a real sense of what colleges and universities are like, you need to visit the campus, speak with students and alumni, and get to know the school in a more intimate manner.

—*JEAN JORDAN*
DEAN OF ADMISSION
EMORY UNIVERSITY

CAN BE HELPFUL although imperfect reference, but not always best indicator of which colleges are best matches for particular students.

—*MATS LEMBERGER*
ASSISTANT DIRECTOR OF ADMISSIONS
DARTMOUTH COLLEGE

MY MOM AND DAD wanted me to find a well-rounded school, and the closer to them, the better. I just wanted to get as far away from my high school as possible. I remember my parents watching over my shoulder as I completed my applications. I needed one more to apply to, and I was out of ideas. My dad had a little sparkle in his eyes and a slight smirk as he suggested that last school. I didn't know much about it, and it was in the mid-range: not a top school, but definitely not one of the worst. I ended up going there. My university is only an hour and fifteen minutes from my parents' house, but I love it.

—*K.C.*
DAVIS, CALIFORNIA
UNIVERSITY OF CALIFORNIA, DAVIS

 IECA⁺ *COUNSELOR'S CORNER*

STUDENTS SHOULD BE LESS CONCERNED with the name of the college and more concerned with what they enjoy most and what they would like to accomplish. Students spend four years in a new home with a new family. Academics are important, but the social, spiritual, emotional, political, and general environment make a significant difference in getting the most out of a college education.

—*RACHEL WINSTON*
EDUCATORS WITH A VISION COLLEGE COUNSELING CENTER

THE PRINCETON REVIEW'S TOP 10 PARTY SCHOOLS

1. University of Florida
2. University of Mississippi
3. Penn State
4. West Virginia University
5. Ohio University
6. Randolph-Macon College
7. University of Georgia
8. University of Texas (Austin)
9. University of California-Santa Barbara
10. Florida State University

THE PRINCETON REVIEW'S TOP 10 SCHOOLS WITH THE HAPPIEST STUDENTS

1. Clemson
2. Brown
3. Princeton
4. Claremont McKenna College
5. Frankin W. Olin College of Engineering
6. Stanford
7. University of Dayton, Ohio
8. Bowdoin College
9. The College of New Jersey
10. Tulane

KIPLINGER'S BEST VALUE PRIVATE COLLEGES

1. California Institute of Technology
2. Yale
3. Princeton
4. Rice
5. Duke
6. Harvard
7. Dartmouth
8. MIT
9. Emory
10. Stanford

KIPLINGER'S BEST VALUE PUBLIC COLLEGES

1. University of North Carolina at Chapel Hill
2. University of Florida
3. University of Virginia
4. University of Georgia
5. College of William and Mary
6. SUNY Geneseo
7. SUNY Binghamton
8. New College of Florida
9. University of Maryland, College Park
10. University of California, San Diego

First Impressions: Applications & Essays

t's impossible for admissions officers to meet even a majority of the students who want to get into their schools. That's why the application essay plays such a pivotal role: It's the school's first impression of the student—a window into the student's life and a crystal ball that reveals the person's potential. In this chapter, we asked college students for essay advice and topics. We also sought their tips on filling out those tedious applications. For more detailed, expert advice about the college application essay, see Brody's Guide to the College Admissions Essay, *beginning on p. 453.*

DON'T PROCRASTINATE. Know the deadlines beforehand and work in advance. Try to send out your applications by the end of October so you can focus on scholarships and last-minute things in November and December.

—SARAH BORMEL
BALTIMORE, MARYLAND
BOSTON UNIVERSITY

BE YOURSELF. IF YOU ARE FUNNY, WRITE A FUNNY ESSAY; IF YOU ARE SERIOUS, WRITE A SERIOUS ESSAY.

—DAVE CROSS
CAMPBELL, OHIO

HEAD**LINES**
Best Advice and Top Tips

- Keep a list of everything you've done so you won't leave something out.
- Let your personality shine through in your essay.
- Switch roles: Look at your applications and essay as if you were the reader.
- Find fresh eyes to look over your application, both for errors and for impact.

Apply online. Some online applications do not require a fee.

—*Phyllis Briskman Stanfield Pittsburgh, Pennsylvania Washington and Jefferson College*

KEEP A LIST OF YOUR ACTIVITIES, awards, jobs, and volunteer service. It is too difficult to remember everything that you did for the last four years. You want to put your best foot forward and it is frustrating to feel that you could have included something else.

—*Jayne Roberts Edmond, Oklahoma University of Oklahoma*

• • • • • • • •

START OFF WITH SOMETHING that will draw the reader in. These people are reading thousands upon thousands of essays. If yours starts off interesting, you have a better chance.

—*Dana Lawrence, New York Harvard University*

THE COMMON APPLICATION is a high school student's best friend. All of the schools that I applied to were Common Application schools. I focused on one idea and really got to concentrate on my application and make it the best that it could be.

—*ROB FEHN*
BASKING RIDGE, NEW JERSEY
LAFAYETTE COLLEGE

• • • • • • • •

" Your essay is your time to shine. The people looking at this essay have probably never met you. You need to paint them a picture of yourself. Tell them everything. "

—*KATHRINE NOVAK*
SHELBY TOWNSHIP, MICHIGAN
CENTRAL MICHIGAN UNIVERSITY

• • • • • • • •

THERE IS NOTHING WRONG with blowing one's horn, especially when everyone else vying for a spot at the same school is doing just that. An application is no time to show how modest you can be. This is a time to say, "Look at me, look what I have done, and look at what I can accomplish." The people who write your recommendation letters are going to focus on the best and the brightest aspects of your personality and high school career, and you should do the same to really cement what those individuals have stated.

—*CATHERINE HOWARD*
NEW ORLEANS, LOUISIANA
SOUTHERN METHODIST UNIVERSITY

A GOOD WAY TO AVOID or lessen stress is to become as organized as possible. When application time rolls around (or even beforehand), you should write a list of everything you've been involved with in high school. That way, a resume shouldn't be hard to compile when the time comes. Check out schools' websites. Find out the criteria colleges use for acceptance, so nothing is a surprise. And when you have an idea of who you would want to write your recommendations, ask them; it's never too early.

—*KATIE*
NEW YORK, NEW YORK
NEW YORK UNIVERSITY

. . . .

THE STRESSFUL PART WAS FILLING OUT all of the applications, especially since each one was different and asked different questions. If possible, you should try to write one essay that can be adapted to fit multiple questions for different applications.

—*ALLISON LEVE*
BALTIMORE, MARYLAND
NEW YORK UNIVERSITY

. . . .

Take your time with your applications. Make them look nice and include things that may impress the reader.

—*SARAH BORMEL*
BALTIMORE, MARYLAND
BOSTON UNIVERSITY

WRITE WELL, AND I DON'T MEAN just on the essay. Everybody knows that you have to carefully proof the essays. But you have to write with purpose on the entire application. As applications for limited spots in colleges increase, admissions committees include more variables in their decision making. A sloppy application is not a way to impress the committee. It's just one easy way for them to weed you out early in the process. Read the whole thing front to back and then read it backward. I found two tiny mistakes when I did it backward.

—*G.A.*
FREDONIA, NEW YORK
STATE UNIVERSITY OF NEW YORK AT BUFFALO

OUCH!

Sending bribes doesn't help. I had my mom bake some cookies and I took them to the admissions officer when I had my interview. He was clearly unhappy, but he said he would not hold it against me if I promised not to do anything like that in the future at any other school. He said he often gets home-baked cookies, candies, and nice baskets of food. He said that never once have those things come into play when a decision was made on a student, so it's really a waste of time.

—*LINDA ROADARMEL*
PARKERSBURG, WEST VIRGINIA
WEST VIRGINIA UNIVERSITY

THE WORST PART OF THE WHOLE process for me was writing the essay. It's hard to come up with something you feel would be adequate. A good way to do it, though, is to find an important experience you worked through and talk about its impact on you.

—*MARGARET JUDIN*
LAWRENCEVILLE, GEORGIA
AGNES SCOTT COLLEGE

BE REAL IN YOUR ADMISSION ESSAY. You don't want to read a list of achievements in essay form; neither do admissions people. Use humor; it generally goes over well. Set yourself apart from other students: Have you done something others haven't? Are you somewhat different? Write about it! Put your heart and soul into your essay, believe what you are writing, write about something you care about. It'll make the task that much easier.

—*COURTNEY HEILMAN*
BOSTON, MASSACHUSETTS

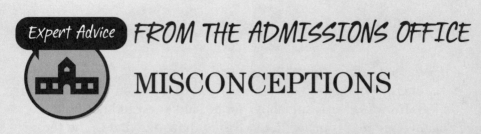

FROM THE ADMISSIONS OFFICE

MISCONCEPTIONS

WHAT IS THE BIGGEST MISCONCEPTION ABOUT THE ADMISSIONS PROCESS?

I THINK THE BIGGEST MISCONCEPTION about the admissions process is that the selectivity of the school is a good way of assessing one's own chance of being admitted. Every year, students are admitted to colleges that admit less than 10%, and the same student is either waitlisted or denied admission to colleges that admitted perhaps 25%-30%. It is not as uncommon as people think. The reality is that each college is looking for different things so, particularly at highly selective institutions, the same applicant may appear unique to one college and commonplace to another, independent of their level of selectivity.

—MARK BUTT
SENIOR ASSISTANT DIRECTOR OF ADMISSIONS
JOHNS HOPKINS UNIVERSITY

• • • • • • • • •

THAT IT'S IMPERSONAL. People who learn about the admissions process are always surprised and pleased at how well we know our applicants, how much we want to understand them as individuals, and how much we're on their side.

—CHRISTOPH GUTTENTAG
DEAN OF UNDERGRADUATE ADMISSIONS
DUKE UNIVERSITY

• • • • • • • • •

THAT TESTING IS THE DETERMINING FACTOR in an application for schools like Dartmouth.

—MATS LEMBERGER
ASSISTANT DIRECTOR OF ADMISSIONS
DARTMOUTH COLLEGE

THAT IT'S FORMULAIC AND HEAVILY WEIGHTED toward tests scores and grades. 90% of our applicants are fully qualified to be here. We're going to look way beyond test scores and grades. The second biggest misconception is affordability. We've made major changes to our financial aid packages; we are very affordable. We are as or more affordable than many of the great flagship public universities now. Many students should be putting aside the issue of cost. One of the reasons we instituted our new financial aid policy is because we heard over and over from students when we were on the road that they weren't even considering Harvard because of the cost. We knew of the big juxtaposition between the great flagship public institutions and places like Harvard—we wanted to close that cost gap. Now we are much more competitive and can allow students that option.

—*WILLIAM R. FITZSIMMONS*
DEAN OF ADMISSIONS AND FINANCIAL AID
HARVARD COLLEGE

THE BELIEF THAT ADMISSIONS is solely about GPA and test scores. The admissions process is about creating a community, so academic measures such as GPA and test scores are important, but so is the curriculum the student has engaged during high school, as well as what the student brings to the community as an individual.

—*CHRIS LUCIER*
VICE PRESIDENT FOR ENROLLMENT MANAGEMENT
UNIVERSITY OF VERMONT

THAT ADMISSION OFFICES take things at face value. We don't. In a holistic review, we are really scratching below the surface to get to know the student as an individual within the context of their educational and home environments. We're going to ask questions and use the information presented to get to know the student as best as possible, which means getting past the numbers and trying to get a sense of the person and how he/she will contribute to our college community.

—*JEAN JORDAN*
DEAN OF ADMISSION
EMORY UNIVERSITY

THAT WE DO NOT THOROUGHLY REVIEW each individual file. That we are simply fixated on "numbers."

 —*DANIEL J. SARACINO*
 ASSISTANT PROVOST FOR ENROLLMENT
 UNIVERSITY OF NOTRE DAME

• • • • • • • • •

COLLEGE ADMISSIONS IS NOT ABOUT the most perfect applicants getting accepted. In college admissions, even selective college admissions, "perfection" is not the standard measuring tool. Students put far too much pressure on themselves to be perfect, which is impossible. Instead, they should focus on their development as an individual. Colleges look for all types of students, especially students who are engaged in their particular interests. But mostly, colleges aren't nearly as concerned with what you have already done as much as they are concerned with what you are capable of doing when you arrive on campus. It's more about potential, not perfection.

 Also, there is way too much hysteria about getting into college. The United States is about the only country in the world where anyone who wants to go to college can get into a college. With over 3,000 colleges, there truly is a college for any type of student. Now, some students face obstacles in funding their college experience, but many students in other countries never even get to that point. In those countries, a college education is reserved for a select portion of the population. The hysteria in the U.S. is more linked to a significantly high percentage of students looking for admission to a relatively smaller percentage of colleges. If students would open up to the multiple opportunities available at a much broader palette of possible college choices, they would realize that a tremendous college experience is available at more than just a handful of schools.

 —*TONY BANKSTON*
 DEAN OF ADMISSIONS
 ILLINOIS WESLEYAN UNIVERSITY

THE BIGGEST MISCONCEPTION ABOUT THE ADMISSIONS PROCESS is that the top 35 colleges and universities in the nation, while outstanding, are the only schools in the country. There are many outstanding schools where students can achieve their goals. Examining the mission statement for each school from year to year often determines the selection process, which includes defining the many forms of merit in the process as well.

—*TED SPENCER*
ASSOCIATE VICE PROVOST AND EXECUTIVE DIRECTOR OF UNDERGRADUATE ADMISSIONS
UNIVERSITY OF MICHIGAN-ANN ARBOR

IT WASN'T SO MUCH *what* I talked about in my college admissions essay, but *how* I talked about it. I compared my grandmother to clementines (the fruit), and I carried the concept throughout. It was quirky, but I made it work, and that essay made every college I applied to think I was a quirky yet interesting person. More than anything else, it showed that I could communicate well, which is one of those "have it or perish!" skills.

—*ERIN*
TACOMA, WASHINGTON

STRESS REDUCERS

- Start your essays early. Many schools have essays with common themes, such as an influential person or experience in your life. It helps to start working on ideas for these general essays over the summer, before the academic workload begins.
- Ask for recommendations before you actually need them. It helps to give people a little extra time to write about why you're a great applicant.

—*BETHANY BLACK*
CHAPEL HILL, NORTH CAROLINA
UNIVERSITY OF NORTH CAROLINA AT CHAPEL HILL

MAKE YOURSELF KNOWN: Call the school you are interested in until you can determine who will be reviewing your application. Don't be afraid to leave that person multiple messages until all of your questions are answered. I felt that it was much less likely that they'd eliminate me for asking too many questions as opposed to showing very little interest.

—*G.A.*
FREDONIA, NEW YORK
STATE UNIVERSITY OF NEW YORK AT BUFFALO

MY ESSAY WAS ABOUT ICE-SKATING and how it wasn't something that I enjoyed doing competitively but I rediscovered it as something I enjoyed doing just for me. I got the idea by thinking about something that made me really happy, and I wrote about it. I was having trouble thinking of something before that. I found it easy to pick an emotion and write about that.

—*EMMA*
HARRINGTON PARK, NEW JERSEY
BROWN UNIVERSITY

I HELPED WITH MY SON'S ESSAYS by talking through the subject with him. I guided him to write about personal experiences and to be creative. For example, one essay he wrote was in the form of an e-mail exchange with his parents.

—*BETH REINGOLD GLUCK*
ATLANTA, GEORGIA
P *UNIVERSITY OF SOUTHERN CALIFORNIA*

• • • • • • • •

" Have a purpose for your essay. Are you telling a story? If so, make sure it is clear. The readers are looking for clarity in your composition, not at your SAT vocabulary. "

—*SARAH BORMEL*
BALTIMORE, MARYLAND
BOSTON UNIVERSITY

• • • • • • • •

I WROTE ONE ESSAY. I wrote it at the last minute and I didn't revise it all. I don't know if that's a good approach. That's my writing style and maybe not for others. Ultimately, they're not going to get a sense of you as a whole person from this one essay. And the throw-it-all-in approach is not as successful because it doesn't sound as true. It sounds as if you're trying to build a resume rather than tell them who you are. Just focus on one thing that shows who you are.

—*ANASTASIA*
BALTIMORE, MARYLAND
YALE UNIVERSITY

KEEP ORGANIZED WITH APPLICATION DATES. I almost missed my housing deadline and would've had to go back in line if that happened.

—*LAUREN SHER*
GAINESVILLE, FLORIDA
UNIVERSITY OF FLORIDA

• • • • • • • •

" Use the thumb test. I put my thumb over my name at the top of my essay and asked myself, 'Can anyone else's name go there as the author?' You want your essay to be so unique that you would be the only possible author. "

—*KELLY TANABE*
CALIFORNIA
HARVARD UNIVERSITY

• • • • • • • •

WHAT TO PUT ON YOUR RESUME: every single leadership/extracurricular activity you've ever done. Make sure to make it all sound very important, if you can. Don't lie, but instead of "wrote and asked questions at poverty discussion," say "codesigner and forum moderator at poverty discussion." And put the dates to anything you can; it makes it sound more legit.

—*DAVID BERNGARTT*
RALEIGH, NORTH CAROLINA
UNIVERSITY OF NORTH CAROLINA AT CHAPEL HILL

DEAR COLUMBIA: I LOVE HARVARD

When you complete and submit essays or letters of recommendation, check to make certain the letters are going to the right schools. In other words, make sure your essay to the University of Nevada doesn't say, "I've always dreamed of attending Arizona State University." I know it sounds like a no-brainer, but it can get hectic when you are sending out so many of these letters. I caught myself with a letter to NYU sealed in an envelope addressed to Buffalo. Luckily, I realized what I was doing before I actually put it in the mailbox. I was imagining myself trying to reach in and get the letter out of there. Getting nailed with a federal offense is not a good idea when you're about to start college.

—ALAN WOLF
FREDONIA, NEW YORK
STATE UNIVERSITY OF NEW YORK AT BUFFALO

I APPLIED TO **16** DIFFERENT SCHOOLS and had to write a variety of essays. I had five different people working with me on my essays, trying to perfect them. This, while balancing the academics of my senior year, proved to be difficult. I lessened the stress by allowing myself time off to play various sports; physical activity has always let me take my mind off work.

—ANDREW WUNG
DIAMOND BAR, CALIFORNIA
UNIVERSITY OF CALIFORNIA, SAN DIEGO

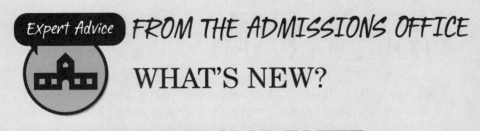

WHAT'S NEW?

WHAT SINGLE FACTOR IN THE APPLICATION HAS INCREASED IN IMPORTANCE IN RECENT YEARS?

IF YOU LOOK NATIONALLY, it has been the increased attention to test scores. At Harvard, as a highly selective institution, there really hasn't been any one factor that's increased in importance. I'd say mostly it's been just competition for admission.

What we tend to look for more than ever are character and personal qualities. It is, of course, a hard thing to measure but what the student has done with his/her time is of high importance to us. We look at interviews, teacher and counselor recommendations, personal statements, etc. to get a sense of the personal qualities and character he/she may bring. We look to anything that might measure what kind of educator that student would be in the dining halls, in the classroom, in our community. We look to the educational effect he or she may have on fellow classmates.

—*WILLIAM R. FITZSIMMONS*
DEAN OF ADMISSIONS AND FINANCIAL AID
HARVARD COLLEGE

• • • • • • • • •

THE HIGH SCHOOL TRANSCRIPT remains the single most important piece of information contained in the application for admission – especially at selective schools. On it, we focus not only on grades and GPA attained, but the rigor of the coursework undertaken.

—*DOUGLAS L. CHRISTIANSEN, PH.D.*
ASSOCIATE PROVOST FOR ENROLLMENT AND DEAN OF ADMISSIONS
VANDERBILT UNIVERSITY

ACADEMIC PERFORMANCE IN HIGH SCHOOL (grades) is still the clear
number one factor considered for a student's admission. Even though
we consider 12 or so primary factors, academic performance carries
the most weight.

As far as which factor has changed the most in importance, I
would say perceived interest on the part of the student, especially for
acceptance at highly selective schools. Twenty-five years ago, before
the Internet, students were applying to three colleges on average.
Back then, if you received an application, you knew the student was
seriously considering your institution. Now the average student sub-
mits applications at 6 to 8 colleges, if not more. With on-line
application programs like the Common Application or the Universal
College Application, submitting another application is simply one
more click of the mouse. So selective colleges with a limited number
of acceptances to hand out are more apt to try and determine
whether they are dealing with a truly interested applicant who will
follow through with investigating the college as a possible option, or
if they are dealing with a student who simply fired off another application to have another fishing line in the water. It's not about a
student making every college feel like "you're the only college for
me," but it is about a student sending a message, whether through an
e-mail, a campus visit, etc. that "I am serious about considering your
institution as a possible college fit."

—*TONY BANKSTON*
DEAN OF ADMISSIONS
ILLINOIS WESLEYAN UNIVERSITY

CONTEXT. As a highly selective college, Dartmouth takes a holistic
approach to reviewing applications. We read for evidence that a student has made the most of the opportunities available in his or her
school context.

—*MATS LEMBERGER*
ASSISTANT DIRECTOR OF ADMISSIONS
DARTMOUTH COLLEGE

THAT THE STUDENT CHALLENGES THEMSELVES based on the rigor of curriculum available to them in their high school. This is often evaluated by the number and progression of academic courses (English, science, social science, math, foreign language) a student takes during high school – freshman through the senior year, and taking honors, AP, or IB courses if available. Senior year curriculum is extremely important. Data indicates that senior year curriculum is one of the most reliable predictors of a student's success during their first year.

—*CHRIS LUCIER*
VICE PRESIDENT FOR ENROLLMENT MANAGEMENT
UNIVERSITY OF VERMONT

• • • • • • • •

CURRICULUM CHALLENGE based upon what is available in the individual student's high school in their academic areas of strength has become increasingly important in recent years.

—*TED SPENCER*
ASSOCIATE VICE PROVOST AND EXECUTIVE DIRECTOR OF UNDERGRADUATE ADMISSIONS
UNIVERSITY OF MICHIGAN-ANN ARBOR

• • • • • • • •

AS COLLEGES HAVE BECOME MORE SELECTIVE, I believe the intangibles, the more subjective parts of the application, have become more important—the impact a person has on the school or the community, the degree to which a student is truly engaged in the learning process—these are the less quantifiable areas that colleges are using to distinguish students more and more. There are so many applicants who are so strong academically, that it doesn't make sense to differentiate applicants on the basis of a fraction of a grade point or thirty or forty points on the SAT's.

—*CHRISTOPH GUTTENTAG*
DEAN OF UNDERGRADUATE ADMISSIONS
DUKE UNIVERSITY

OVER THE YEARS, applications to Johns Hopkins University have been increasing, yet how we read, review applications, and go about making offers of admission has not really changed that much. The major difference is that colleges with more applicants have more people from which to choose.

—*MARK BUTT*
SENIOR ASSISTANT DIRECTOR OF ADMISSIONS
JOHNS HOPKINS UNIVERSITY

•••••••••

THE ACADEMIC RIGOR OF A CANDIDATE'S RECORD remains even more important than ever with more and more applicants submitting high school transcripts with "A's" in virtually all their courses.

—*DANIEL J. SARACINO*
ASSISTANT PROVOST FOR ENROLLMENT
UNIVERSITY OF NOTRE DAME

•••••••••

SPEAKING FROM A HIGHLY SELECTIVE, holistic review process, I believe that everything has become more important. If I had to point to one thing in particular, I think presentation has become increasingly important; the ability to present oneself in an honest, thoughtful, and concise manner is certainly of great value to a student's application.

—*JEAN JORDAN*
DEAN OF ADMISSION
EMORY UNIVERSITY

MY DAUGHTER'S FRIEND, who is a year older, told her to write about something that others wouldn't be writing about. My daughter wrote an essay about the day she persuaded a couple to adopt a pet at a Humane Society adoption center. She wrote it from a very personal point of view, which really conveyed her passion for animals and for people.

—*R.F.*
ATLANTA, GEORGIA
P 🏛 *UNIVERSITY OF PENNSYLVANIA*

• • • • • • • •

I'M TAKING A CREATIVE NONFICTION class right now. Our professor's piece of advice was to think about the thing that really makes you crazy and different from anyone else, something that no one would ever expect. That can be applied to your college admissions essay. Go for the little interesting thing that makes you unique. My essay was about this strange obsession I had with Shakespeare when I was nine years old.

—*CAROLINE*
HAMILTON, MASSACHUSETTS
🏛 *BROWN UNIVERSITY*

• • • • • • • •

DO NOT TURN YOUR APPLICATION IN the night before it is due! No matter what they say, a school will assume you have more interest in going there if you turn in your application a month in advance, rather than a day.

—*MERELISE HARTE ROUZER*
ATLANTA, GEORGIA
🏛 *GEORGIA INSTITUTE OF TECHNOLOGY*

OPENING LINES AT STANFORD

Here are a few "first lines" from essays written by students who were admitted to the Class of 2012 at Stanford, chosen by admissions staff:

- When I was in eighth grade I couldn't read.

- While traveling through the daily path of life, have you ever stumbled upon a hidden pocket of the universe?

- The spaghetti burbled and slushed around the pan, and as I stirred it, the noises it gave off began to sound increasingly like bodily functions.

- I have old hands.

- Flying over enemy territory, I took in Beirut's beautiful skyline and wondered if under different circumstances I would have hopped on a bus and come here for my vacation. Instead, I saw the city from the window of a helicopter, in military uniform, my face camouflaged, on my way to a special operation deep behind enemy lines.

- I was paralyzed from the waist down. I would try to move my leg or even shift an ankle but I never got a response. This was the first time thoughts of death ever crossed my mind.

- I have been surfing Lake Michigan since I was 3 years old.

WHAT *NOT* TO PUT IN YOUR ESSAY

*W*e know – you have lots of funny and interesting stories to tell. But that doesn't mean you should tell them – at least not in your college admissions essay. In case you are unclear on what might not impress college admissions officers, here are a few no-no topics to guide you:

YOUR ABILITY TO DO KEG STANDS: a valuable asset once you reach college, but maybe not what admissions people would like to hear.

> —NATHANIEL COHEN
> WEST HARTFORD, CONNECTICUT
> NEW YORK UNIVERSITY

• • • • • • • • •

ANYTHING ABOUT BOYFRIENDS or music camp.

> —CHRISTIANA
> NEW YORK, NEW YORK
> COLUMBIA UNIVERSITY

• • • • • • • • •

YOU SHOULD PROBABLY LEAVE OUT INFORMATION about how many mailboxes you smashed or about the time you puked in the bathroom at the prom.

> —SCOTT COOLBAUGH
> KNOXVILLE, TENNESSEE
> UNIVERSITY OF TENNESSEE

• • • • • • • • •

ADMISSIONS OFFICERS AREN'T LIKELY to be impressed that you once took 20 shots of vodka in one sitting.

> —COLIN CAMPBELL
> CHARLOTTESVILLE, VIRGINIA
> UNIVERSITY OF NORTH CAROLINA AT CHAPEL HILL

And a few others to avoid:

- The time you and your buddies tore down the goal posts at the high school football game
- Your ability eat large quantities of a certain food in a short period of time
- High school Spring Break stories, in general
- How you managed to avoid productive work all through high school
- How you spent 24 hours straight playing Wii

I MADE SURE THAT I had a lot of different people proofread my essays for me, including my parents and teachers. I didn't want to forfeit my chances of getting into a school because I had simple spelling or grammatical errors.

—*CARRIE BERTOLOZZI*
CHAPEL HILL, NORTH CAROLINA
UNIVERSITY OF NORTH CAROLINA AT CHAPEL HILL

MY COLLEGE ESSAY WAS ABOUT MY MOM telling me when I was a kid that she was gay. It was about that experience. I come from a really stifled conservative town. The essay was about a lot of conflicting ideas that I saw around me. It showed personal awareness. Write something you're passionate about.

—*CHLOE*
LITCHFIELD, CONNECTICUT
🏫 *BROWN UNIVERSITY*

• • • • • • • •

❝Don't go crazy with the colors. While it stands out less, standard black ink is more legible than hot pink. I wrote my first draft in red, and when my dad saw it he nearly blew a gasket.❞

—*C.D.*
NEW MIDDLETOWN, OHIO
🏫 *YOUNGSTOWN STATE UNIVERSITY*

• • • • • • • •

GET YOUR FRIENDS, family, and whoever is good with words and proofing, to read what you write. It's even good just to hear people say, "This sounds funny," or "I don't understand what you're saying here." Have someone on the outside proof!

—*HEATHER HAYASHI*
AUSTIN, TEXAS
🏫 *AUSTIN COMMUNITY COLLEGE*

MAKE THE MOST OF YOUR EXPERIENCES

Almost every school requires an essay—Michigan actually required three—and many of them ask you to write about some obstacle you've overcome. We were a little worried because our daughter really hadn't faced too many obstacles in her life. Not that everything had been easy all the time, but she hadn't been in a hurricane or anything. We decided that in the end, the schools really just wanted to see if you could write. So for one essay, she wrote about the volunteer work that she had done on the Paul Wellstone campaign and how devastating it was when he was killed in the plane crash before the election; and how she had gone on to work on the campaign of Walter Mondale, who ended up losing. On another, she talked about being in Italy as an exchange student in high school and how people there had a really different sense of their body image, being less uptight and letting it all hang out, so to speak, and how she had had to rethink her own feelings about body images. So these weren't really terrible personal obstacles, but they showed that she could think clearly and write a decent essay.

—M.B.
MINNEAPOLIS, MINNESOTA
P ⌂ UNIVERSITY OF MICHIGAN

ESSAY WRITING 'DON'TS'

Don't write what you think a committee wants to hear. The more you try to craft something for them, the more it will fall flat. You never know who will be reading your application or what they are seeking. They just want to know what makes you tick. There are very few topics a reader has not seen, so just be yourself!

Don't write in a style that is not yours. The essay should reflect your personality. It is disappointing to see an essay written in a severe and formal style from someone who is clearly known for a sense of humor. On the flip side, an essay should not be an attempt to entertain the reader, but if you are more casual, you can be a bit relaxed (with proper grammar and language). But please do not attempt humor if you are a serious person; it is simply painful to read.

Don't have someone else write it. A committee knows when something sounds "wrong" in an essay because they read thousands of essays a year. There are also testing data and grades for English in the application, so if the writing is very different from those indicators, a reader will know something is fishy. Do not make this mistake and lose your chance of admission.

Don't vastly exceed page limits or word limits. You can say everything you want or need within the limits of the essay. If you cannot seem to write close to those limits, you are likely going off-topic or talking about unnecessary things. An essay should be about a small, focused thing—not a broad discussion—and this should be kept to about a page or two.

Don't play with margins and fonts to squeeze in more. What you are doing is obvious, and if you happen to be the 30th application of the day for the reader and your font is small, it is not fun.

R.K.

DON'T BE AFRAID TO WRITE about topics that are controversial, because they can make the best essays. When asked to choose a topic on issues that were important to us, I wrote one of my essays on the death penalty. I also wrote one about why I wanted to be a teacher and how I was inspired by my late father's career. I would definitely recommend topics close to your heart, because it's just easier to write when you have a passion for the subject.

—*ELLANA MANDEL*
RIVERDALE, NEW YORK
SARAH LAWRENCE COLLEGE

• • • • • • • •

I DON'T THINK COLLEGES like to read essays that are just an explanation of your activities list. Try to write your essay about a specific quality you possess or a lesson learned. And it always helps to add some humor into your essay. Self-deprecating humor is always very effective in situations like this. I wrote about how I felt that I had the leadership ability to be the captain of the basketball team, but was overlooked. That shows that I feel I am a leader but that I am also big enough to handle defeat well; kind of kills two birds with one stone.

—*ALAN WOLF*
FREDONIA, NEW YORK
STATE UNIVERSITY OF NEW YORK AT BUFFALO

• • • • • • • •

THERE ARE TWO DIFFERENT KINDS of people: the ones who were done with everything in September, and the ones who worked right up until the last day. Remember, it's okay to be early, awful to be late.

—*NATE BATCHELDER*
STRATHAM, NEW HAMPSHIRE
UNIVERSITY OF NEW HAMPSHIRE

Before I started writing, I would talk through my essay with a friend, a teacher, or parent. If you don't want to share your ideas, speak your essay into a tape recorder.

—*KELLY TANABE*
CALIFORNIA
HARVARD UNIVERSITY

PERSONAL ESSAYS

DESCRIBE THE MOST MEMORABLE PERSONAL STATEMENT YOU'VE RECEIVED.

THERE HAVE BEEN MANY; it would be difficult to choose one. I will say that students sometimes think—incorrectly—that the essay has to be an incredible, knock-our-socks-off, compelling piece of writing. It doesn't need to be, and in fact most students don't have enough experience with this kind of personal essay to write something exceptional. I'm happy when I receive an essay that shows me how well a student can write and think, and that is on a subject that allows me to learn a little more about him or her.

> —*CHRISTOPH GUTTENTAG*
> *DEAN OF UNDERGRADUATE ADMISSIONS*
> *DUKE UNIVERSITY*

• • • • • • • • •

IN RESPONDING TO AN ESSAY QUESTION that asked the student to say how they were different or unique, or what they brought to the campus community, a young woman started the essay with: "I have orange hair. No, not red hair, or what you think of when you say someone has red hair, I have glow-in-the-dark, see-me-a-block-away-at-night, natural orange hair." She went on to talk about how, since she was young, her bright orange hair has helped shape her attitudes and her relations with others.

> —*CHRIS LUCIER*
> *VICE PRESIDENT FOR ENROLLMENT MANAGEMENT*
> *UNIVERSITY OF VERMONT*

A STUDENT SHARED HER CONCERNS regarding not having been exposed to students and ideas different from her own. She indicated that she wasn't quite sure what diversity was but she thought she needed plenty of it to grow and learn as a student.

—*TED SPENCER*
ASSOCIATE VICE PROVOST AND EXECUTIVE DIRECTOR OF UNDERGRADUATE ADMISSIONS
UNIVERSITY OF MICHIGAN-ANN ARBOR

• • • • • • • •

NOT EVERY STUDENT HAS AN INCREDIBLE STORY to tell, and they shouldn't feel bad for not having one! Again, I think honesty is the key to an effective essay. There is one essay I read years ago that I still remember vividly. It was from a male student-athlete who was watching his father do landscaping work in oppressive summer heat and humidity. The student was watching his father through a window as the father was shoveling rock, and he was initially struck by the previously unnoticed strength of his father. The student commented how after working that hard he would have come back inside and collapsed on the couch for a couple of hours, but his father came back into the house, washed up, and immediately began making dinner for the entire family. The student ended by relaying how this was the type of man and father he hoped to become some day. It is a simple story, and I've abbreviated it quite a bit, but it relates the importance of family, work ethic, and commitment engrained within the student. This is the type of person you have confidence in joining your campus community, contributing, and succeeding. These are the messages students should look to convey in a personal essay.

—*TONY BANKSTON*
DEAN OF ADMISSIONS
ILLINOIS WESLEYAN UNIVERSITY

ONE IN PARTICULAR DESCRIBED a student's passion to make a difference in how health care works in America. This student had to overcome a tremendous amount of indifference to receive the care needed, but took the steps necessary to prevail in the end. Inspiring story.

—MATS LEMBERGER
ASSISTANT DIRECTOR OF ADMISSIONS
DARTMOUTH COLLEGE

ONE THAT PARTICULARLY STANDS out was about a student's daily journey by train from his inner city neighborhood to a suburban private school that he attended on scholarship.

—JACINDA OJEDA
REGIONAL DIRECTOR OF ADMISSIONS
UNIVERSITY OF PENNSYLVANIA

WHEN, AT THE END OF READING THE STATEMENT, I could figuratively "see" the student in front of me and wanted the get to know him or her even better.

—DANIEL J. SARACINO
ASSISTANT PROVOST FOR ENROLLMENT
UNIVERSITY OF NOTRE DAME

I PORED OVER MY ADMISSIONS ESSAY for Columbia for three months. I wrote, rewrote, edited, proof-read, and scoured it for any imperfection. I really tried to give the admissions committee a clear picture of my roots, my ambitions, and my achievements. Clear, effective, and concise prose is the best way to make a statement in your admissions essay. Also, humor is fine if you're a comedian. I am not, so I stuck to a serious tone. Bring your admissions essay to at least one of your high school English teachers to edit—not just for content but also for grammar. Even the smallest typo or grammatical no-no can tarnish an otherwise great personal statement.

—*DANIEL*
WHEELING, WEST VIRGINIA
COLUMBIA UNIVERSITY

" Write about something that makes you unique but not weird. "

—*ALLISON LEVE*
BALTIMORE, MARYLAND
NEW YORK UNIVERSITY

DON'T BRAG A LOT ON YOUR ESSAY; there's a temptation to show off. One of my essays was about how I failed three driving tests. That shows more about character. It shows you can over-come something.

—*PAUL*
CHAPPAQUA, NEW YORK
YALE UNIVERSITY

When you're spending hours on applications and essays, don't forget music; it's a great stress reliever.

—*BRIANA*
  SONOMA,
  CALIFORNIA
  SONOMA STATE
  UNIVERSITY

I WROTE MY ESSAY ON BEING EDITOR of my yearbook, and my three years involved with it. I think it made a difference, since I could convey a hard-work ethic (staying at school until 3 a.m., taking work home with me), as well as a passion for what I did. It's good to write honestly and candidly about something that has touched you, since it's harder to BS something you feel strongly about; and over-the-top, SAT-word-saturated essays can definitely set off the BS alarm.

    —*TRICIA POWELL*
     HUNTINGTON BEACH, CALIFORNIA
     UNIVERSITY OF CALIFORNIA, BERKELEY

· · · · · · · ·

MAKE SURE TO USE ACTIVE and not passive verbs. Instead of writing "I was given the award by the local chapter of the NAACP," write "The local chapter of the NAACP awarded me ..." See how much better that sounds?

    —*TABITHA HAGAR*
     WILMINGTON, DELAWARE
     UNIVERSITY OF DELAWARE

· · · · · · · ·

THE MOST IMPORTANT ASPECT of the essay is picking the right subject. And how do you do that? Ask yourself this: What are your major accomplishments, and why do you consider them accomplishments? Don't limit yourself to only accomplishments for which you have been formally recognized. The most interesting essays often are based on accomplishments that may have been trite at the time, but become crucial when placed in the context of your life. I used teaching my little brother to ride his bike as the subject of my essay.

    —*K.R.*
     WINCHESTER, VIRGINIA
     UNIVERSITY OF VIRGINIA

HEADS UP: THE COMMON APPLICATION

Launched in 1976, the Common Application is offered by a group of more than 275 U.S. colleges and universities. Using the Common App for admission streamlines the process, since you only have to fill out the form once. Yet some experts believe there are bad as well as good aspects of the Common App:

PRO

- It takes less time and effort so you can apply to more schools
- You can choose among four essay topics or write your own
- Easier to use than a lot of schools' applications
- If you fill it out online, you can save it at any point and go back to it
- You can cut, paste and move things around

CON

- Makes it easy to apply to *too many* schools
- Less opportunity to show specific things about yourself
- Not as much depth

ASK THE EXPERT

What is an AO? Do AO's have special training?

An admissions officer, or AO, is responsible for visiting high schools, making presentations, reading and evaluating applications, and managing a section of the admissions office's internal responsibilities. An AO is rigorously trained in evaluating applications for his school, and this also includes training about understanding applicants' environments.

R.K.

Expert Advice *FROM THE ADMISSIONS OFFICE*

HIGH SCHOOL PROFILES

HOW DO YOU UTILIZE THE HIGH SCHOOL PROFILE?

THE PROFILE PROVIDES ACADEMIC AND SOCIAL CONTEXT. Academic context is provided by information about the curriculum the school offers, average standardized test scores, the proportion of graduates that attend college and where they go, among other things. Social context is provided by demographic information about the school and the local area and school activities available to students.

—*CHRIS LUCIER*
VICE PRESIDENT FOR ENROLLMENT MANAGEMENT
UNIVERSITY OF VERMONT

• • • • • • • • •

IT HELPS TO CONTEXTUALIZE the student's academic record. If the student has not taken any AP courses and the profile indicates that they offer twelve, this helps us. If the school just does not offer any, this helps us to understand why the student didn't take any.

—*DANIEL J. SARACINO*
ASSISTANT PROVOST FOR ENROLLMENT
UNIVERSITY OF NOTRE DAME

• • • • • • • • •

THE HIGH SCHOOL PROFILE IS ESSENTIAL to helping admissions officers understand the context you come from as a student. It allows us to evaluate the rigor of your curriculum, and helps us understand your high school's grading scale and other academic policies in a way that is invaluable to holistic evaluation.

—*DOUGLAS L. CHRISTIANSEN, PH.D.*
ASSOCIATE PROVOST FOR ENROLLMENT AND DEAN OF ADMISSIONS
VANDERBILT UNIVERSITY

THEY ARE VERY IMPORTANT FOR US, since from them we learn about the opportunities and limitations of a high school's curriculum, the school's grading scale, special course offerings, often something about the community, just a whole host of things that help us understand the student within the context of his or her school.

—*CHRISTOPH GUTTENTAG*
DEAN OF UNDERGRADUATE ADMISSIONS
DUKE UNIVERSITY

* * * * * * * * *

THE HIGH SCHOOL PROFILE PLAYS an important role in the admissions process. Admissions offices encounter thousands of high schools across the country and around the world. As such we rely on the profile to help us get to know an applicant's school and community. When I evaluate a student's high school record, I read the transcript in conjunction with the school profile. This way, I can evaluate a student within the specific context of his or her school—some schools offer 25+ APs, some offer none; a "B" in one high school is very different from a "B" at another; is this a community that sends 95% of its graduates to 4-year colleges, or is it rare that this student is even considering pursuing higher education?

Clearly, "context" is a vital part of the evaluation process, and we rely on the school profile to provide it for us.

—*JACINDA OJEDA*
REGIONAL DIRECTOR OF ADMISSIONS
UNIVERSITY OF PENNSYLVANIA

* * * * * * * * *

THE HIGH SCHOOL PROFILE HELPS provide context on the level of rigor in course selection and extent of opportunities and resources available to a student.

—*MATS LEMBERGER*
ASSISTANT DIRECTOR OF ADMISSIONS
DARTMOUTH COLLEGE

THE HIGH SCHOOL PROFILE is a great resource for our office. We try to climb inside the application and understand the academic environment, the school community, and the local community in order to better understand the student within the context of his/her high school experience. The profile allows us to be better informed about the curriculum, the grading system, the way students may progress over four years, and what type of school activities or leadership opportunities are available to them when class ends. The more informed we are in the application review process, the better decisions we can make.

—*JEAN JORDAN*
DEAN OF ADMISSION
EMORY UNIVERSITY

• • • • • • • •

PRIMARILY, WE USE IT TO GET A BETTER FEEL for high schools with which we may not be as familiar. But being admitted isn't about coming from the most impressive high school. It's about what each student has done with the opportunities they have been provided at whichever school they happened to attend. If you are looking at course rigor, you can't give an advantage to a student with AP course work from a high school that offers 30 AP courses over a student from a rural high school that offers no AP courses. Instead, we focus on whether or not each student has independently challenged himself or herself within the curriculum they were offered at their respective schools.

—*TONY BANKSTON*
DEAN OF ADMISSIONS
ILLINOIS WESLEYAN UNIVERSITY

MAKE SURE THE COLLEGES that you apply to know how thoughtful and thorough you were in the process of selecting them. Make them feel special, not as if you just picked them out of the phone book. You can do this by making reference to specific and distinctive characteristics of the college and how those characteristics fit your abilities, personality, and style particularly well. I told schools that I was good at working independently and didn't require much interpersonal interaction with the teachers. I knew this would appeal to bigger schools where many of the freshman classes could number more than 100 students.

> —G.A.
> FREDONIA, NEW YORK
> STATE UNIVERSITY OF NEW YORK AT BUFFALO

Consider

• • • • • • • •

KEEP THE FOCUS ON YOU. Whether you are writing about your favorite book, an influential person, or your favorite subject, remember that your essay needs to convey something about you to the college.

> —KELLY TANABE
> CALIFORNIA
> HARVARD UNIVERSITY

Write from the heart.

> —DELAN
> LOS ANGELES,
> CALIFORNIA
> UNIVERSITY
> OF SOUTHERN
> CALIFORNIA

• • • • • • • •

STAY ON TASK WITH EVERYTHING. I missed applying to one school because the deadline was in August; I assumed that, because applications to all the other schools I was looking at were due in January or February, this one was, too. But then I looked online and found the application deadline had passed.

> —DANE KARL SKILBRED
> SAINT PAUL, MINNESOTA
> SANTA CLARA UNIVERSITY

THE PRINCETON ESSAY QUESTION WAS, "Who would you have as a roommate?" I mentioned Brooke Shields, since she used to go to the school. It was a silly answer, but I had fun with it. I also mentioned that I've seen the movie *Clash of the Titans* 40 times, and how when I'm bored I recast movies in my head (e.g.: "How would Danny DeVito do as Robin Hood?") I explained that this little game in my head is my escape; it is one random thing that gives me pleasure and provides an outlet for my imagination. I'm sure it's what helped me get into Princeton, because there are 8,000 other Brians who applied to the school who also had good grades and played sports in high school.

—*BRIAN ROSEN*
NEW YORK, NEW YORK
PRINCETON UNIVERSITY

I'M TAKING A CLASS NOW and the professor was talking about the definition of literary criticism, the purpose of the field. Her point was that literature is something that can improve the human experience and make better people. That's the best material for a college essay. Your essay and the way you approach college should all move toward this idea that you're going to be a better person through college. You're going to learn from the experience. Put that in a college essay.

—*CHRISTIANA*
NEW YORK, NEW YORK
COLUMBIA UNIVERSITY

WRITE WITH CONFIDENCE. Don't be cocky, but be straightforward and clear.

—*SCOTT COOLBAUGH*
KNOXVILLE, TENNESSEE
UNIVERSITY OF TENNESSEE

OTHER SIDE OF THE DESK: HOW AO'S SEE YOU

We admire and respect you, but be realistic:

- You may be a big fish in your community, but compared to other big fish, you may not be so big.
- It is *very* hard these days to do anything truly unique that an AO has not seen, so don't feel pressure to be unique.
- AO's read hundreds, or sometimes thousands, of applications each year, so they can easily spot exaggeration or insincerity in applications.

IT TOOK ME ABOUT THREE WEEKS to do the college essay. I had to write about an experience that changed the course of my life. I knew I would write about Lyme disease, which I suffered through, but I kept thinking, "How in the world do you sum up the most difficult years of your life in 500 words?" It just seemed impossible no matter how hard I tried. Then, at about 1 a.m., I sat down with a notebook and a pen, and I wrote the essay in about 30 minutes.

—*KELLY*
HERNDON, VIRGINIA
GEORGE MASON UNIVERSITY

Papers get lost in the mail. When you send anything to a college, make copies first and send everything "Return Receipt Requested."

—*ANONYMOUS*
NORTH POTOMAC, MARYLAND
BRANDEIS UNIVERSITY;
CORNELL UNIVERSITY

PARENTS' PAGES

ENGLISH TEACHERS CAN BE A GREAT RESOURCE for those college essays. The first part of the year my son's teacher helped him with the planning and writing of the essays, and then once he had finished she took the time to look them over and tweak them a bit. Just having someone read them who knew a little more about what admissions officers were looking for was really helpful for him.

> —*DONNA*
> *CINCINNATI, OHIO*
> *P ⚬ MIAMI UNIVERSITY*

• • • • • • • • •

OUR SON DID MOST OF HIS APPLICATIONS ONLINE. He sent them in at 10 p.m. on the night of the deadline, New Year's Eve. He went down to the wire. We were ready to strangle him, and meanwhile he pushed that button to send off his applications and went out for New Year's Eve. There is no easy way to encourage them. Sometimes you just have to let them fail in order to learn. Our son is that kind of kid. But it stressed out the whole family.

> —*ANONYMOUS*
> *BROOKLYN, NEW YORK*
> *P ⚬ BROWN UNIVERSITY*

• • • • • • • • •

HAVE YOUR CHILD COMPLETE the college essays early. Writing an essay doesn't sound that difficult, but once they sit down to do it they realize what a challenge it is. My daughter turned in her essay to her first-choice school about three weeks before it was due. Her friends were actually writing their essays three hours before they were due! And some of them missed the deadline because the schools' computers were jammed with too much traffic from everyone else trying to submit their essays.

> —*ANONYMOUS*
> *LOS ANGELES, CALIFORNIA*
> *P ⚬ UNIVERSITY OF CALIFORNIA, SANTA BARBARA*

I LITERALLY INTERVIEWED MY SON and then we sat down together and wrote the resume. I didn't just say he played soccer for four years. We wrote about the teamwork and expounded on what he learned from the experience. We determined his best assets and listed those attributes at the top of the resume. We did it as if for a job interview.

—*KATHY THOMAS*
DALLAS, TEXAS
P ▄▟ TEXAS CHRISTIAN UNIVERSITY

• • • • • • • •

ADVISE YOUR KIDS TO KEEP THEIR ESSAYS to one page. If someone with ten years of work experience can fit their resume on one page, then a 17-year-old kid should be able to edit his essay down to a page. The admissions officers are really busy and have so many applications to read. You don't want them to lose interest. One school we went to explained it really well; they said it's an application, not a dissertation.

—*JANE*
SCOTTSDALE, ARIZONA
P ▄▟ UNIVERSITY OF MIAMI

• • • • • • • •

I HIRED A WOMAN WHO HELPED my son with the application process. I knew it was a lot to deal with, and was aware that kids will generally respond more quickly and thoroughly to someone who is an expert in the field, as opposed to a parent. There are just too many buttons that get pushed with parents and kids. That said, even with my intention to back off and stay relaxed, there were moments when I found myself checking in with him more often than I should have. When he told me he had it covered, I just had to trust that he did, because ultimately he was the one who was going to have to live with the result.

—*LINDA SALAZAR*
PALOS VERDES, CALIFORNIA
P ▄▟ BROOKS INSTITUTE OF PHOTOGRAPHY

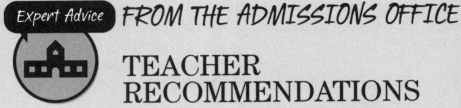

Expert Advice *FROM THE ADMISSIONS OFFICE*

TEACHER RECOMMENDATIONS

WHAT MAKES A TEACHER RECOMMENDATION TRULY COMPELLING AND HELPFUL IN THE ADMISSIONS PROCESS?

HONESTY. I am more likely to give weight to a letter of recommendation that points out some of the student's challenges as well as his or her merits. When I see a transcript with inconsistent performance, and then read a letter of recommendation that talks about the student being "outstanding" academically with no reference to the inconsistent performance, I immediately dismiss the value of the letter. I'd rather have someone say, "Hey, this kid loves English and is one of the best students I've ever had in my literature class. But, when it comes to math and science, the concentration level isn't always as strong. I've talked with Susie about the importance of putting in the best effort possible in all of her courses in college, and I have confidence she will do so." That is a recommendation I can believe in.

> —*TONY BANKSTON*
> *DEAN OF ADMISSIONS*
> *ILLINOIS WESLEYAN UNIVERSITY*

• • • • • • • • •

LEARNING ABOUT HOW the student impacted the classroom environment is really helpful for us since our educational environment is very collaborative and participatory. How did he/she interact with and inspire both his/her peers and the teacher?

> —*JEAN JORDAN*
> *DEAN OF ADMISSION*
> *EMORY UNIVERSITY*

TEACHER RECOMMENDATIONS WHICH TELL STORIES which shed light on the applicant's "life of the mind" are wonderful, and compelling to read. We want to hear about that great history project you wrote, about the fact that you are a catalyst for in-class discussion, or that people love being your lab partner because you think outside the box and get good lab results. Stories like this can really bring your grades and test scores to life for the admissions committee.

—*DOUGLAS L. CHRISTIANSEN, PH.D.*
ASSOCIATE PROVOST FOR ENROLLMENT AND DEAN OF ADMISSIONS
VANDERBILT UNIVERSITY

• • • • • • • •

TEACHER RECOMMENDATIONS ARE IMPORTANT in our process because they can really give an insider's perspective on who that student is in the classroom—which is something that we as admissions counselors never get to see. These letters can tell us about how the student thinks, what sorts of questions they ask, and the quality of their academic work.

—*MARK BUTT*
SENIOR ASSISTANT DIRECTOR OF ADMISSIONS
JOHNS HOPKINS UNIVERSITY

• • • • • • • •

WHEN THE TEACHER USES DESCRIPTIVE WORDS and provides examples to support these words. Anecdotes are also quite helpful in supporting the teacher's description of the type of applicant in his or her class-room setting. Avoiding any "re-hashing" of what we can learn simply by looking at the student's extracurricular section of the application is wise.

—*DANIEL J. SARACINO*
ASSISTANT PROVOST FOR ENROLLMENT
UNIVERSITY OF NOTRE DAME

• • • • • • • •

THOUGHTFUL AND SPECIFIC INSIGHTS regarding a student's aptitude and ability to adapt in a competitive academic environment.

—*TED SPENCER*
ASSOCIATE VICE PROVOST AND EXECUTIVE DIRECTOR OF UNDERGRADUATE ADMISSIONS
UNIVERSITY OF MICHIGAN-ANN ARBOR

WHEN IT PROVIDES INFORMATION that isn't in the rest of the file and it provides intellectual and social insights into the student.   In other words, saying that the student does well, and we already have the transcript that shows the student gets A's in the course material, isn't as important as insights into intellectual curiosity, risk taking, interactions with peers, passion, etc.

> —*CHRIS LUCIER*
> *VICE PRESIDENT FOR ENROLLMENT MANAGEMENT*
> *UNIVERSITY OF VERMONT*

. . . .

BEING CANDID AND DETAILED. It is important to understand that rarely does one particular part of an application result in the final outcome. A decision is based on how all the parts of an application fit together. Giving concrete examples contributes to a clearer overall sense of the applicant.

> —*MATS LEMBERGER*
> *ASSISTANT DIRECTOR OF ADMISSIONS*
> *DARTMOUTH COLLEGE*

. . . .

THE MOST HELPFUL RECOMMENDATIONS come from teachers who know the student very well, on both an academic and a personal level. The teacher who gave you the A+ isn't always necessarily the one who knows you best, and a student should consider this when asking a teacher to write on his or her behalf.

The most useful recommendations tell us about how the student contributes to the classroom environment and performs in comparison with his or her peers. They give us little anecdotes about the applicant that make him or her come alive for the admissions committee.

> —*JACINDA OJEDA*
> *REGIONAL DIRECTOR OF ADMISSIONS*
> *UNIVERSITY OF PENNSYLVANIA*

YOU SHOULD NOT PUT SOB STORIES in your essays. A lot of people have deceased loved ones; it's not going to make you a special individual to a college admissions officer. Don't worry so much about writing something that is going to reflect your intelligence so much as your personality. I wrote about an improvisational comedy class that I took. I had a friend who wrote an ode to his favorite pair of socks; he's at Brown now.

—ZACHARY KLION
 SUFFERN, NEW YORK
 YALE UNIVERSITY

• • • • • • • • •

SCHOOLS GET THOUSANDS OF ESSAYS and it's difficult to stand out from the pack. I opened my essay with an anecdote, one that captured my personality and my experience, and I think this caught attention. In my essay, I also stressed unique reasons why I wanted to attend the school I was applying to. I didn't keep it general (saying something such as, "your school has a great history department"); instead, I mentioned professors' names whom I wanted to learn from and why, and I mentioned some of the special qualities that I felt the school had.

—ANDREA
 TORONTO, ONTARIO
 QUEEN'S UNIVERSITY

Keep it short and to the point. You're not writing *War and Peace*. And these people have tons of essays to read.

—MILLER SMATHERS
 FINDLAY, OHIO

MY LIFE, THE GAME

Think your application is creative? Claremont McKenna College in California says one applicant sent in a homemade board game based on this applicant's life. Chocolate dice and trivia questions on things such as the student's pet rat highlighted the game. For all that creativity, the student was wait-listed.

WHEN FALL IS HELL

Stressful doesn't begin to describe it! In retrospect, I applied to far too many colleges (nine), so from November to January, I was wrestling with a barrage of applications, essays, recommendations, and test scores. Eventually, I learned to relax and even laugh a little at the whole song-and-dance routine. At my school, when the early-decision letters started arriving, we held a "Wait-Listing Party," complete with cake and "Hello, my name is _____ and I was wait-listed at _____" stickers. It's important to realize that after you send in the application, there's nothing more to be done. Relax!

—*EMILY WACHTEL*
LOS ANGELES, CALIFORNIA
UNIVERSITY OF CALIFORNIA, LOS ANGELES

PROOFREAD, PROOFREAD, PROOFREAD. And when you are sure it's good, proofread it again. Nothing says, "I did this at the last possible moment" like an "are" instead of "our." And your computer's spell-checker is not going to pick that up for you. Another good thing to do is to read it backwards. That helps. On my last reading I found a "their" that was supposed to be a "there": That was close!

—*MILLER SMATHERS*
FINDLAY, OHIO

As you're applying for college, look at each application in a different way. In my USC application, I was basically being myself. For my University of California applications, I was more serious and more formal. I didn't really care about USC when I first applied, so my app was very informal and fun. I guess that made me stand out. That's the school I attend now.

—*Delan*
Los Angeles, California
University of Southern California

PLAN YOUR ESSAYS

From each school's application, take all the essay questions—even the short-answer questions—and make a list of them. See if there is any overlap. How can you figure out what to write? Think about the following:

- Map out an outline for each question—what do you want to say? What does this story tell about your personality or what is important to you?
- If given options for essays, choose the one that's the most appealing to you—the committees have no preference and there isn't one "right" one to pick—so whatever is most comfortable to you will flow the best and will make for your best essay.
- Use the same essay idea (or full essay) where you can, BUT if a topic does not directly answer a question on a second application, do NOT re-use an essay—this is obvious to the admissions staff, and is a huge turn-off for them. It can get a great candidate (like you!) wait-listed instead of admitted.

R.K.

EXTRA CREDIT?

DON'T BE LURED into one of the biggest psychological traps in the college application form—supplementary material. This fairly standard invitation to submit extra work implies that there's more that can be done to influence the individual admissions decision. It may subtly pressure you to come up with creative things to send that are not appropriate. A student may not feel he has done all he can without sending "something."

Good applicants are admitted based on the regular criteria. You get 'full credit' for all the activities listed on the application—admissions officers know how to interpret them by the time commitment and length of commitment—and frankly, if you are committed to an activity, your degree of talent (even if zero) doesn't matter.

If you nonetheless feel you must submit supplementary material, make sure it isn't any of the following:

- Doodled drawings, if art is a hobby
- Full scientific papers. Give the summary elsewhere in the application.
- CD's of music, unless you are truly a prodigy
- Anything edible
- Anything requiring assembly or explanation

 *Expert Advice* I E C A⁺ *COUNSELOR SURVEY*

How important is it that a student demonstrate "genuine interest" toward a college as a factor for admission?

Very important – 67%
Somewhat important – 28%
Not very important – 5%

DON'T USE INAPPROPRIATE E-MAIL addresses when writing to admissions officers. One of my friends used the address mikelikesithot@somethingor other.com. Things like that make a really bad impression.

—*ALAN WOLF*
FREDONIA, NEW YORK
STATE UNIVERSITY OF NEW YORK AT BUFFALO

. . . .

' Check your grammar and your spelling. Have your parents check your grammar and your spelling. Have your aunts, uncles, and that cousin you never talk to check your grammar and your spelling. ''

—*MAX MALON MALLORY*
NEW YORK, NEW YORK
SARAH LAWRENCE COLLEGE

. . . .

IN WRITING ESSAYS, it's best to focus on what makes you unique. Whether it comes out through the subject you choose or your writing style or both, it's your personality that will make your essay grab the attention of admissions people. Don't just try to say what you think they want to hear: No one's going to buy it if you tell them your favorite activity is studying.

—*COLIN CAMPBELL*
CHARLOTTESVILLE, VIRGINIA
UNIVERSITY OF NORTH CAROLINA AT CHAPEL HILL

WHAT'S DUE WHEN?

Once you've made your final list of schools, figure out what work is in store for you so you can get organized. With so many things to keep track of - essays, testing dates, application deadlines, etc. - in a limited time, you need to be as efficient as possible.

Log on to each application or download them onto your computer. Keep track of the following on a master calendar:

- Final due dates for all documents
- Essay topics and lengths (Are any of them the same?)
- Forms to fill out
- Policies about supplemental material

Then, plan out intermediate deadlines on a wall calendar before the schools' actual application deadlines. This will help you organize your time. And, if you can stick to your personal deadlines on the way to the final deadlines, you shouldn't have to cram to complete your applications, which will also make them more thoughtful and therefore stronger.

Assess all of the pieces of the applications and backdate the work—make up deadlines on your calendar for the following:

- Each essay: Plan to do one a week if you can
- When to turn in forms to teachers and guidance staff at your high school (the sooner the better!)
- Last possible testing dates for re-taking SAT or ACT
- Financial aid form deadlines: These aren't the same as the admissions deadlines
- Dates to check in with your teachers and guidance staff
- For a useful college application schedule, check out www.collegeboard.com.

R.K.

START WRITING!

Starting early and writing your essays slowly over time will allow you to produce your best work. You'll have time to step away for a day or two during the process, allowing you to catch your own mistakes and improve what you say, and you can ask others for input for revisions both for content and grammar.

How to start?

1. Think about essays you have written for your English classes: You'll need an introduction, a body paragraph or two, and a conclusion.
2. Write in a stream of consciousness—let your fingers fly over the computer keyboard—and edit yourself later. You'll get it down to a page eventually, but feel free to over-write for now.
3. Feel comfortable using your own voice. If you tend to be more serious, it's fine to write a formal, five-paragraph essay like you would for English class. But if you're especially creative or funny, you can adopt a more casual tone and structure. The bottom line: Do NOT try to be something you are not. The key to a good essay is how much it reflects <u>you</u>.

Remember, Brody's Guide starting on p. 453 has step-by-step instructions to help with your essay.

R.K.

KEEP TRACK OF WHICH FORMS you've sent to which college. My brother turned in all the necessary information, but never followed up to make sure that his schools had actually received it. As it turned out, his SAT scores never arrived at Rice, so he wasn't accepted there. Be sure to double-check that the colleges you're applying to have gotten your complete application.

—*NICOLINE STROM-JENSEN*
ATLANTA, GEORGIA
AGNES SCOTT COLLEGE

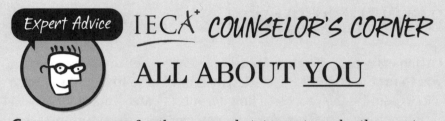

Expert Advice

IECA* COUNSELOR'S CORNER

ALL ABOUT YOU

CHOOSING A TOPIC for the personal statement can be the most challenging part of the essay writing process. Writing about a specific situation that shaped the development of you as a person is an excellent strategy. However, beyond describing the situation, it's important to be reflective and analyze the lessons learned. Also, the personal statement is a great opportunity to add depth and insight to items mentioned in other parts of your application, such as a leadership role in an extracurricular activity, or a summer experience. Above all, when planning the essay, keep in mind that your personal statement should differentiate you in terms of character and interests, so the admissions committee can envision the unique contribution you would have if you joined the campus community.

—*SUSAN JOAN MAURIELLO*
APPLY IVY LIMITED

• • • • • • • • •

ONE MISTAKE MANY STUDENTS MAKE is leaving the *personal* out of the Personal Essay. Use first person pronouns (I, me, my) to tell a vivid story that reveals something about you that won't otherwise get conveyed in your lists of academics, activities, and test scores. Your essay should tell a story that no one else can tell because it is not just about what happened; your personal essay is about how the experience shaped you.

Ultimately, your essay should be 500-650 words of flawless spelling, sentence structure, punctuation and word usage. As you are getting started, however, don't worry about any of these.

There are so many things that matter to you. Focus on one that develops into a good story in which you are the protagonist.

—*MONICA ANDREWS, ED.D.*
PRESIDENT, REELWISDOM

SOME KIDS ARE EXCELLENT WRITERS who simply have an impressive way with words. Other kids try to beef up their papers with cliché lines and "inspiring" statements that are supposed to impress judges. I am neither a talented writer, nor a skilled BS-er, but I am extremely comfortable with being truthful. So, as I wrote my "personal statement," which was supposed to help my judge "know" me, I was simply honest: honest about my hopes, my fears, my struggles and my talents. I didn't talk myself up excessively, yet I never doubted my abilities.

—*SUSI MCGHEE*
DECATUR, GEORGIA
UNIVERSITY OF GEORGIA

BE YOURSELF IN YOUR ESSAY. That's all I did. My essay was about my worst fear, which at the time was sharks. I had learned to surf, and one day when I was surfing I saw two sharks swimming by me. I lifted my legs and arms out of the water and let them go by me. I wasn't hurt, and I realized I had faced my fear. Since that moment, I haven't been afraid of them. That's what I wrote about in my essay.

—*JENNIFER DRAGOVICH*
SEMINOLE, FLORIDA
FLORIDA STATE UNIVERSITY

GET MULTIPLE PEOPLE TO READ OVER your college essay, especially people who know a lot about it, such as a good guidance counselor. Or take it to a university and say, "Can someone read this? Is it good?" I doubt more than two people read my college essays for me. Looking back, the essay is more important than the tests.

—*AHMAD*
BASKING RIDGE, NEW JERSEY
STANFORD UNIVERSITY

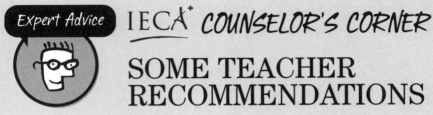

Expert Advice

IECA⁺ COUNSELOR'S CORNER

SOME TEACHER RECOMMENDATIONS

THE TEACHER WHO WRITES your letter of recommendation should be able to describe your contributions to the class or among the school community that they have personally observed either as a coach or club advisor, etc. You should also choose a teacher who teaches you an academic subject, e.g. math, science, language, English, or social studies.

Good letters of recommendation should address your specific characteristics that they observe in the classroom, such as: creative problem solving; unique presentation; critical thinking; helpfulness; work ethic; compassion; ability to overcome challenges; intellectual curiosity; and the ability to think outside of the box - or alternatively to bring a different point of view to the class discussion.

It is helpful to provide the teacher with a summary of a project, report, presentation or classroom activity where you felt like you made an especially good impression. It is also helpful if you can provide the teacher with a graded paper to remind him/her of your work.

When asking for a recommendation, you should also give the teacher the following:

- At least a month's notice.
- A copy of the recommendation form with your name and information filled out. You can download that off of the common application under forms or directly from a non-common application school's website. Some high schools also have their own forms, which are also acceptable.
- A brief outline with reminders of projects and activities that you participated in with the teacher.
- A copy of your resume or "brag sheet"

- For each college: a stamped #10 envelope, with the address of the Admissions Office (unless you want them to submit the form to the high school guidance counselor's office). For the 'return address,' use the teacher's name and your high school address.
- Some schools are moving towards electronic submission of recommendation letters. If your school has this capability, an envelope is not necessary.

Be sure to tell them which school it's for – and what the deadline is.

Always write a thank-you letter to your teachers for their time and effort on your behalf.

—LISA BLEICH
PRESIDENT, COLLEGE BOUND MENTOR, LLC
COPYRIGHT 2008 © COLLEGE BOUND MENTOR. ALL RIGHTS RESERVED

- - - - - - - -

WHEN PLANNING YOUR TEACHER RECOMMENDATIONS, it's important to keep three guidelines in mind:

1. CHOOSE TEACHERS FROM your favorite classes that relate to your academic and career interests. Although it's important that you performed well in the teacher's class, the class itself is also relevant. For example, if you are passionate about history and politics, cover related topics in your essays, are considering majoring in the field, and are involved in related extracurricular activities, ask your history teacher for a recommendation. This way, your recommendation will be much more compelling: beyond highlighting your academic excellence, the teacher can discuss your genuine interest in the subject matter and your intellectual curiosity, which will be very meaningful to the admissions committees.

2. SPEND TIME TALKING TO your teachers before they write the recommendation. Rather than simply providing your teacher with the recommendation form, talk to them about your college plans, specific achievements in their particular classes, and interest in the subject matter studied. This will ensure that the recommendation is as unique to you as possible, rather than a generic letter that could have been written about any strong student in the class.

3. **APPROACH YOUR TEACHERS** for recommendations early in the school year, and remember to say thank you! Your teachers will be submitting many students' recommendations, so you want to make sure they have enough time to write a thoughtful letter, rather than do so in a rushed manner. For early decision applications, you should ask teachers for recommendations at the beginning of the school year; for regular decision, you should approach your teachers by the end of October. After they're done, write them a thank-you note in appreciation for their time.

Two more points to consider:

- *A good recommendation* can be from someone who has watched you struggle and overcome challenges. If you come before or after school for extra help, the teacher can comment on your desire to learn and excel.
- *Do not worry about whether to get* recommendations from teachers who are well known. A new teacher can write a great recommendation and an experienced teacher can write a bad one.

—SUSAN JOAN MAURIELLO
APPLY IVY LIMITED

ASK THE EXPERT

My recommendations are really good, don't you agree?

Do not assume you have "good" recommendations. AOs have a gut feeling about which recommendations are really sincere and which ones are not. AOs are great at understanding the nuances—like the degree to which you are really and truly respected by the person writing the letter. Choose your recommenders wisely, though, and you will be fine.

R.K.

AN APPLE FOR THE TEACHER? THE PERFECT 'THANK YOU'

Teachers can spend hours writing recommendations and filling out forms for you. This is time for which they aren't paid, and you're probably not the only student asking them for a recommendation. It's appropriate to acknowledge the time your teachers have taken to help you.

Here are some suggestions for a "thank you" gift:

- Gift certificate to a book store – or their very own, inscribed copy of *Get Into College*! :-)
- Gift certificate to a favorite local restaurant or coffee shop
- A college insignia item, like a hat or a t-shirt, from the school they attended
- Baked goods or another item you made yourself

R.K.

BIG SHOTS?

Don't assume that a recommendation from the person with the fanciest title in an organization means any more than one from someone lower who actually knows you. Every year, AO's see hundreds of letters from "famous" or "important" people, but if they see that the recommenders do not know the applicants, they essentially ignore these letters. These letters only "work" when AOs understand that the person of power (who *must* have pull at the university) knows you and is really going to bat for you.

R.K.

MY ESSAY WAS ON A RISKY TOPIC: religion. It was about the first time in my life when I questioned my belief in any religion. I was nervous that a controversial topic such as Atheism would offend or turn off some colleges, but in the end I think it made my essay and application stand out. I realized that any school that couldn't have an open mind was not the school for me. However, it should be noted I wasn't applying to any religiously affiliated schools; otherwise I probably would've picked a different topic!

—*MERELISE HARTE ROUZER*
ATLANTA, GEORGIA
GEORGIA INSTITUTE OF TECHNOLOGY

Face to Face: Interviews

T he interview is your bonus opportunity to give the school insight into who you are and what you've done with the life experience you have had thus far. Remember: be yourself, stay relaxed, and be confident. Remember that interviewers are people too. They want you to succeed. If you are scared to death, shy, or intimidated, remember that they are your allies. They respect why you are there and are interested in you.

You can't lose as long as you bring the real you to the interview. It is tough to convey your true self on paper; it should be easier in real life, right? Well, it can be with lots of practice and these tips from Hundreds of Heads.

AS HORRIBLY CLICHÉD AS IT SOUNDS, you have to be yourself in an interview. It's important to be able to act natural, to admit when you don't know something, and even tell a joke or two. Obviously, you should also remain respectful and intelligent.

—KATIE
NEW YORK, NEW YORK
 NEW YORK UNIVERSITY

SMILE.

—CASEY BOND
GRAND RAPIDS,
MICHIGAN
GRAND VALLEY
STATE UNIVERSITY

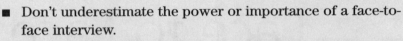

HEADLINES
Best Advice and Top Tips

- Don't underestimate the power or importance of a face-to-face interview.
- Research the school beforehand so that you can show your interest in that school.
- Be sure to ask your interviewer general questions too!

I DRESSED UP A LITTLE for my interview. Just use common sense. Try to be really friendly and nice. Don't try to portray yourself as something you are not. That's not going to work out for you in the long run.

> —*STEPHEN RUSHTON GARTH*
> *NASHVILLE, TENNESSEE*
> *GEORGIA INSTITUTE OF TECHNOLOGY*

• • • • • • • •

MOCK INTERVIEWS WERE MY SAVING GRACE during the college admissions process. Many universities and websites offer sample interview questions, topics, etc. I would print these out and then have someone go through the questions with me in order to simulate an actual nerve-wracking interview. This helped prepare me tremendously. I loved being able to rehearse what I was going to say before I was actually put on the spot.

> —*KAITLYN*
> *ATLANTA, GEORGIA*
> *GEORGIA INSTITUTE OF TECHNOLOGY*

ASK THE EXPERT

What is the school really looking for in an interview?

A school wants to see two things: 1) your character, talent, and interests not shown in the application (or the interests in more detail); and 2) your interest in the school. An interviewer, as an outside third party, "vouches" for you. He observes—and often confirms—what can be read and surmised in other parts of your application. Show that you have something to add to the school. You do not have to be loud to be a leader and contributor, but you need to brag and present yourself. Make sure to convey your research and interest in the school.

R.K.

❝During the interview, smile a lot. When you smile, it shows that your attitude and heart are in the interview; your nerves will also settle down so that you can answer questions clearly.❞

—*MAILE CERIZO*
HAIKU, HAWAII
POINT LOMA NAZARENE UNIVERSITY

BE PREPARED

You're scheduled to meet an alumnus for your interview. To get the most out of it, and to leave the best impression, take some time to think about how you want to present yourself, and prepare some answers to possible questions.

While interviews rarely make or break a candidate, they're still a piece of the admissions process, and it's wise to have a positive interview for your file. An interview is the chance for the committee to have you evaluated by someone in your community, who is (at least somewhat) familiar with goings-on at the college.

Think about the following to give yourself stories and material:

- Your favorite classes
- Your favorite activities and extracurriculars
- Your strengths and weaknesses—and examples of how they've helped you (or how you've overcome them)
- Something at which you excel, or something unusual about your background (this will set you apart from all the other students they meet . . .)
- What you think you might study ('undecided' is fine, as long as you can narrow it down a little)
- Why you are interested in this particular college (and be specific!). This is important – it shows you went to the trouble to learn about the school and have specific reasons for wanting to attend.

Also, prepare questions for the interviewer about himself and the school—things that cannot be found by reading the Internet. This is the alumnus's chance to talk, sell the school, and give you new information. Don't skip this critical opportunity. A student with no questions seems disinterested—a bad sign that will get noted in the evaluation.

R.K.

MAXIMIZING YOUR INTERVIEW

1. Research the school beforehand. Even just a few minutes surfing their website can help. Think about what is actually drawing you to the school.
2. Be yourself. Let the interviewer see what makes you tick. Honest answers about your passions and your personality will help you shine.
3. Engage with the interviewer. Ask what has kept him connected to the school and how the school has affected his life. Ask questions about the school to explore the fit. You have more power in the interview than you think; *they* are trying to sell the school to *you*!
4. Follow up the interview by writing a thank-you note or e-mail. It signifies respect for your interviewer's time and shows your interest.

R.K.

 I E C A⁺ *COUNSELOR SURVEY*

If offered an alumni interview at a school you want to attend, should you take it?

Absolutely – 67%
Only if you believe you'll make a strong impression – 33%
No – 0%

BE PREPARED AND READY FOR ANY QUESTION they may ask and think of an answer that is not obvious. Know the history of the school and the basics of the program that you are applying for.

> —*CASEY BOND*
> *GRAND RAPIDS, MICHIGAN*
> *GRAND VALLEY STATE UNIVERSITY*

• • • • • • • •

I THINK YOU SHOULD TREAT A COLLEGE INTERVIEW like a job interview: Be polite and professional, dress nicely, and send the interviewer a thank-you note afterwards.

> —*ELIZABETH BRISTOL*
> *NORTH ATTLEBORO, MASSACHUSETTS*
> *MOUNT HOLYOKE COLLEGE*

• • • • • • • •

IF YOU ARE ON THE CUSP IN TERMS OF QUALIFICATIONS, a personal appointment to speak with an admissions officer can help a lot. Having a face to go with an application makes it harder to turn that application down.

> —*ALLISON GRECO*
> *YARDLEY, NEW JERSEY*

When being interviewed by a college admissions officer: TURN OFF YOUR CELL PHONE!

—*MERELISE HARTE ROUZER*
ATLANTA, GEORGIA
GEORGIA INSTITUTE OF TECHNOLOGY

YOUNG BUT SMART

Surprised that your AO is a 21-year-old, newly minted college graduate and not a Ph.D. in education? Don't start to think of these AO's as friends. They should still be addressed as "Ms." or "Mr." and be taken seriously. Attempts at friendship with an AO will not get you admitted: AO's all work for the dean, and they see through the flattery.

INTERVIEW 'DON'TS'

Don't wear inappropriate clothing, chew gum, or show up late. Your presentation shows that you take the interview seriously.

Don't tell stories about crazy behavior, or swear.

Don't forget to ask questions—interviews are a two-way street and you will not seem "engaged" if you do not ask a few things in return.

Don't worry about being perfect, or about being a perfect package—you do not know what a school or an interviewer wants. Frankly, "perfect" interviews with too-practiced answers are boring and seem fake.

Don't forget that you are only in high school. Relax—you are not expected to have all the answers or to already have solved world problems.

DURING INTERVIEWS WITH COLLEGES, be prepared to answer questions like, "What could you see yourself doing someday?" "Why have you chosen this major?" If you go into the interview with no idea how you will answer the tough questions, you could be in trouble.

    —G.A.
      FREDONIA, NEW YORK
      STATE UNIVERSITY OF NEW YORK AT BUFFALO

PARENTS' PAGES

MY DAUGHTER INTERVIEWED AT SEVERAL schools and each time the interviewer brought up politics. Fortunately, my daughter is caught up on current events and has strong opinions. When she came to me after the first time she was politically challenged in her interview, I advised her not to back down and to verbalize her opinion along with strong supporting statements. Although I would never suggest that the student start up a conversation on politics, I would definitely engage if asked. Tell your kids not to agree with the interviewer if it isn't what they truly believe. These people are asking these questions for a reason. I think they want to see if you have an opinion, if you know what's going on in the world, if you have passion, and if you can support your position.

> —*ANONYMOUS*
> *PHILADELPHIA, PENNSYLVANIA*
> *P ▪▪ SMITH COLLEGE*

· · · · · · · · ·

I'M AN ALUMNI INTERVIEWER and some of my better interviews involved kids with interests in topics they could intellectually discuss. I remember one kid who was doing research on alternative energy and new fuel options for automobiles. She was very articulate on the subject and it was a refreshing change. The opposite case was when a student said he was really interested in constitutions. He brought up the European Union constitution and talked about how it was coming up for a vote, but he had no ideas or knowledge about its failures in some other countries. He oversold his interest about it. The best way to come across is to have a genuine interest in something and to be informed about it. Trying to search the Internet for knowledge the day or week before the interview probably isn't going to work.

> —*PETER*
> *SEATTLE, WASHINGTON*
> *P ▪▪ SWARTHMORE COLLEGE*

BEFORE MY SON'S FIRST INTERVIEW, he didn't think he needed to prepare because he felt that he was a good public speaker. But public speaking, where you mostly memorize, and an interview, where you are expected to answer on the spot, are entirely different. We practiced interviewing a couple of times until he felt comfortable. We also suggested that he ask questions of his interviewer. This went over really well.

—R.K.
PHILADELPHIA, PENNSYLVANIA
P ⌂ UNIVERSITY OF PENNSYLVANIA

• • • • • • • • •

ONE THING COLLEGE COUNSELORS can help with is preparation for admissions interviews. My son's counselor did a sort of mock interview with him, asking him the questions that are typically asked in real interviews, and helping him prepare questions to ask the admissions officers. It was only a half-hour session, but it really helped him know what to expect.

—CAMILLE
CINCINNATI, OHIO
P ⌂ UNIVERSITY OF KENTUCKY

MAKE A POINT OF LEARNING ABOUT that school's values, because you'll impress the interviewer more if it's clear that you cared enough to do your research. Also, if they've given you an idea of what sort of questions you'll be asked, be sure to think about your answers in advance. I waited until I was in the car the morning of my interview before I even thought about what I was going to say, and I had to brainstorm with my mom the whole way.

—EMILY ROSE
ATLANTA, GEORGIA
⌂ AGNES SCOTT COLLEGE

THINGS NEVER TO SAY TO AN ADMISSIONS OFFICER DURING YOUR INTERVIEW

Sure, guidance counselors and parents will offer coaching advice on acing your interview with a college admissions officer. But sometimes they leave out the obvious – like, what you should *never* say in your interview. That's where we come in. Here's a short list of things you should make sure not to say to an admissions officer:

- "Forget academics. Does this school party?"
- "Why don't you tell me why I should attend your little school?"
- "To be honest, all I'm really interested in is how many dates I can get at this place."
- "If I get in, can you get my friends in, too?"
- "At your school, what's the ratio of good-looking people to ugly people?"

DO SOME HEAVY READING on a couple of new, exciting books before you go to the interview and then work them into the conversation. Interviewers are always impressed to know that you are reading and keeping up with what's going on in the world.

—*ANONYMOUS*
BROWNSVILLE, MARYLAND
UNIVERSITY OF MARYLAND

ASK THE EXPERT

An alum or AO interview? Either way, the little things matter!

You may meet a young, recent alumnus at a local coffee shop for a relaxed chat. Or, you may meet an AO in his office—and feel a little bit of pressure! Here are a few valuable details to help you really nail a great interview:

- A firm handshake is worth a million bucks. Look your interviewer in the eye and smile naturally as you meet him.
- Train your brain. Mock interview sessions with mom - or yourself (in the bathroom mirror)? Do it! Practice how you'll answer several questions the interviewer may ask. Prepare and practice the questions you have for them. Do it over and over again. It's as much about training your brain to answer confidently and knowledgeably, as it is about the content of what you say.
- The "Um" defense. Your interviewer asks a question; you freeze. Don't panic. Don't feel rushed to speak immediately. Say, *"That's a great question. Let me think about that for a moment."* The silence feels much longer to you than it really is. It may seem like hours, but several seconds of silence is comfortable and appropriate. Silence always beats the "Um's."
- Put yourself in his socks. Remember that the interviewer wants you to blow him away. He's vying for you right from the start. Don't fear it; embrace the opportunity to inspire and show the interviewer why you belong on that campus!
- Treat your interview as your moment to shine. The interviewer will sense—and feed off—your excitement.

J.Y.K.

Expert Advice   *FROM THE ADMISSIONS OFFICE*

HOW IMPORTANT ARE ALUMNI INTERVIEWS TO YOU?

ALUMNI INTERVIEWS, LIKE ON-CAMPUS INTERVIEWS, are an optional part of the application process for interested high school seniors. Available in certain areas nationally, and in more limited areas globally, they provide the opportunity to meet one-on-one with a Johns Hopkins admissions volunteer. Interviews typically address your academic background, goals, interests, and what you would contribute to the campus community. More informative than evaluative, these conversations will also allow you time to ask questions of your interviewer and learn about his/her Johns Hopkins experience.

> —*MARK BUTT*
> *SENIOR ASSISTANT DIRECTOR OF ADMISSIONS*
> *JOHNS HOPKINS UNIVERSITY*

* * * * * * * *

AT VANDERBILT, THEY ARE COMPLETELY OPTIONAL, though they are evaluative. The true value of the alumni interview is to the student, for whom it is often helpful to get an outside perspective on the college from someone in their home area.

> —*DOUGLAS L. CHRISTIANSEN, PH.D.*
> *ASSOCIATE PROVOST FOR ENROLLMENT AND DEAN OF ADMISSIONS*
> *VANDERBILT UNIVERSITY*

* * * * * * * *

VERY, DEPENDING ON CASE. Although not mandatory, we encourage alumni interviews because they add an "un-edited" perspective on an applicant. That can be valuable in getting a better sense of intangible qualities.

> —*MATS LEMBERGER*
> *ASSISTANT DIRECTOR OF ADMISSIONS*
> *DARTMOUTH COLLEGE*

FOR PENN, INTERVIEWS are optional and conducted by our alumni. Because we cannot offer interviews to all of our applicants, they tend to be more informational than evaluative. To us, the interview is a way to get to know the student as a person, perhaps in a manner not conveyed by the application. The interview is also an opportunity to let the student learn about the Penn experience through the eyes of an alumnus. Ultimately, a successful interview will personalize the admissions process for both the applicant and the admissions office.

—*JACINDA OJEDA*
REGIONAL DIRECTOR OF ADMISSIONS
UNIVERSITY OF PENNSYLVANIA

WE JUST STARTED A PILOT ALUMNI interviewing program last year so we have not had the opportunity to use alumni interviews in the past. I don't think a great interview will ever overcome a weaker academic record in the world of highly selective admission. But I do think interviews may become a deciding factor when done poorly. In our process, they are likely to help the students on the margins. Generally speaking, students need to be prepared to talk about themselves and the school to which they are applying and there are a number of opportunities within the application to accomplish these requirements successfully--whether that is in the essays, interviews, or extracurricular involvement.

—*JEAN JORDAN*
DEAN OF ADMISSION
EMORY UNIVERSITY

ANOTHER ESSAY?
NO, JUST 'THANKS'

After you complete an interview with either an admissions officer or an alumnus, it's a good idea to write a brief thank-you e-mail or note. Closing this loop will take only 5 minutes, and gratitude may matter.

Remind your interviewer who you are and why he should remember you, by:

- Saying you appreciate his time; and
- Citing something you learned during the meeting.

You might add that you hope you can ask him further questions and that you'd be happy to answer any other questions he might have for you.

R.K.

Extracurriculars & Summers: Activities That Help You Stand Out

*" **G** ot sun at the neighborhood pool": an extracurricular activity that won't impress colleges. "Served as a lifeguard at neighborhood pool for three consecutive summers": an extracurricular activity that will impress colleges. Admissions officers want students who show enthusiasm for activities outside of school and display leadership skills. However, they are trained to spot students who engage in extracurriculars that only serve to pad their resume. Where do you find the balance? We asked students.*

DO ANYTHING THAT DISPLAYS LEADERSHIP.
Practically every job I've applied for over the summer lists "leadership" as one of the primary characteristics. This doesn't have to be formal leadership, but jobs in which you can display some sort of initiative, always help.

—*NAFI ISRAEL*
NEWTON, MASSACHUSETTS
COLUMBIA UNIVERSITY

DO SOMETHING THAT YOU ENJOY; IF YOU ARE HAPPY, YOUR PASSION AND EXCITEMENT WILL BE EVIDENT.

—*NICOLE SPENCE*
WYCKOFF, NEW JERSEY
EMORY UNIVERSITY

HEADLINES
Best Advice and Top Tips

- Choose activities you're enthusiastic about.
- Explore your options: classes, volunteering, travel, or summer job.
- Try something new and different to expand your horizons.
- Don't let your demanding activities steal time from your schoolwork.
- Try not to burn yourself out before you even get to college.

ONE WEEK EVERY SUMMER for three years, I went on a church mission trip to the Appalachian Mountains to repair flood-damaged homes. I didn't realize it before I applied, but the parts on UNC's application concerning extracurriculars were based on the activities you spent the most time on. That is, they weren't going to be impressed if you did 10 or 12 things, but only spent a few weeks on them during your entire course of high school. They were looking for activities that continued over the years. That is why I am glad that I completed the service project three summers in a row instead of just doing it once.

—*CARRIE BERTOLOZZI*
CHAPEL HILL, NORTH CAROLINA
UNIVERSITY OF NORTH CAROLINA AT CHAPEL HILL

I **WORKED AT A LOCAL RADIO STATION** as a newscaster and DJ most of my summers during high school. Given that my academic and professional interest is in journalism and broadcasting, I think this experience looked good to admissions people. Also, it's unique: Working retail or being a camp counselor is all well and good, but lots of people are putting that stuff on their application and it probably won't make you stand out from the others.

—COLIN CAMPBELL
CHARLOTTESVILLE, VIRGINIA
UNIVERSITY OF NORTH CAROLINA AT CHAPEL HILL

• • • • • • • •

AS SOMEONE WHO WORKED in the admissions office as a student, I can say that extracurricular activities play a huge part in acceptance. Obviously, if you are a straight-A student your chances are good, but if you are an average student, extracurriculars help a lot. Showing that you can multitask, take the lead, and be involved means a lot to admissions officers.

—ALLISON GRECO
YARDLEY, NEW JERSEY

• • • • • • • •

THE SUMMER OF MY FRESHMAN YEAR, I interned at a local law firm. There, I learned the skill set it takes to be a successful attorney. Besides that, I worked a job in retail and enjoyed my free time. My summer had a perfect balance: It kept me busy, but left me in a low-stress environment. I would recommend any possible internship that piques your interest. It is important to keep an active lifestyle, as you don't want to be cooped up at home all summer watching reruns of *All in the Family*.

—SCOTT
CHESTERFIELD, MISSOURI
UNIVERSITY OF ILLINOIS

College admissions officers just want to know that you weren't sitting around all summer with Cheez Doodle crumbs all over your shirt.

—D.T.
BRUNSWICK, MARYLAND
AMERICAN UNIVERSITY

I BUILT MY OWN WEBSITE about my life; it was so easy. I think admissions officers like to check out sites like that. It shows them that you are willing to try new things.

—*LINDA ROADARMEL*
PARKERSBURG, WEST VIRGINIA
WEST VIRGINIA UNIVERSITY

• • • • • • • •

" I became involved in one club at my school, the National Forensics League. I decided to pick one club that mattered to me, and to stick with it. "

—*KRISTINA*
RALEIGH, NORTH CAROLINA
UNIVERSITY OF NORTH CAROLINA AT GREENSBORO

• • • • • • • •

I DID A LOT OF TRAVELING during the summer. I went on a tour to Israel with the Birthright Oranim program. It was amazing; I ended up staying in Israel for 10 days, touring and visiting family, and loved it. It was my first time on a plane by myself and I think that was good prep for college. After the Israel trip, I went with my family to Costa Rica for a week. I had the time of my life last summer and I think my experience gave me a lot more independence. I can now do laundry. Who would've thought?

—*BARAK KRENGEL*
DALLAS, TEXAS
UNIVERSITY OF KANSAS

Expert Advice

IECA⁺ *COUNSELOR'S CORNER*

AN 'AUTHENTIC' SUMMER

THERE'S A NEW BUZZWORD in college admissions that should guide your summer plans. The word is "authenticity" and it means living your teenage years in a purposeful way. It means choosing activities that teach you new things, allow you to make new contacts and perhaps play a meaningful role in someone else's life.

This is not as difficult as it may seem. In an academic setting look for programs that involve your potential major or career. There are summer classes in a wide range of subjects that reach beyond the curriculum of most high schools. Though admissions officials yawn at exotic community service trips, such an experience is meaningful if it is part of your ongoing involvement in similar activities at home. If your goal is business school, get an actual paying job, or, if you see your future in international relations, spend a summer living with a family abroad. Alternatively, put your skills to use helping someone else. Be the varsity lacrosse player who teaches the game at an inner city camp or the computer whiz who unravels the mystery of the Internet at the local senior citizens center.

It is not the activity that is important as much as the purpose it serves in enriching your life. Do not collect activities just to fit the profile of some imaginary school. Use the uncluttered weeks of summer to immerse yourself in experiences, as well as to relax and renew your energy for the coming school year. "Authenticity" means there is no rulebook for summertime, no magical plan. It is the long-overdue idea that the way to success and that "perfect" college is to work hard at finding and improving upon the innermost and real you.

—*DORETTA KATZTER GOLDBERG, ESQ.*
PRESIDENT, COLLEGE DIRECTIONS, LLC
© COPYRIGHT 2008 COLLEGE DIRECTIONS, LLC

Don't overextend yourself. It's more impressive to be editor-in-chief of your school newspaper and a junior varsity track runner than a member of 15 varied clubs.

—*Tricia Powell*
Huntington Beach, California
University of California, Berkeley

I USED TO BE AFRAID OF FLYING when I was 13, but I got over it. I noticed on the Web how there was no community for fearful flyers. I wanted to take advantage of that and so I started a website. Colleges like to see that sort of thing. It wasn't only the fact that I had a website; it was that I had a fear, overcame it, and tried to help other people, as well as make a business out of it.

—*Dov Kaufmann*
Ra'anana, Israel
Princeton University

• • • • • • • •

SINCE I WANTED TO MAJOR IN DANCE IN COLLEGE, I attended summer dance programs just about every summer in high school. Auditioning for summer programs really helped me prepare for auditions for colleges. Noting what you've performed on resumes, and what choreographers you've worked with, is also very important.

—*Jennifer Keys*
Baltimore, Maryland
New York University

• • • • • • • •

I WAS REALLY INVOLVED in my high school's speech and debate team and spent a great deal of my summer reading and preparing for fall competition. I also had the opportunity to travel with my family to all sorts of exotic locations, including Thailand, China, and Singapore. I was able to see the world before I needed to buckle down and work, and it was nice to have those opportunities early. In addition, I worked retail during the summer and helped coordinate and coach a summer enrichment camp for middle school students looking to improve their public-speaking skills.

—*Coral A. Schneider*
Cherry Hills Village, Colorado
University of Southern California

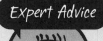 IECA⁺ *COUNSELOR SURVEY*

Although colleges may differ, in general terms is some form of community service/activity important in gaining acceptance to the college of your choice?

Very important – 50%
Somewhat important – 28%
Not important – 22%

GET INVOLVED BECAUSE you *want* to get involved, not because you think that is the key to getting into college. You will excel most in the activities that you enjoy the most. It is in these activities that you will be most likely to assume leadership positions and make the greatest contributions. And this is what colleges are looking for when they analyze your activities.

—*C.D.*
NEW MIDDLETOWN, OHIO
YOUNGSTOWN STATE UNIVERSITY

SEARCH FOR VOLUNTEER OPPORTUNITIES outside your school. Something that has your school's name attached to it makes it seem as if you didn't work very hard to set this up yourself. If you go out there and say, "I'm a high school student, I'm underage, I can't drive, but I do want to help out your organization in some way," you will stand out.

—*CONOR KENNEDY*
WHITESTONE, NEW YORK
BROWN UNIVERSITY

HEADS UP:
SUMMER ACTIVITIES

Contrary to popular belief, there is no "right" summer activity that admissions officers want to see. You should have two main choices:

If you need to earn money, find a summer job. Scooping ice cream is just as valid an activity as any if you need to earn money. If you need to take care of siblings or babysit, you should feel confident that these are important and valued. Do not feel the pressure to do something "meaningful" if there are other, more pressing, priorities.

Follow your interests and explore. This can mean taking that summer class in psychology that your high school doesn't offer, or travel or summer camp. You should pick activities you love and pursue them to their maximum. Do not waste your time on something merely "resume building." You will not be judged by your activities, only by a lack of activities. Fill in that space of summer activities with something every year, but make sure you are also taking a small break; admissions officers do want you to have a break!

R.K.

IT'S PRETTY OBVIOUS TO COLLEGES when you're just filling up your resume. There's no point in doing something you're not excited about just to put it on a resume, because colleges can see through that anyway. I did a summer sailing program with kids who were released from drug treatment centers or going through drug rehab programs.

—*ANASTASIA*
BALTIMORE, MARYLAND
YALE UNIVERSITY

· · · · · · · ·

AT MY COLLEGE, TEST SCORES weren't as important as things I'd done outside of school and other experiences I'd had. My school looks for students who have applied their academics to their outside life. I had been living in Ethiopia for two years and Bosnia for four years, and the experiences I had in those countries gave me an upper hand in my application. I think expanding your life outside of academics makes a big difference.

—*DAHVID CASTILLO-REMINICK*
BRONXVILLE, NEW YORK
SARAH LAWRENCE COLLEGE

· · · · · · · ·

BE SOCIALLY ACTIVE IN HIGH SCHOOL. Join clubs, sports, and as many organizations as you can. Once you're involved in lots of activities, you can highlight them in your application and show how diverse you are. You've got to stand out. I played soccer and lacrosse in high school; both these activities show team spirit. I was also a member of the National Honor Society. I tutored and was a mentor to younger classmates. I joined the Asian club, and this showed I was in touch with my roots.

—*MISTRY KALPANA*
OLD BRIDGE, NEW JERSEY
RUTGERS UNIVERSITY

MY EXTRACURRICULAR ACTIVITIES were possibly the strongest part of my resume. My summer has always consisted of a day camp where I am a counselor. It's fun, and it pays surprisingly well. Also, I participated in all kinds of clubs in high school and held lots of leadership roles. I served three different leadership positions in the Raleigh Youth Council, including president my senior year. I suggest students join service organizations such as Key Club, and then remember to individually list all the events that you participated in, because it really helps bolster your resume.

—*DAVID BERNGARTT*
RALEIGH, NORTH CAROLINA
UNIVERSITY OF NORTH CAROLINA AT CHAPEL HILL

. . . .

❝❝I did volunteer work for the local athletic association, helping youngsters grow and learn about teamwork. Well, that's what I wrote on the application. All that meant was that I umpired some Little League games. Wording on the application is important, too.❞❞

—*D.T.*
BRUNSWICK, MARYLAND
AMERICAN UNIVERSITY

ASK THE EXPERT

Does everyone have to be a leader?

What is so important about being a leader? And what, exactly, is leadership? AOs have no written definition of leadership, but they look for students with passion and an outside recognition of this passion. To be a leader, you might be the director of the play or the team captain, but you might also be the quiet, effective stage manager or the unspoken heart of a team. Starting and following a personal project, especially if it is school- or community-wide, is leadership. The point is that schools want students who will engage in and make a contribution to the academic and social life of the school, besides partying.

R.K.

DURING THE SUMMERS I always worked as a tennis counselor for my country club, teaching little kids how to play tennis. It also gave me a greater sense of responsibility and patience.

> —*ERICA ROGGEN*
> *SYRACUSE, NEW YORK*
> *SYRACUSE UNIVERSITY*

IF I HAD TO DO SOMETHING DIFFERENT, instead of working at Jamba Juice, I'd have gotten an internship in some field that was meaningful to me. The internship work experience gives you a better glimpse into a particular profession or field of study.

> —*DAVID LICHTENSTEIN*
> *SAN DIEGO, CALIFORNIA*
> *UNIVERSITY OF SOUTHERN CALIFORNIA*

Being the president of this or that organization looks great on your application. But if you're not the type of person who's interested in that sort of thing, then what's the use?

—APRIL
CHICAGO, ILLINOIS
PURDUE UNIVERSITY

EVERYONE WILL TELL YOU IT'S IMPORTANT to be well rounded. I had a really impressive resume: I was president of my high school, spent a semester abroad during my sophomore year, was an AIDS peer educator, volunteered at a summer camp in Hungary. Be involved in the things you enjoy, but don't leave your grades and board scores behind.

—ELANA BROWNSTEIN
BALTIMORE, MARYLAND
UNIVERSITY OF MARYLAND, COLLEGE PARK

• • • • • • • •

ONE SUMMER ACTIVITY THAT I participated in was Presidential Classroom, a weeklong program in Washington, D.C., focusing on various issues in politics today. We had seminars, met with representatives of our Congressional offices, visited the State Department and the Saudi Arabian embassy, and celebrated the Fourth of July on the Mall. Colleges love to see that you've challenged yourself during the summer months. It's important to show your desire to continue learning throughout the year, especially outside of the classroom.

—BETHANY BLACK
CHAPEL HILL, NORTH CAROLINA
UNIVERSITY OF NORTH CAROLINA AT CHAPEL HILL

• • • • • • • •

LIFE IS TOO SHORT (as cheesy as it sounds) to do something you don't enjoy; we're much better off being happy people doing what we love.

—NATALIE ROSE SPITZER
DECATUR, GEORGIA
GUILFORD COLLEGE

SUMMER IS THE BEST TIME TO BECOME involved in activities that could combine your recreational interests with productive work. I was fortunate to find a perfect combination to focus on two of my passions. I began as a camper at a theater arts camp and attended it for several years. Then I became an intern and continued to work there for six years. My involvement with one special group showed my interest in both children and the arts. The long history hopefully reflected my commitment.

—*ELLANA MANDEL*
RIVERDALE, NEW YORK
SARAH LAWRENCE COLLEGE

❝Do community service. There is something even more rewarding about working for free that you will never experience unless you do it. ❞

—*JOSIAH WHITE*
CARROLLTON, TEXAS
OKLAHOMA BAPTIST UNIVERSITY

DURING HIGH SCHOOL SUMMERS, I volunteered in a library and a hospital. Volunteering is a huge part of boosting your resume for college. I think schools really like people who are ambitious and involved and do things. It shows you have character and that you'll bring that to the school.

—*MARY KATE TAULANE*
HUNTINGDON VALLEY, PENNSYLVANIA
LOYOLA COLLEGE

Admissions offices like to see leadership, participation length, and a variety of activities.

—*ANGELA MASSINI*
CHICAGO, ILLINOIS
BUTLER UNIVERSITY

IF YOU LIVE NEAR A COLLEGE, get a job on campus. The pay is comparable to a lot of part-time jobs, they are extremely flexible, and not all that difficult. You can also make very valuable contacts with administrators and higher-up people in the campus community.

—*ALLISON GRECO*
YARDLEY, NEW JERSEY

• • • • • • • •

I FOCUSED ON THINGS I was passionate about. For example, I swam when I was growing up and through middle school, so during a few high school summers I taught swimming lessons in addition to lifeguarding. I have also always had a passion for writing, so another summer I attended a creative writing workshop for two weeks through Duke University. Find what you're interested in, be ambitious in pursuing it, and your resume will build itself.

—*WHITNEY TRITT*
ATLANTA, GEORGIA
WAKE FOREST UNIVERSITY

I KNOW WHAT YOU DID LAST SUMMER

Not sure how to describe your summer experience on a college application? Heed the three golden rules:

1. Keep it real and focus on what your summer actually meant to you.
2. Avoid talking about how privileged you were to have had the opportunity to do what you did.
3. Find a way to relate your experiences over the summer to your day-to-day life.

THE WORK I DID OVER THE SUMMERS of my high school career has given me a considerable leg up in college. I knew I wanted to study journalism, so I became one of the youngest co-producers and anchors at a community television station in my area. I also spent a summer training younger people to use the equipment, which allowed me to hone my skills, learn new editing techniques, and earn some money. In addition, I wrote for the teen section of my local paper, *The Buffalo News*, throughout high school. I interviewed everyone from Jeri Ryan, star of *Boston Public* and *Star Trek*, to kids struggling with drug and alcohol addictions. I loved every minute of reporting, and I was able to apply to college with impressive writing samples and a resume tape.

> —*JASON PAUL TORREANO*
> *LOCKPORT, NEW YORK*
> *STATE UNIVERSITY OF NEW YORK, BROCKPORT*

• • • • • • • •

MY ACTIVITIES WERE MOSTLY SCHOOL CLUBS for art, math, foreign language, Honor Society, things like that. While they were great, I wish I had done more community service, because the scholarships I applied for had a heavy emphasis on community service and philanthropy.

> —*DAVID*
> *MUNCIE, INDIANA*
> *ANDERSON UNIVERSITY*

• • • • • • • •

ANY EDGE IS GOOD NOWADAYS, but don't make yourself miserable. I took time off during my summers, and I don't regret it. I just loaded up on my college resume activities during the year. Do what feels right during your summers.

> —*MARTIN*
> *GARDEN GROVE, CALIFORNIA*
> *UNIVERSITY OF CALIFORNIA, LOS ANGELES*

OVER THE COURSE OF FOUR SUMMERS, I went to an engineering camp and played in the pit orchestra for three musicals with a local theater group, in addition to summer school and holding a job. I always felt guilty about not doing more, but when I started filling out applications, I realized that there wasn't even enough space to put down everything I *did* do. Of course, summer activities do leave an impression on the application readers, but not every waking moment of every summer needs to be college focused. Given the chance, I would go back and choose just a few activities that really sparked my interest.

—*EMILY WACHTEL*
LOS ANGELES, CALIFORNIA
UNIVERSITY OF CALIFORNIA, LOS ANGELES

. . . .

" Show them that you are motivated. Get out and do something worthwhile. And if you can help someone in the process, man, they eat that stuff up. "

—*D.T.*
BRUNSWICK, MARYLAND
AMERICAN UNIVERSITY

SUMMER COLLEGE CLASSES

If you are interested in exploring a subject further to broaden your experiences, either at a local college or at one in another city, go for it. However, know that a summer course or other academic experience that requires a fee to participate is not valued any higher than other activities. Choose something for the experience and for your passion, not for your resume.

I WORKED AT AN ELEMENTARY school summer program for four years well before I was concerned with my college resume. I did it because I enjoyed it. I also took a class at the Academy of Art University in San Francisco and had an internship in video editing. I thought at that time that I wanted to go to film school, so I wanted to start learning. I also had a part-time job in an architecture firm and with an interior designer. My family was in both of those fields, so it was easy for me to get little jobs. A genuine interest in learning and the confidence to try new activities is appealing to most universities.

—*KATHERINE SINNOTT*
BERKELEY, CALIFORNIA
UNIVERSITY OF CALIFORNIA, BERKELEY

It's important for college admissions officers to see that you have a life outside of school and playing Xbox (unless, of course, you play on the school Xbox team).

—BENN RAY
BALTIMORE,
MARYLAND
SALISBURY
UNIVERSITY

ADMISSIONS OFFICERS have really good BS detectors. They know a lot of kids do lots of extracurricular activities just to get in. Look for avenues in which you have a passion. Follow your real interests, as opposed to embellishing your application with a lot of random activities. Even if you don't know, ultimately, what you want to be, your choice of activities should be passion-driven.

—TAI MILDER
UKIAH, CALIFORNIA
UNIVERSITY OF CALIFORNIA, BERKELEY

• • • • • • • •

I SIGNED UP FOR EVERY CLUB so I could put them on my applications. If you do that, you also get in all the pictures of the clubs in the yearbook. It's pretty cool. (If I had it to do over again, I would also have been a male cheerleader!)

—MITCH ROYER
WINAMAC, INDIANA
INDIANA UNIVERSITY

• • • • • • • •

I THINK EXTRACURRICULAR ACTIVITIES are a good idea for more reasons than looking good on your college application. During high school, I volunteered for everything under the sun. I also took part in research projects and worked at the Center for Disease Control. All of this made me realize that there was more to life than academics. When I got to college, where I didn't need so many extra activities, I ended up doing them anyway, just for fun.

—JANET
LOS ANGELES, CALIFORNIA
UNIVERSITY OF CALIFORNIA, LOS ANGELES

PARENTS' PAGE

ENCOURAGE YOUR CHILD TO PICK two or three extra-curricular activities that he or she really cares about. My son was heavily involved with a youth robotics competition, and he was always asked about it. His other major activities were Scouts and a varsity letter in track. Every admissions officer told us that a strong record of commitment to a few things is a lot better than a scattershot listing of dozens of things.

> —*RICHARD TYLER*
> *REDMOND, WASHINGTON*
> P ⚑ *NEW MEXICO INSTITUTE OF MINING & TECHNOLOGY*

• • • • • • • • •

IF YOU HAVE THE MONEY AND THE TIME, sign up for a study program at your first-choice school. My daughter attended a summer program at Smith College. She interviewed with an admissions officer while she was there, and was told that the college looks favorably at applicants who attended the program. She did get in, along with all the other girls who were in her class that summer.

> —*ANONYMOUS*
> *PHILADELPHIA, PENNSYLVANIA*
> P ⚑ *SMITH COLLEGE*

Expert Advice

IECA* COUNSELOR'S CORNER

EXTRA-CURRICULARS: CHOOSE WISELY

CHOOSE AN ACTIVITY OR TWO in which you have a genuine interest. Don't choose them because you think it will look good for college. Too many students today think about this first, before considering their genuine interests. This is your time that you're spending, so spend it on something you've wanted to try but the opportunity wasn't easily available. Maybe you have a hidden talent—writing for the school literary magazine, trying out for a sport you've always wanted to play, or auditioning for a part in a play!

Second, don't overload yourself with too many commitments. Students today think they need to be involved in everything. You don't! The end result is stress and burnout. The depth and breadth in a couple of activities pursued during your high school years say more about your commitment than a laundry list of many. Your high school years are supposed to be a time of self-discovery, learning and fun. So challenge yourself to try something new. It just may turn out to be a passion! And there's another possible benefit: A whole new set of friends!

—*JUDY ZODDA*
ZODDA COLLEGE SERVICES

I spent all four high school years on the varsity soccer, cross-country, and track teams. This lengthy involvement shows that I put significant amounts of time into these teams. Universities also search for signs and indications of leadership. By the end of my four years in high school, I had worked my way up to becoming the captain of two of these sports teams. Being a leader doesn't necessarily have to include a title (captain or president), but running for these positions and putting yourself out there is never a bad idea. Although I was busy with sports and academics, I found free time to involve myself in other organizations. I busied myself with yearbook staff, National Honor Society, Girl Scouts, and Key Club (volunteer club). My participation in a variety of clubs showed universities that I had multiple interests.

—SUSI MCGHEE
DECATUR, GEORGIA
UNIVERSITY OF GEORGIA

Have passion in your extracurriculars. It will show.

—ANU PARVATIYAR
ATLANTA, GEORGIA
GEORGIA INSTITUTE OF TECHNOLOGY

'I WAS A POMMES-FRITES MASTER CHEF'

No matter what your activity, make the most of it:

- Serving fries? Do your best to make yourself the perfect employee - that reference from the boss could come in handy.
- Got an internship? Volunteer for any and every task, and NEVER say no - you'll be surprised how you can turn "filing" into "filed over 5,000 documents" on your resume.
- Got a big trip planned? Start a travel blog, which you can share with admissions officers.
- Taking classes? Make sure you build in some unwinding time, too.
- Visit colleges! You know you want to...

R.K.

I think you should join things not because they look good, but rather because they are activities you enjoy. As long as you like to do it, I think you'll do a good job. I was the President of International Coalition, a DJ for KWEB, a tour guide, an orientation leader, a math tutor, a cross-country runner, a water polo player, a hurdler, a summer reading program leader, a piano player, and some other stuff. I loved doing all of it, and if the colleges didn't think they were impressive, screw them.

—*DIANA*
ROWLAND HEIGHTS, CALIFORNIA
UNIVERSITY OF SOUTHERN CALIFORNIA

" If you have to change your life in an effort to meet application requirements, you don't want to be attending that school. You should be involved in extracurriculars because you want to be involved, not so you can appear to be someone you're not. "

—*KYLE PACKER*
LILBURN, GEORGIA
KENYON COLLEGE

A YEAR OFF? PRO AND CON

IT'S FINE TO HAVE A YEAR OFF BETWEEN GRADUATING high school and starting college. I've had college admissions people confirm that to me. But you have to be able to account for that year. To admissions people, it's like a gap on your resume. It's OK as long as you can explain it away. Don't just say, "I needed some time off," or "I wanted to hang out with my friends for a while." I was able to show them that I used that year to take some classes at a junior college and, in effect, better myself. And I think it helped me emotionally. I'm not sure I would have done as well if I had gone to a four-year school right out of high school. Some people need a little extra prep time. Just make sure you don't waste it.

—*DAN MONTOYA*
YOUNGSTOWN, OHIO
OHIO STATE UNIVERSITY

DON'T TAKE A YEAR OFF BEFORE COLLEGE. I know it's tempting, but don't do it. It's going to come down to you explaining what you did with this lost year, and there's no way to put a positive spin on mooching off your parents for a year while you spent most nights drinking with your friends. You'll have plenty of time for that after you put in your eight years of college to get a four-year degree.

—*D.T.*
BRUNSWICK, MARYLAND
AMERICAN UNIVERSITY

I TOOK A YEAR OFF BEFORE COLLEGE TO HAVE SOME FUN. It's good to get to know your hometown. If you didn't have that much time in high school, it can be nice to give yourself the summer or spring to do all the things you've wanted to do. I went to a bunch of museums and investigated neighborhoods and did weekend jaunts to different places. That gave me an appreciation for what I was leaving, and it gave me something to come back to.

—*ANASTASIA*
BALTIMORE, MARYLAND
YALE UNIVERSITY

COOL SUMMER?

The Juneau Icefield Research Program, started in 1946, takes students from colleges all over the U.S. to study glaciers just outside Juneau, Alaska during the summer months.

Love at First Sight? Visiting Schools

(& what to do when they visit you)

Visits to college campuses are a great way to get a feel for the life you might be living over the next four years. They are also a great way to cut colleges off your list: Many students have taken one look at a campus they thought they would like and decided they would never set foot there again. Others have visited a campus that was low on their list, and they never wanted to leave. What are the most important questions to ask during a visit? How do you get the inside story from students? Before you visit your favorite colleges, stroll through the following stories and advice.

KEEP AN OPEN MIND: There are many comparable schools and you shouldn't decide you would only be happy by going to one of them. I intentionally did not visit any of the campuses before I found out whether or not I was accepted to the school.

—ALLISON LEVE
BALTIMORE, MARYLAND
NEW YORK UNIVERSITY

FIND A RANDOM PERSON TO TALK TO: STUDENTS ARE BRUTALLY HONEST.

—SARAH BORMEL
BALTIMORE, MARYLAND
BOSTON UNIVERSITY

HEAD**LINES**
Best Advice and Top Tips

- Ask any questions you want; you'll be investing four years and thousands of dollars.
- Timing is important; try to go when students are around and the weather's nice.
- You will do best where you thrive; decide if you can thrive there.
- Jot down your impressions so you'll remember how you felt; it's also material for your essay or interview.
- Politeness counts; always follow up with a thank-you note.

NEVER VISIT ON A WEEKEND MORNING. Several of the colleges were dead when I visited. No one was on campus and there didn't seem to be any atmosphere. Then it hit me: Everyone was still asleep. Now that I am in college, I completely understand why everyone is sleeping. The most important time to visit is later in the afternoon on a spring day. There are more people on campus and I could get a feel for what the school was really like. Spring is amazing: people lying in the quad getting sun, everyone is happy. That is the best time to visit.

—*ROB FEHN*
BASKING RIDGE, NEW JERSEY
LAFAYETTE COLLEGE

I KNEW A FRIEND ON THE TULANE CAMPUS and went to visit him. This visit definitely influenced me when I was applying to schools. I fell in love with the city and the campus, and even though my friend wasn't a deciding factor, knowing he was there was a plus.

—*JAMES AROGETI*
ATLANTA, GEORGIA
TULANE UNIVERSITY

• • • • • • • •

" Visit your number one choice last. That way you can compare it to the others with an open mind. If you go to your number one choice first, your opinion of the others will be tainted because you think you have seen what you want. "

—*BETSY LILIENTHAL*
WILMINGTON, DELAWARE
UNIVERSITY OF DELAWARE

• • • • • • • •

SPEND A FEW DAYS IN THE CITY OR TOWN nearest the university. Often campus life is affected by the city or town it's located in or near; if you don't like the city, there's a possibility you won't like the campus.

—*AMANDA NELSON-DUAC*
ST. AUGUSTINE, FLORIDA
GEORGE WASHINGTON UNIVERSITY

I VISITED SEVERAL SCHOOLS and I liked the fact that the University of Cincinnati was an urban school with a lot to offer around campus. Later, I gave campus tours, and I was told that most students decide within their first 20 minutes of being on campus whether they want to consider that school or not.

—*ANDREW J. BURKE*
CINCINNATI, OHIO
UNIVERSITY OF CINCINNATI

WHEN I VISITED THE SCHOOL I ultimately chose, I knew I wanted to go there. It was the most miserable day ever. There was black ice on the sidewalk, and my eyelashes were freezing together. And I still wanted to go there, so I figured, "This must be the place." It was a small campus. They had small classes. Everyone was very friendly, I just felt really comfortable there.

—*JULIE COLLINS*
DES MOINES, IOWA
DRAKE UNIVERSITY

THE REAL STRESSFUL PART was taking trips to the colleges with my parents. Road trips with only your parents aren't fun!

—*ADRIENNE LANG*
OLATHE, KANSAS
TEXAS CHRISTIAN UNIVERSITY

VISIT THE COLLEGE WHEN SCHOOL is in session before making any final decisions; you're going to spend the next four years of your life there! Prospective students should not only look at the buildings when visiting the schools; they should take a look at the students walking around the campus. Do they look happy to be there?

—*ERICA GOLDENBERG*
BLOOMINGTON, INDIANA
INDIANA UNIVERSITY

RIVALRY 101

I toured UNC on a Friday afternoon in February. It was gorgeous outside, and I remember thinking that the weather was never like this at home in upstate New York. My most vivid memory from the tour came when our guide was discussing the Robertson bus, which runs continuously between UNC and Duke. "It's really great, especially if you have friends at Duke," she said. Without missing a beat, a woman in the back of the tour called out, "Why on earth would we have friends at Duke?" I got my introduction to the Duke-Carolina rivalry right then and there. When you're taking a tour, try to envision yourself living there, studying there, sitting on the quad. If it's hard to picture yourself there, it might not be the place for you. Most importantly, no one can make this decision for you. Just because your grandfather's best friend's nephew went there and loved it, doesn't mean that you will.

—BETHANY BLACK
CHAPEL HILL, NORTH CAROLINA
UNIVERSITY OF NORTH CAROLINA

IT'S IMPORTANT TO REALIZE that a formal tour is formal. They're taking you to see buildings and see what the school physically looks like. To get a real feel for the school, you have to walk around and hang out with people. It's very easy to get in touch with students who are at the school. You can go through the school admissions office, and students are very happy to talk about the school. Ask students questions. The first question I ask is, "Are you happy with the school? Why or why not?" Every student has an opinion.

—DANA
LAWRENCE, NEW YORK
HARVARD UNIVERSITY

PARENTS' PAGES

TRY TO CONVINCE YOUR KIDS to get a little bit out of their comfort zone when they are looking at potential schools to go to. As a ranch kid from Texas, where our closest neighbor is two miles away, my daughter only wanted to go to a very small and rural school. So I let her pick the colleges she wanted to visit and when we planned our trip there I would say, "Since we're headed to Kentucky, let's just stop in Memphis on the way and take a look at some schools." We ended up checking out 40 schools this way, and she ended up at that school in Memphis, where she never would have thought about going had I not convinced her to expand her horizons.

> —*TOM*
> *WACO, TEXAS*
> *P* ⚓ *RHODES COLLEGE*

· · · · · · · · ·

FIND SOME KIND OF BACK-DOOR ENTRANCE to introduce your kids to college campuses. You want to start early, but if you push too much before your kids are ready, they will just run. We live in Atlanta, pretty close to Emory. Emory has an Egyptian museum, so I planned a trip there. We also planned a lot of our college tours in conjunction with our vacations. A lot of families go to school after school; by the time they get to the last one, the kids are burned out. We would ski, then go look at a school, go to a park, then look at a school.

> —*J.M.*
> *MARIETTA, GEORGIA*
> *P* ⚓ *RICE UNIVERSITY*

· · · · · · · · ·

WE TOOK MY DAUGHTER ON COLLEGE visits the summer before her senior year and made a family vacation out of it. We camped along the way, stopped at local parks, and tried local restaurants. Yes, it's a serious time to gather information, but it should be enjoyable, too.

> —*V.A.*
> *AUSTIN, TEXAS*
> *P* ⚓ *RICE UNIVERSITY; UNIVERSITY OF TEXAS, AUSTIN*

MY HUSBAND AND I ASKED our daughter if she wanted us to visit the campus with her or if she wanted to go on her own. She decided she wanted to be left there, so I drove her to the admissions office and we made a plan to meet later. My advice to other parents: You're there to help your child debrief during the college admissions process. You don't have to go with them to see everything. You'll be in the way if you're physically with them as they're figuring it out.

—*NANCY*
GREENBELT, MARYLAND
P *OBERLIN COLLEGE*

• • • • • • • • •

CASUALLY VISIT SOME LOCAL SCHOOLS that aren't of any interest before you even start the application process. We visited several schools in our town and nearby that our daughter knew she didn't want to attend, and it really helped her identify what she did and didn't want in a school. When she did get serious about applying, these background visits gave us a good foundation of knowledge and a good template with which to compare the schools she actually wanted to attend.

—*LESLIE KUHLMAN*
CINCINNATI, OHIO
P *FRANCISCAN UNIVERSITY OF STEUBENVILLE*

• • • • • • • • •

WE ASKED A LOT OF QUESTIONS on the school tours. Most people ask very few. It became a family joke. I said to my husband, "These people on the tour with us are lucky. They're getting a lot more information than they would have gotten without us." We each had our favorite questions to ask. My favorite was, "How late can you get food on campus?" My son is a night owl and I thought this might be an issue. Asking a lot of questions just gave us more information. They had to answer off the cuff. The more questions you ask, the more you get off the script.

—*ANONYMOUS*
BROOKLYN, NEW YORK
P *BROWN UNIVERSITY*

TOO MUCH INFORMATION?

When we went on the tour for Tufts, my daughter had already been accepted, so it was her second visit to the campus. The rest of the group was made up of high school juniors and their parents. The student guide must have made a dozen references to what she considered the college's major draw: "great parties," including an annual naked quad run, where hundreds of students rip off their clothes and run bare-assed across the campus! She felt compelled to share that she had participated in her sophomore year, prompting a visual I did not want to visualize!

Because we had seen the campus before, and had gotten lots of input about the academic environment, we knew that the school had great things to offer, but I'm pretty sure some of those other parents were mentally crossing it off the list. It's important to visit a campus more than once and to talk to staff, department heads and a variety of students to get a true reading of the school. Don't let one immature, party-happy tour guide dissuade you.

—D.J.S.
EASTON, PENNSYLVANIA
P ᴀ TUFTS UNIVERSITY

BEING ON THE CAMPUS LETS you see what you're getting into. I went to one college I'd been pretty interested in, but the people I met were unfriendly and the campus was really ugly. I realized I could never be happy there for four years; that's something you're not going to figure out by reading the brochures.

—EMILY ROSE
ATLANTA, GEORGIA
ᴀ AGNES SCOTT COLLEGE

TRUST YOUR FIRST IMPRESSIONS. I went to a small private high school. When I visited Michigan, I didn't really like it, but I went there anyway and was miserable. I wasn't into the whole party scene and the academics weren't what I wanted either. I left for Brown.

—*ANNE*
PITTSBURGH, PENNSYLVANIA
BROWN UNIVERSITY

* * * * * * * *

"My parents took me on college tours, though on several occasions they dragged me on tours of schools I had no interest in. You, not your parents, should pick your tour itinerary. "

—*COLIN CAMPBELL*
CHARLOTTESVILLE, VIRGINIA
UNIVERSITY OF NORTH CAROLINA

* * * * * * * *

A BAD VISITING EXPERIENCE doesn't mean you won't be happy at the school. You might have a bad tour guide or host, or the weather might be gross, making the campus look uglier than you had imagined it. So if you're not sure, visit again; it's worth a second trip to make sure you'll spend the next four years in a place where you feel comfortable.

—*ELANA BROWNSTEIN*
BALTIMORE, MARYLAND
UNIVERSITY OF MARYLAND, COLLEGE PARK

FROM A TOUR GUIDE'S MOUTH

I'm a campus tour guide at my school, so I know that most of the information we give you is important. You should not focus so much on which buildings you will see, but on what the tour guide is saying as you go through them. Focus on which residence halls you would like to live in and take the suggestions that the tour guides give you. If they recommend a certain hall, they are not only giving you advice from a university standpoint, but also from personal experience. Take notes and pictures during your visit. And, most important, ask questions.

—DAVID DANENBERG
KENT, OHIO
KENT STATE UNIVERSITY

CONVINCE YOUR PARENTS that you want to get a feel for college life by visiting campuses that some of your friends go to, without your parents coming along. Look up a couple of old friends through Facebook or MySpace, take some road trips, and see what college is really like when you're not walking around with a tour group and your parents. You're not going to choose a particular college because your father pointed out on the tour that they had the largest research library in the region. The quality of life on campus is a big part and there is no way to know whether you want to go urban or rural, or big or small, unless you actually go and see what it is like to live there.

—DOMINIC BERARDI
CINCINNATI, OHIO
UNIVERSITY OF CINCINNATI

WHEN YOU VISIT CAMPUSES, find out what the social scene is like. It could make or break your experience. It's a really important outlet, especially if you're going to an educationally rigorous university. And ask about diversity. Find a place that's more diverse than your high school; it makes it fun to learn about other people.

—*AHMAD*
BASKING RIDGE, NEW JERSEY
STANFORD UNIVERSITY

• • • • • • • •

ASK STUDENTS ABOUT THE RELATIONSHIP they have with their professors. How many professors do they have that relationship with? Are professors accessible? Can you talk to them on a regular basis? That is something that is lacking here. I've had a hard time having one-on-one talks with my professors.

—*EMMA*
HARRINGTON PARK, NEW JERSEY
BROWN UNIVERSITY

• • • • • • • •

SOME SCHOOLS OFFER AN OVERNIGHT PROGRAM in which you can be housed with a current freshman and be taken to their classes, experience their activities, and just get to know them. Take advantage of this! Visiting Emory opened my eyes to the multiple opportunities available at this university. I was able to see what the other students were like, sat in on classes (getting a decent feel of the structure, professors, other students' work ethic), talked to current undergrads, and just got a general feel of the school. Because of the opportunities, the happiness of the students, and the proximity to the city, my decision was sealed.

—*NICOLE SPENCE*
WYCKOFF, NEW JERSEY
EMORY UNIVERSITY

Bring your parents, if you can. They'll feel better and be more understanding later when you're at school.

—*LAUREN SHER*
GAINESVILLE,
FLORIDA
UNIVERSITY OF
FLORIDA

IECA* COUNSELOR'S CORNER

MAKE THE MOST OF YOUR CAMPUS VISITS

JUNIORS: **N**OW IS THE TIME TO START VISITING COLLEGES! If you plan ahead, you'll avoid being overwhelmed later by fuzzy memories of campus centers, dorm rooms and lecture halls. Here are some tips:

CONSIDER THE FIRST FEW VISITS as "discovery visits" and stay open minded. Visit colleges that you've always dreamt of attending, but also select all types of institutions - large-small, urban-rural, public-private, single sex-coed. You may be surprised. It happens more often than you think that those who have their hearts set on attending a big-city school, for example, suddenly discover the benefits of rural liberal arts colleges.

BE PROACTIVE. The "visit campus" links on the admission websites have all the tools you need - including schedules of campus tours, information sessions, directions and lodging information.

CONTACT THE ADMISSIONS OFFICE. Tell them you are coming. Make appointments for a campus tour, information session, and optionally, an admission interview. Information sessions, are generally given by admissions officers and the tours by students. If you have time, and you like the school, I recommend doing both. Plan to spend a minimum of two hours on each campus.

ARRANGE FOR AN OVERNIGHT STAY. Colleges organize student volunteers to show you what life is really like in the dorms and in their classes.

PAY ATTENTION TO YOUR SPECIAL INTERESTS. Whether you're most interested in advanced neuroscience research, athletics, political clubs, music, or drama, you'll find it worthwhile to meet with representatives of these programs. Faculty and coaches welcome visitors if the appointments are made in advance.

DON'T HESITATE TO ASK ANY QUESTION! The student tour leader or admission professional recognizes that all of your concerns are important. Also, talk to other students and faculty on campus. People's views vary widely, so ask the same question to several people.

DON'T RELY ON YOUR MEMORY ALONE. Take notes and bring a camera or video recorder. These useful tools will serve you well when your memory blurs on the plane ride home.

GET HELP IF YOU NEED IT. If the thought of organizing itineraries and driving for miles and miles leaves you anxious, you may want to consider a pre-arranged college tour. Offered by many agencies and independent education consultants, a scheduled tour will provide you with a personalized itinerary, access to the admissions offices, and expert advice on the college admission and financial aid process while you travel.

—*THERESA LEARY, M.ED.*
TLC EDUCATION PLANNING FOR GLOBAL LEARNING

I DID CAMPUS OVERNIGHTS AT THE COLLEGES I was looking at. These were great experiences and really helped in the decision-making process for college. Great things to look for when on those visits are: campus security, what the dorms are like, the quality of the food served on campus, entertainment for the campus community, facilities. Try to find out what the personality of the student body is at that school.

—*KELLY PARMET*
HOUSTON, TEXAS
SOUTHWESTERN UNIVERSITY

" During the interviews, make sure people are being level with you when they're talking about the school. Keep saying, 'No, seriously ...' until you get them to really talk honestly about the ups and the downs. "

—*KATHRYN*
PHILADELPHIA, PENNSYLVANIA
SARAH LAWRENCE COLLEGE

HAVE CONTACT WITH ACTUAL STUDENTS; you'll get a better sense of things.

—*COLIN CAMPBELL*
CHARLOTTESVILLE, VIRGINIA
UNIVERSITY OF NORTH CAROLINA

DON'T LOOK AT SCHOOLS that everyone knows and talks about. You need to find a college that is good for you. When I decided to look at Muhlenberg College, most of my friends said, "Muhlen*what*?" Ignoring their naïveté was the best decision I have ever made. When I visited Muhlenberg I felt right at home. There is no better description than to say that it just felt right. There is no such thing as a "good college." Good is something that one needs to decide for oneself. I suggest having an open mind and not deciding anything about a school until you see it with your own eyes.

—*MELISSA BERMAN*
MANALAPAN, NEW JERSEY
MUHLENBERG COLLEGE

• • • • • • • •

WHEN I WAS APPLYING, I'd always ask questions about the kind of food that the college served. I knew if they talked about fast food places nearby or dorms that had kitchens, the food must be bad.

—*ELIZABETH MILLER*
DECATUR, GEORGIA
AGNES SCOTT COLLEGE

• • • • • • • •

IF YOU PLAN TO PARTICIPATE IN AN ACTIVITY, such as the newspaper or the radio station, during your visit speak to students who take part. It's a good way to find out what the people are like and what your chances are of getting involved. I was planning on studying journalism, so going to the student newspaper was one of the first stops I made during my first visit to campus. The students were very supportive and told me to go for it. It puts your mind at ease once you've made the initial contact with those groups.

—*BRIAN SNIDER*
YOUNGSTOWN, OHIO
YOUNGSTOWN STATE UNIVERSITY

Visit the school during a tour. Walk around campus with your family; see if you feel the right vibe.

—*LAUREN MARCINIAK*
BURR RIDGE, ILLINOIS
BRADLEY UNIVERSITY

PARENTS' PAGES

THE COLLEGE SEARCH PROCESS is all about the student. Allow them to take charge, even if their style is not like yours. One idea that I like is for parents and students to split up and take separate campus tours (if possible) – this makes the experience more personal for both the parents and students.

> —*PAUL*
> *MIDDLEBURY, VERMONT*
> *MIDDLEBURY COLLEGE*

• • • • • • • •

WE USED THE SUMMER before my daughters' senior years to visit campuses. My strategy was to group the schools that they were interested in into geographical areas, and then organize two to three trips spaced throughout the summer, with each trip covering two to four schools. The planning took a considerable amount of organization—you have to figure out driving time and where you will be staying, sign up for the campus tour and interview, and map out your route between colleges. The actual visits to the campuses are fun, but also exhausting. You have to plan well and know your limitations.

> —*LUCY RUMACK*
> *BROOKLYN, NEW YORK*
> *P SWARTHMORE COLLEGE*

• • • • • • • •

MY DAUGHTER WENT WITH AN organized group to visit college campuses. I would have liked to go with her to see the culture at each campus. As far as her needing Mom to tag along; I did not think that was necessary. My wanting to go with her was more about my need to have *her* need *me*, and I don't think it is fair to place that burden on your children. I know we all want to spend as much time with them as possible, but the truth is that they are going to be on their own in college, so why not get them used to it?

> —*TRACY*
> *CHICAGO, ILLINOIS*
> *P WASHINGTON UNIVERSITY*

HEN YOU BEGIN VISITING COLLEGE CAMPUSES, make sure you don't schedule
e same types of schools together on your first visit. If you are going to see
veral schools on your first visit, include a private and a public school and a
rge and a small campus or maybe a school in an urban area and one in a
ral area. The first trip is really about ruling out kinds of schools, not figur-
g out where you want to be.

—KATHIE
COOPERSBURG, PENNSYLVANIA
P ⚐ PRINCIPIA COLLEGE; ROANOKE COLLEGE

• • • • • • •

M NOT A BELIEVER IN VISITING COLLEGES before making a decision. I've
und that the influencing factors that emerge from visits to schools are
perficial. Students report on the weather, the coolness of their tour guide,
e size of the dorm rooms, the age of the buildings. None of these aspects of
school determine the overall educational or social experience. I believe that
e significant factors defining a school can be identified from talking with
ople and reading up on the school.

—BETH REINGOLD GLUCK
ATLANTA, GEORGIA
P ⚐ UNIVERSITY OF SOUTHERN CALIFORNIA

• • • • • • •

Y SON WENT TO INFORMATION SESSIONS for all of the schools he applied to.
ometimes he was the only one there, so he was able to spend time talking
ith the person who might ultimately decide his fate. He was also able to get
rsonal e-mail addresses at these events; and after each one, he followed up
ith an e-mail or a letter thanking the person for meeting him.

—R.K.
PHILADELPHIA, PENNSYLVANIA
P ⚐ UNIVERSITY OF PENNSYLVANIA

• • • • • • •

YOU ARE GOING TO VISIT a campus, make sure classes will be in session before
ou plan your trip.

—J.M.
SCOTTSDALE, ARIZONA
P ⚐ LOYOLA UNIVERSITY NEW ORLEANS

THE FIRST TIME I VISITED DELAWARE was on a rainy, cold day in March my sophomore year of high school. My mom dragged me there on a day off because my older brother wanted to look at it, and I could not have wanted to be there less. The next year, though, when I started visiting other schools, I found myself comparing them all to Delaware. I ended up seeing Delaware about six times before I actually started school, including going to a football game and taking a few tours, and every time I felt like I could see myself there. If you feel interested enough in a school to go back six times, there's probably a reason.

—*LAURA DATTARO*
ELKRIDGE, MARYLAND
UNIVERSITY OF DELAWARE

• • • • • • • •

" I did a university-sponsored visit with my parents, and a visit with friends; both are a good idea. If I just relied on my friends, I'd only get a feel for the social scene (which was fun to experience, too!). "

—*JESSICA NEWMAN*
WEST BLOOMFIELD, MICHIGAN
MICHIGAN STATE UNIVERSITY

IF YOUR CAMPUS TOUR GUIDES give you their e-mail addresses, don't hesitate to contact them with any questions you might have. They're likely to give you honest answers regarding anything from professors to social activities and Greek life.

—AMANDA NELSON-DUAC
ST. AUGUSTINE, FLORIDA
GEORGE WASHINGTON UNIVERSITY

" I was very direct while talking to people about the school. It's OK to be critical; you are investing four years and thousands of dollars. It's a big deal. Don't be afraid to ask what you want to know. You aren't being rude; you are being smart and proactive. "

—ZACH HANDLER
ST. LOUIS, MISSOURI
BRANDEIS UNIVERSITY

ASK ABOUT THE SOCIAL LIFE when talking to students. What do they do on the weekends? How much do people drink? Is it a big deal if you don't drink? If you're not comfortable with that kind of social life, you might not fit in.

—EMMA
HARRINGTON PARK, NEW JERSEY
BROWN UNIVERSITY

A Q-TIP
Ask only open-ended questions of the tour guide, the information session leader, and any students you happen to meet. By asking a question that only requires a "yes" or "no" response, you will not really receive the information you are seeking.

BE CAREFUL WHICH STUDENTS you hang out with on your visit. I visited with this kid to see how he lived and what he did. He made the college seem a helluva lot more interesting than it actually was. He wasn't worried about academics. He had a party lined up every Saturday. He was like, "Oh, you'll learn stuff. It's not too hard." I bought the story, and I attended the college. But now I'm transferring because I don't like it. If I had to do it again, I would try to hook up with more mainstream students to get a clearer picture of what campus life is like.

—*WILLIAM ALVAREZ*
LYNDHURST, NEW JERSEY
LA GUARDIA COLLEGE

• • • • • • • • •

THREE QUESTIONS EVERY STUDENT should ask college students when they visit colleges are: What is the atmosphere of each of the dorms on campus (party oriented vs. studying, etc.)? How is the food? Who are the good professors, and what classes are 'must-takes' for any major?

—*CARLOS*
ST. LOUIS, MISSOURI
UNIVERSITY OF SOUTHERN CALIFORNIA

• • • • • • • • •

WHEN STUDENTS VISIT COLLEGES, the number one question they should ask students (when no member of the administration is around) is if they honestly love or even like their college. The second question should be what the worst thing about the college is. The third should be what the best thing about the college is. Colleges, like life, have ups and downs and it is important that you can handle them both.

—*BRIEONNA CROSTON*
TEMPLE HILLS, MARYLAND
UNIVERSITY OF SOUTHERN CALIFORNIA

I VISITED ALL THE CAMPUSES that I applied to. If possible, you should stay with someone you know at the school, or have the school arrange for you to stay with a student. In my case, I had sent in my deposit to another school that I thought I loved. But when I stayed with a friend of mine, I had the most miserable time and I ended up not going. Then I stayed with a friend at my current school and I had an *amazing* time. It helped me decide on which school I wanted to spend the next four years at.

—MATT BORTNICK
EAST BRUNSWICK, NEW JERSEY
INDIANA UNIVERSITY

ONE OF THE MOST IMPORTANT THINGS to look at when visiting a college campus is how people live. What you want is real, candid views from students who attend the school. The day-to-day routine of students will give you an idea of what to expect if you decide to go to the school. It's also an interesting insight into how they've adjusted to the school themselves.

—MAILE CERIZO
HAIKU, HAWAII
POINT LOMA NAZARENE UNIVERSITY

Expert Advice IECA⁺ *COUNSELOR SURVEY*

Visiting a school before deciding to attend is:

Essential – 72%
Pretty important – 22%
Not important – 6%

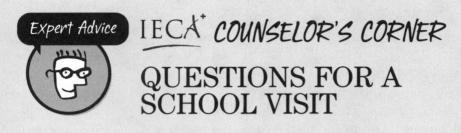

QUESTIONS FOR A SCHOOL VISIT

WHEN VISITING A COLLEGE, focus on the following areas:

ACADEMICS: How are the majority of classes taught? Are they lectures or class discussions? How intense is the work load? Is there a core curriculum that all students are required to take? How difficult is it to meet these required classes? Does the college have a strong program in your intended field of study? How much time do students spend studying?

STUDENT LIFE: What are the students like? Do they seem like people you would be friends with? What do the students do for fun? Are they more artsy or athletic? More studious or more interested in partying? Are there fraternities and sororities? How much do they dominate the social scene? What percentage of kids stay on campus over the weekend? How easy is it for kids to participate in sports? Theater? The newspaper? You fill in the blank for your passion.

CAMPUS: How does the campus make you feel? Can you see yourself here for the next four years? What are the dorms like? How easy is it to get to town or a nearby city? What amenities does the campus offer in terms of a gym, theaters, transportation to town or local attractions? What is nearby - and are those things you enjoy doing?

GENERAL LEARNING ENVIRONMENT: What is the general feel of the campus in terms of learning and community? Are professors accessible? How so? What is the political climate, are all views accepted or does the campus lean more towards conservative or liberal views? Is the curriculum more focused on liberal arts, hands-on learning, pre-professional programs, etc.? How does this type of learning style match your own?

FINANCIAL: How much does it cost for tuition, room and board? What percentage of students receives aid? Is it needs-based or merit-based aid? Are merit-based scholarships available? How many students receive them, and do you think you would qualify?

After your visit, write down your overall impression of the school in 2-3 sentences and determine whether you want to keep it on your list. Also, make sure you sign in with Admissions, so that they can make a note that you visited the school.

—*LISA BLEICH*
PRESIDENT, COLLEGE BOUND MENTOR, LLC
COPYRIGHT © 2008 COLLEGE BOUND MENTOR, LLC. ALL RIGHTS RESERVED.

THANK-YOU CARDS REALLY leave a positive impression. After any sort of meeting with a college representative, I made sure to get their contact information. Once at home, I immediately sat down and wrote an eloquent and complimentary thank-you letter while our meeting was still fresh in my mind. College representatives keep all these thank-you notes on file.

—*BRITTANY RYAN*
DALLAS, TEXAS
UNIVERSITY OF OKLAHOMA

TOUR ANY COLLEGE CAMPUS that you are interested in. You get an entirely different feel for the school when you pull your head out of college books and Web pages and walk around the campus. I knew when I walked on the Wake Forest campus that it was where I wanted to be. Something about being there felt right, a feeling you cannot get looking at any staged picture on a brochure or reading any statistics.

—*WHITNEY TRITT*
ATLANTA, GEORGIA
WAKE FOREST UNIVERSITY

• • • • • • • •

❝ I looked for an institution in which I could grow academically as well as socially. It is important to keep both factors in mind. ❞

—*SCOTT*
CHESTERFIELD, MISSOURI
UNIVERSITY OF ILLINOIS

• • • • • • • •

I WISH I HAD VISITED ONE SCHOOL that was pretty far from home. I limited myself to schools that were within about three hours from home. But I later realized that in many ways they were all very similar. For a different perspective, I wish I had taken a trip to a school in Michigan or Missouri just to get a sampling of how things could be different.

—*BURT EMMET*
NEWARK, DELAWARE
UNIVERSITY OF DELAWARE

THE MAIN QUESTION I HAD WAS, "Can I see myself walking across this quad and talking to these people for the next four years?" When I visited Harvard, it took me about three minutes on the campus before I looked at my father and pleaded with him to get me out of there. Listen to those instincts.

> —*CATHERINE HOWARD*
> *NEW ORLEANS, LOUISIANA*
> *SOUTHERN METHODIST UNIVERSITY*

· · · · · · · · ·

THE BEST QUESTION I ASKED WAS, "How much reading and writing is assigned in the first year?" I wanted to know this because it would allow me to figure out how many credits I thought I could realistically carry the first year. Don't sign up for 18 credits and then find out that the school is big on tons of reading and writing in the first year.

> —*SHAUNA VANARDEN*
> *WINCHESTER, VIRGINIA*
> *UNIVERSITY OF VIRGINIA*

OTHER SIDE OF THE DESK: ON RECRUITING

Colleges hope to raise the number of applications they receive annually. The goal is to have a wider range of talent from which to choose, and to increase selectivity by admitting a smaller percentage of the pool of applicants. Every year, *all* colleges across the country recruit, both to inform students and parents about their programs and opportunities, and to develop the largest, most talented, and most diverse pool they can. In the fall, AOs can work extremely hard, visiting four to five high schools a day for months straight and making numerous large, public presentations.

R.K.

IECA⁺ COUNSELOR'S CORNER

WHAT TO DO ON A SCHOOL VISIT

VISITING COLLEGES is an incredibly important (not to mention fun!) part of the college search and admissions process. After all, you're checking out schools where you might be spending the next four years of your life! Here are some tips for making the most of your time on campus:

THE TOUR: Use the tour as both an opportunity to see the campus and a chance to ask the guide (usually a student) questions. If you have a choice between student guides as the tour commences, you should try to choose the guide whose academic or extracurricular interests are most similar to your own.

INFO SESSIONS: Plan to attend one of the college's information sessions, which are usually hosted by admissions officers who will go into detail about academics, extracurricular life and the admissions process. Bring a list of questions - this is your chance to have them answered in person by an admissions officer at the college. Take good notes - as you visit several colleges on a trip, you will find that it can become hard to remember who said what!

MEETING WITH ADMISSIONS OFFICERS: When you call to arrange tours and information sessions, ask for the name and contact information of the admissions representative in charge of your high school or region. It is generally a good idea to make contact with that person. If it's a small school, you could ask the receptionist if you could schedule a meeting with that person; if it's a bigger school, it's likely better to e-mail them yourself. If you send them an e-mail, and they aren't able to meet, at least they've seen your name and had some indication of your interest in the school!

ATTENDING CLASS: Try to attend a class by making arrangements in advance through the admissions office. Or, if you have a friend or know a graduate of your high school who is a student at the college, contact them to see if there is a class you could attend with him or her. Most professors welcome visitors - just be on time!

MEETING WITH PROFESSORS: An increasingly common question from students and parents is whether or not they should arrange a meeting with a professor while on campus. Meeting with a professor in a particular subject area in which you are interested can be helpful – but remember that you need to know what you're talking about! If you do arrange such a meeting, you need to be well-prepared ; you should know a substantial amount about that subject, and the department at that school, be able to discuss the reasons for your interest in that subject, and have several questions for the professor about his classes and/or research.

INTERVIEWS: If the school you're applying to offers on-campus interviews, and you are a rising senior, you should take advantage of the opportunity to schedule an interview along with your tour and information session. This chance to meet with an admissions officer (or in many cases, a rising senior) can be a great way to demonstrate your interest and also to learn more about the college – just be sure to spend some time preparing for the meeting.

THANK YOU NOTES: Remember to send thank-you e-mails to any admissions officer, teacher, or student interviewer with whom you met while you were on campus!

—*SHANNON DUFF*
  COLLEGE COACH AND DIRECTOR, COLLEGIATE COMPASS LLC

CONTACT ALUMNI

As part of your fact-finding mission about schools, contact local alumni to get to know a school's personality from the inside.

Alumni can be good information resources—especially alumni who keep strong ties to their alma maters. Talking to them can help you learn about schools – as long as you don't expect to make friends or convince someone to champion your application.

Contact your colleges to ask about events hosted by local alumni for prospective students or look on their websites for contact information for local alumni clubs (this can often be found on the alumni relations Web page, not the admissions Web page). If an alumnus will meet you or speak with you, ask some of the following questions (also plan to ask these in your alumni interview later).

- What was your favorite part of your college experience at X University?
- What was your least favorite part?
- How often do you get back to campus and what differences do you see today from when you attended?
- What do you consider the unique aspects of the college?
- What type of student fits the best there: in terms of personality, interests, lifestyle, etc.?

R.K.

THE SUMMER BEFORE MY SENIOR YEAR, I went on a road trip with my mom to see different campuses. A school may be totally different than you think. St. Mary's College of Maryland was really nice, but when I got there, I realized that it's in the middle of nowhere. I had been thinking about going to American University and planned to visit it. But when I got there, it was too crowded. The visits showed me what the campuses and dorms were like, and what the kids were like.

—MAREK JAROSLAW DUDZIAK
BAYONNE, NEW JERSEY
LOYOLA COLLEGE

• • • • • • • • •

BEING A RECRUITED ATHLETE IS TOUGH. You're trying to take care of the recruiting trips while not letting your grades slip in high school. But it's only as stressful as you let it become. I had to cut things out. I had to skip a couple of practices during the school year. You can't do everything. You can't keep all the plates spinning.

—MATTHEW BAKER
SILVER SPRING, MARYLAND
YALE UNIVERSITY

ASK THE EXPERT

If you came to the school for an overnight visit and your host hated you or you partied hard...will it get back to the AO?

Rule of thumb: Don't do anything to jeopardize your chances of admission. Your behavior can always get back to an admissions officer. AO's do not require you to be pure and sweet, but give them only reasons to love you. At schools where character is a big part of the admission process, positive stories about you can only help.

PARENTS' PAGES

IF YOU HAVE A YOUNGER CHILD, bring her along when you go on trips to colleges. We brought our daughter along on some of the trips when my son was looking, and because of this she had a head start. For example, she already knew that she wanted to be in a big city. My first child's list was all over the map, but since my daughter had seen some campuses already, her initial list was much more refined.

> —R.K.
> PHILADELPHIA, PENNSYLVANIA
> P ▪️ UNIVERSITY OF PENNSYLVANIA

· · · · · · · · ·

A LOT OF PARENTS TAKE THEIR KIDS to tour different campuses after they get accepted, but I think it's better to go on tours even before you apply. First of all, the application process is really cumbersome; you can't use the same essay for every school, so why not eliminate some work? The application fees are expensive, so why not narrow down your choices early on? And also, once you get accepted, you have such a short time to make a decision; you probably wouldn't have time to see everything. For us it worked out great.

> —J.H.
> PASADENA, CALIFORNIA
> P ▪️ UNIVERSITY OF SOUTHERN CALIFORNIA

· · · · · · · · ·

IF YOU WANT TO TIP THE SCALES, visit the dean of the department your child is trying to get into. My son had a specific skill, which was music. Once my son chose his two top schools, I called the music department in both of those schools, spoke to the dean and said we would be in the neighborhood and would like to stop by and say hello. Just be proactive and call the department yourself. This way, your child is no longer just a faceless application; you actually get to meet the person who ultimately will decide if your kid gets accepted.

> —ANONYMOUS
> BEVERLY HILLS, CALIFORNIA
> P ▪️ NORTHEASTERN UNIVERSITY

MAKE SURE YOU VISIT YOUR TOP CHOICES because colleges want to be courted by students. My son was a 'legacy' at his second-choice school. He was overqualified and I was certain he would get in. He applied to nine schools and was accepted at all of them except the legacy school. When I called the school to inquire, they said they rejected him because he never made an official visit. Because he didn't schedule an interview, they just thought that he wasn't that interested.

—ANONYMOUS
NEW YORK, NEW YORK
P ⚏ CORNELL UNIVERSITY; DUKE UNIVERSITY

• • • • • • • • •

AN ADMISSIONS COUNSELOR TOLD US, "Watch and listen to your child's initial reaction when they first arrive for their visit." Based on this counselor's experience, your children will know if they are comfortable in this setting within the first 10 minutes on campus. Listen to your kids! Their gut reaction is usually right on.

—DEBBIE
PITTSBURGH, PENNSYLVANIA
P ⚏ OHIO UNIVERSITY

• • • • • • • • •

MY HUSBAND AND I were on a college tour with our daughter: right up in front, first in the group to raise our hands and ask questions, so close to the tour guide that when she stopped we almost bumped into her. Our daughter gradually sank back into the group until she had completely distanced herself from us and was at the very end. We realized then that we were way too into it and that we needed to back off.

—TERESA OEFINGER
PETALUMA, CALIFORNIA
P ⚏ UNIVERSITY OF CALIFORNIA, DAVIS

• • • • • • • • •

START BY LOOKING AT THE AREA, not just the college. Don't blow off the college tours, either. Go spend time and money visiting. It's worth your peace of mind.

—DEBBIE
HOMEWOOD, ILLINOIS
P

PARENTS, THE STUDENT NEEDS TO VISIT small campuses and large campuses, inner-city and college-town environments. Ask yourself, "Can this child succeed far from home?" Some kids at this age think they want to get as far away from home as possible, but once there, they feel unsure and start questioning their choice.

—*SUSAN*
YARDLEY, PENNSYLVANIA
P ⚐ UNIVERSITY OF OKLAHOMA

. . . .

START EARLY AND TAKE an informal approach. We took a campus tour with our son during a visit to his grandparents in his sophomore year of high school. We called a nearby school and scheduled a tour, just to let him get a feel for what a college visit is all about. There was no pressure because it was so early, and it helped him get an idea of what he wanted to look for in a school.

—*DONNA*
CINCINNATI, OHIO
P ⚐ MIAMI UNIVERSITY

. . . .

MY DAUGHTER PROBABLY wishes she had visited more schools. As a parent, I think 10 to 12 campus visits are plenty!

—*DEBBIE*
PITTSBURGH, PENNSYLVANIA
P ⚐ OHIO UNIVERSITY

NO GIFTS

Bringing gifts to an admissions officer is a bad idea. Gifts are appropriate, if ever, only after your child has been admitted and has had a great deal of correspondence with the admissions officer. Gifts are for saying thanks, afterwards.

Inviting admissions officers to dinner is not appropriate when they are traveling in your area. Admissions officers cannot appear to be partial: they cannot spend time with you outside this process in any social way, especially in any way related to money.

MY SON HAD TWO DIFFERENT EXPERIENCES on the trip. When we visited one of the schools, they were having their accepted-students weekend. They assign you to a student guide and there are all kinds of organized programs and activities going on. At another school we visited, he spent the morning there with a professor and the afternoon going to classes and visiting students. Ultimately he chose the school where he was able to spend time with the professor. The first was a hard-sell job and the second was low-key and much more about the school and what his daily experience there would be like.

—*MARYANNE LAGUARDIA*
SANTA MONICA, CALIFORNIA
P 🏫 *BELOIT COLLEGE; UNIVERSITY OF ARIZONA*

TOUR TIPS FOR PARENTS

PARENTS: HERE ARE A FEW TIPS to keep in mind, to avoid fatally embarrassing your student during a campus visit:

ASK INTELLIGENT QUESTIONS. Admissions officers should always be polite about any questions; it is their job to provide information. But don't step over the line and challenge the admissions officer, especially in a public presentation, on controversial issues. These questions may be posed in a private conversation.

ASK THE TOUR GUIDE ABOUT STUDENT LIFE and how the system works at the school. But don't ask questions based on your child. ("My son is really quiet and wants a room of his own.") Wait until after the tour to ask about the availability of quiet dorms.

DON'T BE THE FAMILY SPOKESPERSON. If your child isn't asking questions, it's not a good sign. Make sure he asks some of the questions himself.

R.K.

WHEN COLLEGE COMES TO YOU: LOCAL RECRUITING EVENTS

Colleges want to provide you with information, so they often will send recruiters to college fairs near you. It's worth attending one of these events to learn more about more schools, especially if it is on your list and far away; the more you know, the more you will be sure of your "fit." Also, while these presentations don't replace campus visits, they can expose you to schools about which you may never have thought - and inspire you to go and visit.

Five ways to know if a college will be coming to you:

- **GET ON THE MAILING LISTS:** You may receive a notice in the mail.
- **READ THE WALLS:** Colleges send posters to high schools with dates and times of scheduled visits.
- **SURF THE WEB:** Colleges will post large-scale public events on their Web pages. You usually do not need invitations to go, although they may request RSVPs.
- **VISIT THE GUIDANCE OFFICE,** college counseling office, or career center and ask the staff for a schedule of visits.
- **E-MAIL A SPECIFIC COLLEGE YOU ARE INTERESTED IN:** You may not receive an answer, but you can try.

What happens at these events?

- You will hear a presentation about the school and its admission policies
- You may see slides, a video, or a Power Point presentation
- You can ask questions of the "expert" who reads applications for your region
- You can meet and speak with local alumni who may also attend
- You can get a better feel for a school

R.K.

Expert Advice IECA* *COUNSELOR'S CORNER*

FAIR GAME

EVERY YEAR MY STUDENTS WONDER why, if they have a college counselor, they should attend their local college fairs. There are numerous answers, all of which can impact your final college choices. First, it is impossible to visit all of your potential options for reasons of both time and cost. A college fair offers the opportunity to meet with many school representatives to get to know more about their colleges. Frequently, the booths are manned by admissions counselors and by alumni, offering two different perspectives about the college. What better way to get updated information about a particular school's current admission's profile than to talk to someone who is doing the admissions for your area? Did you know that admissions offices divide the country by regions, and the people you meet at a fair locally will most likely be the ones reading your application?

Secondly, alumni can give you the "Insider's Scoop" on the happenings on campus, what they liked, what they didn't like, and what has been most helpful to them since they graduated. They can provide an idea of what services the alumni network and job placement services provide for graduates. They can also give great tips on restaurants, school events, etc. that they most enjoyed while on campus.

Finally, in today's extremely competitive admissions market, interest shown by a student becomes a key factor in admissions for the colleges. All schools want to admit students who will attend, and making the effort to meet representatives is another way to demonstrate how interested you are in a given college. Providing a representative with a face to connect with a name can be the turning point in a positive final decision. This is your opportunity to let your personality connect, so take advantage of it.

—*SUSAN M. HANFLIK, M. ED., CEP*
SUSAN HANFLIK AND ASSOCIATES, EDUCATIONAL CONSULTING

WHEN I STEPPED ONTO CAMPUS I did not get that feeling that everyone talks about where they "just know that this is the one place for them." I knew that my school offered the academic and social atmospheres that I desired and, most importantly for me, they had given me a very large amount of financial aid. I know that this may not apply to everyone, but for me, money was a huge issue going into my collegiate years and so when choosing the school that I wanted to attend, financial aid, along with academic structure, played much bigger roles than some ethereal "clicking" feeling that I may or may not have felt.

—*MAX MALON MALLORY*
NEW YORK, NEW YORK
SARAH LAWRENCE COLLEGE

Show Me the Money: Scholarships, Financial Aid & Loans

A *ll this talk about getting into the college of your choice, but how are you going to pay for it? The cost of college has risen far faster than inflation in recent years; even in-state tuition can cost more than $10,000 a year. A part-time job delivering pizza just won't cover that. From need-based aid to merit or athletic scholarships, as well as federal grants and private donations to college education, plenty of options are available. We asked college students to show us the money. Read on for valuable advice.*

GET FINANCIAL AID DONE EARLY. As soon as you apply to a school, start the process. There are always forms that are missing or ones that you filled out wrong. If you wait too long to do this, you won't get financial aid.

—*JENNIFER DRAGOVICH*
SEMINOLE, FLORIDA
FLORIDA STATE UNIVERSITY

THE FINANCIAL AID FORMS ARE NOT DIFFICULT. JUST JUMP IN THERE AND DO IT!

—*BETH REINGOLD GLUCK*
ATLANTA, GEORGIA
P UNIVERSITY OF SOUTHERN CALIFORNIA

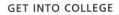 **HEADLINES**
Best Advice and Top Tips

- Be prepared to be patient; it's just not a quick and easy process.
- Be a good detective: there are scholarships out there, even in your local community.
- The costs add up, in application fees, but in odd expenses, too—save where you can.
- Negotiate: Schools can be more flexible than you think.
- Work out a budget for school; it's easy to live beyond your means.

BE WILLING TO REALLY WORK on financial aid if you need to. A kid from my hometown got about $100,000 in aid by winning a ton of smaller scholarships that he found on fastweb.com.

—*KAYLEIGH SHEBS*
AMBRIDGE, PENNSYLVANIA
AGNES SCOTT COLLEGE

• • • • • • • •

APPLY FOR WORK-STUDY OR ASSISTANTSHIPS right after you are accepted, to have a better chance at getting the most sought-after jobs. These positions often pay a portion or all of your tuition, and include a stipend for spending money.

—*CASEY BOND*
GRAND RAPIDS, MICHIGAN
GRAND VALLEY STATE UNIVERSITY

TALK TO THE FINANCIAL AID COUNSELORS as soon as you arrive at your college. Try to build a relationship with one of them. This will be important, especially when you start applying for new or renewed scholarships or grants. I regularly discuss deadlines and payment plans with my counselor. The last thing you want to worry about as a college student is payment deadlines.

> —MAILE CERIZO
> HAIKU, HAWAII
> POINT LOMA NAZARENE UNIVERSITY

• • • • • • • •

THERE ARE ENDOWMENTS that fund literally millions of scholarships. Don't just browse the Internet for full rides. Take the time to write essays for the smaller $500 and $1,000 scholarships. First, they add up quickly. Second, once you write a couple of essays, you'll find there is a pretty straightforward model to most application processes. Once you write four or five letters, you can make little changes and send them to other groups. This expedites the process and gives you a much better chance of getting the scholarships.

> —DOMINIC BERARDI
> CINCINNATI, OHIO
> UNIVERSITY OF CINCINNATI

TOP FIVE COLLEGE FINANCIAL BLUNDERS

1. Not applying for aid
2. Saving in a child's name
3. Missing scholarships
4. Sending in forms too late
5. Paying financial planners to do it

APPLY FOR EVERY SCHOLARSHIP POSSIBLE. Need-based money is great because you don't have to pay it back and there are usually low GPA requirements. Watch out for merit-based scholarships that require 3.5 or 3.3 GPA's. College GPA's are not like high school: they're much harder to maintain or raise.

—*SARAH BORMEL*
BALTIMORE, MARYLAND
BOSTON UNIVERSITY

" Saving up before going to college was a really good idea. Even if you just take less than half out of what you earn from baby-sitting or doing the odd job, it really adds up and comes in handy in the long run. "

—*ELANA JUDITH SYRTASH*
NEW YORK, NEW YORK
YESHIVA UNIVERSITY

CALLING IN THE FEDS

The Free Application for Federal Student Aid (FAFSA) is mandatory if you'll be applying for any federal financial aid. The FAFSA website is www.fafsa.ed.gov.

ROOM TO NEGOTIATE?

BE PERSISTENT. I was accepted to Agnes Scott but needed more money, so my dad kept calling the swim coach and saying, "You know, my daughter would really like to swim for your team, but we need help." That worked; they increased my scholarship.

> —*DANA NOTESTINE*
> *EAST POINT, GEORGIA*
> *AGNES SCOTT COLLEGE*

• • • • • • • •

DON'T LET THE MONEY STAND IN THE WAY. You don't have to accept the first package a college gives you; keep reapplying. Schools that supposedly won't give you anything usually try to find a way to get you in if you've been accepted.

> —*HANNAH ASSADI*
> *SCOTTSDALE, ARIZONA*
> *COLUMBIA COLLEGE*

• • • • • • • •

THEY TELL YOU THAT YOU CAN NEGOTIATE YOUR FINANCIAL AID. My experience is that it's not the case. I tried to negotiate with MIT and they weren't having it. The good schools are less willing to negotiate because they have so many applicants. I ended up going to Villanova, but even the little bit I tried to push them, they really wouldn't budge. My general feeling is that the negotiating process is overrated.

> —*DAVID*
> *NEWARK, DELAWARE*
> *VILLANOVA UNIVERSITY*

OTHER SIDE OF THE DESK: IMPROVING YIELD WITH SCHOLARSHIPS AND LOANS

Schools that offer merit aid or merit scholarships do so to try to enroll the students they most want and love. Some scholarships are awarded for measurable GPA or SAT criteria, and some are awarded for more intangible reasons, such as "leadership" or "talent." Recipients are often selected by committees and AO recommendations, so there is some element of randomness in this process, too; many deserving candidates will not receive this aid.

FASTWEB.COM IS BY FAR the best resource available to young students looking for free money. I applied for more than 10 different independent grants and scholarships through this site. There is literally a scholarship for everyone if you look hard enough. I was very active in community service, for instance, and received $10,000 from the Toyota Motor Company. Many companies offer grants such as this, so take advantage of them. The biggest mistake of the admissions process often comes through overlooking the immense financial opportunities available to incoming students. Also, fafsa.ed.gov is the site for federal financial aid. Always fill out a FAFSA. It's an important element of your application, regardless of your current financial standing. You may get more grant money than you anticipate.

—*LAUREN ELIZABETH LEAHY*
DALLAS, TEXAS
SOUTHERN METHODIST UNIVERSITY

MY FAMILY WASN'T REALLY there for me financially, so I didn't have anyone when I was applying telling me, "Go into debt if you need to; it'll pay off in the long run." If I had it all to do over again, I would have focused more on where an education could get me, not how much it would cost.

—*MARY PERALTA*
BATON ROUGE, LOUISIANA
LOUISIANA STATE UNIVERSITY

● ● ● ● ● ● ● ●

IF I COULD DO ANYTHING DIFFERENT, I would have demanded more help and guidance with financial aid. Although my memories of Seton Hill are very fond, it was not the school I should have chosen, financially speaking. I am in severe debt due to my education. At the time, I didn't care how much school would cost; I just wanted to make sure I could get in. Figure out ahead of time how you're going to pay for your education later on!

—*JODI*
PITTSBURGH, PENNSYLVANIA
SETON HILL UNIVERSITY

A FEW UNUSUAL SCHOLARSHIPS

- The United Daughters of the Confederacy offers $400–$1,500 in scholarships to lineal descendants of Confederate soldiers.
- Harness Tracks of America offers $2,500–$3,000 in scholarships to students who are actively involved in harness racing.
- Two/Ten International Footwear Foundation offers up to $2,000 in scholarships to children of workers in the footwear industry.

I BECAME BORDERLINE OBSESSED with applying for scholarships. Fastweb.com is a great website that provides much information on many scholarships. I can't even remember how many scholarships I applied for. At the end of it all, I was a finalist for some scholarships and even managed to schedule interviews for some. Though I did not make the final cut on many of them, the entire process was a good learning experience that taught me excellent essay-writing and interviewing skills. Also realize that colleges have many scholarships out there just waiting to be seized by willing students. I ended up with three different, significant scholarships from OU alone. Not only did they provide me with considerable scholarship money, but they also gave me some sort of prestigious title that will be regarded highly on campus.

—*BRITTANY RYAN*
DALLAS, TEXAS
UNIVERSITY OF OKLAHOMA

• • • • • • • •

APPLYING FOR FEDERAL STUDENT loans is a very confusing and painful process. The forms are impossible, and if I didn't have my dad helping me, I would never have figured them out. One thing I learned, though, is that the phone number on the FAFSA application is very useful. The customer service people there are very helpful, even when you call them 100 times.

—*ANONYMOUS*
LOS ANGELES, CALIFORNIA
UNIVERSITY OF CALIFORNIA, LOS ANGELES

SCHOOL LISTSERVS CAN BE a valuable source of financial aid information. Check out your school's listserv for scholarship and leadership opportunities. For some reason, students aren't interested in them; they just delete them, and don't bother to read them. That's a mistake if you are looking for money.

—*JOSH GELLERS*
NEW YORK, NEW YORK
UNIVERSITY OF FLORIDA

MY GUIDANCE COUNSELOR directed me to some scholarships, but I found a lot more online. It's just a matter of finding them and applying. From my experience, the more you get involved in while in high school and the more varied the activities you are involved in, the more you'll have opportunities to find scholarships that you are eligible for.

—*JULIE COLLINS*
DES MOINES, IOWA
DRAKE UNIVERSITY

NATIONAL SCHOLARSHIPS ARE FINE AND DANDY, but you're competing against a nation of kids. There are many businesses in your community that give out scholarships to local kids. Those are to your advantage, because not only do you have a better chance of getting them, but you can actually get more of them. I had a friend who got more than $24,000 in local scholarships because she applied for every single one.

—*MAR-Y-SOL*
MARTINDALE, TEXAS
TEXAS STATE UNIVERSITY

RESEARCH SCHOLARSHIPS

Even if you're in the lucky position where your parents can afford to send you to college and pay the entire cost, it's worth looking into scholarship possibilities, either need-based or merit-based.

College is expensive, so it certainly makes sense to check out any possible financial assistance. And hey, you can brag that you are a scholarship recipient! But if you haven't even chosen your school, why do this now? Because some scholarship applications require essays, it's important to ensure you meet deadlines.

Need-based aid: Here are just a few common starting places, among the many websites that list scholarships. Think creatively about who you are and what you offer - there may be a scholarship out there for you.

- FastWeb (www.fastweb.com)
- Student Advantage (scholaraid.studentadvantage.com)
- Scholarship Search Engine (www.studentaid.ed.gov)

Merit-based aid: Many schools offer merit-based aid. This can come as money either for the top applicants in their pool or for applicants that bring something they want: a talent, like athletics or music, for example. What do YOU do?

- Go to all your favorite colleges' websites and look at the financial aid section - if there are scholarships, you'll see them listed, along with the policies about how they are awarded.
- Think creatively - perhaps get a list of all schools with such scholarships and add one or two new schools to your list to increase your chances of earning one.

R.K.

SOME WEBSITES, such as msn.com, have really helpful tuition calculators that give you a very realistic and personal idea of what college will cost. It allows you to enter your state, and in some cases even your school as well as other personal information, so that you really know what to expect. After I did the calculations there, I found that it was going to cost me about $1,500 more per year than I was figuring. And that amount is nothing to sneeze at for a student.

—TABITHA HAGAR
WILMINGTON, DELAWARE
UNIVERSITY OF DELAWARE

DON'T FORGET, as I did, that work-study wages are subject to state and federal withholding taxes and Medicare. Once you deduct those amounts, work-study may not seem like such a good idea. I had pretty much my whole first check spent already in my mind before I got it. Then I was pretty disappointed to find out that taxes were going to come out of it. Keep that in mind when trying to figure out if work-study is worth it to you.

—KEN KEEL
WINCHESTER, VIRGINIA
UNIVERSITY OF VIRGINIA

DATA ON DOLLARS

In recent years, $134 billion in financial aid has been available to college students and their families. About 62 percent of all full-time college students receive some form of grant aid.

WHEN IT COMES TO SCHOLARSHIPS, always go for it. My college gave me a full ride in theater. I was quite lucky to get it. I had applied for it two months after they had already done the auditions for it. I begged the professor to give me a shot. He let me audition, and as it turned out, they liked me and they gave me the full ride. I really needed it.

—*HEIDI*
YERINGTON, NEVADA
TEXAS SOUTHERN UNIVERSITY

" Most people make their parents do the financial aid stuff. I was a lot more hands-on with my process to go to school. I think it makes you more appreciative of where you are and what you are doing. "

—*DAMILOLA OSUNSANYA*
ATLANTA, GEORGIA
EMORY UNIVERSITY

My dad offered to give me the difference in tuition if I chose a less expensive school. I was expected to go to Washington University, but UC Berkeley is much less expensive.

—*DANIEL J. SEIGLE*
WEST DUNDEE, ILLINOIS
UNIVERSITY OF CALIFORNIA, BERKELEY

A MAIN REASON I stayed in my home state of Michigan was financial. I didn't want to put my parents through more expenses, and there are good schools here. I'm getting financial aid and I got student loans, and that's how we're paying for college now.

—*JESSICA NEWMAN*
WEST BLOOMFIELD, MICHIGAN
MICHIGAN STATE UNIVERSITY

• • • • • • • • •

IF YOU CAN'T AFFORD your "dream school," and you really, honestly think it is the right school for you, apply for financial aid early. The whole process is very confusing, and even when you think you're finished you might not be, so you should get started as soon as you've assessed your financial situation. If you get any information about financial aid from any schools you think you might be interested in, reply ASAP to it. I stopped replying to letters about financial aid from a school I assumed I'd get into, and I wasn't accepted. It was a very small school and I'm sure they took my lack of response as disinterest in attending their school and didn't want to offer an invitation to someone they thought wouldn't accept.

—*MERELISE HARTE ROUZER*
ATLANTA, GEORGIA
GEORGIA INSTITUTE OF TECHNOLOGY

Get your parents' help when applying for financial aid. It's really confusing. I did part of it, but it wasn't something I could do on my own.

—*WILLIAM ALVAREZ*
LYNDHURST,
NEW JERSEY
LA GUARDIA
COLLEGE

TOP SCHOOL DISCOUNTS

For families with financial need that make less than $100,000, Stanford will waive tuition. At Harvard, students whose parents make $120,000 to $180,000 will pay, on average, 10 percent of that income; the percentage declines steadily for families making less, until hitting zero at the $60,000 mark.

HEADS UP: FINANCIAL AID

Your financial situation will dictate how much colleges can help you overall. If you and your family have little money, schools can be very generous with financial aid and scholarship money, and private schools can be just as affordable as public schools.

TIP: Apply for aid even if you suspect you may not qualify for it. Colleges take into account many factors you may not realize, such as how many of your siblings are in college, as well as assets and income tax forms. Families making $100,000 or more can still qualify for aid. If you do not apply for aid at the outset, you usually can't apply for aid at a later date.

Some private schools will not tie admission to financial aid requirements, but some will. You will find *need-blind* schools, where the admissions committees make decisions without seeing financial aid forms and without considering your financial situation, and *need-aware* or *need-sensitive* schools, in which their admissions decision hinges in part on ability to pay.

R.K.

COLLEGE – FREE!

Berea College accepts only applicants from low-income families, and it charges no tuition. The school carries a $1.1 billion endowment. Also, every student has a 10-hour-a-week campus job.

THE SQUEAKY WHEEL GETS THE GREASE: Call, complain, do what you need to do to get scholarship money and financial aid. I originally received no scholarship money from USC, but my father (having no connections to anyone important at the university) made a couple of phone calls and I received a $4,000 annual scholarship in the mail, which was pretty neat!

> —*DAVID LICHTENSTEIN*
> *SAN DIEGO, CALIFORNIA*
> *UNIVERSITY OF SOUTHERN CALIFORNIA*

• • • • • • • •

BE CAREFUL, THERE ARE MANY WEBSITES out there designed to look like the FAFSA site, but which require a money deposit. I was very close to falling for one of these scams, initially believing that a down payment was required. Any scholarship or financial aid scholarship that asks for money is illegitimate.

> —*BRITTANY RYAN*
> *DALLAS, TEXAS*
> *UNIVERSITY OF OKLAHOMA*

• • • • • • • •

THE FINANCIAL AID PROCESS is brutal but well worth it. Be prepared to fill out more forms than you'll believe. I honestly think they try to break your will by asking for the same information over and over. Just know going in that it's not an easy or a quick process. But if you get aid, it is a big help. My freshman year I got about $3,000 in free money, so I thought all the paperwork was well worth the effort.

> —*C.L.*
> *NEW MIDDLETOWN, OHIO*
> *YOUNGSTOWN STATE UNIVERSITY*

PAYING THE PIPER

College debt is real debt. Six to nine months after graduation, you'd better be prepared for a chunk of your income to go toward paying it off. Before taking an admissions offer to an expensive school, think long and hard about whether student loans are worth it for you.

Work out a budget for yourself. It's way too easy to live beyond your means in college.

> —*DANIEL*
> *WHEELING, WEST VIRGINIA*
> *COLUMBIA UNIVERSITY*

ALL YOU HEAR WHEN YOU'RE APPLYING IS, "Don't worry about the money," but that's not always the best advice. I didn't realize how much that debt would affect my life. Now I'm about to graduate, and I'm facing all these loans. You have to wonder, was it worth it?

> —*ANONYMOUS*
> *DECATUR, GEORGIA*
> *AGNES SCOTT COLLEGE*

• • • • • • • •

I HAVE TWO JOBS TO HELP PAY for my education. I pay for 75 percent of my schooling, and my dad pays the rest, so I feel a big difference from high school. If I screw up, it's my problem. I'm jealous of people who have their parents pay for school, sometimes they take advantage: they drink, they skip classes. I take it seriously.

> —*MICHAEL ABRAMOVITZ*
> *TUCSON, ARIZONA*
> *UNIVERSITY OF ARIZONA*

I CHOSE **CALIFORNIA STATE UNIVERSITY, FRESNO** because I earned the Smittcamp Family Honors College full-ride scholarship. Out of 575 seniors in the Central Valley, only 50 to 75 are chosen for this prestigious academic scholarship. My parents could not afford to send me to college; an English teacher told me about this program, and said it was for any senior who wants to go straight into college at Fresno State. It was an academic scholarship, meaning you usually have to get pretty good grades. But it is also based on merit, need, and community involvement. The program paid for my tuition, campus room, parking, a laptop and printer, a book stipend, and other perks. Best of all, I could live "away from home" and still be near my family and friends in Fresno.

> —*EMILY TUCK*
> *FRESNO, CALIFORNIA*
> CALIFORNIA STATE UNIVERSITY, FRESNO

• • • • • • • • •

I HAVE A COUPLE OF RANDOM scholarships from outside organizations; they mostly cover the cost of books. There's probably a scholarship out there for everyone. When I was searching, I think I found one that applied to left-handed California female students of eastern European descent with a GPA of 3.0 or above in a public school. Or something like that. Not even kidding.

> —*JESSICA*
> *SARATOGA, CALIFORNIA*
> UNIVERSITY OF SOUTHERN CALIFORNIA

I have a friend who got a disability scholarship because of being color-blind!

> —*RACHANN MCKNIGHT WALKERTON, INDIANA*
> *INDIANA UNIVERSITY*

If you've participated in the College Board's SAT Program Fee-Waiver Service, you may also be eligible to waive application fees at the colleges to which you're applying.

APPLY FOR EVERY SCHOLARSHIP; it helps. Also, don't stop once you're in college. I've received a second scholarship from TCU the past few semesters because of my work in my department.

—ADRIENNE LANG
OLATHE, KANSAS
TEXAS CHRISTIAN UNIVERSITY

66 Jump on every cent they will give you. I had too much pride to take advantage of the fact that I am from an underrepresented minority. I'm over that now. 99

—SETH
SUNNYVALE, CALIFORNIA
UNIVERSITY OF CALIFORNIA, BERKELEY

AS AN ATHLETE, the most important thing to do in the beginning is to put yourself out there, sell yourself. I sent out e-mails and my personal player profile (stats and measurements) to a list of maybe 50 schools I was potentially interested in. I felt this type of sharing my abilities would contradict my modesty, but in the end I learned it is all part of the game. Put yourself out there and make sure the coaches or schools in general know how serious you are about attending the school. If there are opportunities for a meeting or interviews at any point, by all means take them!

—JACKIE ADLAM
MILL VALLEY, CALIFORNIA
COLGATE UNIVERSITY

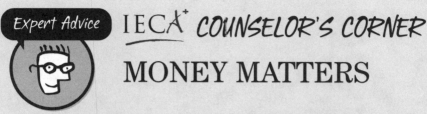

Expert Advice IECA⁺ *COUNSELOR'S CORNER*

MONEY MATTERS

1. When figuring the cost of attending college, include tuition, fees, room and board, books, supplies (notebooks, art materials, computer), transportation, and personal expenses like laundry and entertainment.
2. The deadlines for applying for aid are not the same as those for applying to college. Make sure you know them.
3. Apply early - and on time.
4. Find out which forms a particular college requires: FAFSA, and/or CSS PROFILE, and/or the college's own application. And, yes, filing the FAFSA is free.

—*BETSY F. WOOLF*
WOOLF COLLEGE CONSULTING

I KNOW THAT I'M NOT GETTING a lot of financial aid from the state, because my parents can afford college. I'm doing my best to find outside scholarships. I'll soon know my high school class ranking, which determines what financial aid the college will give me. Being at the top of the class, or being valedictorian or salutatorian, has an impact as well. I applied for several different scholarships: Comcast is giving me one, as is the high school (for community service), and I've applied for theater scholarships. There's a lot you can apply for.

—*JESSIE SCHOREN*
LINDENWOLD, NEW JERSEY
ROWAN UNIVERSITY

Consider

PARENTS' PAGES

PARENTS, YOU HAVE TO GET your tax information together much sooner than you're used to. Every school has a different date for financial aid forms, and if you miss it, tough. We had to have our taxes done at the beginning of February, which was a really big change for us.

> —*M.B.*
> *MINNEAPOLIS, MINNESOTA*
> *P* 🏫 *UNIVERSITY OF MICHIGAN*

● ● ● ● ● ● ● ● ●

WHEN WE APPLIED TO COLLEGES for financial aid, they said that my son had to contribute 35 percent of his savings to his education, while I only had to contribute five percent of my savings. When I found this out, I told my mother to stop contributing money to my son's account. If I knew that early on, I would have just saved money for my son's education in my own account.

> —*JILLIAN*
> *OAKLAND, CALIFORNIA*
> *P* 🏫 *CALIFORNIA INSTITUTE OF TECHNOLOGY*

● ● ● ● ● ● ● ●

GET HELP FROM YOUR HIGH SCHOOL. Perhaps because my husband passed away in my daughter's sophomore year, her school's administration and faculty were exceptionally caring. They knew her strengths and weaknesses and clearly knew our financial limitations. Therefore, I was surprised when many of her advisers strongly urged her to apply to Sarah Lawrence College. It seemed odd to try for such a high-end school, since we couldn't afford for her to "accept an acceptance" if she succeeded. When we asked about our economic concerns, all her advisers had the same response: First, show them you belong there, then ask them how to make that happen! I guess they got the big picture we were missing. They pushed hard for her.

> —*MICKIE MANDEL*
> *RIVERDALE, NEW YORK*
> *P* 🏫 *SARAH LAWRENCE COLLEGE*

DON'T WASTE YOUR MONEY by allowing your child to apply to schools that you know you cannot afford or will not allow your child to attend. This will only set them up for disappointment. Set your child up for success.

> —*MERYL SHER*
> *WESTON, FLORIDA*
> P ⚓ *UNIVERSITY OF FLORIDA*

* * * * * * * *

WE WANTED OUR DAUGHTER to apply for as many scholarships as possible, so my husband thought up a little "incentive." We told her we'd give her 10 percent in cash of whatever scholarships she earned. If she got a $300 award, we gave her $30. Then she felt like there was something in it for her. She was eventually successful getting over $4,000 in scholarships!

> —*TERESA OEFINGER*
> *PETALUMA, CALIFORNIA*
> P ⚓ *UNIVERSITY OF CALIFORNIA, DAVIS*

* * * * * * * *

I LEARNED A REALLY HELPFUL TIP IN A SEMINAR. The speaker said that if you get accepted to your first-choice college but get a better financial offer from one of your other choices, you should use the other offer to try to get more money from your first choice. He told us to write a letter to our first choice, include a copy of the financial offer from the other school, and explain that you would prefer to go to the school you are writing to, but would like them to match the financial offer from the other school. He told us that 95 percent of the time the school you want to attend will give you the extra money.

> —*LAURA*
> *ESCONDIDO, CALIFORNIA*
> P ⚓ *UNIVERSITY OF ARIZONA*

* * * * * * * *

THERE ARE SO MANY SCHOLARSHIPS out there; you just need to do a lot of research to find them.

> —*KAREN BARCHAS*
> *TRUCKEE, CALIFORNIA*
> P ⚓ *UNIVERSITY OF CALIFORNIA, BERKELEY*

A LOT OF SMALL, PRIVATE SCHOOLS offer merit-based scholarships to good students, which helps defray tuition costs. Don't be afraid to ask about that, and then be proactive! Once we started getting scholarship offers, we went back and asked if they could be increased at all. We weren't shy about asking for more and the schools often came back with it. Some people might think what they offer is all you can get. But if that school really wants your child to come there, they'll do what they can to get him.

—*MONA GLOVER*
CINCINNATI, OHIO
P ᴂ KENYON COLLEGE

• • • • • • • •

FINANCIALLY, IT HELPS THAT OUR DAUGHTER is working. It's just in a coffee shop, but in addition to making some money, it really motivates her and helps her organize her time. And since the coffee house has wireless technology, she can do all her homework there and hang out with her friends. It's been a big benefit all around.

—*M.B.*
MINNEAPOLIS, MINNESOTA
P ᴂ UNIVERSITY OF MICHIGAN

• • • • • • • •

MAKE SURE THAT YOU GET all of your financial forms in with your applications. After my son was rejected at Yale for early decision, we were certain that he would also be rejected from Duke, so we didn't send in certain supplemental financial information that was requested. But guess what? He was accepted to Duke University and there we were with an acceptance letter from the school of my son's dreams, but no financial aid package to go along with it.

—*BERURAH RUNYON*
DERBY, KANSAS
P ᴂ DUKE UNIVERSITY

I WORKED OUT A DEAL WITH MY DAUGHTERS before they started school. I told them that I would pay their tuition and related expenses and they would have to pay their room and board. I told them that they could either take out loans or work as resident advisors to cover their room and board. College is a whole package, and you don't want to do everything for them. They need to learn to live independently and I don't have a problem with making them shoulder just a little bit of the burden.

—*J.H.*
PASADENA, CALIFORNIA
P ♟ *UNIVERSITY OF SOUTHERN CALIFORNIA*

• • • • • • • • •

I AM A SINGLE MOTHER and I have three children. I don't make that much money, but I own a home, so my daughter did not get as much aid as she thought she would. Someone advised me to have her call her school's financial aid office to explain our circumstances. She spoke to someone there, who advised her to write a letter and told her what she should put in the letter. I couldn't believe it, but it worked. They are not paying for everything, but at least it is manageable for me now.

—*J.M.*
SCOTTSDALE, ARIZONA
P ♟ *LOYOLA UNIVERSITY NEW ORLEANS*

• • • • • • • • •

PRIVATE SCHOOLS ARE VERY EXPENSIVE. Even if your kid is on a full scholarship, it is still hard. Your kids' friends are going on ski trips, camping trips, and lavish vacations, and you don't want to say, "No, you can't go." It's the culture there and a lot of the kids are doing it. And even if you don't send them on the trips, everything at school is expensive. It's like shopping at Macy's as opposed to Saks; you can get the same thing, but at Saks it's going to be triple the price. So if you go to Harvard, as opposed to Boston College, your dollar gets spread a lot thinner.

—*HENRY NOYES*
CHICAGO, ILLINOIS
P ♟ *HARVARD UNIVERSITY; WELLESLEY COLLEGE*

AID: A FAMILY MATTER

It is best to know your family's financial situation and financial values so that you don't waste time on colleges you won't be able to attend. Remember, though, that schools can be generous with aid and/or scholarship money, if you qualify – so don't be too quick to focus only on public schools over private schools, for example. Couple the answers to the following questions for your parents with research about your schools' financial aid policies – which vary from college to college – to determine how financial aid will impact your applications and choices.

Questions you need to ask:

- How much can the family afford to contribute?
- Can you take loans and be okay with that? Who will pay them back after you graduate?
- Do you want to look only at state schools where the sticker price is cheaper?
- Should you consider private schools, assuming they could be as cheap as public schools if you qualify for need-based financial aid?
- Are you interested in searching for and applying for scholarships?

R.K.

ALWAYS APPLY FOR SCHOLARSHIPS that are specific to each school. I applied for full scholarship programs at a couple schools. I was not given either scholarship, but both schools offered me lesser scholarships that were still substantial.

> —*PAUL*
> *MIDDLEBURY, VERMONT*
> *MIDDLEBURY COLLEGE*

• • • • • • • • •

APPLY FOR EVERYTHING. Ask older students who already graduated what they applied for. Also, use the Internet. There are thousands and thousands of unknown scholarships out there. And most schools are great about giving out financial aid. If they accepted you, they want you at their school, so they will be willing to help out any way they can.

> —*BRIAN HUEFNER*
> *PEACHTREE CITY, GEORGIA*
> *UNIVERSITY OF SOUTHERN CALIFORNIA*

DOUBLE THE FUN

A number of colleges offer scholarships or discounts for twins and triplets:

- Carl Albert State College in Oklahoma (Paula Nieto Twin Scholarship)
- George Washington University in Washington, D.C. (50 percent discount for second sibling)
- Lake Erie College in Painesville, Ohio (each twin gets the scholarship in alternate years)
- Sterling College in Kansas (50 percent discount for each twin)

ATHLETIC SCHOLARSHIPS

IF YOU'RE AN ATHLETE AND WANT TO PLAY ON A COLLEGE TEAM, arrange a meeting with the coach. Bring your scrapbook, statistics, or other information that will help give a clear picture of your talents. Consider asking your high school coach to send a letter to the college on your behalf. As soon as I met with the baseball coach, I knew we were going to be able to work well together. I don't think you can be sure of something like that until you meet face-to-face. He put my mind at ease about some concerns I had.

—*BRIAN SNIDER*
YOUNGSTOWN, OHIO
YOUNGSTOWN STATE UNIVERSITY

WHEN YOU'RE AN ATHLETE LOOKING FOR A SCHOOL, you have to market yourself. I was in the newspaper; I was First Team A State and played on select teams. I sent profiles to universities to tell them what I had accomplished; I was recruited by several colleges. I went to the school that offered me the most money – a full scholarship. It was all about the money: who was going to give me the most.

—*ANDREW*
DEARBORN, MICHIGAN
WAYNE STATE UNIVERSITY

I HAD A COACH IN BASKETBALL WHO HAD BEEN AN ALL-AMERICAN, so he had been through the recruiting thing. I had many questions, and it was nice to be able to turn to him. Even if your coach wasn't recruited, chances are that you are not the first athlete he or she had who was recruited. So ask the coach for help.

—*LINDA ROADARMEL*
PARKERSBURG, WEST VIRGINIA
WEST VIRGINIA UNIVERSITY

I WON A **$48,000**-A-YEAR SCHOLARSHIP. And I needed it. I did my research and found a school that was in the Northeast (I am from the South), had a 78-percent female student body (I am male), and very few athletes (I play basketball). I made sure to make it clear in my application that I possessed all of the aforementioned traits, knowing that it would increase my chances of being accepted. Once I was accepted, I knew that the college would see my FAFSA, and if they really wanted me would be forced to give me a scholarship.

—MAX MALON MALLORY
NEW YORK, NEW YORK
SARAH LAWRENCE COLLEGE

6 Fill out scholarship applications in the downtime you have during boring summer days. It may seem like a tedious task to keep plugging at in your last summer before college, but using just a few of those lazy days can really pay big benefits, no matter how much aid you have. 99

—ANU PARVATIYAR
ATLANTA, GEORGIA
GEORGIA INSTITUTE OF TECHNOLOGY

GO FOR IT, WHETHER YOU THINK you'll get it or not. Apply for those $1,000 and $2,000 scholarships for writing a paper. I know people who have gotten a few of those, which added up to $5,000. That's a good amount of money to help pay for college.

—*TRENT*
GRAPEVINE, TEXAS
UNIVERSITY OF COLORADO

· · · · · · · ·

" Every college has a financial aid office. They offer all kinds of weird aid. Apply to all that you can. The Hastings Milledge Grant for Left-Handed Republican Narcoleptics has your name all over it. "

—*ADAM DREYFUS*
SAN FRANCISCO, CALIFORNIA
UNIVERSITY OF CONNECTICUT

11

Help! Getting Support From Counselors & Parents

F ew things can cause family arguments like the college admissions process. Even so, it is possible for parents and their almost-adult children to work together to ensure the process has a successful outcome. We asked students and parents for advice on this topic. We also asked them about the importance of guidance counselors and private admissions counselors. We realize you're probably getting advice from most or all of the above. But please read on: We really want what's best for you!

MY PARENTS, SPECIFICALLY MY MOTHER, felt it necessary to repeatedly remind me how many days I had left until the applications were due! Her pressure helped me realize that I really needed to get started on the process (although I believe that I would have completed them anyway).

—*NATHANIEL COHEN*
WEST HARTFORD, CONNECTICUT
NEW YORK UNIVERSITY

LET YOUR PARENTS HELP. TWO OR THREE MINDS ARE BETTER THAN ONE!

—*LAUREN SHER*
GAINESVILLE, FLORIDA
UNIVERSITY OF FLORIDA

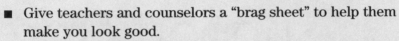

HEADLINES
Best Advice and Top Tips

- Give teachers and counselors a "brag sheet" to help them make you look good.
- It's your job to make sure people send letters and transcripts; make sure it gets done.
- Be clear with your parents; let them know when you need more help, or less.
- Remember, two (or three, or four) heads are better than one.
- Politeness counts: thank those who helped you with a card or gift.
- Regular communication with your parents on your SAT studies will help reduce stress—for them, and for you!

USE YOUR TEACHERS AND COUNSELORS to help you. Our dean helped us out with college admissions. He gave us books to read and talked to us about schools we were interested in. He helped me write my essay. And he also helped me get recommendations from my teachers.

—ADAM JOHNSON
LIBERTYVILLE, ILLINOIS
WESTERN ILLINOIS UNIVERSITY

• • • • • • • •

Consider

ASK FOR HELP AND IF YOU DON'T GET IT, take initiative. Call your school and be a pain in the ass, because you will definitely benefit from it. Ask questions even if they are the most ridiculous questions you have ever thought of.

—TILLIE
HOUSTON, TEXAS
CHATHAM COLLEGE

AT THE BEGINNING OF YOUR SENIOR YEAR, it is your responsibility to meet with each teacher you will ask for a recommendation. You should give them an addressed and stamped envelope and all the required forms. It is also helpful to provide a "brag sheet" so they have a complete view of your achievements and activities outside their classroom. One of my teachers told me that she had no idea how involved I was in my church and wouldn't have known to include that information in her letter if it wasn't on the brag sheet.

—EILEEN DAILY
FREDERICK, MARYLAND
EAST CHRISTIAN COLLEGE

• • • • • • • • •

Hire an outside expert to help with the application. It was the single smartest thing we did.

—LINDA SALAZAR
PALOS VERDES, CALIFORNIA
P BROOKS INSTITUTE OF PHOTOGRAPHY

THE WORST PART WAS that I felt as if I was by myself in the search process. At my high school, if you weren't interested in the stereotypical big state school, you were pretty much on your own. Our guidance counselors tried to be helpful, but they were pretty clueless. I had to figure out a lot by word of mouth and the Internet.

—A.M.
DECATUR, GEORGIA
AGNES SCOTT COLLEGE

• • • • • • • • •

DON'T BE AFRAID TO LOOK STUPID. Ask questions of your teachers and especially of your guidance counselors. I'd ask them, "What would you do if you were me? Where would you go to school if you were me? What did you do wrong during the process that you wish you could do over?" Most kids are afraid of looking dumb by asking a lot of questions. But everyone working at your high school already has a college degree, which means that at one time they were standing exactly where you are now.

—PAMALA BURNSWORTH
MORGANTOWN, WEST VIRGINIA
WEST VIRGINIA UNIVERSITY

SUCH A GOOD BOY

The most important person to rely on when you're going through the college application process and the transition, is Mom. Here are the essentials that mine taught me:

- How to cook mac and cheese.
- How to dress.
- About dating and how to kiss girls (very important in college).
- How to take notes in class (she's a great note-taker).

Finally, I wish I could've taken my mom with me to school so she could be my wingwoman. My mom's great at picking up gals. I know she would brag to college girls about how great I am. Don't underestimate your parents: They're older and wiser.

    —DANIEL
      TORONTO, ONTARIO
      YORK UNIVERSITY

SOME PARENTS ACTUALLY WRITE ESSAYS, send e-mails to schools in the name of the student, fill out applications, and push schools. Parents who have neither the time nor the interest hire consultants to craft their child's accomplishments so they will be presented in a more interesting light. I believe that supporting my children has been an ongoing process since they were born. The most influence I had on my son and daughter was brainstorming possible essay topics. Also, I helped with proofreading.

    —SHARON
      PHILADELPHIA, PENNSYLVANIA
      P   WESLEYAN UNIVERSITY;
      WASHINGTON & LEE UNIVERSITY

MY PARENTS HAD THEIR EYES SET on the Ivy League. When I got rejected from my top two choices, Wharton and Stanford, they were extremely disappointed. They blamed my unsatisfactory performance on my habit of procrastination -- I didn't study for the SAT, I didn't spend enough time on my college essay, I didn't do enough extracurriculars. On the other hand, I actually accepted my rejections pretty well since I had already lowered my expectations so that I would not be devastated when the reject letters come. Those were my only rejections, but my parents would not let me forget. Although I hate it when my parents nag me about working on my stuff, I must agree that if I had spent more time studying, writing, doing, I would have probably done much better.

—*DIANA*
ROWLAND HEIGHTS, CALIFORNIA
UNIVERSITY OF SOUTHERN CALIFORNIA

● ● ● ● ● ● ● ● ●

" My parents were very involved- they were picking out colleges for me! If it's too overbearing, tell them that you'll do it on your own and that you'll ask them for help when you need it. "

—*LAUREN MARCINIAK*
BURR RIDGE, ILLINOIS
BRADLEY UNIVERSITY

PARENTS' PAGES

BE DILIGENT. STAY ON TOP OF THE SITUATION. Work with your children, not against them. Guide them but don't force them. This is one of those situations where parents have to earn their keep. This is a real test of parenthood. Don't screw it up.

> —*COLLEEN BAKEY*
> *FREDERICK, MARYLAND*
> *P* 🏛 *GEORGETOWN UNIVERSITY*

• • • • • • • • •

MY CHILD'S SCHOOL EMPHASIZED THAT THERE IS A SCHOOL for every kid out there, and that is absolutely true! Parents, don't get caught up with other parents who panic and stress out. Find parents who have been through the process with their older kids, because they tend to be more relaxed about the whole experience. And the more that parents can stay away from the "keeping up with so-and-so" game, the more they can support their child in making a choice that suits his personality and academic level, and help their child feel good about his decisions.

> —*LINDA SALAZAR*
> *PALOS VERDES, CALIFORNIA*
> *P* 🏛 *BROOKS INSTITUTE OF PHOTOGRAPHY*

• • • • • • • • •

I WASN'T ALWAYS SUCCESSFUL IN STEPPING BACK, but my daughter was not shy about letting me know that I had already given her my opinion and she didn't need to hear it again. My daughter had gone to her grandparents' home in Florida for a week prior to the start of her senior year. She did not complete her applications before going, which she had promised to do. When I called her about it, she got so mad she said she was not coming back home, was going to stay in Florida, and wasn't going to college. Obviously, things calmed down, but that let me know I needed to back off.

> —*R.F.*
> *ATLANTA, GEORGIA*
> *P* 🏛 *UNIVERSITY OF PENNSYLVANIA*

HERE'S THE IRONY: After the offers, the accepted-student days, the commitments—in other words, by June of my daughter's senior year—my entire point of view had changed. I could now clearly see that her results were in order with her grades and scores, gender, academic interest, geographic location—and effort. When my friend Jeanne's son began the process, I applied what I knew to his case and told her to relax, he'd do fine. And, in fact, I called eight out of nine of his applications correctly: He was wait-listed at one school I thought he'd get into. But if there'd been a pool, I would've won.

—*ANONYMOUS*
NEW YORK, NEW YORK
P ⌂ *CARLETON COLLEGE*

I STAYED TOTALLY OUT OF MY DAUGHTER'S DECISION about where to go. I didn't even give an opinion, especially since she was considering the college that I attended. Since that college was close to our town, I felt that any enthusiasm that I showed for University of Oklahoma would appear to be self-serving. Actually, keeping my mouth shut was easy because she never considered any other school; in fact, she never even applied to any other school. I do feel good, though, knowing that the decision was hers and that I didn't try to influence her.

—*JAYNE ROBERTS*
EDMOND, OKLAHOMA
P ⌂ *UNIVERSITY OF OKLAHOMA*

EVERY TIME YOU'RE TEMPTED to give a piece of advice to your kid on applying to school, bite your tongue. Let your child think about what he or she wants. I don't listen to that advice, but it *should* open up more conversation!

—*WENDY LUKEHART*
TAKOMA PARK, MARYLAND
P

JUST AS WITH ANY LARGE ASSIGNMENT or project, I had to learn how to budget my time. My parents helped me create "due dates" for my nine college applications, and organize on a spreadsheet what I needed to get done by when. It is possible to get through, as long as you keep organized.

—*DAVID LICHTENSTEIN*
SAN DIEGO, CALIFORNIA
UNIVERSITY OF SOUTHERN CALIFORNIA

* * * * * * * *

THE FIRST TIME I WALKED INTO MY ACADEMIC advisor's office in high school, there were papers scattered all over the place and the desk was very unorganized. I realized the scope of this advisor's job and took things into my own hands. Advisors are not there to make decisions for you. They provide resources and help you find outlets to information.

—*DOMINIC BERARDI*
CINCINNATI, OHIO
UNIVERSITY OF CINCINNATI

* * * * * * * *

KEEP MOM AND DAD AT BAY: One counselor told me that admissions offices see lots of applications that were clearly filled out by the parents and they don't like to see that. At the very least you should be able to fill out your application by yourself. Don't think that the school won't know if someone else does it for you.

—*DIANE KOTCHEY*
FREDONIA, NEW YORK
STATE UNIVERSITY OF NEW YORK AT BUFFALO

PARENT TO STUDENT

Some parents can be extremely overbearing, more so out of fear, since the competition to get into certain schools can be so intense. With that said, kids need to remember that their parents simply want the best for them, and that this is an overwhelming process. It helps if they can let their parents know up front, "The more you push and the more anxious you are about this, the harder it is for me." Of course, those parents may not always be willing to hear those words. This is really tricky, depending on the family dynamics.

—*Linda Salazar*
Palos Verdes, California
Brooks Institute of Photography

BECAUSE MY PARENTS KNEW they would not be playing a financial role in my college career, I refused to let them play a role in my decision about where to attend. This was difficult, because they really did not want me to attend a college that was far away, but they had no leverage to keep me close to home. Be very honest with your parents about your financial needs and your career goals. They should respect that you are serious enough to know what you need and what you want.

—*Stefanie Fry*
Knoxville, Tennessee
University of Tennessee

THE APPLICATION PROCESS was actually a lot of fun for me. I used researching and applying to schools as a sort of stress *reliever*. The stressful part for me came when I received acceptance and rejection letters. That's when the real decision came and when my list of pros and cons for schools helped a lot. My guidance counselor was invaluable as a source of information and advice. Once I finally made my decision, my mom and I had a little shopping trip and ate at my favorite restaurant to celebrate.

—*JESSICA PAULEY*
CHILLICOTHE, OHIO
UNIVERSITY OF CINCINNATI

• • • • • • • •

WHATEVER YOU DO, take responsibility for yourself. Your college admission is not anyone's job but your own. I've met all too many high school kids who have a hundred "if only" statements to say about their admissions process. Fix that on the front end by handling your part. You can do it. So get up, get out, and get it done!

—*LAUREN ELIZABETH LEAHY*
DALLAS, TEXAS
SOUTHERN METHODIST UNIVERSITY

• • • • • • • •

MY PARENTS TOOK ME to college campuses to visit, motivated me to sit through yet another admission presentation and campus tour, helped correct my essays, and provided me with constructive criticism. They provided me with SAT classes and a private counselor for one session. They gave me the tools, and I used them; this is how I believe all parents should interact with their children during the admissions process.

—*DAVID LICHTENSTEIN*
SAN DIEGO, CALIFORNIA
UNIVERSITY OF SOUTHERN CALIFORNIA

HEADS UP:
PRIVATE COUNSELORS

In addition to the resources in your high school, you may want to get outside help in the admissions process from a private counselor. These counselors are not a replacement for your own research and work, but they can help you focus your college search and your applications.

PRO
1. A good private counselor or consultant will get to know you well and can help you figure out a personal game plan: where you should be applying, what you should do to stand out, etc.
2. They help expand your knowledge of colleges and universities and their environments.
3. They provide extra emotional support throughout the process.
4. They help you strategize about what to highlight in your essays and your applications.
5. They help manage your expectations (and Mom and Dad's) to make sure that you will be admitted somewhere that is a great fit for you.

CON
1. Private consultants are expensive.
2. They cannot "get you in," no matter what they promise. You will ultimately rise and fall on your own merits.
3. They generally do not have access to admissions offices. Most admissions offices will speak only to your high school counselor.
4. Anyone can work as a private consultant. It's up to you to make sure you are hiring someone who is knowledgeable and experienced.
5. In the Internet age, you can do a lot of research on colleges on your own.

R.K.

NEITHER OF MY PARENTS went to college and they really weren't involved with the process. They did pay for all of my applications, but it was up to me to do my own research and decide where to apply. You just have to get motivated and do things on your own, because in the end, it's your choice on where you're going to spend the next four years of your life.

—*SCOTT COOLBAUGH*
KNOXVILLE, TENNESSEE
UNIVERSITY OF TENNESSEE

" When you start applying to colleges, it's important to learn how to delegate. Figure out what parts your parents and your counselors can help you with, and ask them to do it. Never be afraid to ask for help; you don't have to do the entire thing on your own. "

—*DANA NOTESTINE*
EAST POINT, GEORGIA
AGNES SCOTT COLLEGE

ALTHOUGH I APPRECIATED the support and help my parents gave me in my college search and application process, we butted heads when they told me my first- and second-choice schools were too expensive. They didn't want me to be up to my neck in debt after graduation, and at the time I didn't understand the implications of a $47,000-a-year price tag. Today, I don't have any regrets about choosing a less expensive college. It served me well, and the program is a good fit for me.

—*JASON PAUL TORREANO*
LOCKPORT, NEW YORK
STATE UNIVERSITY OF NEW YORK, BROCKPORT

• • • • • • • •

MY PARENTS DIDN'T HELP AT ALL, except with some of the financial aid forms. I think their view was that if I wanted to go to college, I should get myself there. That ended up helping me out because I learned a lot about each school through the process of trying to navigate their admissions department. Because I had to sort through all the mail I was getting from schools, I noticed that I was getting a lot of it from Delaware, and what I got from them felt the most genuine. If my parents had been going over the letters with me—or for me—I don't know that I would have picked up on that. Plus, you want the admissions board to get the best sense of who you are, and parents reading over or helping to fill out applications can obscure that.

—*LAURA DATTARO*
ELKRIDGE, MARYLAND
UNIVERSITY OF DELAWARE

ASK THE EXPERT

Don't AO's and guidance counselors work out acceptances between them?

Guidance counselors can and do call AO's to talk about students. They can help push for their students, but only so far. Ultimately, colleges will do what they want, and they keep in mind that a large portion of the applicants do not come from schools where counselors have the time or ability to make a call. They do not hold this against the students when making final decisions.

R.K.

MY PARENTS WERE REALLY not involved that much. But it can work to your advantage: You have them as a resource that you can tap if you want  to, but *only* if you want to. If you feel that you can handle it without their involvement, as I did, then you have that option as well. I chose to keep them at arm's length, but still within grasp if I needed them … or their checkbook!

—*BETSY LILIENTHAL*
WILMINGTON, DELAWARE
UNIVERSITY OF DELAWARE

● ● ● ● ● ● ● ● ●

LISTEN TO YOUR PARENTS' and guidance counselor's input, but be honest about what you are thinking and feeling. This is your life, not theirs!

—*K.F.*
BASKING RIDGE, NEW JERSEY
P LAFAYETTE UNIVERSITY

THE BEST RESOURCE MOST KIDS HAVE—and the one that for some reason they don't want to use—is their parents. Pick their brains as much as you can. Some kids just don't want to believe that their parents have any insight into anything. But if someone has been through the process, that person will have something to pass along. I was lucky because both of my parents are college grads. They had tons of tips for me.

> —*C.L.*
> *NEW MIDDLETOWN, OHIO*
> *YOUNGSTOWN STATE UNIVERSITY*

• • • • • • • •

MY PARENTS HAD DEFINITE opinions about certain schools and where they thought I fit best. They were really set on Vanderbilt, which was the only school I didn't get into. I remember feeling relieved that I wouldn't have to fight them on that, and that I'd be able to go exactly where I wanted to be. Your parents want the best, but follow your heart in the college process. You're the one who has to be there for four years, not them. Make the decision yourself.

> —*WHITNEY TRITT*
> *ATLANTA, GEORGIA*
> *WAKE FOREST UNIVERSITY*

• • • • • • • •

MY PARENTS HAD THE ULTIMATE say on where I went to college, because of cost and location, but I chose the schools within reasonable distance from my home. I applied on my own and knew what criteria I was looking for. Listen to your parents, but make known what you need and want in a school.

> —*ADRIENNE LANG*
> *OLATHE, KANSAS*
> *TEXAS CHRISTIAN UNIVERSITY*

I realized I went a bit overboard when I called up the college and the receptionist said, "Hi Gloria, what can I do for you today?"

> —*G.V.*
> *HOUSTON, TEXAS*
> *P UNIVERSITY OF TEXAS, AUSTIN; UNIVERSITY OF MICHIGAN*

PARENTS' PAGES

MY PARENTS WERE VERY HELPFUL with college applications, and when we were visiting campuses. They helped me debrief after each visit: what was good, what wasn't good, how did this compare to other schools, and so on. The one thing they did that really stressed me out was to wait until late in the process to make their suggestions. If you have any opinions about where your son or daughter is going to college, state them in September, not in December.

> —B.B.
> WYNNEWOOD, PENNSYLVANIA
> P 🏛 BROWN UNIVERSITY

· · · · · · · · ·

I HAVE TWIN DAUGHTERS, and they're going to different schools by design. In the months of college applications, be prepared for some extremely stressed-out children. It's too much pressure! Get up early in the morning, fix them breakfast, and take care of some of their minor day-to-day needs, so they can concentrate just on what they need to do.

> —LENORA WANNIER
> LA CAÑADA, CALIFORNIA
> P

· · · · · · · · ·

MY SON'S NOT LOOKING at what colleges have to offer in terms of education; he's looking at questions like "Can I skateboard there?" My daughter checked the University of Kentucky because it was the number one cheerleading school. I told her, "You're not going to college to cheer!" But the school was a good price and it's what she really wanted. The reality is that even though you think you know it all, parents, you haven't been to school in many years. Your kids know more than you think, and it's good practice for them. They'll soon be adults having to make decisions for themselves.

> —DEBBIE
> HOMEWOOD, ILLINOIS
> P

ENCOURAGE YOUR CHILD TO ASK lots of questions and talk with people she knows who graduated ahead of her and who can offer their perspective on schools. We tried to speak with as many people as we could about the schools she was interested in. My daughter was introduced to two Penn alums, who wrote letters of recommendation for her. One was especially helpful in that he met with us and, after speaking with my daughter, he tried to focus on one aspect of her accomplishments that might help her stand out. He felt that her work in a political campaign was something that many high school kids would not have, so his recommendation letter to Penn emphasized that part of her background. She applied early and was accepted.

—*R.F.*
ATLANTA, GEORGIA
P ♣ *UNIVERSITY OF PENNSYLVANIA*

• • • • • • • •

ENCOURAGE YOUR KID TO SLEEP. Have sympathy! My son was up at 6 a.m. Saturday mornings for the SAT prep class. Help your children find other outlets while going through it. Outlets can be creative and fun (like music or sports). The most important thing is to help them find balance.

—*WENDY LUKEHART*
TAKOMA PARK, MARYLAND
P

• • • • • • • •

KEEPING YOUR EXPECTATIONS AT BAY begins well before college, when you learn that living your life through your child is not always healthy. They have their own goals, which may not be your goals; you and your child will be happier if you can realize that. My daughter made very good decisions, so it's easy to be philosophical now. But parents whose egos are all wrapped up in where their kids go to college are depriving their children of the opportunity to grow and mature.

—*R.F.*
ATLANTA, GEORGIA
P ♣ *UNIVERSITY OF PENNSYLVANIA*

I THOUGHT THAT VOLUNTEERING at my son's high school would give me a little edge over other parents in terms of needing things from advisors and teachers at the high school. I didn't set out to volunteer with that goal in mind, but as I spent more time and got to know the principal and the advisors, I realized that I could use the newly formed relationships to my advantage. I feel that when they do things for him, like write recommendations or get his transcripts out, they know me and might use a bit more care.

—*L.R.*
SCOTTSDALE, ARIZONA
P ▫ *UNIVERSITY OF CALIFORNIA, BERKELEY*

• • • • • • • •

CALLING OTHER PARENTS AND ASKING for advice is a great way to get information, but think about whom you're asking and what kind of position you're putting them in. People who have already been through the whole college process were more than happy to tell me things and give me advice, but it's a different story for other parents who are still in the middle of it all. There are just so many spots and scholarships to go around, especially from any particular high school, so it's understandable if those people don't want to give out too much information—and you shouldn't feel pressured to, either.

—*CAMILLE*
CINCINNATI, OHIO
P ▫ *UNIVERSITY OF KENTUCKY*

• • • • • • • •

AFTER GOING THROUGH THE COLLEGE application process four times in six years, the best advice I can give is not to get overinvolved or worried. It's the guidance counselor's job to help your child apply and get accepted. Step back and enjoy those junior and senior years. Enjoy your children, because they will soon be gone and your job as parents will be over.

—*DEE A. MARTIN*
MADEIRA, OHIO
P ▫ *UNIVERSITY OF DAYTON; WITTENBERG UNIVERSITY;*
BOSTON UNIVERSITY; SAINT LOUIS UNIVERSITY

AS A PARENT YOU WANT THE BEST for them. This is a teaching moment for you; it's a way to help your kids make big decisions, so in the future when you aren't there for them, they will be able to make these tough choices on their own.

—*PETER*
SEATTLE, WASHINGTON
P ⚑ SWARTHMORE COLLEGE

• • • • • • • •

PARENTS CAN DO THEIR OWN RESEARCH of the schools that interest the students. When the parents do this they can contribute when the students try to put together a list of pros and cons for each school. This can be especially helpful since the student may not remember everything with all of the work that they are required to do, and especially if the parents honestly know their children and what they're looking for in a college. Parents can also help by giving their children ideas for essays, especially for those that ask students to explain their best qualities. In addition, parents can ask questions that students are afraid to ask during the many receptions and meetings that colleges have.

—*BRIEONNA CROSTON*
TEMPLE HILLS, MARYLAND
P ⚑ UNIVERSITY OF SOUTHERN CALIFORNIA

• • • • • • • •

I THINK PARENTS CAN MAKE THE COLLEGE APPLICATION PROCESS easier for students by supporting their decisions to apply wherever they'd like – even if parents are hesitant to the idea of letting their children attend schools on the other side of the country or even in another country. The reality is, you really don't know what schools you're going to get into.

Parents can also make the application process easier by not constantly nagging or doing anything that may cause distractions from the process. Students must write meaningful essays during this time and it can sometimes be exceedingly difficult to write a personal essay that illustrates your persona when you're extremely upset with your parents.

—*CINDY VUONG*
FULLERTON, CALIFORNIA
P ⚑ UNIVERSITY OF SOUTHERN CALIFORNIA

I WORK IN THE OFFICE OF ADMISSIONS at my college and I have received hundreds of phone calls from parents calling to do research on behalf of their child, to schedule their child interviews and tours, and many other things that the student should be doing for themselves. Along with being a good exercise in intellectual achievement, the application process also offers the opportunity for the student to gain vital communication and networking skills, and if the parent takes on any of those responsibilities they are doing their child a disservice. A student who is applying to college should be capable of calling and scheduling a meeting with an admissions counselor all by themselves. The admissions counselors would much prefer to speak with your student themselves and most of the time the person you are talking to is a student worker who has absolutely no say in the matter anyway.

　　—MAX MALON MALLORY
　　NEW YORK, NEW YORK
　　🏫 *SARAH LAWRENCE COLLEGE*

A HARMFUL PARENT . . .

- Puts his needs first and makes this process about himself;
- Fills out forms for his child;
- Writes the essays for his child;
- Pressures his child to gain admission to a specific school;
- Contacts the universities about the applications because his child is "too busy";
- Abdicates responsibility in the process and puts it all on his child;
- Argues with the guidance counselor and the high school;
- Blames failure on his child and not on the process.

WHAT ARE YOUR EXPECTATIONS?

Take time to investigate your own expectations, values, and biases about both the application process and your child's success. Are there certain schools you secretly—or not so secretly—wish he could attend? Is there a magic test score you want him to achieve? While you want the best for your child, you should be honest with yourself about what you really wish will happen. It is better to see, recognize, and process any selfish needs you may have so you can recognize when your expectations are being unfairly put onto your child. As all parents do, you have hopes and dreams for him, but you will all be happier if you can be honest about whether your child shares them. Putting your expectations on him may, in fact, harm your child through unrealistic pressure. Your dream school could be a mismatch. The car window decal that would make you proud could mean a miserable four years for your child. Set goals and share your dreams, but adjust your expectations to fit his dreams and ability.

A HELPFUL PARENT . . .

- Asks his child his dreams and listens to him;
- Attends high school presentations and guidance counselor meetings (where appropriate);
- Assesses his own selfish needs and tries to separate them from his child's;
- Puts together a list of possible schools, insuring that his child will have several good places for himself;
- Visits schools (where possible);
- Helps plan essays to help his child highlight his strengths;
- Pushes his child to work hard, but celebrates his hard work;
- Insists that his child run the admissions process (e.g., call admissions officers and write e-mails to them directly).

MY DAD IS AN ACCOUNTANT, so he handled all the student aid forms and what-not, and my mom is really good at writing resumes and essays, so she helped me out a lot. The whole process was collaborative, because my parents had my interests in mind. They let me do whatever I wanted with the process, and I usually wanted more direction from them. They even said, "You know, David, you don't have to go to college if you don't want to." To which I promptly responded, "Of course I want to go to college." But giving me the option was nice.

—*DAVID BERNGARTT*
RALEIGH, NORTH CAROLINA
UNIVERSITY OF NORTH CAROLINA AT CHAPEL HILL

• • • • • • • •

SINCE THE COLLEGE COUNSELORS at my high school weren't very helpful, my parents enrolled me in a private counseling center. I was able to go to the center, where they had computers and snacks and counselors on hand to answer questions and edit essays. It was so helpful to take the application process away from my home. It also helped relieve a lot of stress, since the center was quiet, calm, and specifically dedicated to college admissions.

—*JESSICA*
SARATOGA, CALIFORNIA
UNIVERSITY OF SOUTHERN CALIFORNIA

• • • • • • • •

MY PARENTS DIDN'T REALLY UNDERSTAND the complexity of the process. Their greatest gift to you would be to connect you to someone who does (or to become someone who does).

—*LAUREN ELIZABETH LEAHY*
DALLAS, TEXAS
SOUTHERN METHODIST UNIVERSITY

 Expert Advice

IECA⁺ COUNSELOR SURVEY

What should students do to make best use of their guidance counselors?

- Remember that how well your counselors know you is up to you, so the student should make regular (say, once a month) meetings with the counselor from March of the junior year through December of the senior year. Come to each meeting with one specific question to ask or issue to address and one thing you want the counselor to know and understand about you.
- Get to know them well so that they can write a genuine, enthusiastic letter of recommendation.
- Fill out completely any informational forms you receive from Guidance; counselors will use the info on these forms to write recommendations.
- Stay organized, prepare questions ahead, take notes.
- Meet early and often, share with them the schools you are interested in and your reasons. Help them get to know you – your passions, strengths, hobbies, personality.
- Treat them with respect.
- You need to develop relationships with several adults at your school and in your community to build a team of support – no one guidance counselor can meet the needs of all the students that the school assigns him/her ...
- Respect deadlines so that your counselor can meet her deadlines.
- If you don't do your job, your counselor can't do hers.
- Know that your guidance counselor is working hard on your behalf.
- Let her know that you appreciate her efforts. A special thank-you note when it's all over would be nice.

ASK FOR HELP! At first, I was very discouraged by the complexity of the entire process. Before I even delved into the land of deadlines, applications, and loans, I had to figure out where I wanted to attend. I felt stressed by the emphasis on having a reputable 'top five' choice list, stressed by rejection letters, and stressed about making one decision that would change the course of my life. It wasn't until I asked for help that I began to be more proactive about my decision-making and more self-assured in the process. By asking one person for help, I was suddenly connected to an extensive and diverse network of schools, possibilities, counselors, and alumni.

—*HEATHER MUNTZER*
SANTA ROSA, CALIFORNIA
CALIFORNIA COLLEGE OF THE ARTS

· · · · · · · · ·

THE BEST WAY THAT A PARENT can make the process easier for the student is to guide without pressuring. The process in itself is a stressful one, so parents are most helpful in assisting in the decision-making process without projecting their own opinions. Another way that a parent can be really helpful is in the organization of materials, trips, and school information. It's easy to feel overwhelmed during the process with the number of materials needed and information to access. In my own experience, my mom was most helpful in keeping the information I needed readily available and helping me with keeping deadlines.

—*CASEY HEERMANS*
DECATUR, GEORGIA
UNIVERSITY OF NORTH CAROLINA AT CHAPEL HILL

YOUR PARENTS AREN'T TRYING to torture you; they are just thinking about your future. I think people should appreciate it when their parents put pressure on them to go to college. My dad worked really hard to get a college education. He left his family to study, and knows how much value there is in an education. The pressures he placed on me positioned me to be a better person. I think parents just want what's best for their kids.

> —ANONYMOUS
> LOS ANGELES, CALIFORNIA
> UNIVERSITY OF CALIFORNIA, LOS ANGELES

❝ Don't take your parents', friends', boyfriend's, teachers', or the newspaper's college rankings into account. It's just you. ❞

> —DIANA
> ROWLAND HEIGHTS, CALIFORNIA
> UNIVERSITY OF SOUTHERN CALIFORNIA

WHICH COLLEGE TO ATTEND is a decision that, while guidance is appreciated, needs to be largely the student's decision. College marks an entrance into adulthood, and it's an important part of maturity to be able to analyze your options and make your own choice. It can be and should be a very empowering event in a student's life.

> —ANU PARVATIYAR
> ATLANTA, GEORGIA
> GEORGIA INSTITUTE OF TECHNOLOGY

ASK THE EXPERT

Do colleges share information about applicants?

The days when colleges shared information about you are over. Schools really only find out where else you have applied if you let them know yourself, or if you accidentally send an "I love you, Harvard" essay to Yale. Schools know you have many applications out there, and as long as you prove you are a good match, they should be happy to take you.

R.K.

THE APPLICATION PROCESS was very stressful. I was trying to determine my life for the following four years, which is *not* an easy task. One major thing that helped cut back on all the stress was to use a computer that was not at my house. I always went to the counseling center to do college applications, and making the process completely separate from everything else helped me focus and get things done. I would suggest going to a library to fill everything out and write essays.

—*JESSICA*
SARATOGA, CALIFORNIA
UNIVERSITY OF SOUTHERN CALIFORNIA

• • • • • • • •

MY PARENTS WERE VERY INVOLVED with the process. They filled out my paperwork for me and scheduled my visits. I had to learn to be more laid back, because my mom was just as excited and controlling as I was.

—*RACHANN MCKNIGHT*
WALKERTON, INDIANA
INDIANA UNIVERSITY

YOUR SCHOOL'S COLLEGE COUNSELOR

In most high schools, a staff member is assigned to aid with the college application process. They do much more than just mail out forms: College advisers can be a valuable resource. They visit the schools, attend professional conferences, and forge relationships with the admissions staff at the colleges.

Your guidance counselor knows about the admissions process, has a sense of the admissions history of students from your high school and what profile gets in where, and can help you plan your courses and applications. Often, they are in a better position to make the right match than you would be. And they are advocating for you. Remember: You are never bugging the counselor too much!

Additionally, many schools request that a "Counselor Report" be attached to the transcript, so it's really important to get to know your counselor (and have him like you!). At your appointment, make sure to ask:

- What can I tell you about myself?
- How competitive are my grades and courses for the schools I want?
- Are there other schools you would recommend?
- Can I provide you with any info to help you in writing my recommendation?
- What resources do you think I should investigate?

R.K.

PARENTS' PAGES

MY SON WANTED TO HANDLE the entire application process on his own and I knew he was completely capable, but my own fears and insecurities got the best of me. He didn't want to talk about anything or show me any of his essays and completed applications. So to satisfy my curiosity, I went through his things when he was out of town for a weekend. My son actually anticipated this and totally set me up. He left an essay on top of his pile that was titled, "My Mother Is Crazy." It wasn't what he turned in with his applications but he clearly communicated to me how disturbed he was by his overbearing mother.

—*J.M.*
RENO, NEVADA
P ⚏ *UNIVERSITY OF PENNSYLVANIA*

DON'T EVER USE THE PHRASE, "I am sure you will get in." When my daughter was rejected from her top-choice school, she felt like she'd disappointed me.

—*ANONYMOUS*
NEW YORK, NEW YORK
P ⚏ *NEW YORK UNIVERSITY*

PARENTS, SOFTEN 'ADVICE' WITH a short IM or e-mail. It takes the 'in your face' aspect away from the communication.

—*BETH REINGOLD GLUCK*
ATLANTA, GEORGIA
P ⚏ *UNIVERSITY OF SOUTHERN CALIFORNIA*

A PARENT LEARNS A LESSON

MY DAUGHTER WROTE A SURREAL ESSAY to send to her first-choice college. She wanted to be creative, but it came across more like she might be on drugs. Her father and I told her she needed to rework it, but she was quite confident that it showed her uniqueness and sent it off. She wasn't accepted, and I'm pretty sure that the essay was at least part of the reason. Subsequently, she wrote another essay for another college. It was similarly cryptic, and again I told her she needed to rework it. She didn't necessarily agree, but she became unsure of her abilities based on her first experience, so she went along with me. I made major changes and found the process thrilling and gratifying as the essay took shape. I tinkered, nipped and tucked over a period of days, and thought "Hey! Maybe I'll get into college one day!" It became a personal challenge. In retrospect, I felt it was cheating, but more than that, I saw that she felt devalued by what I had done. As tempting as it might be to step in, just give your observations, and stick to objective things like spelling and grammar. Beyond that, you're doing more harm than good.

> —*ANONYMOUS*
> *PENNSYLVANIA*
> *P* ⚑ *TUFTS UNIVERSITY*

* * * * * * * *

WE WENT TO AN OUTSIDE, private-school advisor who was very helpful and offered a lot of information that we were unaware of until our meeting. He was organized and clearly had years of concrete experience to draw from. The advisor from our school was overburdened, impatient, and gave deadlines that kept changing. I never felt she had an overview of the schools—or perhaps more important, strong connections that could be helpful. I think outside help in our case was useful. Get referrals for advisors from other parents.

> —*ANONYMOUS*
> *BROOKLYN, NEW YORK*
> *P* ⚑ *PURCHASE COLLEGE, STATE UNIVERSITY OF NEW YORK*

PARENT OVERBOARD

Here is a hard and fast rule for you. If you break it, you are going too far, doing something wrong, and/or hurting your child. Getting caught doing any of these things can easily sideline your child's application: If you ever find yourself signing your child's name, writing in his voice, speaking in his stead, contacting every alumnus you can find, or contacting the admissions office on a regular basis—you've gone overboard.

PARENTS, WHAT DO YOU STAND FOR?

The college admissions process is a wonderful opportunity to model your family's values and behavior. Do you encourage your daughter to lie in her application (for example, to create a leadership title in her favorite organization to make herself look better)? Do you act as if it is OK to apply to more than one school on a binding early decision basis? Do you encourage your son to play games of flattery just to collect a trophy admission letter, knowing that he will certainly turn down the offer? Do you send in a deposit at more than one school because you and your child simply cannot decide which school he wants, when you are required to commit to one—and only one—school? Do you back out on a school (to which you have sent an admissions deposit) without warning or explanation in the spring or summer before entry?

By doing any of these things, you are telling your child that he should be self-centered and do anything to get ahead in life; that it is OK to be irresponsible to others; and that it is OK to break rules. Your actions in these moments are very powerful. A good parent puts a lot of responsibility on the child to act responsibly—and that is the best tool you can bestow, to prepare and empower him for his college career and beyond.

R.K.

MY PARENTS WERE INVOLVED heavily in the decision-making process. They wanted to know what college I was interested in attending, and visited campuses with me. They stayed hands-off with the actual decision, but if your parents want to get involved, deal with it—*especially* if they are paying for it!

> —*ANGELA MASSINI*
> *CHICAGO, ILLINOIS*
> *BUTLER UNIVERSITY*

• • • • • • • •

WHEN DECIDING WHETHER TO STAY in state or go out of state, I think most parents would prefer their kids to stay in. Mine encouraged more independence, and I think my mom was neat in that way. When I was trying to decide which way to go, my mom told me if I stayed home, my college life would just be an extension of high school. She said nothing would change, and I would always have her there to fall back on. She said if I went away, I would learn to make decisions on my own and be more independent, which is an important step in moving to adulthood.

> —*JANET*
> *LOS ANGELES, CALIFORNIA*
> *UNIVERSITY OF CALIFORNIA, LOS ANGELES*

Expert Advice | IECA⁺ COUNSELOR SURVEY

What is the most important role an independent counselor plays?

Research/developing the college list – 39%
Emotional support/guidance – 0%
Managing parents – 0%
Planning/strategizing – 56%
Editing – 5%

Expert Advice IECA* *COUNSELOR'S CORNER*

AN EDUCATIONAL CONSULTANT – WHY? HOW?

- We are aware of a full range of colleges and we visit campuses on a regular basis to update our knowledge of campuses and of admission practices.
- We provide an informed, objective atmosphere in which to discuss realistically the student's strengths and weaknesses as well as educational objectives, choices, and plans.
- We give students help weighing college selection factors such as cost, location, and curriculum, and we offer advice regarding the nature of the admission process.
- Often students respond to the interest of an expert outside the family circle, and 'catch fire' as they begin to put priority on their own education.

Before hiring an educational consultant, ask these questions:

- How long have you been an educational consultant? ("Tell me about your background in working with students, consulting, and college admissions.")
- How do you keep up with new trends, application changes, laws?
- How often do you visit campuses and meet with admission representatives?
- What professional associations do you belong to? Are you a Certified Educational Planner? (See www.iecaonline.com, www.nacacnet.org and www.aicep.org.)
- How often do you attend professional conferences, workshops, and seminars?
- Do you adhere to the ethical guidelines for private consulting established by the Independent Educational Consultants Association?

- Are all fees involved stated in writing, up front, indicating exactly what services will be provided for those fees?
- Do you ever accept compensation from a college in exchange for referrals? (The answer should be 'no'!)
- Do you guarantee admission to a school or a certain minimum dollar value in scholarship? (The answer should be 'no'!)
- Will you enter data on admission applications, write and/or re-write essays for the student? (The answer should be 'no'!)
- Will you use your personal contacts to get my child into a top college? (The answer should be 'no'! A consultant doesn't get students admitted - they help students demonstrate why they deserve to be admitted.)

—*DIANE GELLER, MA*
CERTIFIED EDUCATIONAL PLANNER, DEFELICE & GELLER, INC.
PRESIDENT, INDEPENDENT EDUCATIONAL CONSULTANTS ASSOC. (IECA)

• • • • • • • • •

HIRING AN INDEPENDENT COUNSELOR is extremely valuable. Most parents hire one to give their child the best chances to get accepted, but this is not why they are worth the investment. The right advisor can provide perspective, insight, wisdom, coaching, mentoring, planning, and support. They can help students ponder majors, careers, and facets of college life they never considered. Without a college coach, parents and students are likely to attend a school based upon reputation and rankings alone and never consider the programs, internships, student life, and spiritual components that provide the foundation for the rest of their life.

When students choose a school because it is a good fit for them, they are more likely to enjoy college, do better in their classes, and get the most out of their experience. College is one of the biggest investments a family will ever make, and the choice of a college will begin a grand journey into the future. Unrealized potential leaves people wondering, "What could I have accomplished?"

—*RACHEL WINSTON*
EDUCATORS WITH A VISION COLLEGE COUNSELING CENTER

THINK NEW THOUGHTS

Just because you haven't heard of a school before doesn't mean it's not the right one for you. Private counselors think of things you wouldn't have thought of. For instance, is a particular school you're interested in, too rural for you? Too urban? They'll discuss interview techniques with you, and how to look at schools, as much as which schools to look at. They can often provide more personal attention; you can talk to them any time, not just during school hours, and you can ask trivial questions. This is definitely a situation where two heads can be better than one.

THE COLLEGE SEARCH did not go without some rocky moments. My mother and I argued about possible majors, cities I could live in, financing my education—you name it. It was hard not to get frustrated. I think when you're 17 or 18 years old, the idea of doing things on your own seems incredibly appealing, and it's easy to forget just how knowledgeable your parents can be. There will be days when you and your parents will fight endlessly and days when those fights subside. Ultimately, it's important to be patient, to make the right choices for *you* and not your parents.

—*Coral A. Schneider*
Cherry Hills Village, Colorado
University of Southern California

• • • • • • • •

TENSIONS WILL ARISE: Be prepared to fight with your parents. It's not exactly enjoyable, but if you know it's coming and understand it's a result of the application stress, it will be easier to handle.

—*Jessica*
Saratoga, California
University of Southern California

The "Mailbox Diet": Fat Envelopes, Thin Envelopes

*A*ll *the studying, filling out of forms, writing of essays, debating with your parents, visiting schools, trading stories with friends, and dreaming—eventually comes down to one moment: You arrive at home, or you log in to your computer, and you have mail from your top-choice school. Did you get in? Will you survive if you didn't? And how about the other schools you applied to? We asked students to relive their moments—good and bad, acceptance and rejection. Take a deep breath and read on.*

THE MOMENT I GOT MY ACCEPTANCE letter, I ran outside to my parents and attempted to read it to them. After the first sentence I started crying and then went inside and danced all over my house. It was an amazing moment.

    —JENNIFER KEYS
    BALTIMORE, MARYLAND
    NEW YORK UNIVERSITY

EVERYTHING HAPPENS FOR A REASON.

—JENNIFER DRAGOVICH
SEMINOLE, FLORIDA
FLORIDA STATE UNIVERSITY

Best Advice and Top Tips

- Accept that this is a time of intense emotion.
- It may be hard to imagine, but things often work out for the best.
- Taking a gap year is a great option; Prince William did it!
- The admissions process is a learning experience.
- It seems like the end, but it's only the beginning.

IT WAS A HUGE BLOW NOT TO GET into Williams, the biggest failure I ever experienced in my life. Even though it's hard to believe at the time, things do happen for a reason. I ultimately think I would have been unhappy if I had gone to Williams. I don't think it was a good fit.

—*ANNE*
PITTSBURGH, PENNSYLVANIA
BROWN UNIVERSITY

• • • • • • • • •

NOW THEY SEND ACCEPTANCE LETTERS through e-mail. I got home from school and saw the e-mail. I read it and I screamed a lot. My parents and I were very happy.

—*HANNAH ASSADI*
SCOTTSDALE, ARIZONA
COLUMBIA COLLEGE

I DIDN'T EVEN KNOW WE HAD GOTTEN MAIL. One evening, my parents came downstairs with the video camera and a FedEx package. I opened it up. Princeton sends out a big "yes" with an exclamation point. So I saw the "Yes!" and I was just beside myself. I didn't care about anything, I was so happy. I think it was a good idea that my parents videotaped it: I would recommend it. I really want to go find that videotape and watch myself.

> —*Dov Kaufmann*
> *Ra'anana, Israel*
> *Princeton University*

• • • • • • • •

BESIDES WAITING FOR THE MAIL OR E-MAIL every day, beware the random phone call! I was notified over the phone and I was in shock. Normally you receive a big package in the mail, so you have time to stand over it, contemplate the implications of what's inside, lock yourself in a windowless room, and then slowly peel open the envelope. I had no such preparation; I just hung up on the man who called to tell me of my acceptance.

> —*Nathaniel Cohen*
> *West Hartford, Connecticut*
> *New York University*

• • • • • • • •

IF WE HAD IT TO DO OVER AGAIN, I would recommend to my son that he apply to a broader range of schools. He applied to seven schools, and while the advice is always to apply to some schools that are a "reach," some that are a "match," and some you know you'll get into, Ben pretty much 'reached' with all of them. That meant he had to deal with rejection, which was hard.

> —*Victoria Johnson*
> *Minneapolis, Minnesota*
> *P Skidmore College*

OTHER SIDE OF THE DESK: YOUR AO PRESENTS YOU TO THE COMMITTEE

Believe it or not, schools try to keep this process fair, from the first application evaluated, to the last. AO's read, evaluate, and advocate for all students equally with the same set of criteria throughout the whole process. There are systems to make sure that each applicant has his or her fair shot, and usually there is more than one reader-evaluator, especially on complicated applications and on ones that will be rejected. A few weeks before decision letters are sent, the "admitted student" statistics are evaluated and then some decisions shift according to the school's needs: Too many students from New York? Pull a few back to the wait-list. Too few engineers for the School of Engineering? Pull a few over from the wait-list to admit. There are students who were admitted to the class but will never know it because they were yanked to the wait-list at the last minute. Those are the hardest phone calls for admissions officers to take after decisions are sent, because they really loved those students.

R.K.

IT WAS THE DAY BEFORE THEY SAID it was going to be announced: Someone called me and told me that decisions were out. I was home alone except for my younger sister. I went online and typed in my password, and a big bulldog, the school mascot, popped up on the screen and said, "Welcome to the Class of 2009." It was probably the happiest I had ever been in one moment. I remember a blur of jumping and yelling. I called my mom; she started crying on the phone, which was awkward because she was in a line of people at the store.

—*ZACHARY KLION*
SUFFERN, NEW YORK
YALE UNIVERSITY

• • • • • • • •

❝ When I found out I didn't get into my first-choice school, I cried, and I never cry. I feel so much better now because it was not the place for me; I think I did end up at the right school. ❞

—*ANONYMOUS*
BEAR CREEK, NORTH CAROLINA
UNIVERSITY OF NORTH CAROLINA AT GREENSBORO

MY FIRST CHOICE WAS THE UNIVERSITY OF FLORIDA, but the school wanted a 3.6 GPA and I only had a 3.5. So I didn't make it in. I was devastated. At first, I said I wasn't going to college. But then I realized that I wanted to get out of my house and live my own life, so I applied to Florida State University. I ended up liking Florida State more than I would have liked UF. Everything happens for a reason.

　　—JENNIFER DRAGOVICH
　　SEMINOLE, FLORIDA
　　FLORIDA STATE UNIVERSITY

· · · · · · · · ·

ONCE YOU GET INTO YOUR COLLEGE, it's really amazing to hit that moment where you realize all your grades and your SAT and your AP's and IB's and tests and quizzes and exams from high school—are all wiped away. Once you get into college, their purpose is served, and you never have to worry about them again. Makes the whole thing seem kind of pointless (almost).

　　—DAVID BERNGARTT
　　RALEIGH, NORTH CAROLINA
　　UNIVERSITY OF NORTH CAROLINA AT CHAPEL HILL

WORTH THE WAIT

More students are being accepted from wait lists at elite schools this year because colleges found it harder to predict how many graduating seniors would join the freshman class. University of Wisconsin-Madison took 800 students from their wait list in 2008, compared with only 6 in 2007.

HARD WORK PAYS OFF

Sarah Lawrence was always my daughter Ellana's first choice, and although Ellana was wait-listed, she was very determined. She worked hard her freshman year at another school and was admitted to Sarah Lawrence for her sophomore year. Now, we both see the admissions process as being a potentially valuable coming-of-age experience. Most students and their families would never choose to spend an additional year waiting to reach last year's goal. Ellana decided to make her freshman year reflect more of her potential. She amazed us with her resolve to regroup, rethink her strategy, reapply, and eventually earn admission to Sarah Lawrence.

I was concerned about the obvious possibility that even an intensive effort might not change anything. But it did. And yet the lesson we both gained had little to do with the usual success lessons. It was worth everything because she realized she would be happy in either situation. Ellana told me that she was happy to have had a chance to work with the teachers and students she met during her freshman year. It was important to know that if she had to remain there, she would have been fine.

—MICKIE MANDEL
RIVERDALE, NEW YORK
P 🏛 SARAH LAWRENCE COLLEGE

THE ACCEPTANCE LETTER CAME two days late, so naturally I was at the edge of my very uncomfortable seat for two long days. Once it came, though, everything fell into place. I realized that it wasn't just one grade or one SAT score or what I did every day after school or even how many community service hours I had. It was the whole package they were looking for, and it was an incredible moment to read that they had chosen me. At that moment, all of your hard work is commended, and you should feel great about what you have just achieved.

—JACKIE ADLAM
MILL VALLEY, CALIFORNIA
COLGATE UNIVERSITY

• • • • • • • •

MY SON DID NOT GET INTO HIS FIRST OR SECOND choice of schools. He was very upset. Rather than let him attend his "safety" school, which he was not at all excited about, I encouraged him to take a year off and do something meaningful. He ended up finding a program called National Outdoor Leadership School (NOLS) and was accepted into its Semester in the Rockies. He is studying under the big sky and stars of Wyoming, Utah, and Colorado for the whole fall semester and is earning 16 college credits. He plans to reapply to college this January for next fall.

—LISA
POUGHKEEPSIE, NEW YORK
P

Three high schools – Collegiate, Brearley, and Chapin – all of them private schools in New York City (which cost almost as much to attend as many private colleges!), got more than 20% of their (small) graduating classes into one of 8 top US colleges.

ASK THE EXPERT

I was not accepted at a college I really love. Can I appeal their decision?

Some schools will revisit your application if you think they made an error or if you have new, compelling information that may change their decision. First, check their website or call the admissions office for information on their appeal process. Next, send a short, concise letter—ideally to the AO who reviewed your application—as soon as possible. This shows genuine interest, concern, and initiative. You may follow up with a short e-mail or call to verify that they received your letter, but do not do more than that. Your letter should synopsize the facts they already have, but focus mainly on the new and compelling reason(s) you have for appealing. Schools will normally not reconsider your application unless there is a real error or substantive change in your application.

J.Y.K.

I WAS WORKING AT A RETAIL STORE at the mall and felt like I had been waiting forever for my acceptance letter to arrive. I took my 15-minute break in the middle of the afternoon, and I noticed that there were five or six phone calls from my parents. I came back to the sales floor a few minutes later, and my mom was standing there, in the middle of the store, with the big red package and a huge smile on her face. We started screaming in the middle of the mall and made absolute fools of ourselves.

—*CORAL A. SCHNEIDER*
 CHERRY HILLS VILLAGE, COLORADO
 UNIVERSITY OF SOUTHERN CALIFORNIA

GAMING THE WAIT-LIST:

DO...

- *Immediately send back the form* you get, indicating that you want to remain on the wait-list.
- *Ask your guidance counselor to call the admissions office* to help show that you are serious.
- *Try to assess whether there are any weaknesses you can address.* Usually there is nothing to do at this point, but you can ask what the AO would like to see.
- *Contact the AO responsible for your application* to tell him that the school is your top choice and that you would definitely come if admitted.
- *Know that this is personal*—the AO knows you and remembers you. He is human, so the more polite and sincere you are, the more you make your case.

DON'T...

- *Call when you are crying or angry.* Make your reasoned case yourself (your parent should not call!); it will be noted in your application, and you should be put on a shorter list.
- *Become a pain.* E-mailing or calling every day can become annoying and cause the AO to dislike you instead of wanting to be your advocate. Send letters and call, but be judicious.
- *Do nothing.* Schools will only offer admission to interested students (they want 100 percent yield from the wait-list) so they will not extend offers to students who have not continued to express interest.
- *Forget that often this is not about you*, but about internal admissions needs. Schools wait-list for a number of statistical reasons, and there are applicants AO's love that they will be dying to take from the wait-list later, if they are able to. Your phone call can help assess this.

R.K.

ONE THING THAT YOU MIGHT NOT HEAR from your parents but is important to know: Do not *freak out* if you don't get into your college of choice. Sure, there might be some school that fits perfectly into your life's grand scheme, but odds are, you're not even gonna stick with whatever plan you have right now. The most important thing about college is – college! It's about going off on your own, meeting new people, getting involved, being responsible for yourself. Whether you go to State or Tech or A&M or whatever, you're going to learn a lot both in and out of the classroom. All the rankings and name recognition of schools sometimes gets people's heads in a spin about which school is a "good" school and which school is not. But college is what you make of it. You should be excited about getting out there on your own, no matter where you're going.

—*DAVID BERNGARTT*
RALEIGH, NORTH CAROLINA
UNIVERSITY OF NORTH CAROLINA AT CHAPEL HILL

• • • • • • • • •

THE DIRECTOR OF ADMISSIONS ACTUALLY called me to say that all my references were in, and she said that my chances looked good. It was several years before I realized how amazing that phone call was—didn't everyone get that phone call? When I got the letter, I did that whole thing about "Oh, it's a thick letter—that's good news." But then I thought, well, maybe they just had a lot of bad things to say. I was frozen for a minute or two. I was so overwhelmed at what I'd gotten myself into.

—*NANCY MITCHELL POEHLMANN*
GRANGER, INDIANA
AGNES SCOTT COLLEGE

Contrary to popular belief, it is my experience that a "Yes!" can come as easily in a small envelope as in a big manila one.

—APRIL
   CHICAGO, ILLINOIS
   PURDUE UNIVERSITY

I FOUND OUT BY E-MAIL. They tell you to check your e-mail at 8 o'clock. I checked and it wasn't there, so I got into the shower, and my little sister went onto my computer and the e-mail had come in. She clicked on it, it opened, and she saw what it was. Right away, she clicked the "minimize" button and ran out of the room. I came back to the computer and was trying to figure out why the screen looked different than when I left it. Then my sister tiptoed in and said, "I think you got your e-mail." So I made everybody leave the room, I shut all the doors and I gave myself a moment to meditate. I opened the e-mail and the first thing I saw was, "We are delighted to inform you …" I was pretty ecstatic. Then I screamed and told my family. Everybody was screaming and shrieking and I thought the house was going to fall down.

—DANA
   LAWRENCE, NEW YORK
   HARVARD UNIVERSITY

• • • • • • • •

AFTER MY EARLY DECISION APPLICATION to Brown was deferred, I applied by regular admission. I wrote the admissions office a letter saying Brown was still my first choice. I think that follow-up letter was really important. I had done some interesting things since I had first applied to school. I also had more grades. Anything you can do to help yourself stand out, is good.

—B.B.
   WYNNEWOOD, PENNSYLVANIA
   BROWN UNIVERSITY

Students from abroad now take up a growing number of spots. At the University of Pennsylvania, 13% of the class of 2011 is made up of international students, up from 11.8% the previous year.

PUBLIC MEANS PUBLIC

WATCH OUT WHEN CONTRIBUTING to websites that discuss colleges. AO's visit those sites, too, to read students' comments and impressions about schools. Sometimes AO's can actually figure out who you are.

Don't take advice from students on any of these sites about "chances for admission." Professionals in the field cannot predict your chances with accuracy, so random students, who know nothing more than your statistics, certainly can't. These forums are full of misinformation about the application process, the committee processes, what games to play, and schools' weaknesses. If you have questions, approach the AO directly!

Also, beware what you say about yourself on Facebook, MySpace, or other social or school websites. Your comments might be read by those considering you for admission; it's happened before. Make sure you show only your best self to the public.

KEEP FOLLOWING UP

MY DAUGHTER WAS WAIT-LISTED at one of the schools she applied to, and then rejected. The college admissions office said they never received her high school transcript, but the high school gave us proof that they sent it. My daughter got copies of everything, walked into the college's admissions office and handed everything over in person. We still had to wait two weeks and it was time to say yes or no to the other schools. They ultimately accepted her, but it was too little too late. The lesson we learned from all of this is how important it is to follow up. Some colleges offer an online checklist where you can see what they received and what they are still waiting for. Keep following up until you get a confirmation that everything has been received.

—*D.G.*
SANTA MONICA, CALIFORNIA
P ⬛ DREXEL UNIVERSITY

HEADS UP: ON TRANSFERRING

You've already heard that you should apply only to schools you'd want to attend. If you're now looking at your acceptances and thinking, "I can always transfer," you're right—but there's a catch. Transferring, from a social point of view, is not a lot of fun.

- Many friendships are forged in freshman year.
- You might get the worst choice in dorms.
- Your course credits may not transfer.
- You have to be more assertive to assimilate.
- You bond more with the college in your first year.
- Your freshman year is the most exciting, when everything is new and no one knows anyone else.

So, do your best to make your first choice the right one!

WHEN I HEARD I GOT IN, I ran out of the admissions office. My mom and I were going crazy. I called my dad and then my boyfriend. I went to my high school theater teacher, who had been helping me. Later, we went out to dinner. We had Chinese food, my favorite takeout.

—*JESSIE SCHOREN*
LINDENWOLD, NEW JERSEY
ROWAN UNIVERSITY

A FEW WORDS ON REJECTION

- Rejection is not personal: You are still a worthwhile person.

- Getting into colleges will continue to be especially difficult for the next several years simply because of the population trends—it's a seller's market right now.

- Even the top schools turn away a certain percentage of the valedictorians and salutatorians who apply each year. As William Fitzsimmons, Dean of Admissions at Harvard College, noted elsewhere in this book, probably 90 percent of the students who apply there would be worthy of admission; the problem is, they simply can't take that many.

- If you are rejected by every school you applied to, fear not: Counselors receive a list of schools that are still accepting students in April. And sometimes they can even get students into a school that has officially stopped accepting applicants.

Expert Advice *FROM THE ADMISSIONS OFFICE*

THE SCENE INSIDE

WHAT IS IT REALLY LIKE IN YOUR ADMISSIONS OFFICE DURING READING SEASON?

IN OUR OFFICE, READING SEASON IS a lot like winter hibernation! Admissions officers hunker down in their offices or homes and read applications, sometimes very late into the night and through the weekends. We take reading breaks by knocking on each other's office doors to share our enthusiasm for applicants that we think are special — the ones that made us perk up and take notice when it's late at night and we're still surrounded by piles and piles of folders.

> —*JACINDA OJEDA*
> *REGIONAL DIRECTOR OF ADMISSIONS*
> *UNIVERSITY OF PENNSYLVANIA*

• • • • • • • • •

INTENSE . . . and tiring.

> —*DANIEL J. SARACINO*
> *ASSISTANT PROVOST FOR ENROLLMENT*
> *UNIVERSITY OF NOTRE DAME*

• • • • • • • • •

HIGH ENERGY, busy and exciting!

> —*TED SPENCER*
> *ASSOCIATE VICE PROVOST AND EXECUTIVE DIRECTOR OF UNDERGRADUATE ADMISSIONS*
> *UNIVERSITY OF MICHIGAN-ANN ARBOR*

• • • • • • • • •

IT'S VERY, VERY QUIET yet there is a lot of organized movement for the first half of reading season. College admissions offices are often well-oiled machines. For the second half, there is a lot of discussion and debate.

> —*MARK BUTT*
> *SENIOR ASSISTANT DIRECTOR OF ADMISSIONS*
> *JOHNS HOPKINS UNIVERSITY*

AS TO BE EXPECTED, busy with reviewing applications and communicating with students via e-mail or by phone.

—CHRIS LUCIER
VICE PRESIDENT FOR ENROLLMENT MANAGEMENT
UNIVERSITY OF VERMONT

• • • • • • • • •

QUIET. Most admissions officers find that they do their best application reading away from the distractions of the office.

—CHRISTOPH GUTTENTAG
DEAN OF UNDERGRADUATE ADMISSIONS
DUKE UNIVERSITY

• • • • • • • • •

WE REVIEW BY COMMITTEE, and most decisions end up being relatively easy to make. About 15-20% of the decisions are hotly debated, and in most of those cases there is a consensus on the final decision. However, there are always a handful of decisions that could have gone either way, but that is a very small number. Overall, the review process is an exciting and enjoyable time for our office.

—TONY BANKSTON
DEAN OF ADMISSIONS
ILLINOIS WESLEYAN UNIVERSITY

• • • • • • • • •

QUIETER than usual.

—MATS LEMBERGER
ASSISTANT DIRECTOR OF ADMISSIONS
DARTMOUTH COLLEGE

• • • • • • • • •

THE ADMISSIONS OFFICE IS A STRESSFUL PLACE during reading season. Each of our readers and file evaluators takes their job seriously, and we are reading files looking for the reason to ADMIT you. This is a huge responsibility that we take extremely seriously. Your interest in our institution is not something we take for granted, so we are honored you are considering our school. The least we can do is give your file a thorough and careful evaluation before we send you our decision.

—DOUGLAS L. CHRISTIANSEN, PH.D.
ASSOCIATE PROVOST FOR ENROLLMENT AND DEAN OF ADMISSIONS
VANDERBILT UNIVERSITY

I got turned down from five colleges before I found one that would have me. Hey, it happens to the best of us!

—*TRINA COOKE*
STRUTHERS, OHIO

IF YOU DON'T GET ACCEPTED at first, don't waste any time crying. I wasn't accepted the first time I applied to UCLA. When I first received the bad news, I went into hibernation. Then I realized that everything happens for a reason, and there was no point in crying over something I had no control over. Plus, by staying in my room, I was missing out on other things in life.

—*ANONYMOUS*
LOS ANGELES, CALIFORNIA
UNIVERSITY OF CALIFORNIA, LOS ANGELES

• • • • • • • • •

BECAUSE MY GRADES WERE SO-SO, Purdue sent me a "Get grades of B or better this semester and we'll let you in" letter. Apparently, all I needed was a little motivation to get my grades up. I was really excited and proud of myself once I got the acceptance letter, partially because I wanted to go, but mostly because I wasn't sure what I would do if I didn't get in.

—*APRIL*
CHICAGO, ILLINOIS
PURDUE UNIVERSITY

• • • • • • • • •

IT WAS VERY STRESSFUL TO WAIT to hear from schools, thinking about the uncertainty of where I was going to be the next year. Also, knowing I was competing with my friends proved to be stressful when the results came in, especially when I got accepted in places they didn't. I thought the stress would end after we got the acceptance letters back, but it didn't. It's helpful that most people around you are going through the same thing, so you're stressing together.

—*B.B.*
WYNNEWOOD, PENNSYLVANIA
BROWN UNIVERSITY

LIKE PULLING TEETH

I was at the dentist having wisdom tooth surgery. I was in the recovery room and my brother called to tell me that I had received a letter from my top school. I said, "If you open it, I will kill you." What came out was "Iurgh oou opfeen ish, Ih vielll kihs ouu." He somehow understood me and replied that he wouldn't, but that it did not matter anyway because he already knew what the decision was. I mumbled at him, asking if it was because the envelope was thick or thin. He said no, and then proceeded to read these words off of the outside of the envelope: "Congratulations, here is your big fat envelope." I started freaking out, which involved a lot of drool and giddy laughter. It was amazing. When I got home and opened the letter, I found out that I had received a full scholarship as well, and the slobbering started anew. It was a fantastic day. And then I realized that I was in terrible pain and I had four holes in my mouth.

—MAX MALON MALLORY
NEW YORK, NEW YORK
SARAH LAWRENCE COLLEGE

EMORY HAS A PROGRAM FOR MINORITIES – they let you stay on campus and go to class to see if you like the school. That really persuaded me. Look for a community that is open and makes you feel welcome.

—DAMILOLA OSUNSANYA
MIRAMAR, FLORIDA
EMORY UNIVERSITY

PARENTS' PAGES

FROM THE BEGINNING, OUR DAUGHTER WANTED to go to University of Florida. She did not get in. That was extremely disappointing, for her as well as for us. The parents are part of the process. We drove five hours to appeal the university's decision. People told us, "You're wasting your time." But we went, and we spoke to people at the school admissions office. Our daughter had a meeting with them and still did not get into the school. It was very hard. We gave her a lot of encouragement and support. We also had to tell her that you don't always get what you want in life and you need to learn how to make it work. So she did a year at junior college. After that, she transferred to Boston University. She did well there but she still wanted to go to UF. She applied and got in. She ultimately got what she wanted.

> —MARLA
> BOCA RATON, FLORIDA
> P ⌂ UNIVERSITY OF FLORIDA; FLORIDA STATE UNIVERSITY

• • • • • • • • •

AFTER MY DAUGHTER AND HER FRIENDS submitted their last applications, they all got together for a bonfire and burned everything related to SAT prep, college brochures, etc. They thought it would be a good way for them to ease their suffering during that long waiting period for acceptance letters.

> —KAREN
> SCOTTSDALE, ARIZONA
> P ⌂ UNIVERSITY OF ARIZONA

• • • • • • • • •

I THINK THE HARDEST PART of a deferral and a rejected application is the feelings they drum up—like being last to be picked for a game, or not being asked to a dance or party. So you have to help them to put those "devastated" feelings aside, and do things that will make them feel successful.

> —TERRY
> IRVINE, CALIFORNIA
> P ⌂ MOUNT HOLYOKE COLLEGE

WHEN YOU'RE WAITING TO HEAR BACK from colleges via e-mail, be sure to check your bulk mail or spam mailbox from time to time. Sometimes the college messages end up in the junk mail file.

> —*V.A.*
> *AUSTIN, TEXAS*
> *P ⌂ RICE UNIVERSITY; UNIVERSITY OF TEXAS, AUSTIN*

• • • • • • • •

I SPENT ABOUT $300 FOR COLLEGE TOURS, $100 for two ACT tests, $60 for an ACT prep class, $200 for college application fees, $5 on stamps for college applications, about $60 dollars in ink to print out draft after draft of college entrance essays, $20 in bus fare to attend college open houses, $150 on long-distance calls to colleges to ask about 30 minutes worth of questions every other day, $100 worth of transcripts – and about $500 on clothes and entertainment to console her when she didn't get into her first-choice school.

> —*KEVIN ITSON*
> *CHICAGO, ILLINOIS*
> *P ⌂ UNIVERSITY OF ILLINOIS AT URBANA-CHAMPAIGN*

• • • • • • • •

WHEN MY DAUGHTER DIDN'T GET INTO her top choice, I had her make a list of three things that her top school had to offer. Then I had her write down three negatives regarding her top choice. Ultimately, we were able to find another school with all of the positive attributes she was seeking and only one of the negatives.

> —*ANONYMOUS*
> *CHICAGO, ILLINOIS*
> *P ⌂ BOSTON UNIVERSITY; DUKE UNIVERSITY*

• • • • • • • •

EVEN IF YOU BELIEVE WITHOUT A DOUBT that your child will get into his or her first-choice school, make sure you build up the others, too. My daughter really wanted to get into Stanford, but she didn't. She was really disappointed, partly because I had contributed to making her think that it was more important than it really was. I talked about it all of the time. We gave her the feeling that she would be failing if she didn't get in.

> —*KAREN*
> *TRUCKEE, CALIFORNIA*
> *P ⌂ UNIVERSITY OF CALIFORNIA, BERKELEY*

MY FIRST DAUGHTER WAS A STRONG STUDENT and an athlete, and decided to apply early decision to a top college. She was encouraged by the coach, who thought she was a good fit for the school. Despite her excellent credentials, she was deferred. She found out that a C+ in AP Calculus the first quarter of her senior year was the reason. Since she had her heart set on this school, she worked very hard in her calculus course and pulled up her grade. She then wrote a heartfelt letter to the Dean of Admissions, telling him about her struggle with calculus and how his college was still her first choice. In the end she was admitted to five highly selective colleges, including the school that deferred her. I think the letter she wrote definitely helped.

—*LUCY RUMACK*
BROOKLYN, NEW YORK
P ✦ *SWARTHMORE COLLEGE*

BE CONSERVATIVE

One of the best ways to prepare for decision time is to always talk conservatively about the application process. As chances of admission become less and less predictable, avoiding calling any school a 'shoo-in' will help—imagine what happens if your child is rejected from that sure thing. Keep telling yourself and him—and believe it—that this process can be unpredictable. Putting all your hopes and dreams into any one school can be dangerous. Wish for the best, brace for the worst, and you will survive the storm.

R.K.

ON REJECTION – FOR PARENTS

Your child got the thin envelope—rejected from her dream school—and your hopes are dashed, too. How will you react? Rejection is like a grieving process; there are stages to go through and your strength and health at the end depends on how you progress through these stages of "mourning."

SADNESS/DISAPPOINTMENT: Your heart breaks, knowing that your child will not be on her dream campus in the fall.

ANGER: You think, "How could they not have taken my amazing child?"

LETTING GO: You can finally say, "This was not the place for my child. There are other places where she was admitted, and where she will be happy; I want to help her find her place."

Through the difficult first stages, you are most likely to upset your children further by the way you react. Here are a few critical mistakes you should be sure to avoid, so that your child can move on:

MISTAKE #1: Calling admissions officers and yelling at them in your child's presence. An aggressive, angry conversation will achieve nothing (aside from annoying the admissions officer), and it only models poor sportsmanship. This is neither the first nor the last disappointment you will have in your lives. If your child really needs closure and has to ask why, she can make a calm, rational, investigatory phone call—by herself—to the admissions office.

MISTAKE #2: Encouraging your child to open a new campaign for admission. Sending letters and e-mails, having everyone you know contact every office on campus, and returning to the admissions office to fight in person will only waste your child's time and emotional energy and prevent you from moving on to better choices. Admissions decisions are rarely, if ever, reversed. Focus your energies on real possibilities.

R.K.

WHEN I GOT REJECTED, it was probably one of the worst times in my life. I got six rejections in a row. It was horrible. I'm a white male from Long Island; there wasn't anything to distinguish me. Being upset is all right, but get some perspective that this isn't the last step. The thing that got me through was knowing that this was not the end of the process. You can check out transfer programs to reassure yourself that this isn't the last go.

—CONOR KENNEDY
WHITESTONE, NEW YORK
BROWN UNIVERSITY

• • • • • • • •

I APPLIED EARLY TO MY NUMBER one school and I received my acceptance in early January. While it was extremely exciting, I was also really careful in sharing it with my friends. Everyone who's applying to schools has high anxiety about being accepted or rejected, and it's easy to feel more stress because of your friends. The best way to share it is to do so modestly, while also being really positive and supportive of friends who may not have heard or are dealing with rejection.

—CASEY HEERMANS
DECATUR, GEORGIA
UNIVERSITY OF NORTH CAROLINA AT CHAPEL HILL

HARD-VARD

Harvard's overall admission rate for the 2012 class was 7.1 percent – the lowest of any Ivy League school, and the lowest in Harvard's 370-year history. 1,948 applicants were admitted out of a pool of 27,462 applications.

Decisions, Decisions: Picking the 'Right' School for You

*C*ongratulations! You got into college! Actually, several colleges. Now you've got to choose the place where you'll spend at least four years of your life; set the success standard for your pending career; and possibly meet that special someone or lifelong friend. The good news is that the decision is up to you; the bad news also is that it's up to you! Read on to discover how others made their final choices.

BE TRUE TO YOURSELF ABOUT what you want to get out of school. Don't fool yourself about being someone you're not. Don't base your choice on what other people are doing.

> —*BETH MAYEROWITZ*
> *NEW YORK, NEW YORK*
> *UNIVERSITY OF WISCONSIN*

DO YOU WANT TO GO TO A SCHOOL WHERE YOU KNOW PEOPLE OR WHERE YOU'LL START TOTALLY FRESH?

> —*JOSH TIZEL*
> *TORONTO, ONTARIO*
> *YORK UNIVERSITY*

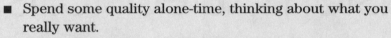

HEAD**LINES**
Best Advice and Top Tips

- Spend some quality alone-time, thinking about what you really want.
- Weigh all the factors: distance, cost, size, curriculum, climate, atmosphere.
- Yes, it can be stressful, but everyone else is going through it too.
- No double-depositing—make a grownup choice and stick to it.
- Remember: It's how you spend your time in college, more than the school itself, that shapes your future.

I THOUGHT I KNEW EXACTLY where I wanted to go, what I wanted to major in, all the little details. But once I got accepted and had to make a choice, I was a wreck, knowing that this would be one of the biggest decisions of my life. Spend some time alone thinking about what *you* want, not what your friends or parents want.

—SHEILA CRAWFORD
CARY, NORTH CAROLINA
NORTH CAROLINA STATE UNIVERSIRY

• • • • • • • •

I'M ORIGINALLY FROM TEXAS and I just wanted to get out for a while. I hadn't been to Colorado before, so that's where I decided to go.

—TRENT
GRAPEVINE, TEXAS
UNIVERSITY OF COLORADO

THE EARLIER YOU CHOOSE A SCHOOL, the more options you have open to you when you try to find a place to live. I waited until almost the last minute to submit my application. Once I finally received my acceptance letter, I had to find an apartment and a job, pack, and move in about three weeks' time. It was a lot of unnecessary stress that easily could have been avoided!

> —*ASHLEY YOW*
> *SAN ANTONIO, TEXAS*
> *TEXAS STATE UNIVERSITY*

"No school makes you happy or smart. You have to do that on your own, so relax about making the choice. What school you get into is not that big a deal."

> —*BETH REINGOLD GLUCK*
> *ATLANTA, GEORGIA*
> *P UNIVERSITY OF SOUTHERN CALIFORNIA*

KNOWING WHAT YOU'RE GOING TO BE "when you grow up" should factor into your decision of which school to attend. I wanted to be a veterinarian, so I chose a college that has a vet school. This school has pre-vet in undergrad, so I took biomedical science and started working towards this career.

> —*JILL*
> *TORONTO, ONTARIO*

REMEMBER THAT YOU'RE THE ONLY PERSON who knows yourself and what you want. The other day, I told my brother, who is applying to college, that he is the only one who knows what he wants. He's getting a lot of information from everyone, including me, and he should filter it. Ultimately, he's the one making the decision.

—*ANASTASIA*
BALTIMORE, MARYLAND
YALE UNIVERSITY

. . . .

BE ABSOLUTELY SURE IT'S WHERE you want to go. It's a hard decision to take back. The first college I went to, Ithaca, there were too many pressures. It was too far away. It didn't have a major I could live with. Now I'm transferring to Rutgers next year. It's kind of absurd.

—*WILLIAM ALVAREZ*
LYNDHURST, NEW JERSEY
LA GUARDIA COLLEGE

. . . .

I KNEW THAT UNC WOULD BE ABLE to offer both academics and a lively social scene—the balance was important to me.

—*JILLIAN NADELL*
GREENSBORO, NORTH CAROLINA
UNIVERSITY OF NORTH CAROLINA

. . . .

I WAS ACCEPTED TO DEPAUL, Tennessee, and Houston. I decided on Tennessee because it was in a completely new place where I didn't know anybody. Houston was a little too far away and DePaul was very expensive, especially since it's in Chicago. I liked Knoxville and how it's centered around the campus.

—*SCOTT COOLBAUGH*
KNOXVILLE, TENNESSEE
UNIVERSITY OF TENNESSEE

Easy decision: I went to school where my older sister went to school!

—*JANNA HAROWITZ*
VANCOUVER, BRITISH COLUMBIA
McGILL UNIVERSITY

PARENTS' PAGE

OUR DAUGHTER THOUGHT FROM THE BEGINNING that she wanted a big school in a reasonably big city, but there was a smaller school in Portland, Oregon, that she was interested in. She was accepted and flew out there from Minneapolis by herself, visited the college on her own, and stayed in a dorm. It was an expensive trip, but I'm glad she went because she realized that even though she really liked Portland, the school wasn't big enough to sustain her for four years. She realized that she was right all along: that she wanted to go to a big school because of all the things it could offer. She ended up at the University of Michigan and has been very happy there.

> —*M.B.*
> *MINNEAPOLIS, MINNESOTA*
> *P* 🏫 *UNIVERSITY OF MICHIGAN*

• • • • • • • • •

LOOK VERY CAREFULLY AT ANY PARTICULAR NEEDS your children might have. If they're reluctant to go to school or lack independence, consider all of that in choosing a school, whether it's large, small, close to home. Don't lock yourself in to thinking it has to be four years of nothing but school. You can consider combining work and school. I think the most important thing to impress upon children going to school is that there's no single way to do it. Don't try to rush it if it needs to be taken slowly.

> —*CINDY*
> *HERNDON, VIRGINIA*
> *P* 🏫 *GEORGE MASON UNIVERSITY*

WE LIKE YOU, BUT ...

I applied to the University of Chicago and Brown. I got an acceptance to the University of Chicago in the fall, but became less enthused about it once I got in. Then Brown did this incredibly weird thing: it admitted me the year after my class, which I've never heard of, but it exists. The school sent me a letter in July that said, "Look, we admitted you in the class for the year behind you." That was kind of shocking, especially since it was in an envelope that said, "Congratulations!" The condition was that I couldn't matriculate anywhere else and I couldn't take classes at Brown even as a shadowy semi-student. I just had to *not* be in college for a year. So I went to the University of Chicago.

—BOBBY
MAPLEWOOD, NEW JERSEY
UNIVERSITY OF CHICAGO

Consider

THE COLLEGE APPLICATION PROCESS often exaggerates the actual importance of where you go to college. More important than *where* you go to college is whether you excel when you are there. In other words, a high average at an average school is almost always better then an *average* average at a great school. Always keep that in mind.

—NATHANIEL COHEN
WEST HARTFORD, CONNECTICUT
NEW YORK UNIVERSITY

. . . .

ASK FOR ADVICE. There was a guy I knew who was a great actor, who recommended the Theatre Program at the University of Toronto, so I trusted his suggestion.

—MICHAEL ALBERT PAOLI
TORONTO, ONTARIO
UNIVERSITY OF TORONTO

I APPLIED AND GOT ACCEPTED to so many schools that the final decision killed me. I can't tell you how many times I walked out to my mailbox ready to send my letter of intent to my chosen school, only to bring it right back in the house to change my mind. I think I practiced this ritual at least five times during the few weeks I had to make my final decision.

—JANET
LOS ANGELES, CALIFORNIA
UNIVERSITY OF CALIFORNIA, LOS ANGELES

. . . .

" Think really carefully about what size you want your college to be. I only looked at schools of 1,500 or less, and that ended up being smaller than I realized. You can get tired of seeing the same faces pretty quickly. "

—KAYLEIGH SHEBS
AMBRIDGE, PENNSYLVANIA
AGNES SCOTT COLLEGE

. . . .

I HAD TO CHOOSE BETWEEN Rutgers University and NYU. Because Rutgers and NYU were the same-caliber schools, my parents and I chose Rutgers because it was more affordable. But if I had to do it over, I would have attended NYU. I love New York City!

—LISA GREENBAUM
NEW YORK, NEW YORK
RUTGERS UNIVERSITY

MAKE SURE THAT YOU RESEARCH YOUR MAJOR and your potential career path. You want to go to a school that offers both the curriculum and the experience that you are looking for. Ask the school about student life, and whether you can speak with some students and visit some student groups. Also, get an outline of the courses that you will be taking; it's important that the major you want has a wide variety of courses to take.

—*ANDREW J. BURKE*
CINCINNATI, OHIO
UNIVERSITY OF CINCINNATI

MY UNIVERSITY IS A VERY LAID-BACK and friendly school. It's easy to fit in with people and it's not too challenging academically. But it is three girls to one guy, so it isn't optimal for dating. You should look at the ratios when you're applying if you're interested in meeting someone!

—*JILL*
TORONTO, ONTARIO

ONCE YOU ARE ADMITTED TO COLLEGE, don't try to meet your future classmates on the "___ College Class of ___" website. Not cool. Your true friends you will meet in person at college.

—*PAUL*
MIDDLEBURY, VERMONT
MIDDLEBURY COLLEGE

AND A SOPHOMORE GETS ...?

Abilene Christian University in Texas is part of a new movement of colleges giving incoming freshmen iPhones and iPods. The school bought more than 600 iPhones and 300 iPods for students entering this fall.

ASK THE EXPERT

This school is a good fit academically, but will I have fun there?

You've succeeded; they've accepted you! Now, you need to change gears and think more critically about why the school is right for *you*. You've done all of your analytical work for the moment. Now, rely on those instincts! Spend time on campus; talk with current students. Do whatever you can to get directly to the source (you're reading this book, right?). Visualize yourself as a student on campus. Stand in the middle of campus and watch; walk through the halls when class gets out; get a cup of coffee at the student union café; take a book to the main library and hang out for a while.

Take advantage of the school visit programs not just as a passive listener. Don't be shy—introduce yourself to a group in the dining area. Pull your tour guide aside. Ask that guy in the dorm you visit what you want to know. If you don't visit, find a friend of a friend who goes to that school. Ask your school counselor if he can put you in touch with a recent grad. Most of all, embrace the fact that this is now a decision you make as much with your heart as with your head. Rely on your gut—you can't lose!

J.Y.K.

IT WAS REALLY IMPORTANT FOR ME to choose a school with an active Jewish community so that I wouldn't have to deal with finding my niche religiously, knowing that college is a tough transition anyway. I was also struggling with going to a huge school after going to a small private school for my whole life, but I've found that wherever you go to school, big or small, a person will be faced with this challenge.

—*ELANA BROWNSTEIN*
BALTIMORE, MARYLAND
UNIVERSITY OF MARYLAND, COLLEGE PARK

PARENTS' PAGES

SPREADSHEETS ARE WONDERFUL TOOLS when it comes to comparing schools, financial awards, tuition/room/board, travel expenses, and pros and cons. The selection process is much easier when you see the information laid out side by side. Our son set up a spreadsheet with all of the schools he had applied to. As applications were sent out and letters of acceptance came in, he made notes of the school, how long it took for a response, the scholarship offers, unusual expenses that are often overlooked (storage, travel, etc.), and notations about the visit. With this process, he trimmed down a list of seven schools one by one until he came to his final decision.

> —*ANONYMOUS*
> *KENT, WASHINGTON*
> *P* *WASHINGTON STATE UNIVERSITY;*
> *UNIVERSITY OF WASHINGTON*

· · · · · · · · ·

MY DAUGHTER'S CHOICE CAME DOWN to two state schools. I thought that would be the easy part, but it was the worst part of all. Her decision came down to one nagging question: "Do I want to go far away, or do I want to stay nearby?" She kept going back and forth. One school was five hours away, while another was one hour away. There were so many reasons to stay: be closer to family and friends; be near the big city; less travel. She also had a thousand reasons to be far away: a new environment; warmer weather; nice road trips; closer to another state. It just went on and on, and I thought I was going to die of Repeated Question Syndrome. One month before school started, my indecisive daughter picked the school that was closer to home. That's the school I thought I wanted, too—until she came home every weekend and wanted her clothes washed.

> —*KEVIN ITSON*
> *CHICAGO, ILLINOIS*
> *P* *UNIVERSITY OF ILLINOIS AT URBANA-CHAMPAIGN*

MAKING THE FINAL DECISION

There are some rational tools you can use to evaluate your choices:

ATMOSPHERE: First and foremost, you are seeking to place your child where he will be happy and therefore succeed. Academically, you want to choose the school offering the necessary majors, as well as a range of academic strengths, in case – as so often happens – he wants to change his mind. Your child may want a place where he is among the smartest, or a place where he is challenged by his peers and may have to work harder; achieving academically will be easier in the right classroom. The school should also be a match for your child's personality. For example, if your child likes crowds, don't push the tiny suburban or rural school. Your child needs a core group like himself and the comfort to feel free to express himself.

COST: After weighing the pros and cons of your financial packages, and/or the pros and cons of the state school at the lower cost versus the private school, choose a school which you will be able to afford without making such a sacrifice that it hurts too much and adds too much pressure on both you and your child.

LOGISTICS: Consider what you value as a family in location and communication patterns. How far away is the school? Is it OK to fly between your home and the college? Does your child need to be close to home and want to come home on weekends? What is the comfortable distance you want between yourselves: a car ride, a phone call, or a couple of time zones away? Be clear about this factor—it can color the whole family's experience for four (or more) years.

SOMETIMES FINANCES HELP YOU DECIDE. I originally applied to Seton Hall because it was in New Jersey, and I was accepted. But when the bill came, it was obvious I couldn't afford it. I took a year off and applied to state schools that I could afford. My sister was dating some guy who went to Rowan, so I went with her to check it out and liked it. It was affordable, and the school accepted me.

—JAMIE HARGRAVE
NUTLEY, NEW JERSEY
ROWAN UNIVERSITY

• • • • • • • •

I WAS RECRUITED BY A NUMBER OF SCHOOLS in my state and out of state, but I only applied to one and got in. The reason for my selection: This school was five blocks from my house, and none of the other schools was willing to move their campuses down the block from me.

—LINDSEY MORRISON GRANT
PORTLAND, OREGON
CONCORDIA UNIVERSITY

• • • • • • • •

GO FOR ENVIRONMENT; go to a school in a place where you'd go to visit.

—IAIN BURNETT
REDWOOD CITY, CALIFORNIA
UNIVERSITY OF CALIFORNIA, SANTA BARBARA

RED OR BLUE?

Hillsdale College in Hillsdale, Michigan, was recently ranked America's most conservative college. Mills College in Oakland, California, was ranked the most liberal.

I BASED MY DECISION ON THE TWO FACTORS that, in hindsight, are probably *least* important: cost and location. If you are going to make the huge commitment of going to college, you shouldn't worry about those things. They are minor details.

—*BRENDA PENDLETON*
NEWARK, DELAWARE
UNIVERSITY OF DELAWARE

. . . .

"My dad wanted me to settle for a school. Don't settle unless you have to. It's your education, so be assertive. If you know you want a school near the ocean and you live in the Midwest, push for the ocean. Otherwise, you're not going to be happy."

—*KATHRYN*
PHILADELPHIA, PENNSYLVANIA
SARAH LAWRENCE COLLEGE

. . . .

IT MAY SEEM SILLY when you're applying for college to think of college graduation, but I wish I'd had that mind-set. If you go to school in a small town, for example, you may not get big firms from New York heading your way to recruit.

—*AMANDA NELSON*
NEW YORK, NEW YORK
UNIVERSITY OF WISCONSIN-MADISON

Consider

OTHER SIDE OF THE DESK: THE JOB'S NOT OVER

Decisions are out, and now you will see the marketing machine back in action. AO's and current students, as well as the academic areas of the college, will be in touch to show you the reasons you should attend their college, and the schools run visiting programs to work on yield. A little secret: AO's often remember you, your story, and your application details well, but when you visit, the receptionist will let the AO know you are there and the AO sometimes quickly brushes up on you by looking at his notes in your application. It is a bit of a game, but it is also a way to have the most informed conversation possible with you.

BE REALISTIC. If you are not the most studious person, don't go to an extremely rigorous school. At the same time, if you have enough potential in your chosen field, opt for a school that will help you to be the best you can be in your field. And absolutely do not base your decision on location!

—*COURTNEY HEILMAN*
BOSTON, MASSACHUSETTS

• • • • • • • •

BE SELECTIVE DURING THE APPLICATION PROCESS. My parents told me to do as much as I could do to narrow my choices so I could focus attention on fewer schools. They said that when you get in, you'll know it's where you want to go. Try to avoid getting into 20 schools. Other people applying to college might get screwed if you apply to a school you don't even want to go to and you get accepted and take their place.

—*BRIAN ROSEN*
NEW YORK, NEW YORK
PRINCETON UNIVERSITY

MY PARENTS HAD SOME STRINGENT IDEAS on which schools were the best for me. I got them to consider other schools by doing research and selling them on things like low student-teacher ratio, the percentage of high SAT's, and the like. If you're trying to convince your parents to let you go to a school other than the one they prefer, I recommend this tactic: Sell, sell, sell!

> —*NANCY MITCHELL POEHLMANN*
> *GRANGER, INDIANA*
> *AGNES SCOTT COLLEGE*

. . . .

THE FIRST THING, OTHER THAN MONEY, that you should worry about is which school is best in the field that you want to get into. I want to get into early childhood education, and my school is one of the best schools in the area for that.

> —*RACHEL LYNCH*
> *FREDERICK, MARYLAND*
> *COPPIN STATE UNIVERSITY*

. . . .

I WAS NERVOUS THAT I KNEW TOO MANY PEOPLE at Maryland. It's my state school and a very popular choice for people from my high school, so I was afraid I wouldn't meet new people. I was so wrong. I have stayed close with some of my friends from high school who are in college with me, but I've met tons of amazing new people in college, through social activities, classes, and even through friends from high school. It has also been nice to see familiar faces when walking around campus.

> —*ELANA BROWNSTEIN*
> *BALTIMORE, MARYLAND*
> *UNIVERSITY OF MARYLAND, COLLEGE PARK*

Pick a school that is not beyond your abilities. Getting good grades from a good school rather than poor grades from a top-tier school puts you in good standing for the future.

—*J.K.D.*
PITTSBURGH, PENNSYLVANIA
P KENT STATE UNIVERSITY

OTHER SIDE OF THE DESK: JUST DON'T DO IT

Playing games with colleges is unethical. Period. Sending in a deposit and your signature reserving your place in the class is a commitment (even if it is not legally binding) and you are expected to honor it. Putting down a deposit at two or more schools is not allowed, and if colleges find out, *both* schools will rescind your admission out of respect for each other. Colleges play fair with each other and will not fight for you if you do this. College deans are long-time colleagues and friends.

To withdraw because you have been accepted off the wait-list at another school, or because an unforeseen major family crisis has occurred, is fine. To withdraw because you simply want a different school is unethical. Schools do plan for a "summer melt"—a certain number of students who will ultimately withdraw—but to fool around with deposits takes away the opportunity for students who really want to be at these schools. Also, you are becoming an adult, responsible for making decisions. It is not ethical to double-deposit just because you simply cannot make up your mind. Grow up and decide.

R.K.

I WAS RECRUITED AS A FOOTBALL PLAYER. When it came down to it, I had to choose between Yale, Harvard, Brown, and a few other places. Even though you're going to be a student-athlete, you're going to be spending the majority of your time in your room or with friends going out to eat. You spend time with people in your dorm and in classes. Go to classes and stay with a student. Visit everywhere on campus to help you make your decision.

> —MATTHEW BAKER
> SILVER SPRING, MARYLAND
> YALE UNIVERSITY

• • • • • • • •

I GOT LUCKY - my close friends and peer group from classes applied to similar schools and had similar successes. I think everyone's so high-stress at that time that they walk around on eggshells, discussing acceptances and rejections, but it helps to bear in mind that there are a lot of great experiences to be had and great educations to get at lots of schools. Ultimately, you'll end up where you need to be.

> —ANU PARVATIYAR
> ATLANTA, GEORGIA
> GEORGIA INSTITUTE OF TECHNOLOGY

'CHAT'

Online chat sessions are often scheduled on college websites near acceptance deadlines. These sessions provide a good opportunity to ask honest questions and get straight answers. And if you receive a phone call from a student representative, take the call and take advantage of the opportunity; ask about everything you want to know.

OTHER SCHOOLS SENT ME A FORM acceptance letter, but Oakland sent me holiday cards when I got in. In November they sent me a Thanksgiving card, then holiday and New Year's cards, personally written by someone in the admissions office. I liked that. It made me feel really special. Before, I thought I was a mediocre student. With the cards, I felt like someone wanted me.

—*MINEHAHA FORMAN*
SAN ANTONIO VILLAGE, BELIZE
OAKLAND UNIVERSITY

• • • • • • • •

THERE WERE OTHER SCHOOLS that would have taken me right after high school, but I wanted to go to Youngstown State. So I went to community college for two semesters and applied again. This time they accepted me. Pick the school that is right for you and then don't take 'no' for an answer. Even if it takes a little longer to get in, you'll have your whole life to reap the rewards of your patience.

—*DAN MONTOYA*
YOUNGSTOWN, OHIO
YOUNGSTOWN STATE UNIVERSITY

TRI-STATE = THREE TIMES THE PARTIES!

Tri-State University in Angola, Indiana, is ranked America's top party school in one survey—42 percent of surveyed Tri-State students said they party three to five nights per week.

INTERACT WITH SCHOOLS – CONTACT STUDENTS

Look on schools' admissions websites for some way to contact current students. If there is no formal program, write to the admissions officer responsible for your area of the country and ask if he can put a current student in touch with you. Talking to ANY student is better than nothing, so even if you are matched with someone completely different from you, you can still learn something. Some suggested questions:

- What do students do for fun during the week and on weekends?
- Is there a Greek system, and do most students rush?
- What are some of the fun traditions?
- What do the students like most—and least—about the school?
- What's day-to-day life like? Are the students stressed out? Always partying?
- Are there other students like you (ethnically, religiously, politically, etc.)?

R.K.

ACADEMICS ARE IMPORTANT, but I considered the whole picture when I was making my decision. While I needed a place to grow academically, I would also be growing socially, physically, emotionally, and spiritually. Determine what your values are, and find an institution that complements your values.

—DAVID
MUNCIE, INDIANA
ANDERSON UNIVERSITY

I DECIDED TO GO TO SCHOOL IN MY HOMETOWN because my plan was to go abroad for a year, and I felt that if I was going away from home, I could be in my hometown for the other years of school. I ended up spending my third year overseas, and it was a great experience.

—*SHIRA*
TORONTO, ONTARIO
YORK UNIVERSITY

66 I went on the websites of schools and found out where the hottest girls were! Nah, that's not true: I wanted to be in a diverse city and my school was in a great area, so that's why I applied to York! 99

—*JOSH TIZEL*
TORONTO, ONTARIO
YORK UNIVERSITY

PEER TO PEER

Most college and university websites lack a sense of the real student life that goes on there. One way to catch that flavor is to check out the Web section that's meant for current students, for a sense of day-to-day campus life.

FOLLOW YOUR HEART

Ever since I was old enough to start thinking about college, I had thought that I would go to North Central College, a tiny liberal arts school in Naperville, Illinois. My parents were alumni of the school, as was my cousin. My parents both majored in business, and several years after they graduated, they were married in the college's chapel. Needless to say, the  school meant a lot to them. So when I began visiting schools my junior year, North Central was still at the top of my list. My parents would tell me about the great times they had there, which of course made the school more desirable.

However, I still wanted to see what was out there. It wasn't until I visited Bradley that I knew I had a tough decision to make. I immediately fell in love with the campus and could even picture myself there. All along, my parents would still tell me how great North Central was, but they never pressured me or made me feel like I had go there. I competed in a scholarship competition at North Central and received a nice amount of money; it was then that I had to make my final decision. Do I accept the award and follow in my parents' footsteps as they hoped? Or do I follow my heart and go where I felt I would be extremely happy?

After much discussion, I realized that I needed to have my own college experience and memories. I decided I would attend Bradley. College is when you grow the most as a person. Having an experience like no other is something you will carry with you for the remainder of your life.

—*LAURA*
TINLEY PARK, ILLINOIS
BRADLEY UNIVERSITY

CHARTING YOUR COURSE

If you are still having trouble deciding between two or more
schools (lucky you!), try this method:

Make a chart, listing each school along the vertical (y) axis, and
the following attributes along the horizontal (x) axis:

- Location
- Climate
- Majors
- Class sizes
- Extracurriculars
- Make-up of students

Add a column for any other attribute you want to evaluate.

For each school, assign a value from 1–5 to each attribute, where
1 is the least favorable, 3 is neutral, and 5 is the most favorable.

When all the boxes are filled in, total the points for each school;
you may have a winner.

A few other factors to consider:
- Where do you feel the most comfortable?
- How much of a financial burden will this put on your family—
  does it go too far?
- Is it worth the free ride at a place you're not excited about, or a
  financial investment in a great match?

I GOT THE LIST DOWN TO MY TWO top choices—Marquette and Illinois Wesleyan—and sat down to figure out the pros and cons of each. Wesleyan is a pretty small school. About 60 people from my high school were going there, and I didn't want to run into them every day. Marquette is in a city, so there's always something to do, but it's small enough that it's easy to get around. It also has a broadcast program, which I wanted, the campus and dorms were nice, and my mom was in love in with the school. And only two other people from my high school were going there.

—*ASHLEY LITTLE*
FLOSSMOOR, ILLINOIS
MARQUETTE UNIVERSITY

Expert Advice — IECA⁺ COUNSELOR'S CORNER

YOU MAKE THE CALL

Whether your interest is politics or philosophy, the colleges you are considering are likely to have an organization devoted to that topic. Many club and activity websites list members or officers along with their e-mail address. A few simple questions, whether related to the organization or to college life in general, are likely to give you insight into college life from someone who shares at least one of your interests. Can't find an organization that interests you? Call the admissions office and ask to be put in touch with someone from your hometown.

—*JOAN BRESS*
DIRECTOR, COLLEGE RESOURCE ASSOCIATES

5 REASONS *NOT* TO CHOOSE A CERTAIN COLLEGE

Choosing which college to attend is a complex undertaking with many factors swaying your decision. Some factors are more important than others. Here are some reasons for attending a college that should be considered very (very, *very*) low priority:

- You're hoping to meet (and date) that person you saw in the quad during your three-hour visit to the school last spring.
- All the students seem hung over, so it must be a good party school.
- On the day you visited, the weather was great.
- You've never visited the school and you like "surprises".
- All your high school friends and your boyfriend or girlfriend are going there.

I APPLIED TO UCLA, UC BERKELEY, AND UCI. UCLA and UCI were particularly appealing at the time, because they were close to home. But I definitely do not recommend this! Living at home may seem like a comfortable, financially sound idea; but it also may be developmentally stunting, and I think moving away is a big step toward independence. That's why I chose Berkeley. It's so different from what I was used to (Orange County), and that's a good thing. I felt I could learn a lot more here outside of the textbooks and problems I would have to plow through. I was right.

—*TRICIA POWELL*
HUNTINGTON BEACH, CALIFORNIA
UNIVERSITY OF CALIFORNIA, BERKELEY

SET YOUR SITES ON THESE

Here are some websites that offer information about specific colleges:

> www.unigo.com
> www.studentsreview.com
> www.ecampustours.com
> www.youniversity.tv
> http://collegemotion.com

IT IS DEFINITELY FRUSTRATING to hear friends and classmates babble on about their big plans as they're accepted to their top-choice schools, especially when college T-shirt day rolls around during senior week and you've got no new threads to sport. As difficult as it may be, my advice is to stay relaxed. You've spent 12+ years being organized as a group of kids, and you're just now beginning the process of discovering independence. This process can often be disconcerting and even a little frightening; you're setting off to shape your own life now and part of defining yourself is pursuing the things that are important to you. So, don't measure your own success on the same scale as your peers. They may be excited about their schools, and rightfully so. Just be confident that if you put in the effort, you'll end up in the place that's right for you.

—*KYLE PACKER*
LILBURN, GEORGIA
KENYON COLLEGE

GO TEAM!

Just in case football is *really* important to your college experience, here are the schools with the top winning percentages since they started keeping stats 140 years ago:

1. Michigan – 74.4%
2. Notre Dame – 73.8%
3. Texas – 71.8%
4. Ohio State – 71.3%
5. Oklahoma – 71.0%
6. Alabama – 70.6%
7. Southern Cal – 70.2%
8. Nebraska – 70.2%
9. Tennessee – 69.5%
10. Penn State – 68.7%

Open Your Mind: Imagining the College Life (while doing enough to graduate high school!)

So, what is it like, really? We're talking about college. Do the leaves turn gold and blanket the quad with an ethereal sheen? Do the students and professors sip espresso and talk about the keys to the universe? Do the dorms feature a continuous soundtrack by Simon & Garfunkel? Or is college more like a Nelly video mixed with a raucous college movie comedy? Should you really expect that much beer and sex? No matter what you picture, the reality is probably different. Read on for a head start on the college life.

AS A HIGH SCHOOL SENIOR, I pictured college people acting much more mature. It's taken me a few years to realize that people don't really change from high school. They just get older and do stupider things!

—MICHAEL ABRAMOVITZ
TUCSON, ARIZONA
🏛 UNIVERSITY OF ARIZONA

I DON'T THINK THAT ANYONE IS TRULY "READY" FOR ANYTHING, SO JUMP IN, AND TRUST YOURSELF.

—BRIANA
SONOMA, CALIFORNIA
🏛 SONOMA STATE UNIVERSITY

HEADLINES
Best Advice and Top Tips

- Surprise! People are the same everywhere.
- Remember, with freedom comes responsibility.
- Prepare to be pushed *and* prepare to push yourself.
- Don't fall for senioritis—those final grades do count!
- Imagine yourself in four years' time, then decide what to do to become that person.

I IMAGINED THAT COLLEGE STUDENTS studied all night. Once I was there, I found that through proper time management, I had more study/social life balance than I anticipated. Plus, I didn't do as perfectly as I imagined I would.

—*WILLIAM WATTS*
BERKELEY, CALIFORNIA
UNIVERSITY OF CALIFORNIA, BERKELEY

• • • • • • • •

I IMAGINED COLLEGE STUDENTS to be serious and snobby and generally to take themselves too seriously. I expected a lot of pretensiousness. I did find that at school, but I also found a group of friends that I will have for the rest of my life.

—*MICHAEL ALBERT PAOLI*
TORONTO, ONTARIO
UNIVERSITY OF TORONTO

I THOUGHT SCHOOL WOULD BE TOUGH and that I would have to work much harder than I did in high school. Turned out, it wasn't as demanding as I had imagined. I was pretty independent to begin with, so living on my own wasn't such a big deal.

—*JAMIE HARGRAVE*
NUTLEY, NEW JERSEY
ROWAN UNIVERSITY

• • • • • • • •

" You find the same people in college you find everywhere else. Bottom line: You find what you're looking for. Keep an open attitude and you'll be fine. "

—*ERIN*
TACOMA, WASHINGTON

• • • • • • • •

MY FRIEND'S DAUGHTER FAILED A CLASS in her last semester and her acceptance was rescinded from the school she had been accepted at. She'd sent in her deposit and she had already gotten an apartment. But when the grades came out, the school said, "Sorry, you can't go here, and you have to reapply next year."

—*SUSAN*
LOS ANGELES, CALIFORNIA
UNIVERSITY OF CALIFORNIA, SANTA BARBARA

THIS IS YOUR BRAIN IN COLLEGE

I imagined the life of a college student to be full of freedom with lots of partying and not too many responsibilities. I was only half right. I did have freedom, but I also had the responsibility of taking care of myself. The hardest thing about college was getting up to go to class. When I didn't, I didn't do so hot. When I did, I did pretty well. It's pretty sobering to know that to do well, all you have to do is go to class and do a little work outside of class.

After a while, you learn to pace yourself. One of the greatest things I learned in college was how to say 'no'. You learn your limits in college: what works for you, what doesn't. I know plenty of kids who can party all night and still function in class the next day. I was not that fortunate, but I learned to deal with it and came away with a degree.

Of course, college is totally what you make of it. Some students prefer to party away their four years; others schmooze with their professors for future letters of recommendation at their weekly office hour. I was somewhere in the middle, and I feel I experienced the full spectrum. I now have a bevy of crazy college stories as well as a periodic e-mail "Hey-how's-it-going?" relationship with one of my favorite professors. I came away with a sense of who I am, a new set of great friends, and great memories.

—*TRICIA POWELL*
HUNTINGTON BEACH, CALIFORNIA
UNIVERSITY OF CALIFORNIA, BERKELEY

COLLEGE AND COLLEGE STUDENTS are not what I imagined! At first, it seems intimidating because college is a new, big step in one's life. However, once you get to college, you'll see that this soon wears off and you become used to your surroundings and classes. You become motivated and this is what guides you through the next four years of your college life.

> —CARLY JACOBS
> PHILADELPHIA, PENNSYLVANIA
> LA SALLE UNIVERSITY

• • • • • • • •

WHEN YOU'RE IN HIGH SCHOOL, you picture college students as mature and sensible. When you get there, you realize they're probably *less* mature than high schoolers because these people are alone for the first time! Don't let your imagination run away with you. Many people preparing for college are going through the same anxiety as you are.

> —JOSH TIZEL
> TORONTO, ONTARIO
> YORK UNIVERSITY

I pictured *Animal House* and wild parties. But we don't really have the Greek system at my school, so it's not even close!

> —MICHAEL NOBLE
> TORONTO, ONTARIO
> YORK UNIVERSITY

KEEP THOSE GRADES UP

Colleges hope that you are continuing your academics strongly throughout your senior year. That means if you have been taking Honors and AP and IB classes, you should still take them. Be careful not to jeopardize your college admission at the end of the race. Senior grades can be critical to your admission; many colleges require that you send them before they'll let you matriculate, and those that don't will call your high school to obtain them if they are unsure about you. This happens regularly.

OTHER SIDE OF THE DESK: WATCH IT! WE CAN STILL SAY 'NO'

Though it is often more of a threat than a reality, colleges can and do withdraw acceptances in cases of bad or illegal behavior. Colleges really do find out about everything, and you may be asked to write a letter about new and uncharacteristically bad grades or a suspension, and explain what happened. Cheating and lying at schools with honor codes is especially serious—make sure you end on a high note your last semester; do not risk your future.

I TRIED TO IMAGINE MYSELF FOUR YEARS in the future. I was trying to picture how my life would have changed in terms of things like, if I had a steady girlfriend or a car or a part- or full-time job. You have to realize that you will not be the same person coming out of college as going in. Your situation will be drastically different.

—SAM ULMER
NEWARK, DELAWARE
🏛 UNIVERSITY OF DELAWARE

• • • • • • • •

I ARRIVED AT COLLEGE AND REALIZED I was on my own and responsible for taking care of myself. I was far from my safety net (home), so it made me become more independent than ever. I really enjoyed the social aspect of it and had fun meeting new people from different backgrounds and cultures. I enjoyed some of my classes and joined a sorority, which was a great experience.

—ANONYMOUS
NEW YORK, NEW YORK
🏛 INDIANA UNIVERSITY

MY HIGH SCHOOL VERSION of typical collegiate life: classes in the day, study at night, party on weekends; deep intellectual conversations on lawns in front of buildings; meeting friends and lovers who are just like you. The reality is nothing like that. Depending on the school, and your schedule, studying will be thrown in whenever you get a chance, partying either all the time or rarely (depending on the type of school you go to), and while you may find a person or two who share your passions, no one will ever be quite like you. And distrust all potential significant others: College is about the exploration of sex, not commitment. College will most definitely be great as long as you take chances, sign up for and try new things, but keep a smart head on your shoulders. Not all risks are to be taken.

—*COURTNEY HEILMAN*
BOSTON, MASSACHUSETTS

Be sure not to worry too much about how things will work out. It all unfolds very smoothly.

—*DAVID DANENBERG*
KENT, OHIO
KENT STATE UNIVERSITY

. . . .

6 MTV's version isn't exactly what college is about. Sure, there are fun spring-break parties, crazy dates, and adventures in college; but the studying certainly isn't glamorous. Studying wouldn't make for good television! 99

—*ANDREA*
TORONTO, ONTARIO
QUEEN'S UNIVERSITY

'SENIORITIS': DISEASE, OR EXCUSE FOR FUN?

Once you're accepted into college, all things associated with high school—such as tests, homework, and showing up on time (if at all) —shrink to microscopic importance. It's called senioritis, and it's real. But is it a good thing?

SENIORITIS: I HAD IT BAD. After I got into Stanford, it was so hard to concentrate on classes because I kept picturing sunny California with palm trees lining the streets. Luckily, teachers were sympathetic as the year ended. I normally wouldn't advocate playing hooky, but for graduating seniors already accepted to college, I'd say reward yourself by "being sick" a couple times so you get to sleep late. Once college hits, you'll wish you had slept more in high school.

> —KATHERINE BELL
> STANFORD, CALIFORNIA
> STANFORD UNIVERSITY

EMBRACE SENIORITIS: LEAVE SCHOOL EARLY FOR NO GOOD REASON. It's a nice feeling. You should have a pretty easy schedule. Load up on afternoon electives so you can go to the diner and then sleep.

> —ZACHARY KLION
> SUFFERN, NEW YORK
> YALE UNIVERSITY

TAKE CARE OF YOUR SCHOOLWORK FIRST. Don't worry about partying. If you work hard now, those partying days in college are going to be even better. It will be more worthwhile.

> —ANDREW
> DEARBORN, MICHIGAN
> WAYNE STATE UNIVERSITY

TO BATTLE SENIORITIS, GIVE YOURSELF A GOAL. For example, graduating with a certain GPA. It will keep you in class and keep you focused, and in the end you'll do better.

> —JENNIFER DRAGOVICH
> SEMINOLE, FLORIDA
> FLORIDA STATE UNIVERSITY

SENIORITIS CAN BE A GOOD THING. Slacking off is a great way to spend time once colleges stop paying so much attention to high school academics.

> —COLIN CAMPBELL
> CHARLOTTESVILLE, VIRGINIA
> UNIVERSITY OF NORTH CAROLINA

I TRIED TO ENJOY THE LAST MOMENTS IN HIGH SCHOOL. When you get to college, you're on your own. Enjoy being taken care of. Be a kid.

> —HANNAH ASSADI
> SCOTTSDALE, ARIZONA
> COLUMBIA COLLEGE

DO NOT LET YOUR GRADES SLIP SENIOR YEAR! I totally slacked off and must have dropped three or four places in class rank. Not only did it cost me the opportunity to be in the top two of the class, but I was wait-listed at my first-choice college and I believe that my grades would eventually have caused me to be denied. I also think that the drop in grades cost me several scholarships.

> —SHEILA CRAWFORD
> CARY, NORTH CAROLINA
> NORTH CAROLINA STATE UNIVERSITY

WORK YOUR HIGH SCHOOL TEACHERS: They can help boost your grades. A few times, my teachers were very forgiving and rounded up!

> —ANONYMOUS
> TORONTO, ONTARIO
> UNIVERSITY OF TORONTO

THE WHOLE POINT OF SENIOR YEAR IS TO HAVE FUN. So, make sure you don't flunk out of school, but realize it's a year when you're the king. Revel in that, because in college you're kind of a small fish in a really, really big ocean.

> —*JENNI LERCHE*
> *BELMONT, CALIFORNIA*
> *BARNARD COLLEGE*

• • • • • • • •

JUST TAKE A DEEP BREATH and enjoy your last days of high school.

> —*DAVID*
> *NEWARK, DELAWARE*
> *VILLANOVA UNIVERSITY*

• • • • • • • •

SENIORITIS SET IN BEFORE I was even accepted to my college. It helped me to get out there and find out what I wanted to do.

> —*JULIE COLLINS*
> *DES MOINES, IOWA*
> *DRAKE UNIVERSITY*

COLLEGE IS AN ENTIRE INSTITUTION created for your development and performance. From the perspective of a current college student, these four years seem like a gift to play around with and learn as much about myself as I can. My experience has been one of facilitated introspection and discovery, with an emphasis on how to carry over my curiosity into my future.

—*HEATHER MUNTZER*
SANTA ROSA, CALIFORNIA
CALIFORNIA COLLEGE OF THE ARTS

. . . .

" Have an open mind. It will be different. It will be tough. It will be the best experience of your life. You will be amazed by how much you grow as a person. "

—*ADRIENNE LANG*
OLATHE, KANSAS
TEXAS CHRISTIAN UNIVERSITY

. . . .

SOMETIMES YOU DON'T REALLY know who you are when you graduate high school, and going to college is really the opportunity to become who you want to be. I would hope that seniors wouldn't stress themselves too much about how they're going to do in college. Just be yourself, and you'll find your right group of people. It will all fall into place.

—*JULIE COLLINS*
DES MOINES, IOWA
DRAKE UNIVERSITY

Remember this: Freshman year is *tough*! It's a *huge* adjustment. Ultimately, be prepared to stick it out because it gets better.

—*Nicole Spence Wyckoff, New Jersey Emory University*

I HAD A PRETTY ROMANTICIZED NOTION of college: you know, sitting in the corner of a café and sipping lattes when I'm not in class, finding The One in one of my classes, and getting on the dean's list so I could go to graduate school. But once I got over the idea of college as a vacation from the immaturities of high school, it became a great place to be stimulated intellectually and socially. Four-year universities are not high schools. Prepare to be pushed, but most of all, prepare to push yourself. Try things that you didn't get to do in high school.

—*K.C. Davis, California University of California, Davis*

· · · · · · · ·

FOR ME, COLLEGE WAS VERY MUCH like high school because I was living at home. I thought it would be more exciting, with lots of parties.

—*Shira Toronto, Ontario York University*

CLING TO CONTACTS

Good advice from admissions counselors: Keep up the relationship with the people you've come to know at your school. Even though you no longer "need" them, now that you've been admitted, those staff members and students you met during the application process may be the only people you'll know (and who know you) on campus at first. Say hi, drop them an e-mail, or share a coffee; never let a good connection wither.

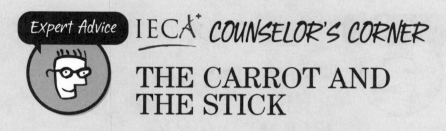

Expert Advice IECA* *COUNSELOR'S CORNER*

THE CARROT AND THE STICK

It's springtime and your college acceptance letter hangs in a place of honor. Prom and graduation are coming up soon, and homework and finals have sunk to the bottom of your priority list. Take care, Seniors, for danger and disappointment lurk in every undone assignment and carelessly written exam.

Colleges believe that you will be the same type of student in college that you are in high school. So, if your grades slip, they may begin to rethink their decision to admit you. Your teachers have warned you that colleges have the right to rescind their offer of acceptance (or impose additional requirements on you). However, unless you know someone who has suffered this fate, you might find it hard to believe that any college would be so cruel. Trust me. While rare, it does happen.

Even if your grades do not put you in danger of losing your spot in next year's freshman class, you'll cheat yourself out of valuable learning opportunities if you slack off now. Brains work like muscles. The longer you let them rest, the harder it is to get them back in shape. Slack off too much now and fall classes will feel like mini-marathons. Finish school with the same enthusiasm and dedication that earned you strong grades all year and you'll be ready for a successful start to your college career.

—*Joan Bress*
Director, College Resource Associates

Expert Advice — IECA* COUNSELOR'S CORNER

SENIOR YEAR: KEEPING UP THE GOOD WORK

Good grades will boost your college applications, since most colleges consider your high school transcript first - before they consider your SAT or ACT scores. Keep up the good work in your senior year, because colleges will be looking at those grades, too. What classes should you take? Ones where you can challenge yourself and still do well. If you think you can get a B or higher in an AP or Honors class, go for it. Colleges will notice.

—*BETSY F. WOOLF*
WOOLF COLLEGE CONSULTING

College is what I expected, because I tried not to expect anything!

—*BRIANA*
SONOMA, CALIFORNIA
SONOMA STATE UNIVERSITY

I WAS EXCITED TO GET AWAY FROM HOME and to experience the party life of school that I had heard so much about. To me, these things seemed very "college." Another thing I expected to get out of my college experience was the education! Shocking, I know, but I did enjoy the access to more sophisticated courses and the encouragement you're given in college to talk about real issues. In high school you can't delve as much into these things, so I was excited to explore different topics and be on my own. I saw college as a chance to grow up.

—*JILL*
TORONTO, ONTARIO

HOMEWORK MINUS HOME

You're going from a structured and restricted high school day of six to eight hours to a college school day of, typically, three hours. Sounds like paradise, but it can be a pitfall. How do you discipline yourself to study or stay engaged and focused? You have freedom, but it's an illusion. The work still needs to be done, but now it's all up to you.

Colleges are aware of the difficulty this transition poses for many students. Most schools provide an enormous amount of tutoring and academic support on campus. You don't have to qualify as a "special needs" student to need help: Go get it, at the first sign that you're falling behind.

FINISH STRONG: ACE YOUR EXAMS

You want to finish your year strong and lock in the top grades you can. Exams can really make or break your averages, so power on and remember the holy grail of summer vacation awaits!

- Make sure you know, to the extent that you can, what will be on the exams and cover all areas.
- Assess your weaknesses and focus on improving them (but don't forget that you have strengths, too!).
- Ask for help if you need it – it's mature to realize that you are not perfect in everything.
- Clarify points with your teachers if material is unclear.
- Get some good sleep the night before.

R.K.

HEADS UP: TAKE ADVANTAGE!

To get off to a flying start academically and socially:

- Take advantage of orientation! This is a freebie period when you will never look stupid asking a lot of questions and bumbling around the campus. Everyone is a freshman in the same boat, so it is a safe period to explore and learn.

- Take advantage of all the school has to offer. The number one regret on everyone's list of what they missed in college? Not doing enough. Make sure you do attend at least a few of those great concerts, lectures, or football games so you never miss out. Getting involved in clubs adds great depth to your social life, too, so remember to force yourself to be brave and check things out.

COLLEGE IS SO MUCH BETTER! Nobody judges you. Everyone is an individual, and respected for it.

—*HEIDI*
YERINGTON, NEVADA
TEXAS SOUTHERN UNIVERSITY

One More Summer: Your Pre-College To-Do List

I s the summer before college your farewell to freedom and youth? Your last moments at home, surrounded by the comforts (and annoyances) of family and old friends? One thing's certain: It's a unique time in your life that won't come again. You want to make sure you spend your time wisely. We asked other students what they did in their final summer before heading off to college. We also asked them what they would take to college, if they could take only one thing. Read on so that you can plan accordingly.

THE SUMMER BEFORE COLLEGE, I worked to save up money for school. If I did it over, I would've spent more time with friends and more time saying goodbye. Now, it's difficult for us to see one another.

—JESSICA NEWMAN
WEST BLOOMFIELD, MICHIGAN
🏛 MICHIGAN STATE UNIVERSITY

I DIDN'T DO ANY-THING TO PREPARE FOR COLLEGE BESIDES SHOP (WHICH WAS IMPORTANT, TOO!)

—DANIELLA KANAL
PITTSBURGH,
PENNSYLVANIA
🏛 STERN COLLEGE

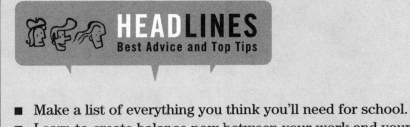

HEADLINES
Best Advice and Top Tips

- Make a list of everything you think you'll need for school.
- Learn to create balance now between your work and your social life.
- Take advantage of your college's orientation program; it really does help.
- Begin to broaden your world-view; explore new magazines or newspapers.
- Spend time with your friends and make plans to stay in touch.

COMING FOR ORIENTATION WAS EXTREMELY important because it helped me decide whether to live on campus, if I'd need a car, what's nearby, and it just gave me an overall feel of things.

> —*MAURA CALLAHAN*
> *TALLAHASSEE, FLORIDA*
> *FLORIDA STATE UNIVERSITY*

ACT LIKE YOU'RE NEVER GOING to see your friends again. Everyone always does, but it feels like you won't. Often, you grow apart from these people. Spend a lot of time with your family; you will miss them so much if you go far away.

> —*ADRIENNE LANG*
> *OLATHE, KANSAS*
> *TEXAS CHRISTIAN UNIVERSITY*

I SPENT THE SUMMER BUYING EVERYTHING I thought I would need, attending orientation, trying to make as much money as possible, and enjoying my time with my friends and family.

—*HALLI LEVY*
SOLON, OHIO
UNIVERSITY OF MISSOURI

● ● ● ● ● ● ● ●

THE SUMMER BEFORE COLLEGE I opted to travel. My goal was to expand my worldview as much as possible before college, as well as have a last hurrah with my high school friends. Some friends and I took a road trip around our state in the first part of the summer. In the month before I started college, I went to Finland and Estonia; it was an amazing experience that allowed me to try out my newly gained independence. I'm really glad I took the opportunity to go.

—*AMANDA NELSON-DUAC*
ST. AUGUSTINE, FLORIDA
GEORGE WASHINGTON UNIVERSITY

● ● ● ● ● ● ● ●

I WORKED AS A TEEN MENTOR and administrative assistant, and then traveled to Israel for a month. While I was there, I studied in a college for four weeks and got credits for school. I got in some traveling, too. I'm glad that I worked a bit and made some extra spending money for the rest of the year.

—*ELANA JUDITH SYRTASH*
NEW YORK, NEW YORK
YESHIVA UNIVERSITY

● ● ● ● ● ● ● ●

HAVE FUN WITH FRIENDS that you know you won't be in touch with. This is what I did; we went sailing and to Cancun. It was a blast.

—*RACHANN MCKNIGHT*
WALKERTON, INDIANA
INDIANA UNIVERSITY

Start packing early. It's not fun spending your last night at home surrounded by boxes and suitcases.

—*JESSICA*
SARATOGA,
CALIFORNIA
UNIVERSITY OF
SOUTHERN
CALIFORNIA

THE PREPARED PARENT

There are many ways parents can help their children prepare for college:

- Make a checklist of all the things that need to be done – for example: doctor visits, get prescriptions filled, purchase dorm furnishings.

- Make a list of all the items that will be needed for school.

- Put together a survival kit of stamps, flashlight, addresses and phone numbers of important people such as physicians and family members.

- Let your child choose what he or she wants for the dorm from stores, then check off the list.

- A 'student shower' would be a great idea to have for your child and help with the endless expense. Some stores even offer a student registry.

—*PHYLLIS BRISKMAN STANFIELD*
PITTSBURGH, PENNSYLVANIA
P ⚓ WASHINGTON AND JEFFERSON COLLEGE

I TOOK A CLASS AT MY COLLEGE, just to feel what it was like to not hear a bell ring when class is over. I took Introduction to Astronomy. It helped me understand how college works. There is really no more homework; it's studying and reading, so you have to have the willpower to actually do some work. It is a great feeling when you can go to class and understand what is being taught.

—*SARAH LOLA PALODICHUK*
NEWPORT BEACH, CALIFORNIA

. . . .

YOUR LAST SUMMER BEFORE COLLEGE, live in that high school moment, but be ready to let go of it when September comes. You want to be as open as you can about meeting new friends and moving on.

—*CANDACE WATSON*
LOS GATOS, CALIFORNIA
SANTA CLARA UNIVERSITY

. . . .

I WORKED THE SUMMER BEFORE my freshman year. I didn't really do anything school-wise. I had to read one book for a freshman reading project, and I had enough time to do that. A lot of kids like to take college-level courses over the summer and prepare before freshman year starts; but the most important thing is to balance academics with your social life. You don't want to go to school and start your university career without relaxing and taking a little break the summer before.

—*ADAM KRESSEL*
MIAMI, FLORIDA
CORNELL UNIVERSITY

. . . .

I RELAXED EVERY DAY. Enjoy it. Don't burn bridges with people who aren't going to the same college as you—you'll be home at Thanksgiving, don't forget!

—*APRIL*
CHICAGO, ILLINOIS
PURDUE UNIVERSITY

Consider

ONE THING TO BRING

As you are enjoying your last moments of youth, you're probably also wondering what you need to bring to college. We asked college students what they would choose if they could bring only one thing. Here are their "desert island" answers.

THE BEST PILLOW I COULD FIND. There is nothing like getting the rest you need...especially when you have only three hours to get it in.

—*LINDSEY MORRISON GRANT*
PORTLAND, OREGON
CONCORDIA UNIVERSITY

. . . .

A SCRAPBOOK. Make sure it has current pictures of friends and family you might be missing. Leave some room to add pictures of the new friends you will be making.

—*STEPHEN MACKAY*
SOUTH ORANGE, NEW JERSEY
UNIVERSITY OF CALIFORNIA, RIVERSIDE

. . . .

PERSEVERANCE. College is easy until you stop showing up; then it becomes brutal and sometimes impossible. People who go to class pass that class. I've never seen someone fail who showed up. Never.

—*ADAM DREYFUS*
SAN FRANCISCO, CALIFORNIA
UNIVERSITY OF CONNECTICUT

. . . .

I'D BRING MY BIKE. I used it to ride to classes after waking up late and being hung over from the night before. It really helped!

—*MICHAEL ALBERT PAOLI*
TORONTO, ONTARIO
UNIVERSITY OF TORONTO

. . . .

MY MOM: She would've done my laundry!

—*BETH MAYEROWITZ*
NEW YORK, NEW YORK
UNIVERSITY OF WISCONSIN

SOMETHING THAT REMINDS you of your hometown. I am a big-time San Diego sports fan and always found it comforting to have posters and other items that represented where I was from.

> —*GARIN FAINSTEIN*
> *SAN DIEGO, CALIFORNIA*
> *UNIVERSITY OF SOUTHERN CALIFORNIA*

A SLEEPING BAG, so that I could hang out at friends' places and have somewhere to sleep!

> —*SHIRA*
> *TORONTO, ONTARIO*
> *YORK UNIVERSITY*

A PLANNER. It's hard to keep track of assignments, events, and activities without some serious organizational tools to help put things in perspective. I figured that out after the first term. Once I learned to budget my time, I noticed it became easier to focus. I set daily or weekly goals for myself and I didn't feel overwhelmed or like I needed to accomplish more than what was reasonable. As a result, I didn't burn out as quickly as other students.

> —*SHANNON*
> *PORTLAND, OREGON*
> *MARYLHURST UNIVERSITY*

AN OPEN AND CURIOUS MIND. College is a wonderful time to explore and learn about yourself.

> —*LISA GREENBAUM*
> *NEW YORK, NEW YORK*
> *RUTGERS UNIVERSITY*

MY CHECKBOOK, preferably loaded! Life gets expensive.

> —*ADAM GUZOWSKI*
> *SOUTH BEND, INDIANA*
> *BALL STATE UNIVERSITY*

HERE IS WHAT I BROUGHT TO COLLEGE: a one-gallon tub of baking sprinkles, about 30 trucker hats, a shopping cart I converted into an armchair, all of my band T-shirts, my high school girlfriend, and all of the toiletries my mom hoped I would use. What of that *should* I have brought? The armchair.

> —SETH
> SUNNYVALE, CALIFORNIA
> UNIVERSITY OF CALIFORNIA, BERKELEY

● ● ● ● ● ● ● ●

MY CAR. Once in a while you need to get away from the campus.

> —JAMIE HARGRAVE
> NUTLEY, NEW JERSEY
> ROWAN UNIVERSITY

● ● ● ● ● ● ● ●

ONE OF THOSE BIG ARMCHAIR-SHAPED PILLOWS. There are never any comfortable chairs in the dorm, so you put this thing on your bed against the wall, and voilà: instant armchair.

> —NANCY MITCHELL POEHLMANN
> GRANGER, INDIANA
> AGNES SCOTT COLLEGE

● ● ● ● ● ● ● ●

PICTURES AND SMALL MEMENTOS from high school and home.

> —JESSICA PAULEY
> CHILLICOTHE, OHIO
> UNIVERSITY OF CINCINNATI

● ● ● ● ● ● ● ●

PROBABLY MY LAPTOP. Actually, *definitely* my laptop.

> —JESSICA
> SARATOGA, CALIFORNIA
> UNIVERSITY OF SOUTHERN CALIFORNIA

I WOULD BRING SOMETHING from someone whom you consider your best friend. I brought a box my sister made me with pictures and letters from everyone whom I could have ever hoped would write to me. A green box with maybe 20 envelopes inside would remind me of people who cared for me and who loved me unconditionally. Oh, and if you go to a place like Colgate, bring a heating blanket for your bed.

—*JACKIE ADLAM*
MILL VALLEY, CALIFORNIA
COLGATE UNIVERSITY

FLEXIBILITY AND COURAGE. College uproots much of what you have known your entire childhood, and things you have never before confronted start to demand your attention.

—*WHITNEY TRITT*
ATLANTA, GEORGIA
WAKE FOREST UNIVERSITY

BE SURE TO TAKE A PHOTO COLLAGE of friends and family to college with you. It's a good way not to get homesick. Also, it's good to share them with new friends so when you talk about those friends and family, you can include your new friends in your life.

—*ANGELA MASSINI*
CHICAGO, ILLINOIS
BUTLER UNIVERSITY

I'D BRING LICORICE TO GIVE AWAY IN RESIDENCE: Candy will help you meet people and make friends!

—*MICHAEL NOBLE*
TORONTO, ONTARIO
YORK UNIVERSITY

I HAD SIX WEEKS OFF BETWEEN HIGH SCHOOL and summer session. I relaxed and baby-sat a lot. I wanted to earn money and do all the things that would be hard in college, like seeing my old friends. These days it's hard to see high school friends; when you come home on breaks, you want to see your family.

—*LAUREN SHER*
GAINESVILLE, FLORIDA
UNIVERSITY OF FLORIDA

• • • • • • • •

Don't worry about saying goodbye to family and friends; you will talk to them often.

—*MELISSA BERMAN*
MANALAPAN,
NEW JERSEY
MUHLENBERG
COLLEGE

I WORKED THE SUMMER before school at the Silver Grill Café. It was a good idea because it gave me something to do and a way to save money. Ah, the Silver Grill!

—*KYLE*
FT. COLLINS, COLORADO
COLORADO STATE UNIVERSITY

• • • • • • • •

I WAS SCARED TO LEAVE. I think everyone gets a little scared to leave home. I was scared because I was going to Illinois from Nebraska! I guess I just didn't want to realize that I was leaving home, so I procrastinated: I didn't start preparing to leave until a week or two before. I should have started getting ready sooner so I didn't feel so rushed. I could have enjoyed the last few weeks of my time at home.

—*ANGELA FRIEDMAN*
PEORIA, ILLINOIS
BRADLEY UNIVERSITY

• • • • • • • •

COLLEGE IS AN ADJUSTMENT. There's suddenly a lack of parental control: do crazy things (like drink) the summer before so it won't mess up your studies later.

—*BENN RAY*
BALTIMORE, MARYLAND
SALISBURY UNIVERSITY

THE SUMMER BEFORE COLLEGE STARTED, I had AARO (Academic Advising, Registration, and Orientation) in which I spent two days with some fellow freshmen learning about the academics that SMU had to offer. I also did summer school at our local community college so that I could rack up some credits without having to spend an exorbitant amount of money. I took three courses that summer and got nine credit hours, which will help me graduate earlier.

> —*JULIETA GRINFFIEL*
> *DALLAS, TEXAS*
> *SOUTHERN METHODIST UNIVERSITY*

* * * * * * * *

START BUYING THINGS IN JUNE OR JULY so you can get your hands on everything you need. By August, the big stores will have less of what you want. Some stores have a registry online, and then the stuff is sent to your dorm so you don't have to overload your car.

> —*MATT BORTNICK*
> *EAST BRUNSWICK, NEW JERSEY*
> *INDIANA UNIVERSITY*

* * * * * * * *

I ENDED UP STARTING A COMPANY with a couple of friends and working all summer to make sure I had some extra cash. I recommend this; school costs more than you think it will.

> —*P.T.*
> *CHICAGO, ILLINOIS*
> *PURDUE UNIVERSITY*

* * * * * * * *

I WENT TO AUSTRALIA for two weeks with my high school on an environmental trip. It was a great idea to do that before arriving on campus. It's good to get away and clear your head.

> —*AMANDA NELSON*
> *NEW YORK, NEW YORK*
> *UNIVERSITY OF WISCONSIN-MADISON*

PARENTS' PAGES

AS MY DAUGHTER PREPARED to leave for college, many of my friends asked me how I felt about it. They said things like, "Aren't you sad?" and "I'll bet you'll cry like a baby when she's gone." But that was not at all how I felt. It almost made me feel like a cold-hearted mother for not feeling sorrow. I thought that maybe later it would hit me and I would suddenly break down in tears. So far that hasn't happened. To me it feels very right and natural that at 18 she's out of the house, experiencing life in a new way. There is no sadness in having her away from home, just joy in her accomplishments. I am truly happy that she is moving on in her life and I enjoy the new relationship we share. She has become very good company, and I look forward to her visits.

> —*ANONYMOUS*
> *EASTON, PENNSYLVANIA*
> *P* ⚏ *TUFTS UNIVERSITY*

• • • • • • • • •

AFTER A ROUGH SUMMER of arguing with my son about curfews, chores, and friends, I was almost relieved to imagine him going thousands of miles away to college in mid-August. But, the day after he left, I went into an unexpected period of mourning; it was two weeks before I could bear to enter his room. When I finally opened his door, the sight jerked me back into reality: The room was a complete pigsty, after he'd sworn he left it clean! Candy wrappers, bottle caps, clothes—even a girl's camisole(!)—were strewn all over the floor. I went straight from grief to anger. Sobbing, picking up dirty socks and wadded-up papers, I worked through my full range of emotions while straightening up that room.

> —*N.L.*
> *ST. LOUIS, MISSOURI*
> *P* ⚏ *TRUMAN STATE UNIVERSITY; CALIFORNIA STATE UNIVERSITY, MONTEREY BAY*

BEFORE YOU LEAVE THEM AT SCHOOL, get a list of phone numbers of their roommates and some of their friends. It made me feel so much better to have those numbers as I drove away.

—*CAMILLE*
CINCINNATI, OHIO
P ⚙ *UNIVERSITY OF KENTUCKY*

• • • • • • • •

BEFORE YOU LEAVE THEM THAT FIRST TIME, define your expectations of how often you're going to communicate and the medium of communication you'll use while they're at school. Even though you're dying to hear about how everything's going, you just can't call them as much as you'd like. We decided to e-mail during the week, and if we wanted to talk on the phone we could do that on weekends. For us, e-mails have worked really well. They let me know enough about what's going on so I'm not dying to call every day.

—*DONNA*
CINCINNATI, OHIO
P ⚙ *MIAMI UNIVERSITY*

• • • • • • • •

WHAT REMAINS WITH ME constantly is the day I took her to the airport. I drove, and three of her best friends came with us. I let them say their goodbyes first. The four of them were so choked up and had tears in their eyes, and it just melted my heart. At that moment, seeing the deep and solid connections she had with these girls gave me the strength to let her go. I knew that she would find new friends at school that would be able to give her the emotional support she needed in tough times. I knew if she could build friendships like the ones she did in high school, that she would not be alone.

—*TRACY*
CHICAGO, ILLINOIS
P ⚙ *WASHINGTON UNIVERSITY*

IT TAKES A VILLAGE

When my son was preparing for college, he said, "Mom, I don't even know how to cook." So a bunch of moms from a group of 14 friends organized a day where all the parents could impart their final words of wisdom.

We came up with a list of all the things the kids need to know before they go away to college. Four of us volunteered our homes. At my house we learned how to clean a toilet—I mean, when else are you going to teach your kid how to clean a toilet? We taught them how to sew a button, how to iron a shirt, how to change a tire, and how to check the fluid in the car. They also learned the essential skill of how to do laundry. A doctor taught them basic first aid.

They learned basic cooking and how to make a salad and cookies. But before they made their salad and cookies, someone met them at the grocery store, where they learned how to choose produce and to shop for the ingredients for the meal they were going to prepare. At the end of the day, all of the boys brought their salads and cookies back to our house, where my husband taught them how to grill. All the parents came over and we had a potluck that night.

—*LAURA*
ESCONDIDO, CALIFORNIA
P UNIVERSITY OF ARIZONA

THE SUMMER BETWEEN HIGH SCHOOL and college is a great time to make some money for college: You'll sure need it when you get there. I found a summer job working at the zoo; it gave me some good experience with animals, as I would ultimately like to be a vet. Those are the kinds of experiences you can put on a resume later to show that you were already thinking ahead.

> —*TED SASKIN*
> *CAMPBELL, OHIO*
> *KENT STATE UNIVERSITY*

* * * * * * * *

TAKE ADVANTAGE OF ANY SUMMER PROGRAMS that your college offers to get a head start. Right before classes started, I entered a program with 40 other freshmen that allowed us to do some volunteer work and team-building activities in the community. It helped me feel like I made my college my home already, and I made new friends.

> —*ANGELA MASSINI*
> *CHICAGO, ILLINOIS*
> *BUTLER UNIVERSITY*

* * * * * * * *

I REALLY JUST PARTIED MY WHOLE last summer away. I traveled around, and I was never home. I didn't have any goals. It was my last chance to have fun with friends at home. Don't just sit home and count the days or get nervous about missing home. Go to a friend's place for the weekend or to the shore for a week.

> —*MAREK JAROSLAW DUDZIAK*
> *BAYONNE, NEW JERSEY*
> *LOYOLA COLLEGE*

IN THE LAST SUMMER before college, every graduated high school student should join Facebook groups associated with their college and start meeting people through Facebook. This will give you an opportunity to learn more about the social aspect of the school and ask upperclassmen questions. This is very helpful, and it is how I found my roommate for USC.

—*REBECCA LETT*
LOS ANGELES, CALIFORNIA
UNIVERSITY OF SOUTHERN CALIFORNIA

• • • • • • • •

THE LAST SUMMER BEFORE COLLEGE, I traveled to Japan as the ambassador for my city's Sister City program. It was a wonderful learning experience that inspired me to spend the rest of my summer traveling to other places in Asia. If you can afford it, I would suggest traveling. And if you can do it with friends or family, all the better. The experience I had traveling to new places helped me be open to new things when I got to campus.

—*JOZ WANG*
LOS ANGELES, CALIFORNIA
UNIVERSITY OF CALIFORNIA, LOS ANGELES

• • • • • • • •

THERE WERE A LOT OF GOOD-BYES my last summer before college. Graduation was in May, but the good-bye period lasted all summer. See if you can organize one send-off event with all your friends. They all leave at staggered times, and it gets emotionally draining to say good-bye over and over. There are things that are sad to leave behind, so don't be afraid to mourn those. But there is a lot ahead for you to embrace!

—*WHITNEY TRITT*
ATLANTA, GEORGIA
WAKE FOREST UNIVERSITY

I RELAXED AND HUNG OUT WITH FRIENDS. I wanted to take it easy before entering a new time in my life; it helped with my adjustment.

—*MAURA CALLAHAN*
TALLAHASSEE, FLORIDA
FLORIDA STATE UNIVERSITY

• • • • • • • •

    ❝ Spend as much time as possible with both family and friends, especially if you are moving far from home. ❞

—*ANESSA PATRICE FAYE MITCHELL*
HOUSTON, TEXAS
UNIVERSITY OF SOUTHERN CALIFORNIA

SERIOUS ANSWER: Get a job. Save some money. Because once you haven't got any, you'll be wishing you had mowed that lawn or taken that nanny gig.

REAL ANSWER: Don't do anything. Lounge. Read. Watch TV. Hang out with friends and family. You'll be so busy come the start of school that you'll wish you had the luxury of being bored.

SILLY ANSWER: Write a poem about each of your friends. I didn't realize how much I appreciated each and every one of my friends until I went away to school. It would have been nice to let them know that they're pretty cool, one-of-a-kind people.

—*NATALIE ROSE SPITZER*
DECATUR, GEORGIA
GUILFORD COLLEGE

PARENTS' PAGES

THE EMOTIONAL SKILLS TOOLBOX

Colleges will provide resources and lists to assist you in buying everything from bedding to meal plans, but there are arguably more important things you can do to prepare your child; you can give him a set of emotional skills. Skills for thriving in a new and challenging environment are the most valuable gifts you can give, not only for his college years, but for his future.

Help your child:

- Learn to make decisions on his own (of course, he should call home when lonely or just to check in).
- Learn to wake up without assistance.
- Learn to take responsibility for strong or weak academic work.
- Prepare to meet new people. He will be exposed to things both fabulous and distasteful; how will he handle both?
- Jump into campus activities. It will enrich his experience, and students always regret not doing enough during the four years.
- Learn how to ask for help—from professors, TA's, and RA's— and know how to find and use campus resources such as offices of Student Life, Religious Life, and Medical Services (including psychological care).

R.K.

WHEN WE HELPED OUR FIRST CHILD pick out things to bring to college, we started out trying to find things that she wouldn't call us to send. We ended up going way overboard. We packed so much food that by the time she graduated, she still had nonperishable items that we bought that day.

—D.F.
LITHONIA, GEORGIA
P 🏫 *DUKE UNIVERSITY; UNIVERSITY OF MIAMI*

I DON'T LIKE THAT MY DAUGHTERS are away. I don't like them not being at home, but it's part of life. The hardest thing was saying goodbye to the first one, even though she moved only 20 miles away. When she left, I knew that was the end of it and that we would never all be living together again. Now it is just something to get used to.

> —ANTHONY ROMANO
> SAN DIEGO, CALIFORNIA
> P ▥ UNIVERSITY OF CALIFORNIA, SAN DIEGO;
> CLAREMONT MCKENNA COLLEGE

• • • • • • • • •

DON'T PLAN ON TOO MANY WARM and fuzzy moments after graduation. I think they go into "I have to separate" mode, and by August you will happily help them pack.

> —KATHLEEN RIDER
> HYDE PARK, NEW YORK
> P ▥ STATE UNIVERSITY OF NEW YORK;
> FORDHAM UNIVERSITY; QUINNIPIAC UNIVERSITY

• • • • • • • • •

THE DROP-OFF SCENE MADE ME LAUGH: all the parents with the Bed, Bath and Beyond bags, bumping into each other. And while the parents are doing all the work carrying stuff in, the child yawns and holds the door for them.

> —MARLA
> BOCA RATON, FLORIDA
> P ▥ UNIVERSITY OF FLORIDA; FLORIDA STATE UNIVERSITY

• • • • • • • • •

THE SMARTEST THING WE DID to help our son make the transition to college was to sign him up for a pre-orientation program. He got into a small one—a rock and river outing—they spent several days whitewater rafting and rock climbing. He made five really good friends. These are the kids he eats dinner with now, and when we get his phone statement we can see these are the people he's communicating with. It really has helped him to have friends right away.

> —VICTORIA JOHNSON
> MINNEAPOLIS, MINNESOTA
> P ▥ SKIDMORE COLLEGE

IF POSSIBLE, GO ON A SENIOR TRIP. I didn't, and I definitely wish that I had. It is kind of a rite of passage, going from a high school student to a college student. It symbolizes that transformation from childhood to adulthood, and from dependence to independence.

—*JULIE ROBERTS*
EDMOND, OKLAHOMA
UNIVERSITY OF OKLAHOMA

16

More Wisdom: Good Stuff that Didn't Fit Anywhere Else

*G*etting into college—and college itself—means challenging *oneself with new experiences, learning from them, and moving on to new and better things. It means developing a personal perspective and living by it. That's about to happen to you. And as you get ready for the best four years of your life, here are some parting thoughts to help you along the way.*

KEEP THIS IN MIND: Getting into college is not a test of your personal worth. When you apply to college, you're not applying to life. You're applying to an undergraduate program at an academic institution. The school has its own needs and wants that simply may not mesh with yours; remember that.

—*BOBBY*
MAPLEWOOD, NEW JERSEY
UNIVERSITY OF CHICAGO

THE PROCESS CLOUDS THE MINDS OF PARENTS. MAYBE OF KIDS, TOO.

—*ANONYMOUS*
BROOKLYN,
NEW YORK
P BARD COLLEGE

HEAD**LINES**
Best Advice and Top Tips

- Determine your own personal velocity—are you a dive-right-in or a toe-in-the-water person?
- College is the time to discover who you are and what you want to become.
- You may leave some old friends behind, but you'll also make some wonderful new ones.
- Find your passion, or be open-minded so it can find you.
- There is no one path to get to where you want to go.

DON'T GO CRAZY, but always follow your own path. An older friend of mine, who is consistently filled with good energy and advice, told me just last night, "Always forward, but never straight." That was the hardest part about preparing for college: staying on my own path. All of my friends were going to similar schools and I was crossing the state alone. I look back now and realize that going away to school without all of my best friends was one of my most fantastic decisions. I graduated and moved west. Most of them are still back in my hometown and have not experienced half the life that I have lived.

—*HILLARY*
BRECKENRIDGE, COLORADO
BOWLING GREEN STATE UNIVERSITY

I'M STILL IN TOUCH WITH MY high school friends. It's "see you later," not "goodbye."

—*DAMILOLA OSUNSANYA*
MIRAMAR, FLORIDA
EMORY UNIVERSITY

. . . .

I TRULY BELIEVE YOU CAN GET a great education and a great launch into adult life at hundreds of colleges, if you are ready for it and open to it. And that's a matter of maturity, which kids have in varying amounts. We have really bought into the consumer marketing junk of colleges, where going to Yale is like buying a BMW. We also believe in the idea of an American meritocracy, when really, it does not exist.

—*ANONYMOUS*
NEW YORK, NEW YORK
CARLETON COLLEGE

. . . .

COLLEGE IS IN SOME WAYS easier than high school because the classes are spread out. On the other hand, it took a while to get used to staying in classes for longer periods. The best thing to do is take notes and meet people in the class whom you can study with or talk to about the class. College is the best time to discover what drives you, what bores you, and what you may want to do with your future. Students need to dig deep down and listen to what their spirit tells them. Do what you enjoy doing. Choose a path that inspires you, so that you don't feel trapped by your decision. Getting a degree and going to college should be a wonderful experience if you allow yourself to apply yourself to something you enjoy.

—*EMILY TUCK*
FRESNO, CALIFORNIA
CALIFORNIA STATE UNIVERSITY, FRESNO

PARENTS' PAGES

TELL YOUR KIDS THAT YOU LOVE THEM, TRUST THEM, and are proud
of them when they are going through applying to schools. Trust
that all the great parenting you've done in the past (and even the
not-so-great moments) has provided a guide and foundation for
your child to make good decisions.

> —BRIANA
> SONOMA, CALIFORNIA
>   SONOMA STATE UNIVERSITY

• • • • • • • • •

I WISH WE HAD KNOWN THAT taking on too many credits at the
beginning and trying to fulfill graduation requirements in your first
semester is not a smart idea. The transition into college is a very
big step involving educational aspects of school, as well as the
entire new experience of living on your own. Taking on too much
at the beginning can cause all the parts of the college experience
to suffer. It is much better to start out a little slower and build
self-confidence, then move on to the harder courses once the student understands the college process.

> —J.K.D.
> PITTSBURGH, PENNSYLVANIA
> P   KENT STATE UNIVERSITY

• • • • • • • • •

IT'S DEFINITELY AN ADJUSTMENT, but this is how it should be. It's
really healthy. We want them to be functioning and independent
members of society. It's time for them to go out and test themselves
to see if they can keep it all together; they have to be responsible
for their own nutrition, clothing and friendships. This is the time
when they become who they really are; how can that be sad?

> —J.M.
> ARLINGTON, VIRGINIA
> P   LEHIGH UNIVERSITY; ELON UNIVERSITY

ADVICE TO PARENTS: It's more important that your child is happy than that you display a 'Harvard' window decal on your SUV. Deep down, you already know this.

—*ANONYMOUS*
NEW YORK, NEW YORK
P ⚑ *BELOIT COLLEGE*

. . . .

A FRIEND OF MINE WHOSE CHILD IS ALREADY IN COLLEGE TOLD ME that at the end of the day it's your child's future, not yours. In other words, you have to know when to back off. The final say cannot be yours because the rewards or failures will not be yours to enjoy or suffer through.

—*COLTON CHAMPNEY*
BALTIMORE, MARYLAND
P ⚑ *UNIVERSITY OF MARYLAND*

. . . .

YOU KNOW THE WHOLE THING is out of hand when applying for college has taken up your child's life and he drops things that were important to him before the process began. If he wants to quit teams he loved being on; if he isn't seeing his friends; if the family stops doing usual things, like eating meals together or going to religious services, then it's too much.

—*TERESA OEFINGER*
PETALUMA, CALIFORNIA
P ⚑ *UNIVERSITY OF CALIFORNIA, DAVIS*

. . . .

WE HAD PLANNED A FAMILY TRIP to Costa Rica the summer before she went off to college. But my husband couldn't get away from work, so my daughter and I ended up spending three days at a beautiful eco-tourist resort. We had a wonderful time together, and it was definitely special because it was just the two of us. It wasn't meant to be this way, but it ended up working out really well. If you can get away to a special place for a few days with your college-bound child, you should do it.

—*LUCY RUMACK*
BROOKLYN, NEW YORK
P ⚑ *SWARTHMORE COLLEGE*

I LEARNED THE HARD WAY that your best friend is not necessarily going with you to college. My friend Beth and I had planned on going through the whole thing together. But toward the end it was obvious her grades were not going to get her into the schools I was considering. It was devastating to both of us. I learned that you need to make your college choice individually. You will become a better person if you are brave enough to strike out on your own.

—*COLLEEN BAKEY*
FREDERICK, MARYLAND
GEORGETOWN UNIVERSITY

• • • • • • • •

I THINK MORE PEOPLE NEED TO GET OUT and spend time in a different region of the country; it's an education that goes beyond the classroom. For me, I left my family and friends behind and didn't know anyone within a 500-mile radius of my campus. I wanted to experience a new place and meet new people; I wouldn't trade my time here for anything.

—*SCOTT COOLBAUGH*
KNOXVILLE, TENNESSEE
UNIVERSITY OF TENNESSEE

• • • • • • • •

NO MATTER WHOM YOU ARE DEALING WITH, whether it's a high school teacher or counselor or an admissions person or an interviewer, don't swear and don't show up late for a meeting. I did both of those the very first time I met with one of my high school teachers to ask for a recommendation. He really got on me about it and said if I did those things at the wrong time, it could affect my future. I took that advice to heart.

—*RACHEL LYNCH*
FREDERICK, MARYLAND
COPPIN STATE UNIVERSITY

WHERE YOU GO TO COLLEGE is nowhere near as important as they make it out to be. College is more a personal growing experience than anything else. While degree A may net you X amount of money upon hiring, as opposed to degree B netting you Y amount, college and post-college is really about making it on your own. If you make the effort, you should have an amazing experience in the long run.

—DAVID BERNGARTT
RALEIGH, NORTH CAROLINA
UNIVERSITY OF NORTH CAROLINA AT CHAPEL HILL

GOING AWAY FROM HOME is a good idea and a good experience, if you or your parents can afford it. My mom really wanted her kids to go away because she felt like it was the best thing she did. Now that I've done that, I agree with her advice.

—JANNA HAROWITZ
VANCOUVER, BRITISH COLUMBIA
McGILL UNIVERSITY

STUDY WHAT YOU ARE PASSIONATE ABOUT, but be smart. At the least, minor in something that will get you a job, be it computer science, business, accounting, or teaching. Speaking as a recent honors grad with a B.A. in English and a 3.79 GPA, no employer cares how smart you are if you aren't proficient with computers and have some marketable skills. Also, what you may think you want to do when you're applying, may change when you get into your classes.

—ERIN
TACOMA, WASHINGTON

> Don't decide what you want to do with your life when you're 18. You don't know yet. Just get into college and get a couple of years out of the way. Then decide.
>
> —KIRA
> ST. PETERSBURG, FLORIDA
> SPC/PTA PROGRAM

Expert Advice *FROM THE ADMISSIONS OFFICE*

WORDS OF WARNING

WHAT IS THE BIGGEST MISTAKE A PROSPECTIVE APPLICANT CAN MAKE?

FILLING OUT THE APPLICATION AT THE LAST MINUTE. Careless mistakes that suggest a student isn't taking the application process seriously hurt the chances of even the most qualified candidate.

> —CHRISTOPH GUTTENTAG
> DEAN OF UNDERGRADUATE ADMISSIONS
> DUKE UNIVERSITY

* * * * * * * *

THE BIGGEST MISTAKE a prospective applicant can make is to not apply to the schools which they believe are a good fit. Never finish the process in May wishing that you would have done things differently. Fill out the extra form, write that extra essay, and if you aren't admitted, at least you know you tried. Regret is a heavy feeling and it should be avoided at all costs.

> —MARK BUTT
> SENIOR ASSISTANT DIRECTOR OF ADMISSIONS
> JOHNS HOPKINS UNIVERSITY

* * * * * * * *

LIMITING THEIR OPTIONS — not doing their best in high school by performing well in a challenging curriculum; feeling they "must" go to college such and such and not researching other choices; procrastinating on applying to colleges until late in the application period; not seeking scholarships late in the junior year or early senior year or completing their FAFSA's by mid-February.

> —CHRIS LUCIER
> VICE PRESIDENT FOR ENROLLMENT MANAGEMENT
> UNIVERSITY OF VERMONT

MAKING ASSUMPTIONS. Assuming they know everything about a college without asking. Assuming all of their application materials are in without checking. Assuming they can't afford a particular college before going through the financial aid process. As with any significant investment, you want to eliminate as much of the guesswork as possible to make the most sound decision. Don't assume anything without valid confirmation.

> —*TONY BANKSTON*
> *DEAN OF ADMISSIONS*
> *ILLINOIS WESLEYAN UNIVERSITY*

• • • • • • • •

THE BIGGEST MISTAKE A PROSPECTIVE APPLICANT can make is overexposure. Multiple phone calls, e-mails, faxes, additional letters of recommendation and visits to the admissions office can initially generate interest but quickly turn out to be too much if an applicant isn't careful.

> —*TED SPENCER*
> *ASSOCIATE VICE PROVOST AND EXECUTIVE DIRECTOR OF UNDERGRADUATE ADMISSIONS*
> *UNIVERSITY OF MICHIGAN-ANN ARBOR*

• • • • • • • •

TO THINK THAT WE LOOK at an applicant's GPA or SAT as the most important part of the file.

> —*DANIEL J. SARACINO*
> *ASSISTANT PROVOST FOR ENROLLMENT*
> *UNIVERSITY OF NOTRE DAME*

• • • • • • • •

NOT APPLYING TO A SCHOOL THAT INTERESTS THEM. Keep an open mind – especially about financial aid and scholarships. You may be surprised at what you and your family may qualify for in gift and grant assistance – even from schools with large price-tags. The only sure way NOT to get into a college is NOT to apply to it!

> —*DOUGLAS L. CHRISTIANSEN, PH.D.*
> *ASSOCIATE PROVOST FOR ENROLLMENT AND DEAN OF ADMISSIONS*
> *VANDERBILT UNIVERSITY*

NOT DOING EXTENSIVE RESEARCH on the schools to which you are applying.

Not giving the application the time and energy it deserves. Sloppy, careless, last minute completed applications send the message that students don't really care about applying to the particular school. You've worked hard throughout high school to prepare yourself for continuing your educational and personal journey. The application is a great way to reflect on all of your great accomplishments; present yourself in the best way possible. An effective application takes time and thoughtful reflection, and can't be whipped out overnight.

> —*JEAN JORDAN*
> *DEAN OF ADMISSION*
> *EMORY UNIVERSITY*

• • • • • • • •

THOUGH THERE'S REALLY no single "mistake" that's going to cause a student to be denied, sometimes students seem to have real difficulty following the application instructions. We'll never actually count an essay that's supposed to have a 500-word limit, but please don't send us a five-page story. Likewise, if we ask for two letters of recommendation, it means that we don't want eight. We often see students doing things like photocopying every award they've ever received, or writing "see attached" in the extra-curricular activities box when it clearly states to pick their favorite activities and fill in the blanks. While we certainly want to know as much about a student as possible, submitting too much information can sometimes make an applicant look insecure. It also causes a lot of "background noise" and often prevents us from getting to the heart of the application. Finally, from a logistical standpoint, we're reading hundreds if not thousands of files in a relatively short timeframe – the instructions are there to facilitate a smooth, thorough, and quick read of every application.

> —*JACINDA OJEDA*
> *REGIONAL DIRECTOR OF ADMISSIONS*
> *UNIVERSITY OF PENNSYLVANIA*

• • • • • • • •

PLAGIARIZING.

> —*MATS LEMBERGER*
> *ASSISTANT DIRECTOR OF ADMISSIONS*
> *DARTMOUTH COLLEGE*

Expert Advice

IECA⁺ *COUNSELOR'S CORNER*

TOO MANY STUDENTS think of the application process as a means to get into college. Here are two problems with this "getting in" mindset: First of all, the research, selection, application, and admissions process itself is a journey of enormous reflection and intellectual growth. Second, the focus on "getting in" is comparable to a pregnant couple focusing entirely on the infant's birth with no thought about what they are going to do with that baby once it is born. This makes no sense!

—*ANONYMOUS*
IECA COUNSELOR

IF YOU DON'T GET ACCEPTED to a place you really want to go, take a gap year and improve the statistics. My daughter was rejected from all of the schools she applied to. Instead of going to a state school or a community college, we decided that she should take a gap year. We set up a timeline with certain goals that she would hit by the time applications season rolled around again. She got an internship and a research position at a lab. Now she was able to include solid work experience on her applications, and letters from her boss. She ended up getting into MIT, which was her first choice the first year she applied.

—*ANONYMOUS*
P ᴀ MASSACHUSETTS INSTITUTE OF TECHNOLOGY

As someone who has been very actively involved both in high school and college, nothing irks me more than prospective students that ask about the "formula" for being accepted. There is no formula! Thank goodness there is no formula. Think of how boring that would make your college experience. Passion will carry you much farther than having the "perfect" resume.

> —*Anu Parvatiyar*
> *Atlanta, Georgia*
> 🏫 *Georgia Institute of Technology*

· · · · · · · · ·

Though at the time it seems like the college admissions process is the most important thing in the world, it's not. Don't lose sight of the bigger, more important things, like developing relationships with your friends and enjoying the memories of your senior year. Be careful not to lose friends over the competition; be happy for one another regardless of the circumstances, because after you graduate, the college admissions process is a trivial detail of the distant past.

> —*Elana Brownstein*
> *Baltimore, Maryland*
> 🏫 *University of Maryland,*
> *College Park*

· · · · · · · · ·

I'm a big fan of the British method of the gap year. When you finish the equivalent of high school, you take off six months to a year and travel and work abroad. I think that's a great thing to do. Give yourself some time to wander around and think about what you want and who you want to be. It's very important for people at that age. There's school, and then there's the school of life.

> —*Jessamyn Goshom*
> *Washington, D.C.*
> 🏫 *University of Maryland,*
> *College Park*

Brody's Guide to the College Admissions Essay

by Jay Brody

Contents

INTRODUCTION

The college essay is a strange, rare creature:

IT'S A ONE-TIME THING. Most students write college essays just once --
in the fall of their senior year of high school -- and then never again.
That means applicants (and often parents) come into this project
completely unaware of what the task entails or requires, having never
done anything like it before.

THE COLLEGE ESSAY IS TERRIBLY IMPORTANT. In a world where students
sometimes write dozens of pages for each graded class, it can be
startling to imagine a 500-word piece holding such sway over something as monumental as college admissions. Yet next to grades and
test scores, the essay is the most relevant part of the college application. When admissions officers read the essays, they not only evaluate
them for quality, but also form unconscious impressions about the
candidate: "Is this a likable person? Does he or she sound intelligent?
Curious? Passionate?" Most important: "Do we want this person at
our school?"

YOU CAN USE ALL OF THE TIME AND RESOURCES YOU NEED. Perhaps the
best part about writing the college essay is this: despite all the stress
and hubbub that surrounds the admissions process, students can
write at their own pace. The essay isn't timed, and it isn't a pop quiz.
Applicants have at least three months (and in reality much more) to
conceive, plan, and write a one- to two-page paper. There's also plenty
of time for students to show their essay to parents and teachers, to
rethink, to revise, and generally to make all of the improvements that
good writing requires.

At Brody Admissions, a national college counseling firm, we saw hundreds of applicants to America's finest colleges and universities
struggle with the admissions essay. Over time, we developed the
advice and guidance that best helped those applicants overcome their
difficulties and express themselves effectively to admissions committees. And when we found that none of the existing college essay

guides provided the instructions that we felt students needed the most, we decided to write our own.

Published here, in its entirety, is *Brody's Guide to the College Admissions Essay*. It includes the gathered wisdom of Brody's counselors as well as seven of the best college admissions essays you'll ever see. I'm proud to see our guide included as part of such a terrific and unique book as *Get Into College*, and I hope you find it worthwhile.

Jay Brody
Chicago, IL

I. KNOW YOUR AUDIENCE

You probably know from your English classes or, better yet, as a matter of common sense, that a writer always writes for a particular audience. A VCR instruction manual is written in a different style than a romance novel, which is absolutely nothing like an economics textbook (hopefully).

The most important reason these styles of writing are different is that they serve different purposes and different audiences. The guy setting up his VCR just wants to know how to understand the process and get each step over with as quickly as possible. The romance reader is looking to escape into a fantasy world. The economics student is trying to understand a complex subject.

You'll write the college essay for just one audience: the college admissions committee member. Who is this person who reads your essays and otherwise decides your fate? Well, that depends on where you're applying.

TOP SCHOOLS

At today's most prestigious colleges (Harvard, Brown, Duke, Amherst, and so on), the people reading your essay are usually devoted admissions professionals. They use complex procedures to select applicants, and the essays are an important part of that process. Sure, the essays aren't always important. If you simply don't have the test scores and grades, you're not going to get in—busy admissions officers don't spend a lot of time reading essays from students who just aren't qualified. Similarly, on rare occasions a student will be so qualified or otherwise guaranteed admission that the essay just isn't important—unless the student writes something egregious, he or she will be admitted.

But for most applicants to top schools, essays will be read with a great deal of care. The person reading the essays is usually a tired, overworked admissions officer (sometimes working from home at night) who reads hundreds of essays each admissions season. With that much experience, the savvy admissions officer can get to the heart of your writing much more quickly than you'd expect.

OTHER COMPETITIVE SCHOOLS

What if you're not applying to a "top" school? Some schools require essays, and read them carefully, but are slightly less competitive than some of the names we've already mentioned. This includes a number of smaller schools with strong regional reputations. Most of the above rules still apply. The difference is that, while the profile of the admissions officer is likely still the same (a harried, experienced professional), the pool of competition may be a little less daunting.

This shouldn't change your strategy at all. You still need to produce stellar work, and take care of all of the other essay essentials we talk about later in this guide. Just be aware that your reader will be less inundated with powerful and perfect student essays. Standing out (for the sake of standing out) will probably be at less of a premium, and demonstrating your writing chops will be crucial.

LESS COMPETITIVE SCHOOLS

Finally, there are some large state schools and local schools that don't have rigorous admissions requirements but still require an essay. Not surprisingly, the admissions process (and thus your audience) is a little different at those places. Often, an administrator or part-timer will be reading your essay (or sometimes, especially if your grades and test scores are too high or too low, no one will be reading it).

Make sure your essay looks well-written and solid to any person who might look it over. Don't write anything weird. Don't write anything too innovative or difficult to understand in a short time period. Write well and clearly, and answer the questions posed. At these schools, the essay is used more like your GPA and SATs than as a way to get to know you. The schools want more information about how well you write and how clearly you express your thoughts.

WRITING FOR THE ADMISSIONS OFFICERS

Why is it important to know that someone who reads tons of these essays will evaluate yours? Why is it also important to know that, at

least at the most competitive colleges, an intelligent admissions officer (often an alumnus of the school) is likely to be reviewing your
application? It's important because you need to realize that *your final
audience for the college admissions essay is not the same as the
teachers and parents who tend to provide the most admissions-writ-
ing advice.*

1. Admissions officers can smell insincerity from a mile away.

Because they read so many essays, these people are great at determining who's truly passionate about something and who's making it
up. Writing about wanting to save the planet may sound great to your
English teacher, who doesn't read these essays very often, but the
admissions officer sees this all the time and it sounds phony. Unless
you can back up what you say with real-life experiences, steer away
from essay topics intended to make you sound benevolent or wise.

2. Admissions officers don't know you.

It's easy to forget that those helping you with your essays generally
know you well. If you take a sarcastic tone in an essay, they're likely to
be familiar with it. If you say something that could be construed as
offensive, they know that deep down you're a good person. If you make
a writing mistake, they remember that you're a great writer anyway.

Admissions officers, on the other hand, have never met you. This is
probably the only thing they've ever read of yours, and they're only
going to spend five to ten minutes, at the most, with your application.
What they see is what you get. Be sure that the essay you write gets
your message across on its own, without the need for any background
or understanding of who you are.

3. Admissions officers have seen it all.

You probably can't come up with anything completely original. That
essay where you pretend to be the family dog observing your life? The

one that's a little weird but so clever? They've read that essay, so you get few or no points for originality.

More commonly, that essay about Outward Bound or visiting Africa is not going to be special solely because you had those experiences. You may not realize it, but a number of applicants to top colleges have done those things. So while they may have been transformative experiences for you, they don't mean much on their own to the admissions officers. Rather than rely on how special you are because of those experiences, explain *why* they were so meaningful to you (if you discuss them)—and have a point.

4. Admissions officers have high standards.

If you're one of the brighter kids at your school, you're probably one of the best writers there. English teachers are impressed by your papers. You don't make grammatical mistakes, and you understand how an essay should be put together. When your parents and teachers read an admissions essay on which you've spent a lot of time, they're bound to be impressed. And they'll tell you so.

Once that essay makes its way to Dartmouth or Northwestern, however, the landscape changes. Almost by definition, the schools where your essays really count are the ones where your competition is, on average, about as gifted as you are. Relatively speaking, you aren't a great writer any more. In fact, even if your essay is well-received by friends and family, it's possible that it's actually not as good as many of the essays of other top students from all over the country applying to the same school.

At the very least, you need to realize that your essay most likely is not going to blow anyone away. Don't become too comfortable in the praise of your readers, teachers, parents, and counselors. This isn't high school—college admissions is a competitive, national game and the judges (admissions officers) are playing by a new and tougher set of rules. Your essay should be the best thing you've ever written.

II. TOPICS

High school kids tell great stories. Why? While it's sometimes hard to realize at the time, life in high school is full of adventure and intrigue, as well as exploration and self-discovery. And as any family with only one phone line can attest, there's no shortage of things to talk about in the high school world. High school students spend hours each week on the phone, talking about everything and nothing. Hours more are spent chatting in school, after school, out on weekends, during the summer, and at just about every other opportunity.

So why, when it comes to finding something to write for a college application, does everyone seem to draw a blank? Why, almost every day during the Fall application season, do intelligent 17 year-olds insist that they suddenly have absolutely nothing to talk about?

Because as a high school student, you don't—and shouldn't—have any clue about what makes a good college admissions essay.

A college admissions essay isn't like a science paper, a book report, a history essay, or anything else you've been taught to write. Frankly, a good college admissions essay might not even resemble what you were told was acceptable by your teachers or counselors.

Each of those other pieces of writing has its own set of rules: How many pages should it be? What should my introduction look like? How should each paragraph be structured? Where does my "thesis statement" go?

Your college essay, on the other hand, is more flexible, and is more of a story. It's very short, and you've got to make this one interesting. So interesting that when someone on an admissions committee reads it, he or she says, "Wow! That's a neat kid; I want that student to be a part of our school."

And before you can write that incredible essay, you need to have a topic.

While everyone has his or her own idea about the "ideal" college essay topic, there are certain basic elements that all admissions officers seem to find important. We've condensed these into three basic rules...

RULE #1: YOUR ESSAY MUST BE ABOUT *YOU*.

Sounds obvious, right? Are you going to write your essay about someone else? Of course not. But this first point is the most important one, and the one most often mishandled by smart kids (and good writers!) who manage to flub this great opportunity to sell themselves.

First-rate, successful college essays let their audience—the admissions officers we talked about earlier—learn a lot more about the candidate. Other than your essay, you're going to send these colleges your grades, your test scores, a couple of recommendations, a short list of your activities, and that's about it. How well do those things represent who you are? Do those five pages or so of information describe the real you?

When you write an essay that resonates at a human level—one that's from the heart and gives readers some insight into your personality— you give them a reason to like you, to understand you, and to want to admit you into their school. When you submit a well-written paper about something or someone other than yourself, you're only telling them that you're skilled at writing papers—information they can get elsewhere.

If you think this first rule is silly and easy and *of course you're going to write about yourself,* keep reading. Writing an essay that really gives insight into your personality is harder than you think.

- **Claudia** wrote about how her experience working with disadvantaged children changed the way she views various aspects of her life.

- **Will** wrote about how tennis had dominated his life since childhood and what it took for him to quit playing when he had been so successful. Giving up his (and his parents') dream of playing professionally was the hardest decision he ever made.

- **Ashley** wrote about coping with a disability and how it affected her decision-making.

- **Ben** told a funny story that described how absent-minded he can be.

- **Fran** wrote a silly essay about how she hates the color pink.

After reading these essays, admissions officers undoubtedly felt as though they knew each of these applicants a little better. That's the key to making the essay about you.

It's not as though students who violate Rule #1 write about something entirely off-topic or impersonal. Rather, they write about some aspect of their lives, but in a way that doesn't really tell us much about them. We hear that they enjoy reading, or traveled throughout Europe, but we don't know how their attribute or experience makes them special. We're left thinking, "Anyone could have written that!"

Some examples of common essay topics that don't work because they're too impersonal:

- **Samantha** wrote about her grandmother and how—immigrating from Europe at age 14 and making a life for herself in Brooklyn—grandma has been a role model for Samantha as Samantha has grown up.

Samantha's essay is probably going to be a lot more about grandma than it is about Samantha. Even if we hear about their interactions, we're probably not going to learn much about what makes Samantha tick. Unless grandma's interested in starting college at age 85, this essay isn't going to help anyone.

- **Robert** wrote about biology, his favorite subject and likely major in college. He has a lot of biology-related predictions about what the future will hold.

Robert's essay is about biology. It could work if he opens up about himself, but unless Robert does something more unique than discuss current issues in the field, we're really not going to learn much about Robert here that couldn't be summed up in a few sentences. Robert, probably an interesting guy, may have wasted his essay.

- **Jessica** wrote about running on the track team and how wonderful it was when her school won the state championship; she loved being on a team and talked about how much better the experience was because it was shared among a group.

Jessica's essay is about teamwork and sharing joyous occasions. Most people probably share Jessica's opinion—while she might (but probably doesn't) have some philosophical insights, they're probably more about teamwork and running track than they are about Jessica. We're left knowing no more about this girl after reading the essay than before we picked it up.

So Rule #1 is easy enough: your essay must be about you. Remember — that doesn't just mean that you're the main character in the essay. Instead, you need to come across as a living, breathing human being—someone who can think about the past few years of his or her life and find something personal and revealing to write about.

The other components of your application let the admissions committees understand your background and—if you do a good job—be impressed by you. But the essays can help them know you and identify with you. This opportunity is too valuable to waste.

RULE #2: YOUR ESSAY SHOULD BE INTERESTING.

When we ask students to brainstorm topics and they come back with something we tell them is "boring," we usually end up regretting having opened our mouths. Not only do we get hurt and disappointed looks from the student, but sometimes we get angry calls from mom or dad. Who are we to judge the value of their child's life? Who are we to say what's exciting and what isn't?

That's nonsense. We have yet to meet a high school student who didn't have anything interesting to say, but we've dealt with hundreds who have a hard time articulating what makes them special. And that's understandable. Thinking outside your daily life and routine is hard. Sometimes it's tough to imagine there's anything you could say that would interest the admissions committee of a prestigious college. Of course, if you've done something truly unique in your life already, there's no reason to overcomplicate matters—you should probably write about that! If you competed in the Olympics, founded a charity, or started a significant business, you can bet the admissions committees will be eager to hear about such a formative experience. Writing the actual essay will still be challenging, but you've got your general subject matter already figured out.

Fortunately, for those among us with less newsworthy credentials, there's still hope. However, before we discuss which specific essay topics might work well, we're going to discuss which topics *not* to choose. Here, the most important thing to remember is to avoid the traps that make an essay unbearably dull or common.

Boring Essay Topics

- Don't write about the death of a pet, or even a family member. Not only are these subjects depressing, but such essays almost always sound the same.

- Don't think you need to necessarily write about the most important thing in your life. Many students tell us how important their friends, or siblings, are to them. Or they want to talk about their relationship with God. Even if you manage to make such an essay sufficiently personal to fit Rule #1, it's very challenging to write a "friends" or "God" essay that doesn't look like everyone else's. (Remember, these readers see thousands of essays in just a few months. Is yours special enough to leave an impression?)

- Beware the sports essay. I've seen good ones, but I've seen many more that put me to sleep before the end of the first paragraph. The thrill of victory. The agony of defeat. Persistence. Teamwork...It's all been done.

- The "I'm sitting down to write my essay, and don't know what to write about" essay. Yawn.

- Explaining that even though your parents are divorced, you now realize that they both still love you.

- Bad comedy. Your friends and family don't want to hurt your feelings, and so they often won't be the harsh critics you need. If most people reading it aren't laughing out loud, it's not funny.

In the end—and we'll talk more about this when we discuss particular topics—an interesting essay is simply one that stands out, engages the reader's attention, and leaves a lasting impression. It's not necessary to write about something super-impressive or particularly quirky.

The key is to pursue some aspect of your life that sets you apart – and to provide as much detail and insight as you can.

Boring vs. Interesting Essay Topics	
Boring	**Interesting**
During my two week trip to Europe, I learned a lot about various cultures.	*During my two week trip to Europe, I learned a lot while trapped in a ski-lift for three hours with an elderly Iranian couple.*
I learned the value of hard work by working summers in a warehouse.	*I learned the value of hard work by working summers in a warehouse alongside three poor immigrants.*
I volunteer in a soup kitchen. (Too routine a topic unless you have something unexpected to say).	*I started a soup kitchen because…*
I'm a very well-rounded person—I'm not only good at academics, but I've also excelled at several sports and somehow find time to help the less fortunate. (Not focused enough…doesn't get deep enough to be insightful)	*To the outside world I appear to be a well-rounded person—but those very close to me know that I'm always just waiting for the opportunity to work on my mystery novel, which consumes all of my spare time.*
I keep a fish tank, and it's a hobby I enjoy because I like animals and it looks nice. I've had the tank since my father bought it for me 10 years ago.	*I have a fish tank with five fish named Lucky, Bob, Stripey, Homer, and Big Earl. Each of them has a personality, and in its own way reminds me of myself…*
Growing up in a family of six children has taught me how to deal with others and the importance of family.	*I live in a house with six children, but for the past four years, every Wednesday after soccer practice, I've eaten a special dinner alone with just my mom.*

A note about passion...

What resonates when I read extraordinary essays from "ordinary" kids is that such essays often show passion. Passion is interesting, exciting, and real. Knowing what an applicant really cares about provides an insight that even the most detailed biography cannot. And a genuine passion for something usually demonstrates intellectual curiosity, a character trait prized by admissions committees.

Does writing passionately about a subject mean that your essay will be interesting? Of course not. We've already mentioned how dull and routine the "my friends are the most important thing in my life" essay can be. And many high school students are passionate about music, yet admissions officers read 20 run-of-the-mill "I love music" essays for every good one.

The most important role of passion in your essays comes during the writing stage, when passion can infuse an already engaging essay with a rare urgency and humanity—we'll talk more about that later. But when you're still choosing a topic, it won't hurt to choose something you feel strongly about—a subject that you can discuss straight from the heart and with a special enthusiasm. That enthusiasm will come through when you write.

RULE #3: YOUR ESSAY SHOULD SAY SOMETHING THAT IS NOT OBVIOUS FROM THE REST OF YOUR APPLICATION.

If you've paid close attention to the first two rules when selecting your topic, Rule #3 often isn't a problem. Yet, it's terribly important. The essay provides you with a great opportunity to talk about yourself in a format more personal and expressive than the rest of the application. If you waste that opportunity by rehashing your accomplishments, you're going to fall one step behind other applicants.

For students who have excelled primarily in one particular area, Rule #3 poses a dilemma. For example, an accomplished debater might really have something interesting to say about his debate experiences. On the other hand, this debater—by writing about debate—risks 1) wasting valuable essay space on something he's already conveyed elsewhere on his application, and 2) foregoing the opportunity to talk about something else meaningful to him—such as a very unusual relationship, for example—that really doesn't fit anywhere else.

The solution is to weigh carefully the risks and rewards of writing about a subject you've already covered. Any such essay should convey at least some new information or insight.

Essay topic that overlaps too much with the rest of the application	Why to avoid it
I worked hard at tennis, rising from JV to quarterfinalist in the state tournament. I'm proud of my hard work.	You can convey on your extracurricular activities list that you rose from JV to state quarterfinalist, and everyone will assume that it must have been hard and you must be proud.
I have had significant academic accomplishments, and have proven myself as a talented young scientist in Mrs. Johnson's biology class.	You've taken three biology classes and Mrs. Johnson is writing you a recommendation. We're already aware of your enthusiasm and talent.
Working for the student newspaper, I've gone beyond the norm in seeking out very challenging stories such as increased gang violence in our neighborhood.	This could be a good essay, but you'd probably get most of it across in an activity description and possibly a clipping of one of your articles. If you've got something else to write about, you should take the opportunity to convey that as well.
Volunteering is important to me. I want to make a difference in	We can read about what you've done on your application. The

my world. For example, I've already volunteered in the following ways....	importance you attach to volunteering can perhaps be explained better in narrative form, but is there really enough insight or new information here to warrant using up your essay?
Essay topic that overlaps with the application but is probably OK	**Why it's OK**
While a counselor at a camp for disabled children, I formed a very special relationship with one girl in particular.	You've probably already shown the committee that you worked at the camp, and so it would be nice to talk about something else. But the lessons you learned from an unusual friendship (as opposed to general observation) can't really be conveyed on a chart.
I used to be shy and reserved, but becoming active in theater has had a positive impact on my life that extends far beyond school.	We already know the extent of your participation and success in theater. But the rest of your application (except possibly a recommendation from your drama teacher) isn't capable of demonstrating the importance this activity has had for you.
A lifelong violinist and soccer player, last year I had to make a very difficult choice about which of these two activities I would pursue full-time, with the hopes of becoming a professional.	Wow! What a decision for an eleventh grader.... We can already tell that you did very well in two activities and eventually dropped one, but your description of this issue will go far, far beyond what's apparent from the rest of your application.

Always remember that the essay is a tremendous opportunity to improve your application. Choose a topic that will allow you to buttress and add to the rest of your story.

Getting More Specific: How to approach the essay questions, and how to find a topic.

The hardest part of our job is telling students that their essays—which they've often spent a great deal of time conceiving, writing, and editing—need to be completely rewritten. Usually, this happens when we're handed an essay that has absolutely no hope of conforming to all of the three rules we discussed above. Why do students choose boring, impersonal, or non-illuminating essay topics? Often they do so because they arbitrarily settled on a topic and began writing, perhaps with the encouragement of a parent or well-meaning teacher. But on many occasions, we find that the student felt constrained by the essay question itself.

Each essay written for a college application does one of the following:

1. It responds to a particular question.
2. It responds to one of several particular questions.
3. It responds to a general request for an essay about almost any topic.

Recent Common Application Questions (used by many colleges, both as part of the Common Application and as questions on their own applications)

1. *Evaluate a significant experience, achievement, risk you have taken, or ethical dilemma you have faced and its impact on you.*
2. *Discuss some issue of personal, local, national, or international concern and its importance to you.*
3. *Indicate a person who has had a significant influence on you, and describe that influence.*
4. *Describe a character in fiction, an historical figure, or a creative work (as in art, music, science, and so forth) that has had an influence on you, and explain that influence.*
5. *Topic of your choice.*

While students dealing with the Common Application might initially think they are deciding among several questions, in reality that "Topic of your choice" option means that any topic is fair game. Yes, you can send an essay about *any* subject to a Common Application school.

Yet 95% of the students we work with who have lousy essay topics for a Common Application school invariably have chosen one of the first four questions. Answering one of these questions is fine, and those prompts can serve to get creative juices flowing, but *don't just pick one of these questions and try to answer it no matter what!*

Own your essay.

When we say that you need to "own" your essay, we mean that you must conform your best ideas to the questions you're given, and not let the questions themselves dictate what you write. If your two major essay ideas are 1) your relationship with your autistic brother and 2) your love of painting, don't choose Common Application Question #1 and then wrack your brain for an ethical dilemma you've faced, completely ignoring that great essay fodder you've already found.

Students who choose questions before topics sometimes write good essays, but they often don't do the best job of portraying themselves to the admissions committees. If chess is your best essay topic, then write about chess! Sometimes, this will be impossible, such as when you are asked to answer a question about, say, an issue of international importance (any way you slice it, chess is probably not an issue of international importance). Usually however, you'll be able to find a way to write about one of your preferred topics.

This is so important that we can't stress it enough. Owning your essay is the key to putting your best foot forward. Don't waste your big essay opportunity discussing a book, historical figure, or social problem that means nothing to you.

The Specific Essay Questions

Of course, you may still face some limitations imposed by specific essay questions. So let's go through some popular questions to illustrate how they might be approached. We're not going to focus here on the Common Application questions, except to the extent they turn up elsewhere, because as we saw above, the Common Application places no limitations on the essay. If you're simply dealing with the Common Application, you should write about your #1 topic, in whatever manner will serve you best.

If you wrote a 300-page autobiography, what would be on page 137?

This question tries to stimulate a little creative thinking. It can also probably be answered in two ways: you can describe an important event in your life, or you can describe a hypothetical event that has yet to take place.

If you choose to write about the past, you want to make sure you follow Rule #2 and make it interesting! Give your audience some context, as well as some drama or suspense. If you're writing about your first day broadcasting on the student radio station, show how that day fit into your life and why it was an important moment. Dry autobiographies are painful to read.

If you write about the future, it's hard to avoid being at least a little interesting. Your bigger concern would instead be following Rule #1, and making sure that the essay is about your own life. Don't write about landing on Mars if you have no credible interest in space exploration. Don't write about being the first woman President if it doesn't follow from the rest of your application. A good autobiographical "page" about the future might describe a former biology student taking part in the cure of a genetic disease, or a former animal shelter volunteer running a charity for abused animals. Try to give some insight into your dreams and ambitions—the person you are today—through your description of the future.

Whatever route you choose, take advantage of the question format to be as creative as possible. You can refer to other unwritten parts of the "autobiography." You can begin or end mid-sentence. Here and on other unusual questions, you will be partially judged on the creativity and vigor with which you tackle the assignment. Put your imagination to work!

If you had to come up with a personal motto that defined a value you hold deeply, what would it be?

or

Choose a famous quotation that you find meaningful.

Some questions are designed to make you choose a value or belief that's important to you. In asking this type of question, the admissions committees are hoping to elicit from you—in a more philosophical way—what you find important.

There's room for a great deal of flexibility here. Good college essays often discuss learning and growth experiences, or defining moments or personal qualities. These fit well with the values/beliefs/quotations type of essay.

Here are some values applicants often write about:

- Commitment
- Charity/Helping Others
- Learning/Education
- Family/Friends/Love
- Compassion/Kindness
- Hard Work
- Happiness
- Perspective
- Loyalty
- Personal Growth
- Honesty/Integrity
- Humor

To find quotations, you can search the Internet (probably the best method) or else pick up a copy of *Bartlett's Familiar Quotations* and start leafing through the index.

The best way to succeed with this type of essay is to decide what you want to write, at least in very broad terms, and then work backwards to fit the topic. Starting with a value or quotation and then deciding how to write about it likely means you'll end up with an essay that you don't own. Remember—don't be controlled by the question prompt!

Bad answers to this question happen when an applicant's thought process goes something like this:

What's a value I believe in? The importance of family. Why don't I write about how important my family is to me? Or, I always liked that Mark Twain quote...why don't I write about how that fits my life?

Being forced to answer a particular essay prompt does not absolve you of the responsibility to write a fantastic, A+ essay that will stand on its own. If you've brainstormed topics and your best stuff comes from your experience with music, then write about that! The quotation can be something about music or art. If you live and breathe fish, you should write about fish. Find an appropriate quotation. Can't find one? Keep looking!

Own your topic.

Discuss a setback or disappointment in your life.

This type of question shows up frequently on applications, often as one option among two or three. Generally, we advise applicants to avoid it unless they have something interesting and not too damaging to write about. "Ethical failures," such as the time you cheated on a test and got caught (and learned your lesson), do not make good essays; instead, they highlight what will probably be viewed as a flaw in your character. Setbacks that make you look impotent or incompetent, while not universally off-limits, more often hurt you more than they help: examples include your struggle to make a JV sports team, or your social or academic difficulties.

We have read some great essays that respond to this question, and what they all have in common is a real sense of personal growth and self-awareness.

- **Deb** wrote about her realization that she wasn't ever going to be a great golfer and how she quit the team. She had a number of other interests, and finally facing the disappointment of her father enabled her to focus on what was important to her as an individual.

- **Javier** wrote about being so nervous about public speaking that he was forced to cancel a speech he was to give at his confirmation ceremony. Angry with himself, he joined an adult speakers' club and took courses in speech and debate at his high school. For the past two years, he has given talks to freshmen and sophomores about overcoming his fear.

The best failure/setback essays put the negative event in the context of an eventual success or a genuinely transformative learning experience.

Why is ⚖ a good match for you?

One of the most straightforward of the essay questions, this is also one of the hardest to pull off well. This essay is usually shorter—often 250 words or fewer. The challenge is to avoid a generic answer and to try to explain why a particular college is right for you (and by implication why other colleges aren't as good a fit). You should usually include more than one reason why Perfect University is the school of your dreams.

Here are some ideas:

- *I need a big/small school because...*
- *I need an urban/rural/suburban school because...*
- *The science/writing/history program is appealing to me because...*
- *I visited and loved the...*

- *My family has long had connections to this school...*
- *I've talked to Coach Smith and am excited about playing on your basketball team.*
- *You have the best drama program in the area.*
- *You have the only marine biology program in the area.*
- *I want to work with professors Johnson and Chang in the biology department.*

Bad Answers:

- *Your school has great sports teams for which I've cheered since I was little.*
- *I want to live far from home and Florida is very far from Seattle.*
- *All of my friends are going to your school, too.*

To some extent, our three rules of choosing a topic may be difficult to apply here. But remember that this essay should still mostly be about you. The colleges ask this question because they want to know that you've thought a lot about their institution and are eager to attend. The best answers explain the school's qualities in the context of the applicant's needs and ambitions. Saying you're excited about a biology program is only useful if you've already demonstrated an interest in biology. Otherwise, you haven't done anything to shine a light onto your own life and experiences.

Discuss an issue that is important to you.

This is a tough one, because it's difficult to integrate yourself and an "issue" into the same essay. So applicants sometimes just say: *"Well, it asks for an important issue, so I'll talk about an important issue. I've always felt that AIDS in Africa was a problem because..."*

Bad idea.

While you could write a solid and persuasive essay about a number of outstanding social or political concerns, you don't want to give away your essay-writing opportunity by ignoring Rule #3 and not teaching the admissions committee anything about you (the fact that you're against AIDS or hunger does not make you special).

You may recognize this question as similar to one on the Common Application. If you're seeing it there or as one of a number of choices on a school-specific application, and you don't know how you're going to tackle it, you may want to consider one of your other options.

If you're stuck with this question, or feel that you have a good response, then you should tackle it with the same intellectual rigor that you would use for any other question. As always, your answer needs to be 1) about you, 2) interesting, and 3) not obvious from the rest of your application.

How can this be done? Here are a few essays that worked:

- **Sara** discussed heart disease. She has been active in charities related to heart disease since her father survived a heart attack. She's also done a great deal of research and has strong opinions related to funding and public awareness.

- **Greg** is an environmentalist with a lot of experience in that area.

- **Harold** wrote about his autistic brother, an area of personal concern for him.

- **Shelley** has never been involved officially in politics, but is constantly reading political journals and debates fiercely with all of her friends and family (she's the only Republican she knows).

The common thread here is a personal connection to the topic being discussed. By demonstrating passion for a particular issue, you show involvement in your world and that you care about events that take place beyond your own little bubble.

Put your best foot forward.

Honesty is important, in college applications as much as anywhere. If you're dishonest on your applications, you'll not only face your own conscience, but you're also likely shooting yourself in the foot: one call to your high school from an admissions officer and suddenly all of your applications—and your academic future—will be in jeopardy.

Yet being honest doesn't mean spilling your guts. Many students feel compelled to portray themselves as directly as possible to the admissions committees. They feel compelled to help the committees get to know "the real me." If they're asked what their most defining value is, they write about their most defining value. If the application wants to know which activity means the most to them, then that's what they put down on paper.

Of course committees want to know the real you! How else will they know whether you should be admitted or rejected? If you're going to be a superstar in college, they want to discover the real you so that they can quickly admit you into their class. But if you're a person with lesser credentials and promise, they want to know that too—so they can politely reject you and keep looking for someone better.

Unless you're perfect, your job is to portray an idealized version of yourself to the admissions committees. That doesn't mean you should iron out your faults and quirks to display a boring and flawless version of yourself. But it does mean that you need to exercise some control over how you are viewed during the application process.

Here are some tips for making the best possible impression:

- **Avoid displaying major character flaws or weaknesses unless it's necessary.** If you don't fit in socially or don't speak English well, try to avoid discussing it. If you're asked about your greatest weakness, don't say you're a compulsive liar—talk instead about something more benign, such as your trouble confronting people.

- **Sound like an interesting person, even on the short questions.** "Hanging out with my friends" is never a good answer for what you most like to do in your spare time, even if it's true.

- **When possible, choose your best activity instead of the one they ask about.** You may be asked to discuss the activity that is the most important to you. For the purposes of your application, starting a charity is more important than babysitting. Creative writing is more important than shopping. Don't avoid out-of-the-way interests that might make good essays, or feel compelled to write about your most "impressive" accomplishment. But remember to give your first priority to creating the best possible application, and not to deciding which of two activities is technically the most important.

- **Think creatively about your accomplishments.** Never lie about what you've done. But it's happened at least a hundred times: we'll be talking to a student in our offices and she'll list the things she's been involved with for the past few years. She'll mention JV volleyball, choir, church youth group, and then—in the middle of a list of about 20 minor activities—she'll throw out, "oh yeah, and in the summer before tenth grade my friends and I set up a Shakespeare class for inner-city kids, just once a week, as a project for our youth group." Because it only lasted for a few weeks, took little of her time, and happened over two years ago, she'll consider it almost not worth mentioning. But expressed properly to an admissions committee, this is gold.

- **Pick the question for which you can give the best answer, not the one you can answer the most easily.** Sometimes it's tempting to write about, say, the person who has most influenced you (simple—your older sister!), when the other questions—such as "Please respond to the following quotation from Emily Dickinson"—sound intimidating. But you need to resist the impulse to take the easy road. Spend some time and come up with your best answer, not the most obvious or "honest" one.

Putting together a great application is largely about writing essays that show committees what kind of person they'd be admitting to their school. When choosing a topic for your essays, focus on show-ing them an applicant they'd be proud to admit.

The Brainstorming Process

When we work with a student, we have a number of questions we use to try to draw out any experiences that might turn into good essay topics. How should you do this on your own?

The best way is to make a list. Take a sheet of paper and label it: *Essay Topic Brainstorming*.

On this page you're going to put anything you can think of that might serve as material for one of your essays.

Then start putting the ideas down on paper. The first few should be easy—just answer the following questions: What are your activities? Your academic interests? Your jobs? What do you do in your spare time? How would you describe yourself? How would others describe you?

Write each topic along the left margin of your page, and leave yourself room to explore each idea. To the right of each idea (e.g. "Debate," "Dance," "Brother," "Chemistry," "Job at senior citizens' center," "Competitive," "Musical"), fill in details about where you think each subject could lead. Next to "Debate," for example, you might write the following:

- Finally found an arena where I could express my opinions
- Learned lessons of civility, respect for others
- First experience being on a real team
- Learned the value of commitment and working hard on something

At this point, don't worry so much about the rules of essay writing or what might make a good topic. You'll be better off just scribbling down everything that occurs to you—good, bad, or ugly—and eliminating all the junk later. Sometimes an idea seems terrible at first and eventually leads to something creative or insightful.

Spend a few days on this. Think about ideas when you're taking a shower and when you're lying in bed at night. Each time you sit down to brainstorm, don't let yourself get up until you've had a few ideas.

Eventually, you'll hit a roadblock. Here are some idea starters to make sure you've covered all of your bases:

- **Academics:** What have you done in school that has truly influenced you? Are you a budding physicist? A reader? A writer? Have you won awards or accolades for any school work you've done? What are your academic interests?

- **Extracurriculars:** What school-related activities have you involved yourself with? The big ones will be easy, but is there anything else you've either forgotten about or hadn't considered important? German Club? Math competitions? What sports have you played at any level?

- **Jobs:** What jobs have you had, both paid and unpaid? Include school-year positions as well as summer jobs. Don't forget about jobs you've had for only a short period of time (one week externships, small projects, and so forth).

- **Other Activities:** What do you do in your free time? Read? Program computers? Build models? Sew? Dance? Play sports that you don't play at school? Church activities? Take classes somewhere?

- **Who are the people who have had an impact on you?** Family members? Probably not friends, unless there are some unusual circumstances. Have you had teachers who have been terrific mentors? How about employers? Role models? We've already mentioned the dangers of discussing relationships in an essay, but it's worth writing everything down and seeing where it leads.

- **Travel:** Where have you gone? What did you do? Did you learn anything?

- **How would you describe yourself?** How would others describe you? Are there specific aspects of your life or personality that might be interesting to discuss?

- **What are some of your strongest memories?**

- **What do you like doing the most? Hate doing the most?**

- **What are your short-term and long-term goals?**

- **Who are your heroes?**

- **Are you artistic in any way? How so?**

- **What issues in the world are important to you?**

It's not important that you answer all of these questions, and you can certainly add to the list. The goal is to come up with a list of topics—as long as possible—that covers just about everything interesting or noteworthy that you could ever say about yourself.

Conclusion—settling on the right topic

So now you've got a list of topics. Some of them seem completely worthless (*I wrote that I love my grandma*, you're thinking. *That is not a good essay topic!*). Some look intriguing, but you're not sure how they might be turned into an essay. Hopefully, a few ideas appear promising.

Now's the time to bring it all together. Everything you've absorbed in this chapter can now be put to use, as you look at the questions you need to answer and try to adapt a topic from your list.

Good luck, and don't forget what we discussed in this chapter:

- **When choosing a topic, remember our three rules of choosing a good topic for your college essay:**
    1) The essay must be about you;
    2) The essay must be interesting; and
    3) The essay must be about something not obvious from your application.

- **Own your essay.** Pay attention to the questions, but write what you want to write.

- **Put your best foot forward.** Never lie or exaggerate the truth. But also never forget that you're trying to put together the best and most persuasive application, not the most technically "accurate" one.

- **Structure your brainstorming process.** Don't just read a question, think of an answer, and begin to write. To properly mine your entire life for good admissions essay fodder, you need to create a written list of all possible topics and give yourself some time.

Finding a topic is, in our opinion, the hardest part of the process. Once you've done that, you're ready to put together that perfect essay!

III. WRITING: PUTTING YOUR THOUGHTS ON PAPER

So you've got a topic. You've got a computer. You've got some time. What now?

After settling on a topic, every applicant seems to have a different way to get started. Sometimes, students sit in front of a computer for hours, not knowing where to begin. Others work in fitful spurts, churning out an introduction or a conclusion but not much else. Sometimes we see outlines that undergo dozens of revisions. A few times a year, a student leaves our offices and returns the next day with a first draft. Some can't even get that first sentence written.

Unfortunately, there's no ideal approach. Writing college essays is hard, and unless you've got everything planned out exactly in your mind, it's going to take some time to get that ideal 200-500 word essay on paper.

Following are some guidelines that our students have found effective over the years.

Give your essays the attention they deserve.

Writing is difficult. This is your first time writing a college admissions essay. The college admissions essay is likely the most important writing assignment you've ever had.

Your full attention is warranted.

Kids today have full schedules, and we know there are a lot of important things going on junior and senior year. But almost all of those sports, lessons, and activities should really take a back seat to turning out stellar applications. It's that important.

Don't wait until the last minute.

By far the most important timing issue related to your essays is getting started early. You can't wait until the last minute and still expect to turn out essays that will impress the admissions committees. Sure, you may be able to come up with something decent, just as you've probably written papers and studied for tests successfully by staying up very late. But this is a project for which you must get an A+. The college at which you may spend the next four years may very well be determined by how much time you leave yourself for the essays.

When should you begin? If your deadline is January 1, as it is for many competitive schools, you should start your brainstorming process no later than the middle of October. By the time November rolls around, you should have topic ideas for each essay and should be working to get each one started.

Why so early? Because writing these essays takes a long, long time:

- It takes a long time to find the right approach—sometimes weeks of writer's block.
- Writing the essay itself is time-intensive.
- You can easily spend weeks editing and soliciting feedback, and still not feel as though you've done enough.
- Sometimes, a seemingly good topic just doesn't lead to a great essay, and you need to start over.
- Other time-consuming issues, both admissions-related and not, always pop up.

Some schools, especially those with rolling admissions, insist that applications sent in earlier will get more attention. This alone is a good enough reason for you to get started as soon as you can.

Give yourself the space and time to work effectively.

The completion of any great project requires tremendous focus on the part of its creator. Sure, J.K. Rowling may have scribbled out the first *Harry Potter* books while sipping coffee in a London café. But she is a uniquely gifted author, and this was even for her probably quite hard to do—it's a safe bet that the *Harry Potter* sequels were written in a quiet office, without distractions, and with a certain amount of time each day set aside just for writing.

You need to create a schedule and a working environment where you can focus your attention fully on your essays. That doesn't mean you need to clear out a room in your house, or lock yourself in the basement for three hours each day. But when you sit down to write, you need to make certain you won't be distracted or interrupted. That means no TV, no video games, no phone calls, and (yes, we're getting ourselves in trouble here) no homework. Also, no working on grandma's kitchen table while everyone watches football during Thanksgiving weekend.

Some people will tell you to set aside a particular block of time each day (for example, two hours right after school). Unless you have serious self-discipline problems, that probably isn't necessary. But it's important to work in a quiet environment with plenty of room to spread out and where you won't be interrupted. When you sit down to write your essay, you should know that you won't need to do anything else for the next hour or two and can devote yourself fully to the task at hand.

Focus is essential.

Let ideas marinate.

The #1 excuse for bad essays? "I knew what I wanted to say, but I just couldn't put it down on paper."

One of the best things about starting early is that you can always take breaks when the creative process isn't going well. While you shouldn't use this as an excuse to procrastinate, the best strategy when you hit a major roadblock is to get up, relax, and try again later.

Sometimes ideas come to us in the car, or during a run. Often a student will try for weeks to write a first sentence, and then one day she'll sit down and write a beautiful essay in about three hours. These things take time, and your brain can't be prodded to do all of its preparation and creative work at once.

Along similar lines, you should avoid forcing yourself to get everything done in one sitting. You don't want to put yourself in this common predicament: "This Saturday I'm going to write a rough draft of my Notre Dame and Tufts essays, no matter what!" What if you're not writing well that day? What if one essay goes well but the other just doesn't seem like your best stuff? Sitting in your bedroom, staring at a blank sheet of paper, is not the way to encourage a stroke of creative genius.

Eventually, your mind will snap to attention and demand that you put pen to paper. Make sure that moment happens *before*, and not *after*, your final deadlines.

Write long.

When you look at word and page limits, always plan on your first draft being longer than it needs to be. Essays are almost always better for being shortened, and it's very satisfying to take out the worst parts of your essay and still be left with a piece that's the right length. If your first draft is the exact length you need, you'll be stuck with everything you wrote; if it's too short, you'll have to awkwardly fill it in somewhere.

Don't procrastinate.

This one is obvious. Just because you're not going to "force it" doesn't mean you can set up your work area, think about essays for a little while, and then go watch TV. If you avoid working on this difficult and time-intensive task, you'll end up in the same position as someone who waited until the last minute (and you'll be wishing in April that you could do it all over again).

Good Essay-Writing Habits

- Start early—at least two months before your essays are due.
- Sit down to work only when you'll have at least 60-90 minutes of completely uninterrupted time.
- Create a workspace that is non-distracting and free of clutter.
- If you're stuck, leave your writing for a while and return when you're more fresh.
- But don't procrastinate.

IV. STRUCTURE AND STYLE

Since you've never written a college admissions essay before, you probably aren't exactly sure what it's supposed to look like. Should it be a story? A paper? Do you need an intro? Should it be in the first person? Should you start with a quotation? Do you need a conclusion?

Believe it or not, there aren't a lot of great answers to these questions. Perhaps because no high school junior or senior has experience writing these essays, they tend to be much more diverse in style than, say, history papers or newspaper columns. And that's a good thing—no admissions officer wants to read a bunch of essays that all look the same.

Nevertheless, it helps to have some idea of what's expected of you. We have included at the end of this guide some "successful" essays that can give you a sense of what works. If you still want to see even more good essays, you can go online or purchase one of the many books available that include sample college essays. Be careful, though—trying to apply someone else's creative format to your experiences is a recipe for disaster. And, potentially, an invitation to a charge of plagiarism.

Here are the basics for understanding how a college essay should—and shouldn't—be put together:

STRUCTURE

High school teachers will frequently suggest a fairly rigid format for any essay you write, which can usually be outlined something like this:

I.   Introduction
II.   Idea
    A.   Sub-idea
    B.   Sub-idea
III. Another Idea

IV.   Yet another Idea
    A.   Sub-idea
    B.   Sub-idea
    C.   Sub-idea
V.   Conclusion

Each idea is usually a paragraph—the outline above would thus be a five-paragraph essay. So if you're going to write an essay about your cat, your English teacher would probably want you to outline it like this.

I.   Introduction—I love my cat
II.   I've known her forever
    A.   My parents brought her home when I was 4
    B.   I can't remember life before we had her
III.   She is cute
IV.   She is smart
    A.   She aced her cat IQ test
    B.   She can juggle balls of yarn
    C.   She always finds the catnip we hide
V.   For all of these reasons, I love my cat

For most high school writing, and for the new SAT and ACT writing tests, this format isn't terrible. But while we can imagine some college admissions essays maybe being organized like this, you probably should avoid such rigidity in your essay.

If you turn to some of the essays at the end of this guide, you'll see that the most heartfelt and interesting ones could never have been written from this type of strict outline. Good college essays progress, rather than transition. Like good short stories, they are primarily about one thing. Introducing that thing, subdividing it, and then summarizing it is usually not the way to go.

Instead of adopting an inflexible, pre-planned structure, you should focus on creating an essay that has a clear start-to-finish path. The best way to understand this is to look at some admissions essays that you liked, and think about how they were structured.

Your Introduction

Your essay should have an introduction. But that doesn't mean you need an introductory paragraph that summarizes what the essay will be about. The best college essay introductions usually pull the reader immediately into the narrative, setting the stage for what will follow. Think about the effectiveness of the following two introductions:

1. Disadvantaged students often struggle academically. Because role models are often not available for them, they need help after school if they are to succeed. Therefore, some friends and I decided that we would start a program where we help kids after school with their homework and other issues. While it was hard at first, we eventually learned several important lessons. I believe that I am a better person for having had the experience.

2. It was the only time I've ever cried in public, and I did my best to hold back the tears. But when I saw Jack onstage receiving his junior high school diploma, I broke down. Just two years ago, this had seemed impossible.

Both introductions are well-written, and would be perfectly appropriate to include as the opening to a college essay. But the second one, in addition to having more emotional impact, does a better job of pulling the reader into the essay and setting a positive forward trajectory.

When writing your introduction, don't try to summarize the essay, but instead focus on *setting the stage* for the essay. Your introduction should make the reader want to keep reading.

Your Conclusion

We think the toughest part of writing the college essay is the conclusion. Sometimes, a conclusion comes naturally. If you're telling a story, the conclusion is usually the place where you explain how the event or ordeal you describe has affected your life. If you're discussing an important decision, the conclusion would be the place to reflect upon the impact of that decision.

But some essays just don't seem to want to conclude well. For example, if you're writing a quirky essay, then almost any ending risks sounding corny. If you're writing a highly emotional essay, many endings may seem too formal or unsatisfying. What you want to do is wrap the essay up tightly in the same style as the rest of the essay, and "leave 'em laughing." Or crying. Or at least nodding.

It's the same problem that comedians face, as well as comedy sketch-writers and opinion columnists. You don't necessarily need a zinger, but you want a final thought that lets you leave on a high note. You probably know exactly what we're talking about: whether at a wedding, a funeral, or a performance or in a magazine, we've all seen "good endings" that made us appreciate the skill of the writer. That's what you want.

And because coming up with that type of ending is much harder than it looks, writing a conclusion for certain types of college essays can be incredibly frustrating.

The best we can recommend is to give it time. Usually, a good conclusion will come to you if you take the pressure off of yourself for a few days. The most important thing is to recognize that your essay needs to conclude in a manner that's satisfying to the reader, and to avoid the temptation—whether in capitulation or deadline-induced panic—to conclude an otherwise superb essay with a trite and standard ending.

Some examples of bad conclusions:

And because of all the lessons I learned from that experience, I feel that I am now ready for college.

And that's the story of why I quit the volleyball team.

Well, it's time to get back to my busy life. Hope to see you soon!

While I miss my grandfather very much, I know that a little part of him is with me wherever I go.

Conclusions, or at least concluding sentences, are more about style than substance. This is no place to try to interject a funny joke or complex, meaningful life lesson. Write something that wraps up your essay neatly, and leaves the reader satisfied that he or she just read something good.

For some examples of how a well-written admissions essay might conclude, take a look at the essays we included at the end of this guide.

Poor structure means boring essays.

We already discussed how your essay topic should be interesting. Similarly, the structure you choose should allow it to be interesting. That doesn't mean using some crazy format or trying to make your essay different from every other one you've read. But it does mean that you should make sure your essay flows forward and stays alive for the reader.

The most boring essays are either overly structured (such as any essay you feel you could predict after reading the first paragraph), or very unstructured (think: meandering essay about all the reasons someone likes basketball). The most interesting essays progress from an introduction, through a logical and sequential thought process, into an orderly conclusion. They're paced well. Their structure gives them a life of their own. The advice we most frequently give our clients on the subject of structure is this: "Tell a story."

STYLE

We've seen excellent college essays written in just about every tone, style, and type you could imagine. Funny. Sad. Dead serious. Slice-of-life. Narrative. Sarcastic. Literary. Intentionally simple. Long. Short. Formal. Casual. Very casual. With dialogue. With transcribed sound effects. With many characters. With many animal characters. In the first person. In the third person. In the second person. Angry. Ecstatic. Plain. Cryptic. Symbolic. Ambiguous.

There are few concrete rules for writing the college essay: as long as your product demonstrates that you are a good writer and would be a good fit at the school to which you're applying, almost any approach is fair game. Yet while every tactic and every essay-writing strategy could probably be applied successfully to a given essay, there are some basic rules about how you should write.

Writing a "clever" or "funny" essay raises the bar considerably.

In principle, there's nothing wrong with writing a funny college essay, or one that takes an interesting and unusual approach. The problem is that few students are successful in constructing such essays, and they thus rarely have the intended impact upon the admissions committees.

First of all, pieces written in a "funny" style usually just don't work from a comedy perspective. They're not funny. That's because 1) even funny students usually aren't experienced at writing comedy bits; 2) senses of humor vary widely, especially between different generations; and, sadly, but true, 3) most people aren't funny.

Unfunny comedy essays, or other unsuccessful attempts at being clever or original, demonstrate a lack of self-awareness or knowledge about the admissions process. It's one thing to be unfunny; it's a whole different thing to be unfunny but to think that you're funny. You don't want the admissions officers' first impression of you to be that you're a poor comedian who thinks he or she has material so great that it's worthy of a college application.

Second, writing something clever or funny distracts you from other tasks you could be pursuing in an essay, such as explaining something you've accomplished, revealing something substantive about your personality, or telling a story that demonstrates something about your experiences. You wouldn't submit a hilarious two-page joke for your essay, even though it was hilarious; similarly, you shouldn't submit a funny essay that doesn't accomplish anything other than to amuse the reader.

The best way to inject comedy, quirkiness, or originality into your essay is to do so subtly, in the context of your broader effort to put together a good essay. Let them know that you're clever or funny if you feel that's important, but don't make it your defining characteristic. That means that there's less pressure for you to succeed on that front, and more opportunity for you to demonstrate your overall personality, skills, and value as a candidate.

Casual vs. formal style?

This is a common question. Obviously, writing in a more casual style allows the writer to connect better with his or her audience. On the other hand, some students become concerned that writing too informally will turn off admissions committees: these students have been trained to write in a relatively formalistic way, and can't imagine doing otherwise on such an important assignment.

Not surprisingly, the answer is that you need to achieve a happy medium. Writing too formally constricts your essay and makes it difficult to establish a relationship with your reader. Writing too informally, however, can indicate a lack of respect for the process and signal to the admissions committees that you lack the savvy or ability to properly use the English language.

Here are some frequently asked questions about formal versus informal writing on essays, and our answers:

Can I write my essay in the first person (e.g. use the word "I")?

Absolutely. The first person creates a more intimate tone and is generally used in admissions essays.

Should I refer to the admissions committees in my essays (for example, "If you accept me to your school...")

Probably not. While it's important to understand who your audience is, addressing them directly breaks the mood of what should be an important and thoughtful piece of writing. It's also very unusual, at least in good essays.

Can/should I start my essay with a famous quotation?

Unless you've been specifically asked to do so, we generally recommend avoiding quotations. Starting with a quotation from Bartlett's is very common in mediocre essays and will look very familiar to weary admissions officers hoping for something original. If you use a quotation, it should be done very well and should be germane to your essay.

Especially avoid claiming that you've lived your life by a particular quotation or mantra, even if it's true. It's just too trite.

Is slang/vernacular okay?

Sometimes, but usually not. If you're writing dialogue for some reason, or trying to convey the way a particular person talked, it might be okay. But don't use phrases such as "I was cool with that" or "He dissed my friends." Not only does casual slang indicate that you may not have perfect command of the English language, but it also makes it look as though you're not savvy enough to write "up" to the admissions committees.

Anything else I should avoid?

Clichés ("I knew the early bird gets the worm;" "Practice makes perfect.").

Sarcasm, which usually doesn't come across well on paper.

Vulgarity.

Length

You should always follow directions on the applications regarding the length of an essay. However, that usually doesn't mean you need to exactly hit word or page limits. If an essay asks for a certain number of pages, using your word processor you should be able to edit spacing, margins, and so forth to make the essay look good and properly fit into the right number of pages. But don't do anything that makes it appear that you were playing with those factors intentionally. Generally, you should have somewhere between 250 and 450 words on each page.

If you're asked to limit your essay to "around" a particular number of words, you should try to roughly hit that figure (unless the application is strict about the word limit). Our general rule is that your essay should be between 85% and 105% of the total word limit. That means that a 500-word essay should be between 425 and 525 words.

Technically, you can always make your essay shorter than the recommended length. But we don't recommend coming in much below ordinary word or page limits. Focus on going over the recommend length, and then shorten your essay so that you're giving them roughly the maximum length they requested.

V. WRITING WELL

While everyone in the running at the most competitive colleges writes well, good writing remains the #1 factor in evaluating college essays, and is without a doubt the hallmark of any good college essay. Good writers demonstrate intelligence, thoughtfulness, and a finely-honed command of the English language. Great writers show, by writing with a skill and flair similar to that shown by past acceptees, that they belong at a prestigious school and have the skills to perform at the level that will be expected of them.

Bad essay writers, on the other hand, demonstrate that they did not care enough about their essays to make sure they were correctly written. It's tough to turn a good essay into a great one, but to make bad writing into decent writing is simply a matter of attention and focus. And, if necessary, seeking help.

This short chapter will not attempt to teach you grammar, punctuation, or proper MLA style. Our thinking is that whatever you know about writing now is what you're probably going to take into the essay-writing process.

But even if you've paid attention to nothing we've written thus far, we want you to take heed of the following advice:

> Your college essay should be the best piece of writing
> that you've ever produced. There should be no mistakes.
> There should be no awkward phrasing. Everything about the
> way your essay is written should indicate that you are an intel-
> ligent young person with a strong command of the language
> and an ability to put ideas to paper.

The following are our simple writing tips that you should keep in mind when putting together your essay.

Grammar/mechanics/usage

Your writing must be flawless. No improperly used semicolons. No incorrectly-used words. No problems with subject-verb agreement. Your pronouns must have antecedents. Your syntax must be clear. If you have questions about an issue, check with someone who knows. If you struggle even a little bit with these technical aspects of your writing, seek help after you write your first draft.

Vocabulary

Speaking like an intelligent young adult is important. But using big words that you don't ordinarily use is likely to get you in trouble. Admissions officers can spot instantly the student who is using big words when smaller ones would do just as well.

Admissions officers have told us that they've seen words such as "myriad," "comprise," and "nuance" (often used incorrectly) more than they care to remember. Speak plainly and in the language that enables you to most effectively convey your point.

For a great essay about clear and simple writing, read George Orwell's *Politics and the English Language.* Another great resource is Strunk & White's *Elements of Style.*

Active voice

Compare the following two sentences:

Vanilla was the flavor that I chose.

versus

I chose vanilla.

The first sentence is written in the passive voice, while the second is written in the active voice. For the purposes of your essay, you should always choose the active voice. Doing so makes your essay livelier, more fun to read, more interesting, and more indicative that you are an experienced writer.

Vary sentence length

An essay with only long and complex sentences is difficult to read. One with only short sentences sounds boring. The most interesting way to write is to have long sentences interspersed with short ones.

Gender-neutral language

Some people will be offended if you use masculine pronouns to represent an unknown person. On the other hand, using combined terms such as "him/her" can be awkward. Avoid both problems by rearranging your sentences to eliminate awkward or offensive constructions.

For example:

> *I was worried that after I met the admissions officer, he or she would decide I wasn't good enough for his or her school.*

becomes

> *I was worried that the admissions officer would think I wasn't good enough for Stanford.*

No mistakes

Your essay cannot contain a single spelling error, misused homonym (their/there), or improperly capitalized (or not capitalized) word. Don't assume that your spelling/grammar program on your word processor caught every mistake. Computers are notorious for allowing major errors to slip by for arcane reasons.

If you're not a great writer, it's going to be tough to write a great essay with absolutely no help, no matter how much time you put into it. Don't be afraid to seek assistance. Everyone loves to help a college applicant, and odds are good you know a teacher or family member who can help you improve the strength of your writing.

VI. REVIEWING AND EDITING

"The first draft of anything is s**t."
—Ernest Hemingway

We just finished explaining that opening quotations and vulgarity should be avoided. So the fact that we start this short chapter by blatantly violating both rules should get your attention.

Of course Hemingway is exaggerating a little, or at least just expressing his opinion of his own writing. But it's definitely true that for most writers of any caliber, the first draft of an essay will be substantially worse than the carefully-improved final product.

For some applicants, guiding the admissions essay from the first draft through the version that eventually gets mailed to colleges is actually the hardest part of the process. That's because, given the importance of this task, you're probably going to want to spend more time reviewing and polishing this essay than you have for anything else you've ever written.

Here are the steps:

Decide if what you've written is any good.

Most essays can be much improved through editing. But if what you've originally come up with seems terrible to you, it probably is; while lots of work might improve it, you'd probably be better off starting from scratch.

What makes an essay worth abandoning? Not mistakes—mistakes can be corrected. We generally recommend stopping work on an essay only when the essay has a fundamental problem that can't be corrected with partial or stylistic changes.

For example, if an essay is *very dull*, there's usually not much that can be done to make it interesting. The problem is unlikely to be related to how the essay was put together—rather, the choice of topic was probably ill-advised.

Your topic must be interesting. Sometimes you can't tell until you've written your essay that it just isn't going to work. In that case, despite all of your hard work to date, you need to scrap it and start over.

When else should you pull the plug? In addition to dull essays, the other type of essays that generally can't be improved are impersonal essays. If you realize after writing it that your essay doesn't really say anything about you or what type of person you are, you'll probably need to select a new topic and start over.

Put it in a drawer

When you've finally written your essay and have decided you've got what looks like a reasonable first draft, you should put the essay away for at least a few days—and preferably at least a week—and completely forget about it.

Looking at your essay again only when you're "fresh" will allow you to see it from the perspective of a reader, rather than someone who's been focused entirely upon being a writer. You'll have a better understanding of which sections are the most (and least) effective, and what sounds trite or forced. You'll also be more easily able to spot grammar and usage errors.

Edit

There are two stages to any good editing process:

A) Content editing

Editing an essay is more art than science: your task is simply to make the essay better, any way you can. At the content editing phase, that primarily means cutting, expanding, rearranging, and clarifying the various components of your essay to ensure that your essay is as interesting and readable as you can make it.

Read your essay over carefully and decide which parts you like best, and which parts seem not to work. Does it flow well? Is it focused, or do some sections seem not to fit with the rest? Have you spent enough time explaining all of the important points? Are there sections that—while well-written—don't really seem necessary?

The most important and underappreciated quality that all good college essays share is focus. Focus means that your essay is about one thing—it flows from one point to the next, not by meandering, but rather by building on what has come before.

The content editing stage is the perfect time to think seriously about focusing your essay. What's your point? If you could add one paragraph somewhere to make the whole essay flow better and make more sense, what would it be and where would it go? Are there parts that just don't click yet? Is every part of your essay *getting you something*, or are there parts that you'd be better off abandoning?

B) Line-by-line editing (or "stylistic" editing)

At this point, it's finally time to begin looking at the details of your essay. However much time you spent making sure that you were crafting each sentence as carefully as possible, there is always a lot you can do to make your essay read more elegantly.

This does not mean, as some students seem to think, unnecessarily complicating your vocabulary. It does mean making sure that each word is accurate and is there for a reason. Eliminate all spelling and grammar mistakes. Improve your transitions. Vary the sentence length. Essentially, implement all of the writing tips we talked about in the previous section.

Most good writers find that such editing is more easily done on a piece of paper than on a computer—editing on the computer, where each letter is changed immediately, can make it difficult to carefully consider the impact of each change. Print your essay, grab a pen, and pretend you're a tough writing instructor attempting to pick your own essay apart.

But don't forget that editing an essay is about more than eliminating mistakes. You don't want to reach for fancy sentence constructions and five–syllable words, but you do want to add to and improve your writing—even if it's already pretty good. Make those sentences active. Think about what will create a more interesting essay. Ensure that you're not using the same sentence structure throughout each paragraph (for example, don't start every sentence with "I"). Make the introduction gripping. The conclusion satisfying. Ask yourself, "Is this something that a great writer would write?"

Seek Help

Should you ask other people to help you review your essay? In a word, yes. Fresh (and often more experienced) eyes can be invaluable in providing constructive ideas, identifying weaknesses, and correcting mistakes that you've missed simply because you've grown too familiar with your essay.

But whom should you show it to, and what are you looking for from that person?

Show your essay to someone who 1) will be honest and 2) will know what he or she is talking about. The best choice would be someone involved in college admissions. That's usually impossible, so the next best choice is either an English teacher or a very smart friend who will have the energy and commitment to really review what you've put together. If that's not possible, show it to an adult who's willing to devote some time to you and who will be honest.

If you can afford it and think it would help, hire a professional admissions counselor.

Whomever you choose to read your essay, you'll need to tell your reader to be brutal. You're hoping that the reader can tell you:

1) Which parts are the best.
2) Which parts are the worst.
3) What's confusing.
4) What's missing.
5) What doesn't belong.
6) Where you've made grammar and usage errors.

A general report on your essay ("I liked it!" or "You'll definitely get into Notre Dame" or "That story about deep-sea fishing was so interesting—I never knew that about you!"), while often reassuring and nice to have, is, essentially worthless for the purpose of improving your essay.

What you want is detailed analysis and red ink. The more analysis and criticism you can get, the more opportunities you'll have to improve your essay.

Remember, though, that in the end you are responsible for the final product. Don't make every correction given to you—instead think critically about your essay and decide which changes will actually make your essay better. Even adults make mistakes—and where writing is concerned, they make lots of them. You also don't want to make changes that, while technically correct, will destroy the flow, consistency, or readability of your essay.

That's it. Once you've given your own feedback and solicited that of others, and made every improvement you can envision, you're ready to send it out.

Good luck!

VII. SUCCESSFUL ESSAYS

Here we've compiled a number of college admissions essays we received from college students and clients. What do these essays have in common? Most notably, they're good. Without exception, the students writing these essays got into top colleges, and their essays probably helped. Don't let that intimidate you, though—everyone, regardless of what they've accomplished or their writing ability, can benefit from what these essays have to teach.

Why are we including them? We hope that by seeing how these students approached the task, and the diversity of their topics and styles, you'll understand better what the college essay is all about. After each essay, we discuss it briefly—why we liked it, what its best qualities are, and what you as a future essay writer can take away from it.

Most of these essays contain minor errors that we, as full-time admissions counselors, would probably correct. However, because such issues are inevitable among even the best and brightest high school students, we generally focus here on what's important for you to learn. Think about what you, as a writer, might be able to absorb from these fine examples.

And enjoy.

Essay #1: A Dissection

I think that the first time that science really made sense was in seventh grade, when a frog lay splayed out on the desk in front of me. The stench of formaldehyde made my eyes water and my stomach churn, but I did not really notice, fascinated by the still form, its innards arranged in neat array under the flap I had incised in its abdomen. Inside were the precise engineering marvels, finer than the gearings within a Swiss watch, each perfectly evolved through a process I had only read about and never truly understood. Here was the basis for religion, the faith in a higher power that actually represents faith in the innumerable and incomprehensible wonders of nature.

I have always enjoyed observing patterns: the point and counterpoint in Beethoven's 15th string quartet and the intricate fingerings and crescendo in his Kreutzer sonata, for example, as well as the rise and fall of the empires of history. It is the intricate patterns of life, however, that particularly fascinate me, and my brief surgery on the frog led me to envision a career in medicine. On the surface it seems simple, painless (for the doctor), and rewarding; just put the jigsaw puzzle of life back together in some semblance of order: a drug here, an incision there, and the patient will be cured.

However, the flip side of the coin terrifies me: what if those jigsaw pieces will not fit back into place? What if something goes wrong, an artery bursts, the patient hemorrhages and dies within seconds? Science is beautiful in an abstract sense when dealing with grand theories, words on a page, even the peaceful revelations of the frog, but perhaps the frog was not a good analogy for the experience of medicine. After all, there was no danger; it had already passed on. If I had to explain to a grieving family why they have lost their young daughter, however, the crushing realities might become just a little too real.

Nevertheless, working hands-on would be more satisfying to me than to remain in abstraction, in a world that, while appealing in its lack of emotional trauma, offers relatively little in the way of direct human application and personal reward. Surely in medicine there must exist great triumphs, something to balance the overwhelming defeats. The common medical adage is that "it never gets easy." I suppose this is true. In a way, I hope that it is because, while some might believe that emotions cloud the mind of a superior doctor, I believe that to truly be a good doctor one must live in constant awe and fear. Those are emotions I possess in abundance: awe at the beauty of life and fear at its fragility.

This is an excellent college essay that helped its author get admitted to Harvard.

The first thing we noticed about this essay is that it's written incredibly well, demonstrating the author's impressive command of the English language—especially for a high school senior. "The stench of the formaldehyde" is palpable, and the reader is struck by the author's fascination by the frog's anatomy.

After hearing about this awakening experience, we're given a glimpse into how this intelligent young man thinks about his world. He listens to symphonies. He studies history. Better yet, while he's doing those things, he's observing and learning.

The author also has a precocious and well-developed sense of what he enjoys and what kind of person he is. He's a doctor-in-training, for one thing, who is fascinated by the "beauty" and "fragility" of life. Admissions officers don't expect high school students to have their careers planned at age 17, but if you're truly passionate for a field, that can provide insight into your personality and character. For this author, we have a real image of someone who knows what's important to him and where he wants to focus—academically, intellectually, and professionally.

Finally, it should be pointed out that, while there's definitely no specific formula for writing an excellent college essay, as admissions professionals we can say that this guy just *feels* like a Ivy League admit. The easy turns of phrase, vocabulary, diction, thematic cohesiveness, and effortless intellectual perspective are all marks of someone ready for a nationally elite college.

Lessons to take away from this essay:

1. Your essay doesn't have to be a story or about a specific incident or accomplishment.

This essay talks briefly about an experience from the seventh grade, but then is primarily about ideas and the passions of the author. We warn against generic essays because they don't always come across as plausible—describing your love of theater doesn't mean much if you don't have any experiences in theater and can't convince the reader that your "passion" isn't just a ploy to sound interesting to colleges. But this author's interest in biology and the delicate nature of life is almost tangible. It seems impossible that he's not being genuine, and it's likely that his extracurricular activities and academic record buttress this heartfelt essay. He also manages to link his abstract thoughts to tangible images ("a grieving family" and "an artery bursts," for example)—bringing the reader into his world and showing off unusual rhetorical skill.

2. Sounding smart matters.

Seeking vocabulary "home runs" is a common way to ruin your essay. Admissions officers can see right through attempts to sound smart and intellectual, and there's nothing worse than appearing phony or otherwise not genuine on your applications. When you use vocabulary words that are technically correct but could easily be replaced by simpler and shorter words, it demonstrates that you're writing in a certain way just to try to impress your reader.

However, as the saying goes, "If you've got it, flaunt it." The above essay is written so well that the author's command of the English language will be noted and will work in his favor. The sentences are well-constructed and vary in length and style. The writing is emotional and evocative without being awkward or difficult to understand. He has an impressive vocabulary and wields it like a well-practiced sword—not like the blunt instrument used by some high school students as they flip through their dictionaries. Here is someone who *must*, simply by virtue of the way he expresses his thoughts on paper, be intelligent, thoughtful, interesting, and intellectually capable.

Essay #2

My mother grew up on a farm, the daughter of a German-Swiss father and American-Swiss mother. My father immigrated to the United States from Cuba following the Communist revolution. Like all who grow up on farms, my mother has come to the belief that a teenage boy can do nothing better during the summer than toil away on a farm.

As such, the summer after my freshman year and each summer since, I have worked at Terry's Berries, a local organic farm.

It started out as a part-time job. I would work from eight in the morning until noon, then go home for lunch. Terry soon asked me to work a bit later and a bit later. Soon, seven became a better hour than eight. By the end of my first summer, I was working seven to four, Monday through Friday. Work I did.

The conversations with the other workers are among the greatest pleasures I have had. Each year, a new group of men would arrive, mostly Guatemalan or Mexican. I value what I have learned from them. Julio, for instance, showed me how to weed without ruining my back, and Manuel explained why I should always vote for Democrats.

Every summer, inevitably, I would be asked about my future. What did I plan to do? I always dreaded this question because I would hate to isolate myself by mentioning college or some profession I wished to pursue. "No sé." I don't know, I would answer. "Ve a la universidad," José would say. "Este es el alternativo." This is the alternative to the university, he said, gesturing to the fields.

It is not that there is no virtue in farming. Holly, another worker on the farm and a college graduate, views her work as fulfilling, and therefore has chosen farming as her way of life. But she made the choice to farm. José and his compatriots have been limited by circumstance, and so appreciate the choices afforded by education.

I hope José's words will always stick with me. They are a moving testament to the power of academic excellence. Beyond those professional inspirational speakers, the chats with my counselor and my parents' advice, José's simplicity has had the most profound effect on me. College gives me a choice in life, and a college of Harvard's magnitude gives me the most choices. Harvard fulfills my highest expectations of higher education, and I believe that my attendance there will satisfy José's mandate.

This author was also admitted to Harvard, but with a much different approach to the essay. While the first essay is intellectual and introspective, this applicant—the son of a Cuban immigrant—writes a much simpler story about working on a farm and what he learned during his time there.

The impressive aspect of this essay is that the applicant took a tough summer job that some would find tedious and apparently turned it into a tremendous learning experience. He understands how important his opportunities have been, and is grateful for the wisdom imparted to him by those less fortunate.

Lessons to take away from this essay:

1. It's possible to write about experiences with those less fortunate than you without sounding self-important or condescending.

The author of this essay comes across as relatively humble, and seems to have truly appreciated the lessons he learned from his co-workers such as José and Manuel. However, far more common are essays that reveal the author to be condescending or overly proud of his or her relatively small contribution to the plight of the homeless, disabled, or otherwise less fortunate.

Especially for those who have led a privileged childhood and adolescence, it's sometimes hard to recognize how skeptical others might be of your reflections on society (and rightfully so—it's not until you head out into the world that you'll really know what it's all about). Write about what you learned, and what it meant to you, and how it felt to be a part of a positive experience. But don't let admissions committee members think that you just put in a few hours of community service to bolster your resume, and that you naively think the world is noticeably better for it.

2. Those with "cultural diversity" should consider exploiting that advantage on their applications.

This lesson doesn't apply to everyone. But if it's relevant to you, you'll want to pay attention.

Colleges want to admit students with different life experiences. One of the most common and identifiable ways for a high school senior to have such experiences is to have a particular cultural or ethnic background.

When you tell a story about immigrating to America, or growing up among immigrants, it adds an extra dimension to your application. Not only do admissions officers often assume that you overcame some difficulties (such as poverty, language issues, or a tricky home situation) in getting to where you are today, but they'll also assume that you'll have something to teach your classmates about your culture, heritage, different worldview, or immigrant experience. This puts you at a unique advantage in comparison with other applicants.

3. You don't need to write about earth-shattering accomplishments.

While we encourage you to write about something impressive, it's not necessary for you to have performed surgery, rescued a drowning man, or won a national tennis tournament. "Regular" people get admitted into all types of schools (even Harvard), and these people simply write about experiences that provide a window into who they are.

The above essay is about nothing more significant than a low-paying summer job. But the author demonstrates not only that he was able to get something valuable from his experience, but also that he is someone who learns from his world, is appreciative of what he has been given, and will likely make good use of educational opportunities.

This applicant could easily have complained that he had "nothing to write about." Instead, he took an opportunity that would sound mundane to some, and wrote about it in an interesting and affecting way.

Essay #3: Analog

Although my relationship with video started before I was in high school, my tools have remained the same: beige Mac G3, video 8 camera, VCR, and AV cables. Most people making video today are using digital equipment. I'm still in analog. Quality is lost, and the picture that is finally imported looks like it was shot in the '70s.

Analog is all give and take. If the computer does not want to render full screen video, I just reduce the picture by half. If the computer will only play a few frames before it cuts out,

I'll go take a walk. Working this way may be frustrating, but when the video performs, diced into tiny fast-moving segments, and the music gets poured over the top as if it is directing it, that's when I'm satisfied.

Analog is grainy, gritty, and shiny. Analog is beautiful the same way some graffiti art is, because it's real. These are all the things I love about it. And these are the reasons why analog is the place to which I return year after year.

I am not proud of my first efforts in film. The camera was my toy—a diversion to pass time, to occupy myself in a creative way. But these early films gave me experience. I gradually gained both the patience and maturity to create something I'd want to show to people other than my snickering friends.

My first real attempt, Gone Wrong, *was a clumsy, hardly-edited, three-scene piece about a kid who gets hit in the "fundamentals." The soundtrack starts with an upbeat jam by Chick Corea but then shifts to a melancholy Gershwin song for the agony scene. Although the music was appropriate, it was not synched to details. The whole piece was unfocused and immature. I had gone out to have fun, not to create a work of art.*

Though Gone Wrong *was childish, it was my initiation into the feeling, rhythm, and method of editing. It was my first taste, my first negotiation, my first exchange. It was also my last film that would have dialog and an artificially-created story. Through my next two attempts, I realized I was much better at recording real life than creating one of my own.*

When I look back on the days of Gone Wrong, *I see myself as a child trying language for the first time. I made mistakes, but I was learning.*

About a year later, I spent a Sunday taping my mom end-lessly watering the garden, and my brother and dad intently building a soapbox car. I put the scene of my mom, and the scene of my brother and dad, into separate boxes on the same screen. The constant jumps between the two jaggedly-cut shots were a great way to show my family's compulsiveness. Each lasted only a few seconds before shifting angles. I chose Miles Davis' "Springville" as a soundtrack. It is a fanciful, carefree piece with a melancholic undertone. Then I edited all the quick cuts to match the music. The movie ended on the last note of the song.

Sunday helped to establish my style. When I finished with it, I had an excellent technical and creative grasp of my workspace. However, as much as Sunday was a huge step forward from Gone Wrong, it was still immature. The quick cuts made the film almost overedited. It was as if, in my quest to show my family's obsessiveness, I had emulated them, becoming obsessive myself in the intricate construc-tion of the film.

I entered Sunday in a student festival. I was surprised when it won first place in the nonfiction category. I think it won because, unlike many of the entries, it wasn't blatant. Sunday was about a family doing what families do. It was fanciful, escapist, and soothing. I could make subtle refer-ence to conflict, without beating the ideas to death.

The award gave me confidence to return once again to my place. By now, my old beige G3 and video 8 camera had become dated. Almost every entry in the South Bay Student Video Festival that year was made in digital video. People were telling me to upgrade, but I held out. My workspace and my equipment were my close companions. Migrating to digital would be a betrayal. I liked being an iconoclast, a stalwart for an obsolete medium. Plus, I loved that grainy quality of the videos. By going to the festival, and compar-

*ing my work to what else was out there, I realized that tech-
nology wasn't the only thing that set me apart. Not only
were the technology and the methodology iconoclastic,
so was I.*

*Sophomore year, I went on a trip to Las Vegas. There, I saw
people mindlessly attached to slot machines. They weren't
just playing, they had become robo-comatose regressed baby
life forms captivated by the glowing lights and hypnotizing
sounds. This gave me an idea for my next film. Unlike*
Sunday, *however, I had a plan for this movie.*

This idea slowly became Slot. *When I got back home, I once
again approached my workspace. After* Sunday, *I knew how
to work. I selected clips of the people who looked the most
robotic, and started going through my CDs for music. By
now, I had learned that, for me, editing, feeling, and mood
for a film is patterned by, and expressed through, the music.
Even the length of the movie itself is defined by the length of
the song. I decided to set* Slot *to Django Reinhardt's "Blues
Clair," an upbeat jazz guitar composition that gave the film
an ironic, turn-of-the-century feeling that complemented my
trademark herky-jerky analog style—itself the byproduct of
using old equipment. "Blues Clair" was perfect. In addition
to its repetitive style, which aurally resembles slot machines,
its structure virtually determined the outcome. For example,
I set one of Reinhardt's guitar arpeggios to a video segment
of a lounge pianist playing an arpeggio.* Slot *was smooth,
gliding along to the swaying tempo.*

According to Kohlberg's Theory of Moral Development, *the
world becomes less about you as you grow up.* Gone Wrong
was all about me. It was an infantile view of existence.
Sunday *was an insular look at family relationships, but still
mostly about me.* Slot, *however, took a stance about the
world and how we, as human beings, inhabit it.*

Last year, my parents traded in the old beige G3 for a new computer, and my 10-year-old brother started using the camera for his own wacky ends. My equipment was disappearing. Even so, I think I'm ready to upgrade. I know that I will always keep my analog aesthetic. And when nobody remembers what it was like before digital video, the sounds of Django and Miles will ring in my ears, and I will remember what it was like to make something grainy, gritty, and real.

This author was accepted to the University of Chicago; his essay, about his evolution as a filmmaker, was undoubtedly a positive force in his application.

This piece has almost everything we look for in an effective application essay. We're shown that the author has passion in a particular field, and has pursued that passion aggressively and with some success. We learn something interesting about the author that probably wasn't entirely revealed in the rest of the application. This essay is also very interesting, which never hurts. The reader can't help but learn a little about filmmaking—not only technically, but also how a young filmmaker views his craft.

Far more than the previous two essays, this author focuses on the substance of what he's accomplished in a particular area.

Lessons to take away from this essay:

1. Your best essay subject, not surprisingly, is often the one thing you love to do and are most passionate about.

Can you imagine this author writing his essay, not about filmmaking, but about some vacation experience or sports accomplishment he had? It sounds preposterous—not because those would necessarily make poor essays, but because filmmaking is such an integral part of his life.

Not only does your "#1 activity" give you something to write about and a chance to show the admissions committees where you've chosen to focus your time, but it also frequently provides the fuel necessary for *you* to do your best writing. Isn't it easier to write about something when you're actually excited about what you're describing?

When students write essays about the activities they've chosen to pursue, those essays are often infused with an excitement and a passion that's contagious. If you have the opportunity to write such an essay, you should think twice about discarding it in favor of something else.

2. Details provide credibility.

In our experience, one couldn't do a much better job than this author in putting together a college admissions essay about filmmaking experiences. To be good, your essay doesn't need to be nearly this complete or full of expert reflection and analysis. However, when writing about your experiences, details are crucial. Details are essential to the telling of an interesting story—perhaps more importantly, they help convince the reader that you've had real-world experiences and that you're not inflating the importance of something for the purpose of the essay.

Too frequently, we read an essay from a student about, say, his love of travel. It turns out, though, that the essay is in actuality based upon a few trips to Europe. The student (often spurred by parents) has determined that this is his or her most "impressive" accomplishment to date. The essay is invariably dull because there's no real evidence that the student enjoys travel or has gained measurably from his experiences abroad. It's lacking *details*—descriptions of experiences or observations that would buttress the author's claim of being passionate about traveling.

Similarly, we also read a lot of essays about charity work that are long on platitudes ("It felt good to help the less fortunate" or "The look on their faces made it all worthwhile") and short on credible details about what the author did to help or how the experience made an impression on her. That's because, usually, the author did *little* to help (served soup five times) and it *didn't* really make much of an impression.

When you can write about such specifics as analog, digital, Django, film festivals, and temperamental editing software, your essay takes on an aura of authenticity that's especially valuable. By providing these details, you *prove* that you've put time and energy into whatever it is that you're writing about. Write about something in a way that *no one else could.*

Essay #4: I, Me, She, Her... Meredith

It is she, number 8971, senior graduating class, who you have met already. Her numbers fill the first pages of this application, these numbers which she uses to quantify and thus represent herself. Her 4.0's and 1480's and 6's establish her identity to the world: she exists purely in the universe of quantification.

She and I are very often confused, although upon glance we seem so very different. She is the intellectual, the academic reputation. She is classified through a series of numbers, while I am only understood through words. I adore poetry, popcorn, and playing tennis in the rain, and while she enjoys these endeavors, she prefers questioning and reasoning. At one time, I claimed she stifled me and tried to push her away, to send her numbers and her analytical questions to some other person, but she kept returning. At the time, I couldn't find a way to make us fit together: to ensure that her scholarly nature wouldn't overtake me. I wanted to be the dominant one, the one people invited places and wanted to see. Because of her intellect, I was being classified into a group I didn't belong in. She was the student, but I was more than that. I was talkative, artsy-crafty, energetic. But because she was in the honors' classes, she was all anyone could see: the one with the impressive numbers. I was being ignored. Yet as hard as I tried to rid myself of the intellect, the curiosity, she returned in full force. I couldn't escape it: she was still there. Gradually, we have become friends. I have begun to appreciate her as a companion; and while at times we hide in one another's shadows, we are now able to work in much more harmony than before: we are teammates with the same goal.

She is the tutor, the aspiring doctor, the perfectionist whose hands shake when public speaking. I am the pianist, the one who fills journals with unspoken words, and the one who starts philosophical arguments over the dinner table. I work comfortably within the universe of creativity and words, while she finds solace in the boundaries of logic and mathematics. Her thought process follows all logic and reason; I search for emotional and moral connections. I am impulsive, irrational, creative; she is sensible. And yet many times I am seen as only her.

Are we really all that different? Every day she and I are more and more intertwined with one another. Our drives match up perfectly; we have the same mantra: adversity is not an adequate deterrent. Each day we draw upon one another's source of energy, the other's inexplicable passion for life and learning, especially finding out the "Why" in everything. Every day, she gives me a little of her scholarly attitude, and every day I release to her a little of my creative spirit. She possesses the adoration of mathematics and science, establishes new ideas, and she also has the drive to succeed in what she takes on. I possess the builder's hands, the mechanism for the ideas to spur to life, to take form and succeed in themselves. We work together, we are friends, partners. We are both scholars, both "creative geniuses," overzealous and outgoing, diligent and driven. Twisted and tangled, we are both Meredith, but one person, just one personality. She is I, I am she, and we are Meredith.

This essay is special because it reveals the author to be a complex individual—academically qualified, but also struggling with the burdens that the academic "grind" imposes upon a maturing young woman. Many smart kids feel the struggle Meredith describes between "she" and "I"; few, however, express it so articulately. While Meredith's talent in describing how she's come to terms with her two disparate halves is the highlight of this essay, it also has several other strengths. The essay's format provides a forum for Meredith to describe some of her passions and interests, and to personalize her a little bit for the admissions committees (notice how she, almost in passing, mentions her plans to become a doctor). And the whole she/I/Meredith construction enables a literary approach that—while not perfect—demonstrates the author as a gifted writer not afraid to take risks with her prose.

Not surprisingly, Meredith was admitted Early Action to Harvard.

Lessons to take away from this essay:

1. Colleges like interesting people.

In our opinion, this essay is interesting to read. But perhaps even more importantly, it reveals an interesting person. Given the choice between a hard-working academic grind and the person described in this essay, any admissions officer would (all else being equal) choose this girl. She sounds fun. She's creative, "artsy craftsy," and argumentative.

She also has come to terms with her academic side and the intellectual pursuits that that part of her personality craves. This is not a nerd-become-rebel who has decided to shun the "uncool" fields of math and science. Rather, Meredith is a well-rounded high school senior with myriad interests and accomplishments.

She is someone who would add to the vitality of any college's freshman class.

2. It's possible to be philosophical and still write an effective admissions essay, but it's tough.

With this lesson we urge the utmost caution: for every successful "philosophical" essay, the college admissions landscape is littered with dozens of meandering, incomprehensible such essays that just don't work. The problem, to be blunt, is that 17-year olds don't usually have much to say about life in general that admissions officers haven't heard before. In fact, applicants usually sound better when they acknowledge that they *don't* already know everything there is to know about the world. As Socrates said: "The wise admits he knows nothing."

This author avoids that trap by explaining her own personal issues without claiming too much wisdom about life. This essay is about *her*, and about letting the admissions committees get to know her a little bit better.

Essay #5

It stands in the corner of a small room, gleaming in all its beauty, waiting for attention. Its silence resonates. During my childhood, it remained the exhibit devoid of touch, existing solely for my eyes. I struggled to resist my urge to tarnish its innocent magnificence with a cacophonous exposure. The day I finally sliced the thick silence, the sounds were devoured by the ravenous air and I thought I would never take my fingers off it again; I had finally struck the ivory of the grand piano.

Ever since that moment, I have wanted to learn everything about music and the majestic instrument I loved. I became the student of two piano teachers and a member of the National Fraternity of Student Musicians for four years. However, despite my interest and growing dedication, it became difficult to play the piano with an increasingly rigorous course-load every year at school. My usual practice sessions were burdened by excessive homework and other activities. Nevertheless, as a conscientious student of both music and high school, I developed a work ethic that allowed me to arrange my schedule making time for not only the things I had to do but also the things I loved to do.

As I am preparing for an audition to become a member of the National Guild of Piano Teachers, my playing has evolved. It has become more than a curiosity or a pastime; it is an escape. Mozart's "Sonata" soothes a stressful day of school; Gershwin's "Rhapsody in Blue" relives a magical outing; Chopin's "Nocturne" heals the bitter wounds left from an argument with a friend. Year after year the legatos of my music have complemented the staccatos of my life—a fantasia of memories. The piano exists as a source of companionship; a sentient with a pulse that throbs with emotion. The most rewarding experience of my life was breaking the silence that once existed in my home and beginning my endeavor into classical piano. I discovered my own soul through music.

This is another essay that "worked" at Harvard.

The author has written a short piece, and the choice of topic—while not unusual—doesn't fit exactly with what we usually preach. Playing a musical instrument, even at instructor-caliber, is impressive but not unique among Ivy League applicants. And there's no talk (at least in the essay) of piano-related accomplishments that might put this author in a class above her peers.

On the other hand, despite a few minor issues, this essay is written beautifully. Some parts are brilliant. Sure, anyone could assert a love for the piano. But reading this essay, do you have any doubt that this author is telling the truth—that she does, in fact, feel she has "discovered [her] own soul through music?"

While sending only this essay to a college might represent a missed opportunity in today's world of hyper-achieving high school seniors, as part of a comprehensive admissions package—including several diverse essays—it would do a terrific job of rounding out an application.

While a talked-about trend in the admissions committee is the "well-rounded class" as opposed to the "well-rounded student"—that is, a preference for people who do one thing excellently over those who do a number of things well—admissions officers are nonetheless looking for individuals who have a life and a self-awareness beyond academic studies and extracurricular, resume-building pursuits. This author's love of the piano, and the instrument's importance in her life, demonstrate that she is not a one-dimensional applicant, and that she takes joy and comfort in her art.

Lessons to take away from this essay:

1. If you're going to write passionately about something "ordinary," you need to make the essay work.

When you write an admissions essay about an amazing accomplishment or truly unique experience, your subject matter can sometimes stand on its own. That's not to say that you don't need to write a good essay. But just as Arnold Schwarzenegger can get away with a few less-than-stellar sequences in an action film (or in a stump speech), an essay about feeding starving children in Africa will always score at least *a few* points.

However, we've read some terrible essays about playing instruments, running, cooking, playing chess, knitting, and many other pastimes. That's because it's very difficult to make an essay about a common leisure activity interesting. It's also tricky to make it "about you," as opposed to something that could have been written by anyone.

It turns out that almost everyone who writes about running describes the meditative nature of jogging alone on a quiet trail. Those who love sailing write about being on the open water and knowing all about the boats, knots, and sails. Applicants who love to read talk about curling up with old friends such as Elizabeth from *Pride and Prejudice*. For admissions officers who read thousands of essays each year, it's hard to provide something of this nature that will make you sound interesting and provide any meaningful information about who you are. Sure, running is an integral part of your life. But that doesn't mean it necessarily deserves a prominent place in your college application. Remember, your job here is to impress and create a personal bond with the reader.

This essay is about playing the piano—something that literally millions of Americans do. But the importance of the piano to this applicant truly comes across in this special essay. Not only do we get the impression that this is an expert piano player, but we are also introduced to a young child who once yearned to play the grown-up instrument, and has now made it a stabilizing influence in her stressful and exciting life. What makes this essay work? Certainly the emotive language helps, and the inclusion of details lends credibility to the author's story. In the end, though, it *just works*; this essay *adds* to the application of which it is a part. By the time we are visualizing the author gratefully banging out Chopin upon the grand piano after a hard day, we know her better than we would have otherwise, and we probably like her more as well.

2. It's the message that matters.

This extremely well written essay has a few awkward spots. Nonetheless, it's often beautiful, and the images painted by the author are memorable: the young girl looking up at the forbidden grand piano, and finally attacking it like a starving man on a loaf of bread; the overworked student relaxing with her instrument after a hard day; the reflective college applicant realizing the importance of the piano in helping her deal with the "staccatos" of her life.

The substance of, and impression left by, your essay matters more than verb conjugation or literary allusions. Admissions officers admit real people, and they want to connect with those people. The essay is not simply a writing test, and should not be treated as such.

Essay #6

Moving to a different country at the age of six was as much of an adventure for me as it was unmitigated torture for my mother. On a voyage that took more than twenty-four hours, the eager, wide eyes of my twin sister and I had not fluttered shut once – and neither had my mother's. At one o'clock in the morning, we squealed and fought for a glimpse out the plane's tiny window, as my exhausted mother apologized continuously to the sleep-deprived passengers. After eleven years, I still remember peeping out and gasping, gazing upon the bright lights of Los Angeles. A million specks of color, each one brilliant and full of possibilities lay beneath my feet. I was coming upon a country full of stars, and according to my mother, it was to be my new country; I could not tear my eyes away.

The first year of my new life in America was a year of firsts. It was the first time I had ever run under a sky so stunningly clear and blue, and so impossibly huge; it was the first time I had played with my sister in our own yard (with grass in it!), and not seen one skyscraper, it was the very first year I held in my chubby hands, the cold, white, amazing substance that is snow; and it was the first year that I fell in love with America.

That love has stayed with me through all the alienation that I have felt in this beautiful country, an alienation I became familiar with as early as elementary school. One day the counselor took my sister and I aside. "Girls," she said, "you are not required to recite the pledge of allegiance with the rest of the class. You may remain sitting." Although I continued to pledge my daily allegiance to the country that I love, a nagging voice always said, "Sit down. Your pledge means nothing. You're not 'required' to recite it." Was my mother right? Will this star-studded country ever let it be mine?

In school, I worked incessantly and passionately—maybe if I just worked hard enough, I would finally be accepted. Not until I was at the top, and better than anyone else, I believed, would I be good enough to be part of this country. So when I was given second chair of the flute section my seventh grade year, I burst into tears of disappointment. As usual, however, the tears quickly dried, allowing the cold-steeled determination in my inner core to shine through. I would just have to try harder and prove to America that I am worthy of its acceptance – and work harder I did. I easily auditioned my way to first chair second semester, and three years later, I was accepted in the All-State Honor Band. When I received an unacceptable B+ on my math test, I skipped tears altogether, and moved on to the determination stage. My days, already filled to the brim with music lessons, cross country, community service, band, and school, threatened to overflow, but my determination, strengthened by all the obstacles I had to overcome, held firm, and I increased my study time, forgoing sleep, food, and friends. I ended the year with the highest grade in all my core class. I tested into Central Academy (a school for gifted and talented students) the next year, and have taken advanced courses there ever since. Even at Central, however, I could not be anything less but at the top of my class.

Alas, however hard I worked, however much my body was drained from exhaustion, my mind weary from lack of sleep, I could not seem to gain ground in my race to be accepted. How can I, when I am labeled an "alien"; when I peer into the mirror and see a strange girl, with slanted eyes, yellow skin, and a flat nose starring back? She is utterly different from the beautiful large-eyed girls with rosy complexions that surround me every day.

Feeling ostracized, I returned to my native country a few years ago, where my mother's roots are, and where I had been too young to leave mine. I do not think I have to say the hope that was in my heart...but I was disappointed. The faces of my relatives crowed around me, unfamiliar and foreign. My mind, indulged with open skies and wide spaces, rebelled against the crowded streets and soot-covered skies of Taiwan. This too, then, was not were I belonged. At that moment, I felt lost – like a dandelion seed in a wild, relentless wind, tossed from one place to another, never to settle down.

Now, in my room, with a Chinese painting on one wall, and a Beatles poster on the other, I stare at my college applications: international student is checked, government financial aid is not. I am all alone. I look out my window, and through my tears, street lamps, lighted windows, and Christmas lights blur into the panorama of stars that called to me in my first glimpse of America. I will belong here some day, I promise. In this land where wishes come true, maybe the wild wind will stop, just for a while, and give me time to grow my roots.

This beautifully written essay is different and unique. It's an immigrant's story of coming to America, and her ongoing struggle to fit in here.

Lesson to take away from this essay:

If honest and not manipulated, emotional prose can have a powerful effect on an application.

To us, this essay is stunning: while poetic and evocative, it also resonates with the innocent longing of a teenaged girl. We won't describe *why* we found the images, metaphors, and succinctly expressed thoughts of this author so powerful, but we urge you to read through the essay again. What does it make you feel? Can you sympathize with this girl's plight? If you were an admissions committee member, how would this essay interact with the test scores and grades you already had for this applicant?

One of the primary goals of your essay is to humanize you for the admissions committee. The essay isn't just for evaluating how well you can write; rather, it's your opportunity to show the committee who you are, what's important to you, and what makes you tick. If you can help the reader to empathize with an emotion you feel deeply—here, a desire to thrive in an environment where the author feels like an outsider—then you can *move* the reader into knowing you *as a person*, rather than a set of numbers and data on a page.

In the best of worlds, you can encourage the reader to actually get behind you and take up your cause (in the case of an admissions officer, to recommend you to the rest of the committee). Just like the underdog at the end of a good movie, the author of the above essay likely has most readers rooting for her to succeed—to finally grasp, through admission to a prestigious college and perhaps financial aid, the elusive American Dream.

Essay #7: Kurt and Me

I am not Vonnegut. He is not me. I did not fight in World War Two. He did not break his arm in the third grade. We are separate people, yet under the light of the literary world we are bonded together - he as an author, and I as a reader. Our relationship began in 1996 when I first read his novel Welcome to the Monkey House. *Sure we had a good time, but it wasn't love. Over the past 5 years our affair has burgeoned with unbridled passion. Today, I stand completely devoted, respectful and honored to have my place with Vonnegut. I am a reader.*

As a lowly pre-teen with no passion for myself, let alone others, I had a shallow relationship with Kurt. We were two strangers at a party, discussing the weather while piling bite-size nachos, cookies, and carrots onto our designer napkins. I was intrigued by Vonnegut's words; I enjoyed his stories for their simplicity and their sweetness. They were my punch to wash down the dry cookies.

Kurt gave me a gift that served to form the base of our relationship. He taught that my writing mattered. His simply constructed sentences and straightforward plots gave me hope; my subject matters could be interesting also. I felt that my sentences, even though not splattered with adjectives and copious description, could be meaningful. I did not lose faith despite the low quality of my work. I knew I could get better, that there could be meaning inside of my words.

Through more schooling I did eventually betray Kurt. I became a mistress to the semicolon, a slave to the adjective. I found myself new lovers. John Steinbeck taught me description. Ayn Rand gave me long sentences with hints of sarcasm. I matured after my relationship with Kurt, but soon found myself yearning to rekindle the old flame. So I did. This was no puppy love. We exploded in passion, I read and absorbed Kurt's words as if they were written especially for me. His philosophies, his conceptions about the American culture were filled with simple truths.

In God Bless You, Mr. Rosewater, the main character has a simple maxim: "God damn it, you've got to be kind." These eight words – twenty-seven letters – sum up a large part of Vonnegut's humanist viewpoints. There is no moral more fundamental than human kindness.

When stress rules one's life, one often acts irrationally, taking on the qualities of an irritable individual. About a month ago, I was very over-worked, over-stressed, and under-slept while finishing up a school project. Many friends with whom I conversed that week were not pleased to have had the experience. And then the phrase lurked into the tightly balled fist of my mind. "God damn it, you've got to be kind." I realized that this adage holds true no matter what the circumstances. Tired or not, courtesy and friendliness should be top priority. The line has stuck close to my heart; it is a picture of Kurt to carry in my wallet.

We're married now, Kurt and I. The wild passion has tamed into deep love and respect. We stand by each other as author and reader. Vonnegut and his influences will forever be a part of me. I will be kind, I will respect my own writing, and I will dream. These I will wear as a wedding band, a symbol of permanence. We are a couple, however I have not remained completely devoted. My adjectives, my semicolons, my circumlocution are all vices; arguments vibrating through the ornately decorated walls of the white picket-fenced home. But I am not Kurt. Kurt is not me. We are each individuals, forever learning and redefining ourselves. We are simply together, author and reader.

This MIT student loves literature, and it shows. Ordinarily, topics such as this one make the essay-writing process difficult, as it's hard to write something unique about an activity as ubiquitous as reading. For the most part, it's all been said before.

However, this author takes a unique approach. Not only does she give the reader a great deal of information about herself as she describes her interest—she was once a "lowly pre-teen with no passion for [her]self"; as a young writer she was encouraged to know she could express herself without a large vocabulary; she cherishes kindness— but she uses an interesting device in comparing her relationship with the author Kurt Vonnegut to a romantic one. While this device isn't perfect and even a little awkward in places, it's a daring and impressive technique for a young writer. It also works—this author views her experiences with Vonnegut as incredibly important, and she's able to convey that importance through this approach.

Lessons to take away from this essay:

1. When writing about a passion, provide details about yourself and how you've been influenced.

Many people write about their love of reading. Such essays generally fail—not because reading is an inherently unsuitable topic, but because the applicants don't reveal anything interesting about themselves or how their experiences have been unique.

To say that you love to curl up with a good book, and to see the characters come alive in your head, merely puts you in the group of tens of millions of Americans who enjoy fiction. To say something worthy of a college application—a forum designed to help you convey a sense of yourself to a competitive school—you need to go beyond the ordinary and pull something special from your own experiences. As this author put it, "we were two strangers at a party, discussing the weather while piling bite-size nachos, cookies, and carrots onto our designer napkins." For many people this type of insight just isn't possible, and so they wisely choose another topic.

This author is also a writer, and she discusses details of her reading history that help us understand her relationship with the activity. She initially enjoyed reading Vonnegut as an easy and fun leisure activity. She later learned to appreciate authors with more complex writing styles, but also returned to Vonnegut and his "simple truths." While we think the author could have included even more details, she definitely does a good job of *showing* (remember your writing teacher saying "show, don't tell"?) how Vonnegut affected her life and why she finds her relationship with his writing so important.

2. One of the most impressive things you can do in an admissions essay is show growth and development.

While colleges obviously want to admit smart and impressive kids, one of the most crucial qualities they seek in applicants is self-awareness and the ability to grow, improve, and learn from mistakes. Colleges often see themselves as laboratories that encourage and nurture developing minds, and as a result they're far more interested in who you'll become than what you've been in the past. That's why, for example, so many schools will look positively at an upward grade trend, even when freshman and sophomore grades (and thus average GPA) are significantly lower.

Great college essays frequently demonstrate that the applicant has learned from life, and that he or she has an active mind that is seeking out new experiences and new ways to grow. A "standard" essay about reading might describe learning to read as a young child, and continuing with that interest through young adulthood. However, this applicant makes clear that she not only reads, but has considered the impact of that interest—and particularly of one author—on her reading, writing, and worldview. Vonnegut taught her that she could write meaningfully at a young age despite a limited command of vocabulary and literary maturity. She later learned to enjoy and adopt more sophisticated writing and storytelling techniques from other authors. She's gleaned philosophical lessons from Vonnegut. Finally, after all of these experiences, she's acknowledged that she is "forever learning" as a reader.

For colleges, finding that person who is "forever learning" and re-examining herself is of the utmost importance. By showing not just what you've done, but also how you've been affected by that experience and what you've learned from it, you can demonstrate yourself to be someone who will continue to grow and thrive in a college setting.

REALLY USEFUL WEBSITES

Check these sites for whatever information you may need. In addition, the websites of each college or university you are interested in will provide specific information.

FUNDING
Ameri-Corps National & Community Service
www.cns.gov

Gates Millennium Scholars
www.gmsp.org

FAFSA Express
www.fafsa.ed.gov

FastWeb
www.fastweb.com

The Financial Aid Information Page
www.finaid.org

Free Scholarship Search
www.freschinfo.com

Sallie Mae CASHE Scholarship Service
Scholarships.salliemae.com
www.wiredscholar.com

Scholarship Search
Cbweb10p.collegeboard.org/fundfinder/html/
fundfind01.html

Student Advantage
Scholaraid.studentadvantage.com

The Student Guide
http://studentaid.ed.gov

Higher Education Services Organization
www.hesc.com

NCAA Guide for the College Bound Student
Athlete
www.ncaa.org

New York's College Savings Program
www.nysaves.org

Unusual Scholarships
http://finaid.org/scholarships/unusual.phtml

David Lynch Foundation for Consciousness-
Based Educations and World Peace
www.davidlynchfoundation.org

Expected Family Contributions Calculator
*http://apps.collegeboard.com/fincalc/efc_*
welcome.jsp

Scholarship Searches
www.collegenet.com
www.scholarship.com

Qualified Minority Scholarship Search
www.molis.org

Hispanic Online
http://hol.hispaniconline.com/HispanicMag/
2008_02/collegeguide.html

Jackie Robinson Foundation
www.jackierobinson.org

United Negro College Fund
www.uncf.org

ASPIRA
www.aspira.org

American Indian Movement
www.aimovement.org

ORIENTATION
GEAR UP
www.ed.gov/gearup/index.html

Campus Tours
www.campustours.com

The U
www.theU.com

College Bound Interactive Guide to Student
Life
www.cbnet.com

FINDING YOUR SCHOOL
The College Board
www.collegeboard.com

Commission on Independent Colleges and
Universities
www.nycolleges.org

Peterson's Education Center
www.petersons.com

College Search
www.citizensbank.com/edu

RESOURCES FOR SCHOOLS AND FAMILIES
Universal Black Pages
www.ubp.com

US News & World Report
www.usnews.com/usnews/edu/grad/
rankings/rankindex.htm

American Universities
www.clas.ufl.edu/au/

College Opportunities Online
http://nces.ed.gov/collegenavigator/

American Association of Community Colleges
www.aacc.nche.edu

Community College Web
www.mcli.dist.maricopa.edu/cc

Database of Colleges
www.collegenet.com
www.gocollege.com

Campus Dirt
www.campusdirt.com/

College Confidential
www.Collegeconfidential.com

College Prowler
http://collegeprowler.com/

TESTING & APPLYING
The American College Testing Program
www.act.org

Educational Testing Services
www.ets.org

TEST.com
www.test.com

The Princeton Review
www.princetonreview.com/

Sylvan Learning Centers
www.educate.com

The Common Application
www.commonapp.org
http://www.collegeview.com/index.jsp

Kaplan On-Line
www.kaplan.com

GRE
www.gre.org

SAT
www.collegeboard.org/sat

TOEFL
Web1.toefl.org

College Link
www.collegelink.com

National League for Nursing
www.nln.org/test

COUNSELING
Independent Educational Consultants
Association
http://www.educationalconsulting.org/

National Association for College Admission
Counseling
www.nacacnet.org

College Horizons
www.whitneylaughlin.com

GAP YEAR PROGRAMS
Gap Year Programs
www.gap-year.com

Year Out Group
www.yearoutgroup.org

Leapnow
www.leapnow.org/

BUNAC
www.bunac.org

The Center for Interim Programs
www.interimprograms.com

Transitions Abroad
www.transitionsabroad.com

Travel Tree
www.traveltree.co.uk

MISCELLANEOUS
College is Possible
www.collegeispossible.org

Trio Programs
www.trioprograms.org

Yes I Can
www.yesican.gov

The Chronicle of Higher Education
http://chronicle.com

CREDITS

Page 4: *The New York Times*, Jan. 17, 2008

Page 14: *The Early College High School Initiative*

Page 19: "Can't Complete High School? Go Right to College," Karen W. Arenson, *The New York Times*, May 30, 2006.

Page 45: Bob Schaeffer of the National Center for Fair and Open Testing, a nonprofit organization based in Cambridge, Mass., quoted in *The New York Times*, May 28, 2006

Page 49: *The New York Times*, April 23, 2006

Page 52: *The New York Times*, Aug. 12, 2008

Page 59: AP, Aug. 22, 2008

Page 60: "The Long (and Sometimes Expensive) Road to the SAT," Julie Bick, *The New York Times*, May 28, 2006.

Page 63: AP, Aug. 22, 2008

Page 65: *The New York Times*, August 26, 2008

Page 67: http://www.cnn.com/2008/US/05/30/test.drop/index.html

Page 78: "Taming the Monster," *The New York Times*, April 23, 2006.

Page 112: "Chewing gum selectively improves memory in healthy volunteers." Wilkinson L., Scholey A., Wesness K., *Appetite*. June 2002

Page 134: "Taming the Monster," *The New York Times*, April 23, 2006.

Page 135: *The New York Times*, Sept. 22, 2008

Page 150: http://wiki.answers.com

Page 158: http://www.princetonreview.com/schoollist.aspx?type=r&id=746

Page 158: http://www.princetonreview.com/bestcolleges/parties.aspx?uidb-adge=%07

Page 159: http://www.kiplinger.com/tools/colleges/ataglance.html

Page 159: http://www.kiplinger.com/tools/privatecolleges/ataglance_prv_univ.html?kipad_id=50

Page 179: Stanford Magazine, Sept./Oct. 2008

Page 191: Kerry Keegan, College Admissions Counselor, Academy of the Holy Names, Tampa, FL; *The New York Times*, March 21, 2006; Betsy F. Woolf, Admit U College and Graduate School Admissions Consulting, Westchester, NY.

Page 197: Questions for Your Visit, *College View*, www.collegeview.com/articles/CV/application/questions_for_visit.html

Page 203: "Ivy League colleges find 2006 is a buyer's market," MSN, April 14, 2006.

Page 244: *The Princeton Review*, www.princetonreview.com/college/research/articles/prepare/summerbook3.asp

Page 254: *The New York Times Magazine*, Sept. 21, 2008

Page 293: "America's Best Colleges 2006," *U.S. News & World Report*.

Page 297: *The Scholarship Book 2003*. Prentice Hall Press: New Jersey, 2002. p vii.

Page 303: *The New York Times*, April 20, 2008

Page 304: *The New York Times*, July 21, 2008

Page 307: www.Collegeboard.com

Page 345: Kerry Keegan, College Admissions Counselor, Academy of the Holy Names, Tampa, FL.

Page 352: Betsy F. Woolf, Admit U College and Graduate School Admissions Consulting, Westchester, NY.

Page 358: Wall Street Journal, May 21, 2008

Page 360: The Wall Street Journal, Nov. 30, 2007

Page 364: The Wall Street Journal, Nov. 30, 2007

Page 366: Betsy F. Woolf, Admit U College and Graduate School Admissions Consulting, Westchester, NY; Kerry Keegan, College Admissions Counselor, Academy of the Holy Names, Tampa, FL.

Page 367: Kerry Keegan, College Admissions Counselor, Academy of the Holy Names, Tampa, FL; Betsy F. Woolf, Admit U College and Graduate School Admissions Consulting, Westchester, NY.

Page 384: *The New York Times*, Aug. 21, 2008

Page 388: "Group names top 10 conservative colleges," *WorldNetDaily*, December 16, 2005.

Page 393: Education Life, *New York Times*, January 2006.

Page 394: www.campusdirt.com.

Page 402: http://lifetussle.wordpress.com/2008/02/19/all-time-best-college-football-programs-is-your-school-on-the-list/

Page 414: Kerry Keegan, College Admissions Counselor, Academy of the Holy Names, Tampa, FL.

Page 417: Kerry Keegan, College Admissions Counselor, Academy of the Holy Names, Tampa, FL.

SPECIAL THANKS

Special thanks to the Admissions Officers who shared their insights and experience with us (and you!):

Tony Bankston
Dean of Admissions
Illinois Wesleyan University
www.iwu.edu

Mark Butt
Senior Assistant Director of Admissions
Johns Hopkins University
www.jhu.edu/

Douglas L. Christiansen, Ph.D.
Associate Provost for Enrollment and
Dean of Admissions
Vanderbilt University
www.vanderbilt.edu

William R. Fitzsimmons
Dean of Admissions and Financial Aid
Harvard College
www.harvard.edu/

Christoph Guttentag
Dean of Undergraduate Admissions
Duke University
www.duke.edu

Jean Jordan
Dean of Admission
Emory University
www.emory.edu/

Mats Lemberger
Assistant Director of Admissions
Dartmouth College
www.dartmouth.edu/

Chris Lucier
Vice President for Enrollment Management
University of Vermont
www.uvm.edu/

Jacinda Ojeda
Regional Director of Admissions
University of Pennsylvania
www.upenn.wdu

Daniel J. Saracino
Assistant Provost for Enrollment
University of Notre Dame
www.nd.edu

Ted Spencer
Associate Vice Provost and Executive
Director of Undergraduate Admissions
University of Michigan-Ann Arbor
www.umich.edu/

MORE THANKS

Special thanks to the Independent Educational Consultants Association (www.educationalconsulting.org) and to the following IECA members, for sharing their advice and wisdom:

Monica Andrews, Ed.D.
President, ReelWisdom
www.reelwisdom.com
monica@reelwisdom.com

Lisa Bleich
President, College Bound Mentor, LLC
Copyright © 2008 College Bound Mentor
LLC. All Rights Reserved.
www.collegeboundmentor.com
lisa@collegeboundmentor.com

Joan H. Bress, LICSW,
CEP-Certified Educational Planner
College Resource Associates,
www.CollegeResourceAssoc.com
joan@collegeresourceassoc.com

Sandra Clifton
Clifton Corner, A Tutoring &
Coaching Center
www.cliftoncorner.com
sandra@cliftoncorner.com

Brigid Dorsey, Ph.D.
IECA, HECA, NYACAC
bkdorsey@gmail.com

Shannon Duff
College Coach And Director, Collegiate
Compass Llc
www.collegiatecompass.com
info@collegiatecompass.com

Elise R. Epner LLC
College Admissions Consulting
© 2008 Elise Epner
www.eliseepner.com
eliseepner@snet.net

Ginger Fay, Fay College Counseling, LLC
www.faycc.com
gfay@faycc.com

Diane Geller, MA
Certified Educational Planner
DeFelice & Geller, Inc.
www.defeliceandgeller.com
dianegeller@gmail.com

Susan M. Hanflik, M. Ed., CEP
Susan Hanflik and Associates Educational
Consulting
www.shanflikandassociates.com
smhanflik@cox.net

Doretta Katzter Goldberg, Esq.
President, College Directions, LLC
© Copyright 2008 College Directions, LLC
www.college-directions.com
doretta@college-directions.com

Theresa Leary, M.Ed.
TLC Education Planning For Global
Learning
www.theresaleary.com
info@theresaleary.com

Susan Joan Mauriello
Apply Ivy Limited
www.applyivy.com
susan@applyivy.com

Rachel Winston
Educators with a Vision College Counseling
Center
math4fn@yahoo.com or
collegeguide@yahoo.com

Betsy F. Woolf
College & Graduate School Admissions
Consultant
Woolf College Consulting
www.woolfcollegeconsulting.com/
bfwoolf@woolfcollegeconsulting.com

MORE THANKS

Thanks to our intrepid "headhunters" for going out to find so many respondents from around the country with interesting advice to share:

Jamie Allen, Chief Headhunter

Alexa Stanard	Jennifer Bright Reich
Andrea Fine	Ken McCarthy
Andrea Parker	Linda Lincoln
Andrea Syrtash	Liz Garone
Ashley Spicer	Lorraine Calvacca
Beshaleba Rodell	Marie Suszynski
Brandi Fowler	Nancy Larson
Carly Milne	Paula Andruss
Daniel Nemet-Nejat	Ruthann Spike
Elana Brownstein	Sally Burns
Gloria Averbuch	Stacey Shannon
Helen Bond	Staci Siegel

Thanks to our assistant, Miri Greidi, for her yeoman's work at keeping us all organized.

The real credit for this book, of course, goes to all the people whose experiences and collective wisdom make up this guide. There are too many of you to thank individually, of course, but you know who you are.

ADVICE FROM:

Agnes Scott College
American University
Anderson University
Austin Community College
Ball State University
Bard College
Barnard College
Beloit College
Boston University
Bowling Green State
University
Bradley University
Brandeis University
Brooks Institute of
Photography
Brown University
Brown University
Butler University
California College of the Arts
California Institute of
Technology
California State University,
Fresno
California State University,
Monterey Bay
California State University,
Northridge
Carleton College
Central Michigan University
Chatham College
Claremont McKenna College
Clemson University
Colgate University
College of William and Mary
Colorado State University
Columbia College
Columbia University
Concordia University
Coppin State University
Cornell University
Dayton University
Drake University
Drexel University
Duke University
East Christian College
Eckerd College

Elmhurst College
Elon University
Emory University
Florida State University
Fordham University
Franciscan University of
Steubenville
Free Will Baptist Bible
College
George Mason University
George Washington
University
Georgetown University
Grand Valley State University
Guilford College
Harvard University
Hunter College
Illinois Wesleyan University
Indiana University
John Hopkins University
Johnson & Wales University
Kent State University
Kentucky Wesleyan College
Kenyon College
Knox College
La Guardia College
La Salle University
Lafayette College
Lehigh University
Louisiana State University
Loyola College
Loyola University New
Orleans
Marquette University
Marylhurst University
McGill University
Miami University
Michigan State University
Middle Tennessee State
University
Middlebury College
Mount Holyoke College
Muhlenberg College
New Mexico Institute of
Mining and Technology
New York University

North Carolina State
University
North Dakota State
University
North Iowa Area Community
College
Northeastern University
Northwestern University
Oakland University
Ohio State University
Ohio State University
Ohio University
Oklahoma Baptist University
Pennsylvania State
University
Pitzer College
Point Loma Nazarene
University
Princeton University
Principia College
Purdue University
Queen's University
Quinnipiac University
Rhodes College
Rice University
Richland College, Dallas
County Community
College District
Roanoke College
Robert Morris College
Rowan University
Rutgers University
Salisbury University
Santa Clara University
Sarah Lawrence College
Seton Hall University
Seton Hill University
Skidmore College
Sonoma State University
Southern Illinois University
Carbondale
Southern Methodist
University
Southwestern University
St. Louis University
Stanford University

State University of New York
at Buffalo
State University of New York,
College at Brockport
State University of New York,
Purchase College
Stern College for
Women
Swarthmore College
Syracuse University
Texas Christian University
Texas Southern University
Texas State University
Tufts University
Tulane University
University of Arizona
University of Arizona
University of Baltimore
University of California
University of California,
Berkeley
University of California,
Davis
University of California,
Los Angeles
University of California,
Santa Barbara
University of Charleston
University of Chicago
University of Cincinnati
University of Colorado
University of Connecticut
University of Delaware
University of Florida
University of Illinois
University of Illinois at
Urbana-Champaign
University of Kansas

University of Kentucky
University of Maryland
University of Maryland,
College Park
University of Massachusetts
Amherst
University of Michigan
University of Michigan
University of Missouri
University of North Carolina
University of North Carolina
at Greensboro
University of Oklahoma
University of Pennsylvania
University of Pennsylvania
University of Southern
California
University of Southern
California
University of Tennessee
University of Texas, Austin
University of Toronto
University of Virginia
University of Washington
University of Wisconsin
Vanderbilt University
Villanova University
Wake Forest University
Washington and Jefferson
College
Washington & Lee University
Washington State University
Washington University
Washington University in
St. Louis
Wayne State University
Wellesley College
Wesleyan University;

West Virginia University
Western Illinois University
Williams College
Wittenberg University
Xavier University
Yale University
Yeshiva University
York University
Youngstown State University

AND FROM ADMISSIONS OFFICERS AT:

Dartmouth College -
www.dartmouth.edu
Duke University –
www.duke.edu/admissions
Emory University -
www.emory.edu/
admissions
Harvard College -
www.harvard.edu/
Illinois Wesleyan University
College - www.iwu.edu
Johns Hopkins University -
http://apply.jhu.edu
University of Michigan-Ann
Arbor -
www.admissions.umich.edu
University of Notre Dame -
www.nd.edu
University of Pennsylvania -
www.upenn.edu
University of Vermont -
www.uvm.edu/admissions/undergraduate/
Vanderbilt University -
www.vanderbilt.edu

PRAISE FOR *THE FIRST EDITION:*

ForeWord Magazine 2007 Book of the Year Bronze Medal Winner

"... a fun, fascinating read ..."
—ABOUT.COM

"Very readable book . . . The information is timeless."
—INTERNATIONAL HONOR SOCIETY OF HIGH SCHOOL JOURNALISTS

PRAISE FOR *HOW TO SURVIVE YOUR FRESHMAN YEAR*

Book of the Year Award finalist, *Foreword* magazine

Recommended Reading, *Positive Teens* magazine

Ingram Library Service "Hidden Gem"

Included in "Ten Good Books for Grads," *Detroit Free Press*

"A guide full of fantastic advice from hundreds of young scholars who've been there …. a quick and fun read."
—BOSTON HERALD, *TEEN NEWS*

"The perfect send-off present for the student who is college bound. The book manages to be hilarious and helpful. As an added bonus, it's refreshingly free of sanctimony."
—THE POST AND COURIER, CHARLESTON, SOUTH CAROLINA

"This book proves that all of us are smarter than one of us."
—JOHN KATZMAN, FOUNDER AND CEO, THE PRINCETON REVIEW

"Honest portrait of the trials and jubilations of college and how to best navigate your own way through."
—NEXT STEP *MAGAZINE*

"Explains college to the clueless."
—COLLEGE BOUND TEEN

"The advice dispensed is handy, useful, and practical. This book will make great light reading for an incoming freshman."
—VOYA

"A great tool for young people beginning an important and often daunting new challenge, with short and funny, real-world tips."
—WASHINGTON PARENT

"This how-to book is jam-packed with hundreds of quick tips and great advice … "
—SAN DIEGO FAMILY MAGAZINE

"Words of wisdom: Hundreds of parents nationwide weigh in with advice on everything from messy bedrooms to driving to sex … "
—THE CINCINNATI ENQUIRER

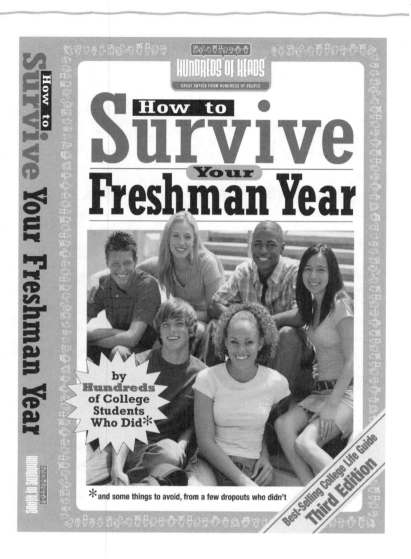

- #1 bestselling college life guide in an updated third edition

- Over 1,000 pieces of advice from students at more than 100 colleges

- All-new tips, facts, references, and checklists for college-bound teens

- Short, entertaining stories make a fun and quick read

- The perfect high school graduation gift!

HOW TO SURVIVE YOUR FRESHMAN YEAR...by Hundreds of Sophomores, Juniors, and Seniors Who Did. THIRD EDITION (320 pages, $15.95)

ISBN-10: 1-933512-14-8
ISBN-13: 978-1-933512-14-3

WHAT THE CRITICS ARE SAYING ABOUT HUNDREDS OF HEADS®:

"Colorful bits of advice … So simple, so entertaining, so should have been my million-dollar idea."

—*The Courier-Journal (Louisville, Kentucky)*

"The books have struck a nerve."

—*CNN.com*

"If you've got a kid going off to college this year, you've got to get this book... It's kind of irreverent and fun..."

—*WGN Radio (Chicago)*

"Entertaining and informative series takes a different approach to offering advice...Think 'Chicken Soup' meets 'Zagats'..."

—*The Sacramento Bee*

"Hundreds of Heads hopes to make life in our complicated new millennium a bit more manageable."

—*The Record (Hackensack, New Jersey)*

CHECK OUT THESE OTHER BOOKS FROM HUNDREDS OF HEADS®

HOW TO GET A's IN COLLEGE:
Hundreds of Student-Tested Tips (304 pages, $14.95)

ISBN-10: 1-933512-08-3
ISBN-13: 978-1933-512-08-2

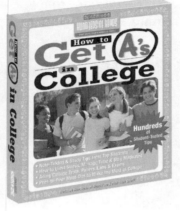

Hundreds of successful college grads share their wisdom, stories, tips, and advice on how to get top grades, find the right major, manage your time, stay motivated, avoid stress, seek out the best teachers and courses, form important relationships, and graduate – happily – at the top of the class. **Special Editor Frances Northcutt is an academic advisor in the Honors Program at Hunter College in the City University of New York.**

Wisdom from hundreds of parents who have successfully navigated the college admissions process. **Special Editor Rachel Korn is a college advisor and consultant, and a former admissions officer at the University of Pennsylvania, Brandeis, and Wellesley.**

HOW TO SURVIVE GETTING YOUR KID INTO COLLEGE...
6 × 7", 256 pages, $14.95

ISBN-10: 1-933512-11-3
ISBN-13: 978-1-933512-11-2

The college graduate's orientation guide to the real world. Filled with hard-won wisdom from hundreds of young adults on everything from finding your first job to renting an apartment to learning how to cook.

Featured on the Today Show and in *USA Today!*

"… the perfect gift for the newly minted college graduates on your list.
—*THE POST AND COURIER (CHARLESTON, SC)*

HOW TO SURVIVE THE REAL WORLD: LIFE AFTER GRADUATION
(204 pages, $13.95)

ISBN-10: 1-933512-03-2
ISBN-13: 978-1933-51203-7

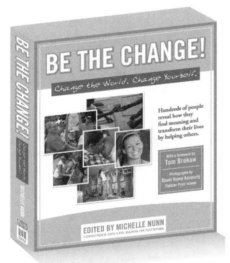

By intertwining practical advice on service and volunteerism with real-life stories of personal transformation, this book is the perfect companion for people who want to be inspired and informed and to take action to change their lives and their world. **Edited by Michelle Nunn, Co-founder and CEO of Hands On Network.**

"This is a wonderful and inspiring book."
—*WALTER ISAACSON CEO, ASPEN INSTITUTE*

"This is a book that could change your life … It's almost magic and it could happen to everyone. Go!"
—*JIM LEHRER, ANCHOR, PBS NEWSHOUR WITH JIM LEHRER*

BE THE CHANGE! CHANGE THE WORLD. CHANGE YOURSELF.
(336 pages, $14.95)

ISBN-10: 1-933512-00-8
ISBN-13: 978-1933512-00-6

ABOUT THE EDITOR

RACHEL KORN is a U.S. college advisor and consultant. She attended
Brandeis University as a Justice Brandeis Scholar, and Harvard University,
where she earned a Master's Degree in Higher Education Administration.
Rachel worked on the admissions staffs at Wellesley College, Brandeis
University, and The University of Pennsylvania, where she visited hundreds
of high schools across the nation, interviewed prospective students, and read
and advised committees on approximately 10,000 applications. She has been
an active member of several professional organizations including regional
chapters of the National Association for College Admissions Counseling and
the College Board. Rachel currently lives in Tel Aviv, Israel.

JENNIFER YETWIN KABAT is the founder of The Way In College
Admissions Consulting, which provides personalized consulting for students
throughout the college admissions process. She has worked in admissions
offices at Harvard College, the University of Michigan, and the UC Berkeley
School of Law. Jennifer was the Associate Director of Admissions at UC
Berkeley School of Law where she reviewed and made decisions on thousands of applications.

Jennifer has her Masters in Higher Education Administration from
Harvard and a B.A. in English from the University of Michigan. Jennifer was
born and raised in Tucson, Arizona and currently lives in Marin County,
California with her husband and two children.

ABOUT THE AUTHOR OF BRODY'S GUIDE TO THE COLLEGE APPLICATION ESSAY

JAY BRODY is a Harvard Law School graduate, former admissions counselor, and author of a popular book about the college admissions essay. He
has appeared on national television to discuss admissions-related issues,
been published widely discussing the SAT and ACT, and served as the Guide
for About.com's college admissions portal. He currently resides in Chicago.

![HUNDREDS OF HEADS]

LOOKING FOR MORE ADVICE AND A PLACE TO CONNECT?

FIND IT at www.hundredsofheads.com

...the COOLEST place to GIVE and GET tips on anything and everything about COLLEGE. Check out:

- Videos
- Blogs & Polls
- Experts
- Illuminating Articles

Search, ASK, discuss, and ANSWER questions on the HOTTEST topics:

- Getting Into College
- College Life
- Exams
- Roommates
- Parties
- Food and Laundry
- Parents' Guide
- Relationships
- Volunteering and Personal Growth
- Life After College

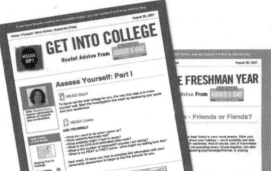

FREE "Advicemails" KEEP YOU in the KNOW

GET Hundreds of Heads' "Advicemails" filled with the best "insider" peer-to-peer wisdom—including STORIES, tips, and guidance from hundreds of college STUDENTS INTERVIEWED across the country—as well as advice from our EXPERTS on today's top issues—all DELIVERED FREE to your INBOX every week.

"HeadsUp! Get Into College" includes SAGE advice from Rachel Korn, a former ADMISSIONS OFFICER at the University of Pennsylvania, Wellesley, and Brandeis – and from IECA Consultants.

"HeadsUp! Freshman Year" shares WISDOM from Fran Northcutt, an academic ADVISOR in the Honors Program at Hunter College at the City University of New York.

VIEW sample newsletters and subscribe (they're FREE!) at www.hundredsofheads.com/advicemail.